THE MUSEUM OF EAST ASIAN ART

INAUGURAL EXHIBITION

VOLUME 2

CHINESE METALWARES AND DECORATIVE ARTS

THE MUSEUM OF EAST ASIAN ART

INAUGURAL EXHIBITION

VOLUME 2
CHINESE METALWARES AND DECORATIVE ARTS

3 APRIL 1993
Circus Lodge 12 Bennett Street
Bath BA1 2QL England

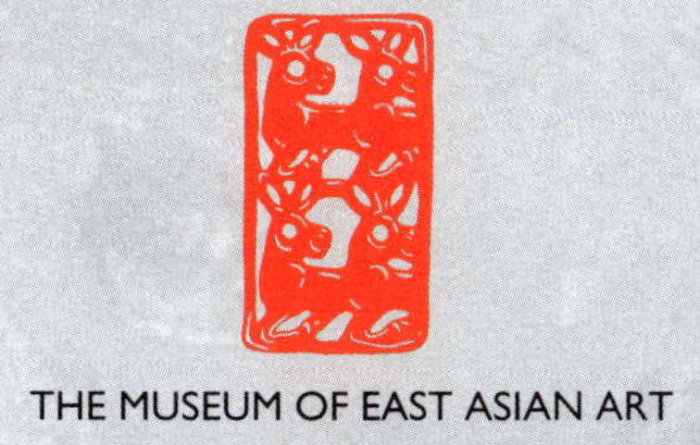

THE MUSEUM OF EAST ASIAN ART

Published by The Museum of East Asian Art

ISBN 1 897734 01 8

Text by Brian Shane McElney, Honorary Curator
Chinese Translation by Ng Kai Yuen
Designed and produced by PPA Design Limited
Designers: Michelle Shek, Leung Yiu Wing
Photography by Arthur Kan
Colour Separations by Fung's Graphic Arts Co., Ltd.
Printed and bound in Hong Kong by
Hong Kong Prime Printing Co., Ltd.

Preface

It gives The Museum of East Asian Art the greatest pleasure to present this, the Inaugural Exhibition of its new museum devoted to East Asian art, at Circus Lodge, 12 Bennett Street, Bath, England. The Museum of East Asian Art was registered as a United Kingdom educational charity on 27th of July 1990. Since registration it has pressed ahead with all speed to establish this, its new museum.

The two volume catalogue of this exhibition commemorates a significant event in the history of East Asian art in England. The opening of The Museum of East Asian Art provides the first new museum devoted entirely to the subject since the Gulbenkian Museum in Durham, now The Oriental Museum, opened its doors in 1960. It also adds greatly to the emphasis on the subject in the southwest of England, which already boasts the fine collection of Chinese art in the City Museum and Art Gallery, Bristol. This new museum will attract visitors from all over the world who can now visit both institutions in one visit to the southwest.

The concept and inspiration in bringing this project to fruition were of course those of Brian McElney, who, apart from the munificent gift of the major part of his private collection, has been the driving force in the acquisition of Circus Lodge and its conversion to a museum, and the employment of and cooperation with the distinguished architect, Michael Polkinghorne. Brian McElney, who has also undertaken the post of Honarary Curator for the next ten years, has also shared with us his insights on the pieces in the exhibition in the essays he has contribued to the exhibition catalogues.

The subjects chosen for the exhibition are Chinese ceramics, metalwares and decorative arts other than jade, rhino horn and ivory. Jade has been excluded as this will shortly be the subject of a separate exhibition and rhino horn and ivory have also been excluded because of the problems involved in exhibiting these items overseas as a result of the treaties on endangered species. It is hoped, however, that a small exhibition devoted to rhino horn and ivory will be mounted by the museum at some time in the future.

The Chinese ceramics in the Inaugural Exhibition cover a period from about 2500 B.C. to about 1820 A.D. and provide a fairly comprehensive display of many of the types produced in China during this long period, including many rare examples. The collection is particularly strong in examples from the Song period, which in the opinion of many experts is the most sophisicated period of Chinese art. The metalwares included in the exhibition range in date from at least 1600 B.C. to 1881 A.D. and include a number of pieces of great academic interest.

Acknowledgment must also be made to several other people, most notably to Robert Primrose and his wife Betty, who worked with Brian McElney in Hong Kong for many years. Robert strove prodigiously as Honorary Secretary from the inception of the project until the advent of Dawn Stollar, who has been the Administrator in the strenuous run-up to the opening and will, I am sure, be a tower of strength to Brian McElney in the future. Ann Sin should be thanked for her work in Hong Kong, Ng Kai Yuen for the Chinese translation of the essays and Elizabeth Carmo, now carrying out the secretarial work in Bath. The Hong Kong photographer Arthur Kan should also be congratulated on the colour photographs for the catalogues.

Finally, but not least, Brian Morgan, well known for his display skills, has given valuable advice.

R. B. Bluett

Chairman of the Board of The Museum of East Asian Art

Author's Note

This volume of the catalogue for the Inaugural Exhibition of The Museum of East Asian Art covers the Chinese metalwares and decorative art objects in the exhibition. There are in the metalwares section a total of 90 exhibits and in the decorative arts section, 43 exhibits. The items of decorative art have been deliberately limited to exclude all objects made of hardstones, such as jade, as they will be the subject of the next major exhibition at the museum and the subject of a separate catalogue. There have also been excluded from the exhibition two categories of Chinese decorative arts, which would normally be included in that designation, namely, rhino horn and ivory carvings, because of the requirements for several licences for these objects under the CITES treaties on endangered species. The bureaucracy of these treaties effectively makes travelling exhibitions, which may include such objects, too difficult to organise. Natural wood sculptures have also not been included because of their size and fragility. However, it is hoped to have small exhibitions of the rhino horns and ivories and natural wood sculptures in the museum's collection at some time in the near future.

The 90 examples of Chinese metalware exhibited span the period from about 1600 B.C. to 1881 A.D. and include objects of bronze, gold, silver, cloisonné, enamel, lead, pewter and copper. A lengthy essay in both English and Chinese introduces this section. Every piece has its own colour illustration and in some cases more than one illustration.

For ease of comparison the Ordos bronze pieces and the bronze mirrors have been grouped together in two sections, the Ordos pieces immediately following the Han bronzes (see Exhibits 254 to 264) and the bronze mirrors immediately following the Tang objects (see Exhibits 270 to 276). Similarly all the gold, silver, cloisonné, enamel and miscellaneous metals have been grouped together after the bronzes in their own individual categories.

The decorative arts in the exhibition fall into several distinct categories namely, lacquers, softstone carvings, bamboo carvings, gourds and miscellaneous objects of wood and inlaid wood. Each of these categories has been given a short introductory essay and every piece included has its own colour illustration. In date, they range from about the 6th century A.D. to about 1850.

The author considers it unsatisfactory that in most museum catalogues in the past only a dynasty date has normally been assigned to a piece, where the piece is not marked by an imperial reign mark. This is particularly unsatisfactory where, as frequently happens, the dynasty assigned covers several centuries and a more accurate estimate of the age of the piece is possible. Whilst firm dating within a century is not really possible for many pieces, prior to the Han dynasty, thereafter, it seems to me that a curator should not avoid the issue and should assign the pieces in question within the correct century of their production. This I have attempted to do in the textual descriptions included in the catalogue. Where this is not possible I have indicated two centuries, with production of the piece probably occurring within the middle 100 years of this period.

Whilst most of the objects in the Inaugural Exhibition are owned by the museum, having been donated by the author, there are a small number of items that are only on long term loan. These items have been designated by an asterisk.

Bath Location Map

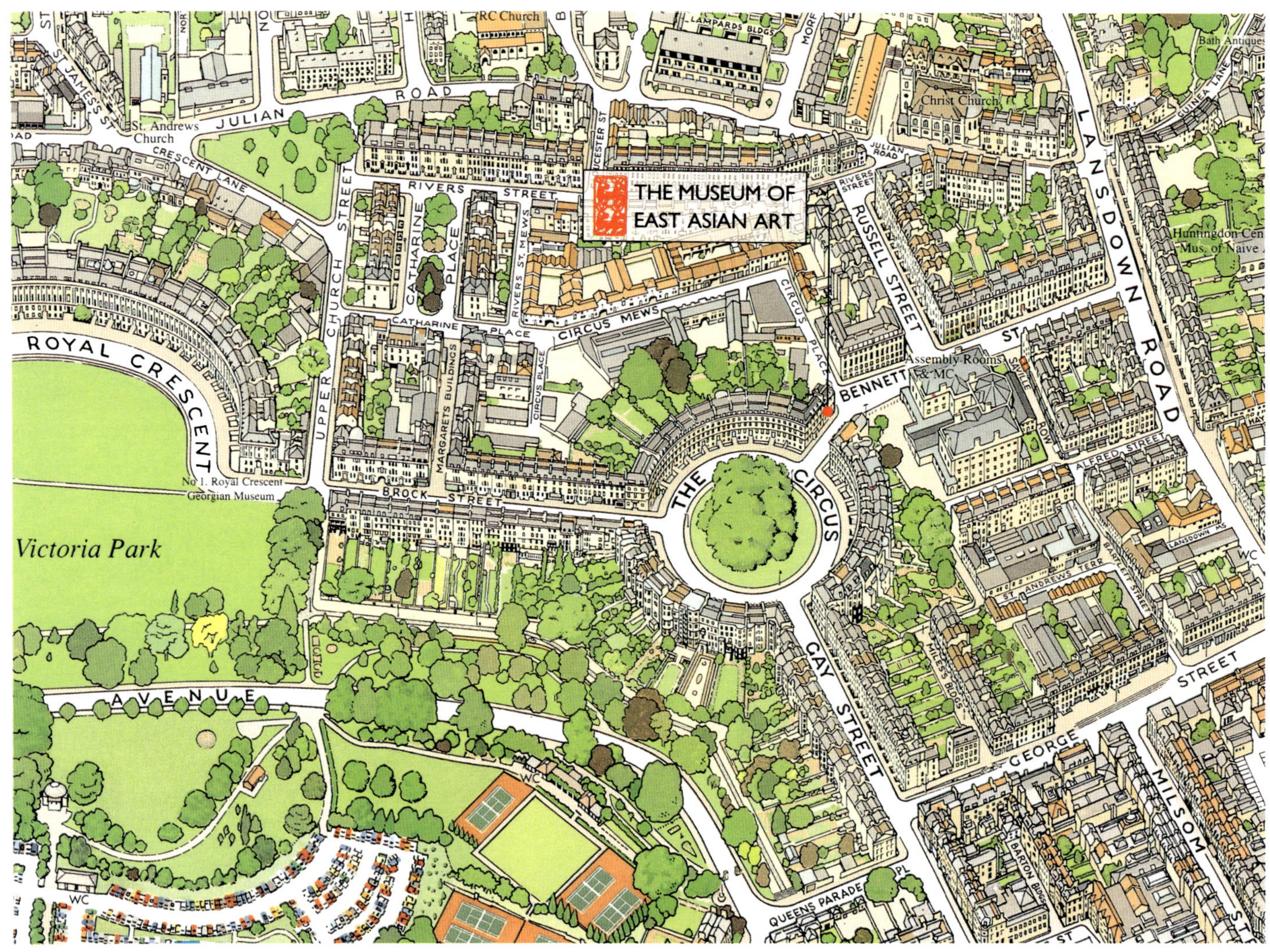

© Copyright 3D Maps Ltd., Bath, U.K. Tel: 0225 442 327.

CHRONOLOGY 年表

				公元前 B.C.
NEOLITHIC PERIOD 新石器時代				c. 7000 — 2000
XIA 夏				c. 2100 — 1600
SHANG 商				c. 1600 — 1100
ZHOU 周				c. 1100 — 256
	Western Zhou 西周			c. 1100 — 771
	Eastern Zhou 東周			770 — 256
		Spring and Autumn period 春秋時期		770 — 475
		Warring States period 戰國時期		475 — 221
QIN 秦				221 — 206
HAN 漢				206 — 公元 A.D. 220
	Western (Former) Han 西（前）漢			206 — 公元 A.D. 8
	Xin (Wang Mang) 新（王莽）			公元 A.D. 9 — 25
	Eastern (Later) Han 東（後）漢			公元 A.D. 25 — 220
				公元 A.D.
SIX DYNASTIES 六朝				220 — 589
	Three Kingdoms period 三國			220 — 280
	Wu 吳		220 — 280	
	Shu 蜀		221 — 263	
	Wei 魏		220 — 265	
	Western and Eastern Jin 西晉東晉		265 — 420	
	Period of Northern and Southern dynasties 南北朝時代			386 — 581
	North 北朝	Northern Wei 北魏	386 — 534	
		Eastern Wei 東魏	534 — 550	
		Western Wei 西魏	535 — 557	
		Northern Qi 北齊	550 — 577	
		Northern Zhou 北周	557 — 581	
	South 南朝	(Liu) Song（劉）宋	420 — 479	
		Southern Qi 南齊	479 — 502	
		Liang 梁	502 — 557	
		Chen 陳	557 — 589	
SUI 隋				581 — 618
TANG 唐				618 — 906
	High Tang 盛唐			684 — 756
	Late Tang 晚唐			757 — 906

FIVE DYNASTIES 五代			907 — 960
LIAO 遼			907 — 1125
SONG 宋			960 — 1279
	Northern Song 北宋	960 — 1127	
	Southern Song 南宋	1127 — 1279	
JIN 金			1115 — 1234
YUAN 元			1279 — 1368
MING 明			1368 — 1644
	Hongwu 洪武	1368 — 1398	
	Jianwen 建文	1399 — 1402	
	Yongle 永樂	1403 —1424	
	Xuande 宣德	1426 — 1435	
	Zhengtong 正統	1436 — 1449	
	Jingtai 景泰	1450 — 1457	
	Tianshun 天順	1458 — 1464	
	Chenghua 成化	1465 — 1487	
	Hongzhi 弘治	1488 — 1505	
	Zhengde 正德	1506 — 1521	
	Jiajing 嘉靖	1522 — 1566	
	Longqing 隆慶	1567 — 1572	
	Wanli 萬曆	1573 — 1620	
	Taichang 泰昌	1620	
	Tianqi 天啓	1621 — 1627	
	Chongzhen 崇禎	1628 — 1644	
QING 清			1644 — 1912
	Shunzhi 順治	1644 — 1661	
	Kangxi 康熙	1662 — 1722	
	Yongzheng 雍正	1723 — 1735	
	Qianlong 乾隆	1736 — 1795	
	Jiaqing 嘉慶	1796 — 1820	
	Daoguang 道光	1821 — 1850	
	Xianfeng 咸豐	1851 — 1861	
	Tongzhi 同治	1862 — 1874	
	Guangxu 光緒	1875 — 1908	
	Xuantong 宣統	1909 — 1912	
REPUBLIC OF CHINA 中華民國			1912
PEOPLE'S REPUBLIC OF CHINA 中華人民共和國			1949

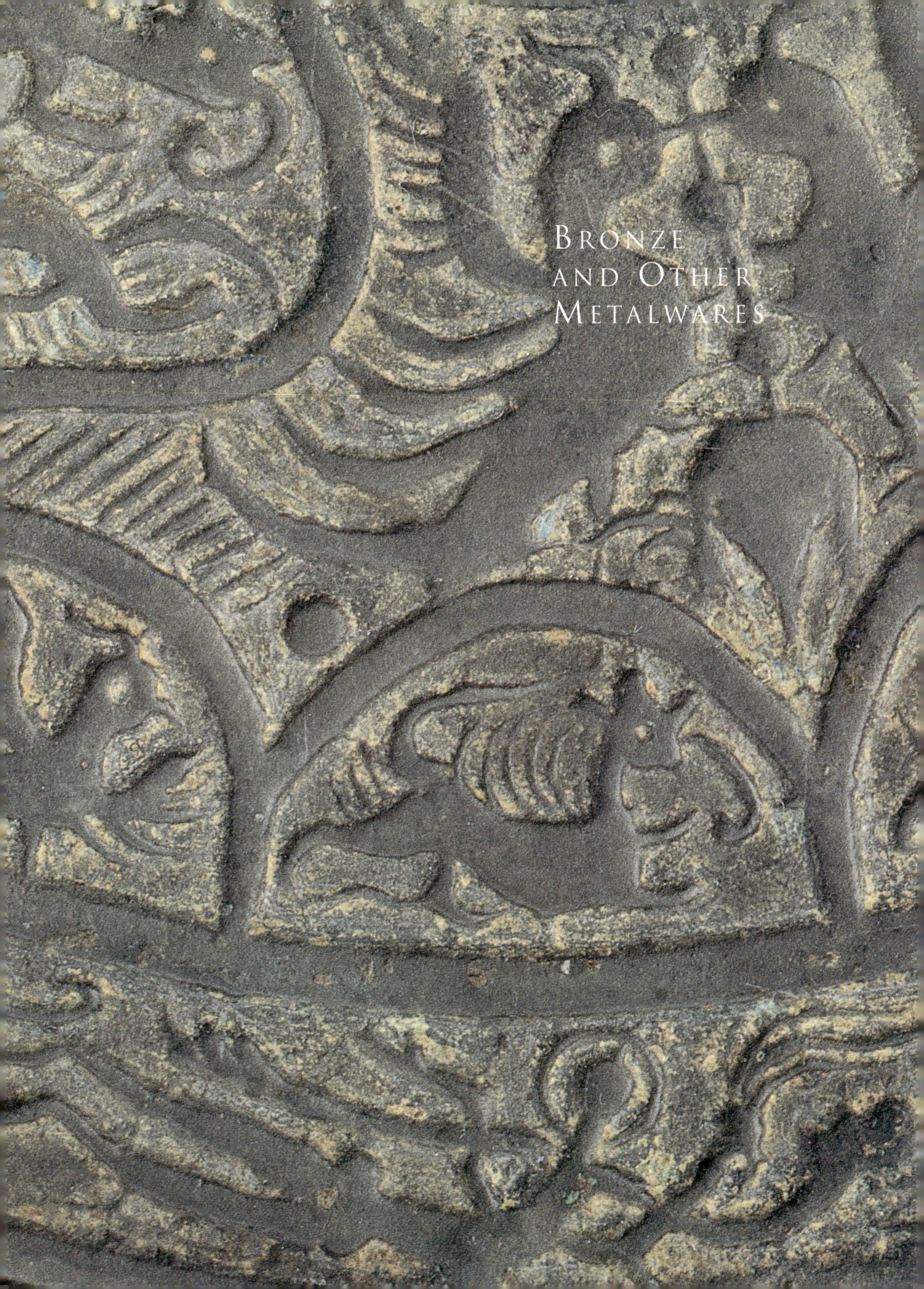

Bronze and Other Metalwares

Bronzes and Other Metalwares

The history of the working of bronze and other metals in China dates back to the earliest period of Chinese history. Indeed, an exhibition I saw in Beijing in November 1990 of recent unpublished archaeological finds included a small bronze bell found in Shaanxi which the Chinese organisers estimated to have approximately 90% copper content and to date to *circa* 2100 B.C. It was billed as the oldest bronze so far found in China. Bronze is an alloy of copper and tin, with lead sometimes being added to the mix.

Bronze ritual vessels seem to have been in production from shortly after 2000 B.C., contemporaneous with the Xia dynasty, but appear to have had their greatest popularity in the Shang dynasty which is traditionally considered to have followed the Xia dynasty. Modern scholarship, however, considers that for some period of time the Xia and Shang were probably contemporaneous. The exact dates of the Shang dynasty are presently uncertain and have been debated by scholars for many years. Pieces belonging to the so-called Erlitou culture, named after the Erlitou site at Yanshi in Henan Province, have been identified. This culture is considered to be of Xia/early Shang dynasty date *circa* 1600 B.C.. Even at that time bronze ritual vessels were being cast from ceramic piece moulds.

The lost wax (*cire perdu*) method of casting was not used at this very early period but was certainly employed at a later date by the still used by the Chinese metal workers for their more detailed work, such as is found on Exhibit 237. I was informed by the bronze expert at the Beijing Palace Museum that the lost wax method seems to have been first used in China in the Spring and Autumn period (770 -475 B.C.).

A flat bottomed *jue* from the Erlitou culture is included in the exhibition, (Exhibit 226). This piece is particularly special in that it has traces of gold sheeting affixed by red lacquer covering the bronze decoration. Red lacquer objects from this early period have been found with gold sheet inlays, and bronze buttons covered with gold were discovered at Anyang in a Shang context. There seems therefore no reason to doubt the gilding is of the period but no other example of such gilding with red lacquer affixative on a bronze of this period seems to have been recorded. It should in due course be possible to confirm the date of this object from a Carbon 14 dating of the lacquer but the amount of lacquer is insufficient, given the current state of Carbon 14 technology, to perform a conclusive test. At this early period, the bases of such *jue*, a type of ritual vessel for warming wine, were flat. A later *jue* from *circa* 1200 B.C. showing the typical rounded base of late Shang period *jue* is also included in the exhibition (Exhibit 227). This particular shape of vessel appears to have left the bronze repertoire shortly after the fall of the Shang dynasty.

Two other ritual vessels are also included in the exhibition. A *ding* from about 900 B.C. (Exhibit 228) and a *gui* from the 9th to 8th century B.C. (Exhibit 229). The *gui* has a long inscription identical on both the top and bottom sections recording the casting of the piece. In contrast to the one or two character inscriptions found on some Shang ritual bronzes, thought to be clan signs, Zhou inscriptions are frequently of considerable length (Exhibit 229), and occasionally record important events such as a marriage or a land or title grant. Ritual bronzes such as this *gui* were frequently made in large sets and their decoration appears rather dull when compared to the fierce grandeur of their Shang predecessors.

Apart from the ritual bronzes, a number of other interesting bronzes are included in the exhibition. These include a group of so-called Ordos bronzes which, for ease of comparison, have been grouped together in the exhibition (Exhibits 254 to 264 inclusive). In the late 1920s and early 1930s, a considerable number of these interesting small bronzes came on to the international market in north China. They consisted of belt plaques, belt hooks, knives, spoons and various small fittings, frequently depicting deer, sheep, birds (generally raptors), tigers, wolves and many other animals. This group of bronzes was named after the Ordos region, part of or bordering north China at the northernmost bend of the Yellow River. The style has also been called the 'animal style' as most of the group are decorated with various animals. Such pieces are found over an enormous area from the Altai mountains in the west to the borders of Korea in the east and Lake Baikal in the north. The style influenced the ancient Near East at one end of the geographic spectrum and central China at the other. Whilst considerable strides have been made in the understanding of this material, a great deal has still to be learned, as became clear at a conference I attended in Pittsburgh in April 1991. The time scale over which these animal style artifacts were produced has also expanded enormously. When they first appeared a relatively brief time scale from the Warring States to the Six Dynasties period was thought appropriate, whereas at the present time, as a result of numerous archaeological discoveries, some pieces are being given a date as early as Shang and as late as the Six Dynasties.

The bronze ferrule from central China (Exhibit 236) shows a sphinx-like animal, which parallels animals at Persepolis in Iran dating from the late 6th century B.C., and the Ordos related swirls on its stylized legs are clear evidence of Ordos influence.

The dating of Ordos bronzes has been problematic for some years. However, extensive excavations in Inner Mongolia and northern and central Shaanxi Province, which have been carried out over the last thirty years, have brought to light many similar bronze artifacts to those in Exhibits 254 to 264. These excavations appear to date the bronzes in question to the period from the Spring and Autumn period of the Eastern Zhou (770-476 B.C.) to the Eastern Han dynasty (25 to 220 A.D.). These bronzes appear to be the artifacts of nomadic tribes, such as the Shanrong, Yuezhi and the Xiongnu, who were active in Inner Mongolia and northern Shaanxi over a long period. The Shanrong were active in the area from the 8th to the 4th century B.C., and the Yuezhi from the 4th to the mid 3rd century B.C., when their dominance of the area was taken over by the Xiongnu, who soon formed a steppe empire as a balance to the Han on the other side of the Great Wall. A number of these interesting plaques with multiple animals (see Exhibit 254) would have been dated, until recently, relatively, late in the period (probably to Western Han 206 B.C. - A.D. 9) with the single animal plaques traditionally being dated relatively early in the period. Recent excavations seem to reverse this traditional dating, however, as multiple animal plaques (such as those included in Exhibit 254) have been excavated at Taohongbala, Hanggin Qi, western Inner Mongolia at a site which has been carbon dated to 711 B.C. ± 115, giving it therefore a 9th to 6th century B.C. dating. Confirming this reversal of the former accepted dating sequence is the discovery of a gilded plaque with a single animal similar to the rectangular gilded deer plaque shown in Exhibit 264, which would traditionally have been dated 3rd or 4th century B.C., in a burial dated conclusively to the 1st century A.D.

In addition to the Ordos bronze pieces, an important gold Ordos fitting of a bear with prominent claws, ruff and ears is included (Exhibit 298). This gold piece shows on its reverse raised textile traces integral to the metal surface. I am told that in the lost wax casting method indicated the textile supported the wax model from which the ceramic master mould was made. The wax textile supported model was invested in clay, which after drying out would then be fired to produce the master mould. In this process the wax and textile were burned off but left a sunken impression of the textile backing in the master mould. The gold was then cast using the master mould. I have seen two gold and two silver pieces cast from the same master mould involved here. Lost textile traces have been found on some gold, silver and high quality gilt and tinned bronze pieces in the Ordos style, including some of the famous gold pieces forming the Peter the Great Treasure at the Hermitage. The place where pieces showing this feature were cast has until recently been a mystery, but in the past year or so a number of animal-style pieces showing this feature and associated casting remains have been found at Yixian, southern Hebei in the ruins of the city of Yanxiadu, the southern capital of the State of Yan from 311 B.C.. The Yan state was overrun by the Qin in 222 B.C. when the site of this city seems to have been abandoned. It is well known that the inhabitants of the State of Yan included numerous people described as "the Di", a tribe from the western regions, who seem to have settled in the Yan and Shanrong states probably in the Spring and Autumn or early Warring States period. It has been suggested to me that whilst the rulers of the Yan state were undoubtedly Chinese, the Di inhabitants may in fact have been one of the nomadic tribes whose artifacts were in the 'animal style'. Whilst this cannot, given our present knowledge, be ruled out, it must be pointed out that lost textile traces are never found on plain bronze pieces but only on prestige pieces in gold, silver and high quality gilt or tinned bronze, surely only affordable by the tribal chiefs. It therefore seems to me more likely that such pieces were made by the Yan metal workers specially for trading to the chieftains of the northern nomadic tribes rather than for the local *hoi polloi* of the Di people, just as the Greeks traded high quality pieces with the Scythian chieftains in the Black Sea area in preceding centuries. The finding of the place of casting, however, helps put a probable time frame on prestige pieces showing textile traces of 311 - 222 B.C.

It seems almost certain, however, that such a casting method was employed contemporaneously in at least one other casting centre since I was told by a Chinese expert that the written inscription shown on at least one such Ordos-style excavated piece was epigraphically not in the style used in the State of Yan. I have also recently seen one fine inlaid bronze piece in the central Chinese style showing tracing of such a casting method. It also seems that the lost wax and lost textile technique was continued into the Western Han as evidenced by several gilded bronze plaques found at Xiongnu sites in both Liaoning and Ningxia.

Another interesting group included in the exhibition shows various gilding techniques or inlays employed from the 6th century B.C. on. These include examples with an inlay of turquoise, Exhibit 238; of silver, Exhibits 240, 243 and 249; of jade, Exhibit 239; of gold, Exhibit 242 and of gold and silver Exhibits 244, 247 and 248. Some of these objects are horse or chariot fittings or belt or garment hooks which became popular in the Warring States period.

Other rare metal objects include:
(1) A *duo* bronze bell of the usual small size with a short rectangular handle (Exhibit 231). *Duo* bells are much smaller than most of the *nao* bells of similar shape with which they are frequently confused. *Nao* bells, however, apart from being generally larger than *duo* bells, have a longer circular handle and all seem to date to the Shang dynasty. Both *nao* and *duo* bells are percussion instruments and generally have no clapper. All previously published *duo* bells I can find are dated to the Warring States period, but the decoration on this bell dates it to the late Spring and Autumn period (6th or early 5th century B.C.) thus making it the earliest published bell of its type. Both *nao* and *duo* bells were apparently played whilst held mouth up on a stick as in the illustration shown in the margin; (2) A spearhead from the State of Yue (Exhibit 233). This state was very famous in the 5th Century B.C. for its bronze weapons of which Exhibit 233 is an example. The patterning of this piece, which is identical to that found on the famous sword of Goujian, King of Yue (reigned 496 - 465 B.C.), is apparently the result of a hardening process which greatly strengthened the bronze and increased the sharpness of the edges of the swords and spear heads so treated. Swords and spearheads showing this technique are rare and appear to have been made in the State of Yue over only a comparatively short period. The technique involved then seems to have been lost and has not been understood until recent times.
(3) A sword with leopard-like spots. The blade of this sword has been examined by metal experts and found to be of a high tin (14%) and low to medium lead (3.5 - 5%) bronze alloy. It is tinned throughout except for its bevelled edges. The leopard-like spots were produced by the masking of parts of the blade during the tinning process. This type of prestige sword was produced by the Wu state and dates to the 4th or 3rd century B.C. (Exhibit 241). The State of Wu was famous for its fine weapons.
(4) A painted bronze basin (Exhibit 246). The painted decoration on this piece is of the type found on lacquers in the tomb of Mawangdui dated 162 B.C.

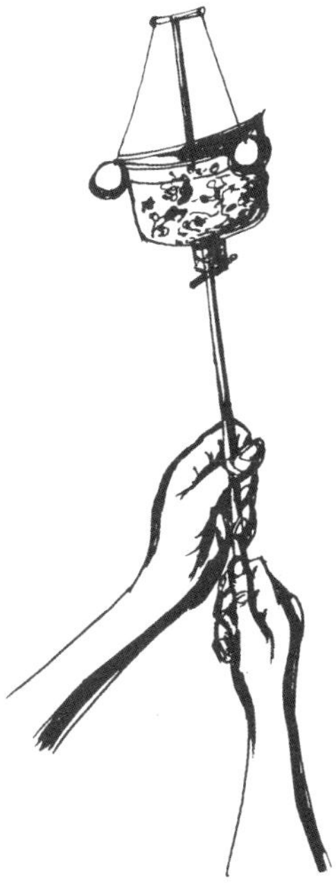

A number of bronze mirrors are also included in the exhibition. Bronze mirrors were already in production in the Shang dynasty though at that time they were simply and crudely cast. However, by the Warring States period, particularly in the State of Chu, bronze mirrors had become a very important art form and were frequently beautifully decorated. A fairly comprehensive selection of mirrors from the Spring and Autumn period to the Yuan dynasty (1279-1368), grouped together for ease of comparison, is included in the exhibition (Exhibits 270 - 276). AChinese artificers' manual from the State of Qi dating from the 5th century B.C. records six recipes for making bronze objects varying from 85% copper 15% tin for bells and cooking vessels to 50% copper 50% tin for mirrors. Some early mirrors are silvery in colour, possibly because of the higher tin content so recommended, though I understand some early mirrors were specially treated with a tin coating and this may be the reason for such colouring.

Most of the mirrors exhibited are in the standard round shape but some of the later ones are square or lobed and are of interest. One of the later mirrors has an incised inscription, which appears to be the official permission for exporting the metal mirror from the south to Jin and Yuan occupied northern China. (Exhibit 275). Laws enacted by the Southern Song prohibited the export of metal objects to the north unless officially sanctioned at that time (1127 - 1279A.D.). Exhibit 276 is unusual in having incised carving on its smooth reflecting surface. I do not know of another mirror that has this feature. Another mirror (Exhibit 272) datable from published excavated examples to the Wu kingdom (mid 3rd century A.D.) is interesting in depicting, among its strange menagerie of mythical animals, flying *apsaras* with haloes, a motif which did not occur in Chinese art until the entry of Buddhism to China in the Eastern Han.

In the dating of mirrors, one of the important points to note is the differing mirror handles over their long history. Such handles generally took the form of central knobs or protrusions, which were threaded with a cord to provide a holding mechanism, but the shapes and sizes varied considerably. In the Warring States and early Han periods, such handles normally took the form of a thin-waisted bridge with three concave sections (see Exhibit 271). In the first century B.C. and thereafter the handle is normally an almost solid circular knob frequently of large size (e.g. Exhibit 272). This type of handle continued into the Tang (618-906) dynasty. Occasionally, particularly in the Sui (581-618) and Tang dynasties, squatting animals such as a frog, lion or tortoise were substituted for the knob (eg. Exhibit 273). After the Tang dynasty, the knob tended to get smaller and sometimes became merely a ring (e.g. Exhibit 275). After the Yuan dynasty, bronze mirrors continued to be made but only it seems as utilitarian objects. The elaborately decorated backs of former times slowly gave way, from the Song dynasty on, to almost undecorated backs. Mirrors with elaborately decorated backs, however, continued to be made in Japan and Korea for several centuries. Chinese mirrors, unlike those serving similar functions in the West, do not normally have handles protruding from the rim. The earliest definitely Chinese mirror I have seen with a fixed handle protruding from the rim is from the late Southern Song. It is recorded that mirrors with handles were considered vulgar by the arbiters of taste in the late Ming (1368-1644), and this may have been the view in former periods. I have, however, seen a bronze mirror with a short hollow handle protruding from the rim, probably originally mounted with a wooden extension. This mirror was simply decorated with bands of nipples and chevrons and was reputedly from south China. From its decoration, I would say that this mirror was probably of the Dongson culture of Vietnam datable to about the 8th century but a southern Chinese provenance cannot be entirely ruled out. In any event mirrors with attached handles protruding from the rim seem never to have been popular in China. Japanese mirrors, however, frequently had such handles from at the latest the 12th century A.D. onwards.

Also included in the exhibition is an unusual container of alms-bowl shape, decorated with bands of small four-petalled flower heads which are inlaid. I believe this piece to be datable to the Tang dynasty (Exhibit 269). After exhaustive scientific tests, which confirmed that this piece is of very considerable age, the container was found to be red brass made by adding approximately 21% zinc to the usual bronze mix. The thick layer of inlay was found to be a copper lead sulphide niello in close to the ideal proportions of 42% lead, 35% copper and 23% sulphur. I have not been able to discover a similar or indeed any Chinese niello-inlaid piece of similar age having been recorded. Niello-inlaid red brass is known from the Islamic world from at least the 7th century but the use of red brass in China proper before the Yuan dynasty does not appear to have been recorded, though its use in western Tibet and Nepal since the 8th century has been demonstrated in recent studies, and its use in China proper in the same century therefore seems a not unreasonable inference. It is well known that there was considerable trade between western Asia and China, with large communities of foreigners, including Arabs, resident at the capital and at Canton until the 860s. The environment was therefore one in which knowledge of the composition of red brass and indeed niello is likely to have been acquired by the Chinese metalworkers of the time. Red brass was also the base material for early cloisonné in China. However, the inclusion of lead in the niello mix does not appear in the comparatively few known Islamic and Western examples from before the mid 11th century A. D. so far tested, although niello with lead has been found on a Byzantine piece of that date . No Chinese niello-decorated examples were included in these tests, no doubt because so few are known. However, the shape and decoration, so similar to Tang *sancai* decorated pieces link this piece to the High Tang period (684-756). There is a small ring inside the rim, probably for a chain to attach a cover now missing. It is interesting to speculate on the use of this vessel. I would hazard a guess that it was used to contain counters for Chinese chess or *weiqi*, which was popular during the Tang dynasty.

Also included in the exhibition is a rare Yunnan bronze lamp datable to the Han dynasty, (Exhibit 252) and a rare large brazier with four identical long-horned *taotie* and three hoof-tipped splayed feet emerging from feline heads (Exhibit 265), which is paralleled by Yue wares of the early Six Dynasties period. I would not rule out a southern Chinese provenance for this piece. There is also an Ordos bronze doe similar to an excavated 5th century B.C. example (Exhibit 257), and a number of other bronze or silver inlaid, gilded bronze or lead animals, which are similar to examples in jade or other media of their respective periods (Exhibits 249, 253, 267, 268 and 278), a so-called Nestorian cross (Exhibit 279), (possibly a personal seal, as the position of similar pieces when found seems to indicate that they were worn suspended from the belt) and two dated later metalwares (Exhibits 281 and 284). The association of such objects as Exhibit 279 with the Ongut Mongols, who were Nestorian Christians, has not been proved archaeologically and is now thought by scholars to be unlikely. The Song/Yuan dating traditionally assigned to such pieces because of this reputed association is now also considered hundreds of years too late.

Exhibits 287 and 289 are also of interest in demonstrating the penchant of the late Ming bronze casters for copying on their bronzes the background diaper patterns found on contemporary lacquers.

Chinese secular sculpture in bronze is a rarity, though Buddhist and Taoist related bronze sculptures are quite common. A bronze sculpture of an official, which can be compared with contemporary ivories, and a bronze *lohan*, the latter with gilding on lacquer, the same technique used on the Erlitou *jue* (Exhibit 226) both from the Ming dynasty (16th and 17th centuries respectively) are included (Exhibits 288 and 291).

Exhibit 292 has the mark of the last Ming emperor Chongzhen (1628 - 1644). This heavy, well-cast gold encrusted item serves as a pointer for the dating to the 17th century of a large group of similar gold encrusted bronzes, which normally have the six character mark of Xuande. The bronzes so marked are very seldom, if ever, of the Xuande period. The Xuande reign was famous for the fine quality of its bronzes, and pieces were so marked right through the 17th and 18th centuries to enhance their marketability. Exhibit 292 is exceptional in having the mark of its real period.

Finally, several interesting metal items are also included in the scholar's studio section of the catalogue. These include a seal paste box with extensive silver inlays and traces of gilding (Exhibit 286), probably dating from the mid 16th century, and a Hu Wenming incense container (Exhibit 289) with Hu Wenming's mark. Hu Wenming was a famous bronze caster who worked during the Wanli period, and seems to have inspired a school of metalworkers in the first half of the 17th century. Some pieces from his school use his mark but they seldom reach the quality of casting on this box, which is probably by the master himself. There is also a gilt-splashed pumpkin waterdropper with shrew handle (Exhibit 290), a Qianlong-marked gilt and splashed-bronze brushrest of two frolicking *kui* dragons (Exhibit 296) and a tripod incense burner with a marbled-metal and black-burnished body (Exhibit 294). The use of the four character Qianlong mark on Exhibit 296 and the general sophistication of the piece renders an imperial provenance likely. Marbled metal, as found on Exhibit 294, seems to have been first produced in China in the 17th century on high quality pieces, but remained rare. Marbled metal was popular in Japan in its high quality 19th century metalware.

Besides the important gold Ordos fitting already discussed (Exhibit 298), a few later gold objects, including a set of gold belt plaques, are also included (Exhibits 299 to 303). Belt plaques of similar shapes (Exhibit 301) seem to have originated in the Liao dynasty (907-1125) and the shape continued into the Ming. The set here is dated to the first half of the Ming or earlier as one of the plaques has what appears to be its original wood backing. Carbon 14 testing gave a 68% probability that this dates to *circa* 1500 A.D., hence the attribution to early Ming. Carbon 14 tests on pieces of this age are not that reliable and I believe the set is more likely to be of Song or at least Yuan date. I do not know of another recorded complete set of gold belt plaques.

A Tang chased and repoussé silver lustral bowl decorated with a three-clawed dragon, fish and crab, ducks and other animals on a ring punched ground, a small silvered-bronze box, a 13th to 14th century niello-enriched silver seal paste box (Exhibits 304, 305 and 306) and a silver filigree box (Exhibit 307) have also been included in the exhibition. The silver lustral bowl with dragon, fish and crab, ducks and other animals amid foliage against a ring punched ground is a fine example from the High Tang period . The silvered-bronze box (Exhibit 305) has the zig-zag key fret found on late Tang silver that was taken into the ceramic repertoire in the Southern Song and Jin dynasties (1115-1234). The deliberate use of cheaper bronze as a substitute for silver, the peony decoration and the existence of a foot rim on this box all point to a dating shortly after the Tang and it is accordingly dated to the Northern Song (960-1127). As regards Exhibit 306, I don't know of another Chinese niello-enriched chased silver example from this early period. The piece can, however, be compared to lacquers of the period of similar shape and decorated with ladies in a garden setting. One of the ladies depicted on this piece is playing a musical instrument, a type of lute, which in the Tang dynasty was held vertically but in the Ming was played in a horizontal position. Here it is held in an intermediate position indicative of a pre-Ming but post-Tang date. The exceptionally finely observed scene of herons by a lotus pond and chasing fish can also be paralleled in art from the assigned period. Niello-enriched silver pieces were particularly popular in Europe from early medieval times and silver products so enriched were produced in the Roman Empire as early as the 1st century A.D.. The use of red brass associated with niello on Exhibit 269 also makes it likely that niello was one of the few decorative techniques introduced into China from the West. One feature, which should be noted on both Exhibits 304 and 306, is the traces or foot prints on the interior of the chasing on the exterior. I was told about a decade ago by Mr. Gyllensvard, a noted expert on Chinese silver, that such a feature normally only occurs on pieces of the Yuan dynasty or earlier and had been eliminated by the Ming, though he added a rider to this that pieces made in Tibet or for the Tibetan market continued to show this feature well into the Ming period. From examples of antique Chinese silver I have seen,

I think both his observations are correct. Deliberate copies of Tang silver made in the 19th and 20th centuries do have this feature but are so coarse that they can be readily distinguished from the genuine period pieces. The decoration on Exhibits 304 and 306 has no connection whatever with Tibet. The silver produced in Tibet or for that market is decorated almost exclusively with Buddhist or Buddhist related motifs.

The silver filigree box (Exhibit 307) is, I understand, good work from Beijing but I understand lower grade silver filigree work was also done in Chengdu, Sichuan Province.

In addition to the gold and silver objects, a number of cloisonné and enamel pieces are included in the exhibition (Exhibits 308-315). Cloisonné and enamel on metal are among the few decorative art objects manufactured in China which did not originate from Chinese invented techniques. An early reference in a Yuan text to cloisonné refers to it as "Dashi" ware (Arabian ware) apparently confirming its foreign origin. Apart from a single enamel example, which has been described as Chinese cloisonné in the Shosoin at Nara, which can be dated by its deposit there to the 8th century, no other example of Chinese cloisonné has been firmly dated to before the Xuande period (1426 - 1435). In later centuries, the reign of Jingtai (1450 - 1457) was considered to be the best period for cloisonné and many pieces are marked with that reign mark, chiefly from the 17th and 18th centuries. The Ming clossonné pieces all have enamels held within wire enclosures called 'cloisons', which are fixed to a metal body made of an alloy of about 70 - 80% copper, and 20 - 30% zinc with generally about 1% each of tin and lead. This metal composition is red brass, which is close to modern commercial brass, and such pieces are comparatively heavy. The exposed surface of the wire cloisons is invariably gilded, though in the course of time the gilding has frequently worn. Post 17th century cloisonné pieces generally have the cloisons attached to a copper body in contrast to the red brass of the earlier period. The changeover in body material seems to have occurred sometime in the 17th century. The almost invariable background colour for Chinese cloisonné pieces is a turquoise blue, and at various periods enamels of certain colours predominated. The pink colour, for instance, shown on Exhibit 312, which has a Qianlong (1736-1795) mark, does not occur before the early 18th century. The pill box (Exhibit 308) has a red brass body and has been given a 15th century dating. This piece has an incised four character Jingtai mark. A recent Chinese publication has suggested that such a four character incised mark is in fact genuine and this piece is therefore a possible candidate for the Jingtai reign period. From its decoration and the colours used in the cloisons it is unlikely to be later than1500.

The final cloisonné piece has the four character Tongzhi (1862 - 1874) mark in enamel cloisons on the base; pieces marked in such a way, which must be of the period, are rare and documentary.

In addition to the four cloisonné pieces, four enamel pieces are included; one, made in the shape of a Queen Anne silver mustard pot (Exhibit 311) is a typical example of Canton enamel. Canton enamels have mixed colour enamels and thinner gilding, if this occurs, than on those produced in the palace workshops in Beijing. Exhibit 310, which is marked with the imperial Yongzheng (1723-1735) reign mark, is a typical example from the Beijing workshop. The colours are not mixed, the gilding is thick and it has the yellow background commonly found on the imperial workshop products. The saucer dish with a Qianlong mark (Exhibit 313) is a fine example of Canton enamel made with an orange-yellow ground in emulation of those from the Beijing imperial workshop. However, it has the thinner gilding and mixed colours typical of the Canton products. The fourth piece is a dated Canton enamel condiment container and spoon made for the Annamese King Minh Minh (ruled 1820 -1840) in about 1830.

Apart from the cloisonné and enamel pieces, one example of gold-enriched pewter (Exhibit 293) has been included. This type of work seems to have been produced in the late Ming and early Qing period. Such objects were apparently made by stamping the desired pattern from a thin gold sheet onto the relatively soft pewter.

The gilded copper brazier and ink stone container (Exhibit 295), which has an internal tray for holding charcoal, is another interesting and rare piece. This would have been used in a scholar's studio in the depths of winter in northern China when it was necessary to keep the water, with which the ink was mixed, from freezing. Exhibit 297, which is dated 1881 and contains a long inscription giving the maker's name and place of manufacture, is a burnished, incised and silver-inlaid copper container for the scholar's studio.

中國青銅器

中國青銅器的製造史可以上溯至最初有歷史記載的時期。一九九〇年十一月我在北京參觀了一些尚未公佈的考古發現材料，其中包括一件在陝西出土的青銅小鈴。主辦者估計銅的成份佔百分之九十，年代約在公元前二千一百年，並聲稱是中國發現的青銅器中，最古的其中一件。青銅是銅、錫的合金，有時還加入鉛的成份。

青銅祭器似乎在公元前二千年稍後一段時間開始製造，時間相當於夏朝，至商代最爲流行。傳統意見認爲商繼承夏，但現代學術界則認爲夏朝和商朝可能有一段時期同時存在。商朝的準確年代至今還未能確定，多年以來，學者們提出幾個不同年份，争辯不決。一些屬於所謂「二里頭文化」的遺物已經被確認。「二里頭文化」是以河南偃師二里頭一地得名，論者認爲是屬夏/早商文化，年代約是公元前一千六百年間。當時已有青銅祭器的製造，其方法是在陶范中鑄成。

失臘法製造銅器在這段草創期雖還未有應用，但肯定在稍後時間內進行採用。中國金屬鑄造者在製作較爲精細的花紋(如展品226)時仍需要用陶製的分范。展品237便是一例。北京故宮博物院一位銅器專家告訴我失臘法似乎是在春秋時代(公元前七七〇年至前四四六年)才開始使用。

展品226一件平底爵屬二里頭文化。此爵異常特別，因爲在紋飾上有金漆的殘留。這時期的漆器罩以金箔(註1)，而安陽商代遺存中也發現蓋有金箔的銅鈕(註2)，因此我們有理由相信這件爵上的金漆是與這件銅器同時製造。據我所知，除這件外，並沒有另一件類似的金漆銅器。不久的將來，碳十四斷代法可能證實金漆的年代。但是，以現在的技術，還不能對這些微量的金漆做一個令人滿意的實驗，以證實它的年代。這類早期的爵都是平底，是暖酒的祭器。展覽中也有一件晚商(約公元前一千二百年)的銅爵。這時期的銅爵底圓，展品227便是這個時期的典型產品。商朝覆亡後，這種造型特別的盛器似乎不再鑄造。

展品中另有兩件祭器。一件是公元前九百年的鼎(展品228)，而另一件是公元前九至八世紀的簋(展品229)。簋的上部及底部記載了鑄造該簋的因由。與商代祭器的一字或兩字的族徽短銘比較起來，周代的銘文便顯得頗長，展品229便是一例。這些長篇的銘文偶或紀錄了一些重大的事故，如婚禮、封地或封爵等。像展覽中的簋這類祭器往往是成批而造，紋飾頗爲呆板，與商器比較，便缺少了後者的瑰麗壯觀。

除以上祭器外，展覽還包括有一些值得玩味的青銅器。它們包括一組稱爲鄂爾多斯的青銅器。爲方便比較，我們把它們放在一起(展品254至264)。在一九二〇年至一九三〇年代，一批爲數頗多的小件銅器在中國北方出現，同時流入國際市場。它們包括銅帶飾、帶鈎、刀、羹和各類小構件。紋飾多是鹿、羊、鳥(通常是猛禽類)、虎、狼和很多其他動物。這類銅器以中國北方鄂爾多斯地區而得名，包括在河套附近的鄂爾多斯地區及與中國接壤的地方。這類器物的風格亦稱爲「動物風格」，原因是它們的紋飾以動物爲主。這類器物的分佈地區甚廣，西起阿爾泰山，東至朝鮮邊境，北達貝加爾湖，横跨古代近東至中國中部，影响了這一地區的銅器製造風格。雖然目前對這些材料的了解已比以前跨一大步，但仍然有很多問題待於研究。一九九一年四月在匹兹堡參加一個研討會後，我有如是看法。根據新的資料，這類「動物風格」銅器的年期比以前所想像的推前了很多。從前論者認爲是自戰國至六朝一段時間所造，爲期甚短，但由於近年來無數考古發現，其中部份有些被定爲早至商代。

展品236是一件中原製造的銅鐏，上有一隻好像獅身人首像的動物，它與公元前六世紀晚期的伊朗波斯波利斯Persepolis地方的動物相類，而有裝飾的腿上的鬈曲紋則明顯地是受鄂爾多斯銅器所影响。

多年以來，鑑定鄂爾多斯銅器都存着不少困難。幸而在過去三十年間，中國在內蒙古、陝西省北部及中部地區進行廣泛的發掘，發現了很多與展品254至264相似的銅器。這些發掘似乎把這些銅器的年代定爲東周(公元前七七〇年至前四七五年)至東漢(公元二五年至公元二二〇年)。這些銅器似乎是游牧民族如山戎，月氏和匈奴的手工藝制品。他們在內蒙古和陝西北部居住了一段很長的時期——山戎在該區活躍的時間是自公元前八世紀至公元前四世紀，月氏則是自公元前四世紀至公元前三世紀。自公元前三世紀以後，匈奴代月氏而興，雄據該區，建立了一個大平原帝國，與長城另一邊的漢族分庭抗禮。鑑定動物紋飾牌的傳統方法是把動物數目較多的一類(參見展品254)定爲較晚的年代(可能是西漢)，而只有一只動物的一類則定得較早。可是，根據近年的發掘資料，似乎推翻了這個傳統斷代方法。在內蒙古西部桃紅巴拉杭錦旗一個遺址中發掘得到一些牌飾，上有好幾隻動物的紋飾，經碳十四探測其他文物，把該遺址的年代定爲公元前七一一年，誤差是加或減一百一十五年，實即公元前九世紀至公元前六世紀。而在一個可準確定爲公元一世紀的墓葬中則發現了一件鎏金飾牌，其中只飾以一隻動物，該件與展品264相似。傳統斷代認爲是公元前三或四世紀的文物，但根據新發現，這看法亦站不住脚。

除了前述銅件外，還有一件重要的鄂爾多斯金構件，上有熊的紋飾，爪、頸毛和耳朵均清晰可見（展品298）。背有凸起的織縷紋成爲表面組成的一部份。據説鑄造方法是用織物支持蠟製的構件模型，然後翻製陶造的主模，待主模乾後即燒結備用。在這一過程中，蠟和襯底的織物會被焚去，同時在主模內壁留下因壓印而留下的織縷紋。在陶製主模注入金液，製成後背面遂留有織縷紋痕跡。我曾經見過鑄自同一個主模的兩件金和兩件銀的構件。在一些具鄂爾多斯風格的金、銀及高質地的鎏金或鎏錫銅件上，包括有名的“Hermitage”收藏的彼得大帝遺珍中的金器，都可見到上有織物的痕跡。有關製造這類留有織物痕跡的飾件的地點，一向説法不定。但在過去一年間，公元前三一一年燕下都（燕國的南都，今河北南部易縣）遺址中出土了一批動物風格的飾件和相關的鑄造用具，飾件上也有織縷紋的殘留。秦滅燕於公元前二二二年，自此燕下都便衰廢。燕地多狄人雜居。狄人來自西域，似乎在春秋時代或戰國早期定居在燕及山戎等地。據悉，燕國統治者雖然是漢人，但作爲其國民的狄人實際上是游牧民族的一支，他們的手工藝製品具動物風格。有必要指出的一點是這種織物殘迹不見於素身銅件，而只見於用金、銀、鎏金或鎏銀銅製的貴重飾件，而這些貴重物品的價值也必然是族長階級才可以負擔得起。因此，我想這類飾件大抵是燕國冶金匠專門所鑄，以售與北方游牧民族的長級人物，對象並非是本國狄人的一般賤民，正如比這時期早幾個世紀的希臘人一樣，他們把高質地的物品售與黑海的斯基泰族長，兩者情況相同。由於鑄造遺址的發現，使我們可以把這一類帶織物遺痕的飾件定爲公元前三一一年至公元前二二二年這一段時間。

似乎可以肯定，在那個時期代至少有另外一個作坊也採用同樣的鑄造方法。因爲有一位中國專家告訴我，至少有一件出土的鄂爾多斯風格銅件上帶有銘文，字體風格與燕地不同；另外我最近見到一件精美的鑲嵌銅件，中原風格，亦是用類似鑄法製成。此外，「失臘」及「失織物」法似乎沿用至西漢時代，遼寧和寧夏的匈奴遺址發現了數件鎏金銅飾牌，可以証實這個看法。

展覽中另一些值得玩味的銅器是一組鎏金或錯金器物。這種技法自公元前六世紀一直沿用。它們包括有鑲松石（展品238）、錯銀（展品240、243和249）、鑲玉（展品239）、錯金（展品242）和錯金銀（展品244、247和248）。部份物品可能是馬或馬車飾、腰帶飾或帶鈎，它們在戰國時代開始流行。

其他罕有的金屬器物包括如下：

（一）鐸——尺寸與常見一樣，均細小。柄呈短長方形（展品231）。它比同形狀的墝小得多。人們通常把兩者混淆，除了大小不同之外，鐃有長筒狀柄，年代似乎都定是商代。鐃和鐸都是敲擊樂器，一般無舌。所有以前著録的鐸都被定爲戰國時代，但這裡的一件依據花紋看來可以定爲春秋晚期即公元前六世紀至公元前五世紀，因此此件可以説是自有著録以來最早的一件。墝與鐸的使用方法是安在木把之上，口向上敲擊，如插圖所示。

（二）越矛（展品233）——在公元前五世紀，越國以生産青銅兵器著名，展品233即此例。上面的花紋與越王勾踐（統治時間是公元前四九六年至公元前四六五年）的寶劍一樣。很明顯，這些花紋有加强銅的硬度的作用，又使劍及矛頭的邊沿更加鋒利。用這技法製造的兵器存世不多，似乎都是在越國生産，持續時間亦非常短暫。技法自後失傳，一直不明，至近始有眉目。

（三）豹斑紋劍——經金屬專家查驗，此劍的刃部含高成份的錫（14%），低至中成份的鉛（3.5至5%），整件是青銅合金所製，除斜尖的劍刃外，劍身整體鎏錫。斑點的形成是在鎏錫時把劍身局部蓋住而成。這類貴重的劍是吴國的產品，製造年代是公元前四世紀至公元前三世紀（展品241）。吴國是以生産精良的武器而著名。

（四）彩繪銅鑑——（展品246），上繪的紋飾與紀年公元前一六二年馬王堆墓出土的漆器相類。

展覽中有好幾面銅鏡。早在商代已有銅鏡生産，但製作粗陋而簡單。至戰國，特別是在楚國，銅鏡已成爲一種很重要的藝術形式，紋飾大多非常精細。展覽中有一系列的銅鏡，自春秋至元代（公元一二七九至公元一三六八年）並陳，使得容易比較風格的嬗變，亦算得頗爲全面（展品270至276）。公元前五世紀齊國一個工匠的記載中紀錄了鑄造青銅器的六種方法（案：即〈考工記〉稱「六齊」）：製鐘及食器的成份是青銅佔85%，錫佔15%，製鏡則銅佔一半，而錫又佔一半。一些早期的銅鏡有銀色光澤，便是根據書中指示加入較多量的錫。雖然根據個人的理解，一些早期銅鏡是在表面上特別加上一層錫衣，可能是這個原因令鏡面呈現銀色光澤。

展覽中大部份的銅鏡都是常見的標準圓形，但有部份晚期的鏡是方形或花形，頗具趣味。其中一面有陰刻銘文，似乎是官方記號，批准銅鏡自南方輸出到被金和元人佔據的北方（展品275）。南宋（公元一一二七年至一二七九年）法令規定禁止金屬製品外銷到北方，若官方批准則不在此限之內。展品276非常特別，因是在平滑的鏡面上陰刻了紋飾。似乎除了此鏡外，我未曾見過具此特色的其他任何銅鏡。另一面銅鏡（展品272）的年代是吳（公元三世紀中葉）。這是根據已發表的出土資料而決定的。這面鏡特別之處是在怪異的神話動物群中，雜有頭帶光環的飛仙。飛仙的紋飾是在東漢時，佛教傳入中國以後才開始出現在藝術品之上的。

對於銅鏡的斷代，其中一個要點是注意其在漫長歷史中，鏡把的不同演變。這些鏡把的形式通常是在鏡背中央墳起的紐或凸起的部份，穿以繩子以便把持。這些紐的形狀不一，大小也不同，差異有時頗大。在戰國和漢代早期，鏡把的形式通常是薄而收腰的橋狀，上有三個凹入的地方（參見展品271）。公元前一世紀及以後，鏡把一般是幾乎實心的圓紐，這些紐往往很大，如展品272所見。這種形式的把持續到唐代（公元六一八至公元九〇六年）。在隋（公元五八一至六一八年）或唐代，這些大紐偶爲蹲伏的動物如青蛙、獅子或龜所取代（參見展品273）。唐代以後，鏡紐趨於細小，有時可能變成僅是一個環狀，如展品275。元以後，銅鏡仍然流行，但這時已全然是一種日用的物品，以前繁縟的鏡背紋飾已不復見。自宋以後，鏡背幾乎全部變成光素無文。繁縟紋飾的銅鏡在中國雖然漸漸式微，但在日本和朝鮮則仍持續了幾個世紀。中國的鏡與西方的鏡作用雖同，但形式有異，一般而言，不會在鏡沿伸出柄來。據我所見，可以肯定是中國製造的帶柄鏡子最早出現於南宋末期。據文獻記載，晚明時（公元一三六八年至公元一六四四年）的鑑賞家認爲帶柄的鏡子是鄙俗的，而在前朝，人們也可能有同樣的觀念。我曾經見過一個帶管狀短柄的鏡子，柄自邊沿伸出，以前可能安有木柄，以加長柄部。這鏡紋飾簡單，只有數圈乳丁紋和“<”紋，據悉是中國南方所造。根據這些紋飾，我認爲它可能屬越南的東山文化，年代約是公元八世紀。但是，我們也不能全然抹殺是中國南部製造的這個可能性。無論如何，自口沿伸出柄把的鏡似乎從來不受中國人歡迎。但在日本，最遲在十二世紀已有這種形式的鏡，往後一直有繼續製造。

展覽中有一件很特別的僧砵式盛器，其上運用填嵌法飾以多列四瓣小花。我認爲此砵形器的年代可定爲唐朝（展品269）。經過多次科學實驗，確定該件確實有相當古老的歷史，同時證實是用紅銅所造，成份是在一般的銅合金中加入21%的鋅；此外，又發現厚厚的填嵌物質原來是一種銅、鉛和硫的合金，成份接近最佳的配合：鉛佔42%，銅佔35%而硫則佔23%。我從來未見過一件類似的、或任何同年代填嵌有硫化物合金的中國器物，這些均從未見於文獻紀錄。填嵌硫化物合金的紅銅器物最少自七世紀起便在伊斯蘭教國家出現，但在中國，元代以前的文獻似乎未有紅銅的使用記載的。然而，近年的研究發現自八世紀起，西藏西部和尼泊爾地區已使用紅銅。因此，中國本部在同一世紀使用紅銅也應是合情合理的推論。事實上，人所共知，在公元八六〇年以前一段時期西亞與中國的貿易頻繁，爲數甚多的不同種族，包括阿拉伯人聚居在首都和廣州。在這樣的環境之下，中國冶金工人遂學到紅銅組成和硫合金的知識。紅銅也是中國早期景泰藍器的基本材料。日本奈良正倉院藏有一件這類早期景泰藍器，假如這件是紅銅所造，那末便可證實在公元八世紀這段時間內，中國已在冶鍊紅銅。可是，經爲數不多的十一世紀中葉以前的伊斯蘭和西方樣本得出的結果進行研究，發現其中的硫合金中沒有鉛的成份，而在當時的拜占庭樣本中，却驗出有鉛的存在。在該等試驗中，並沒有中國樣本，毫無疑問是因爲它們爲數甚少。這罐的造型和紋飾與唐三彩非常相似，所以當是盛唐（公元六八四年至七五六年）的產物。口沿內有一小環，可能是用以把鍊與蓋相連，而蓋則已佚失。對於這罐的用途，我猜想是用以盛放圍棋棋子。圍棋這一遊戲在唐代頗爲流行。

展覽的金屬製品還有一件罕見的銅燈，雲南製造，年代屬漢代（展品252）；一件罕有的大香爐，上有四組長角孖鋪首，外撇的蹄狀足自獸頭伸出（展品265），其形狀可與六朝早期的越窑相比較，我認爲這件也有可能是南方的產品；一件鄂爾多斯銅鹿，它與一件年代屬公元前五世紀的出土樣本相似（展品257）；一組動物，其中有銅製、有錯銀、有鎏金、有鉛製等，它們都可以和相關年代的玉或其他質料的動物相互比較（展品249、253、267、268和278）；一件稱爲景教十字的銅飾件（展品279）（可能是一種私印，因爲依照類似飾件出土的安放位置表明它們是懸掛在腰帶之下）；兩件紀年的晚期銅器（展品281和284）。像展品279一類物件，有人認爲與汪古部蒙古人有關，因爲他們是景教徒。但由於考古資料未能證實這個說法，學者們認爲可能性不大。正由於這個說法，過去的人把這類銅件的年代定爲宋元之間，但現時則認爲應該早定幾百年。

展品287和289也頗爲特別，它們反映晚明銅冶工人的喜好，把同時代漆器的菱形地紋移植到所製的銅器之上。

與佛道有關的銅器塑像在中國甚爲普遍，但屬非宗教的雕塑却極爲罕有。展覽中有兩件明代作品（一件是十六世紀而另一件是十七世紀），（展品288和291），前者是一個文官像，造型與當代的象牙可相互比較；後者是一個羅漢，上罩金漆，其技藝與展品226二里頭時期的銅爵相同。

展品292帶有明朝最後一個皇帝崇禎的年號（公元一六二八年至一六四四年）。這件冶鑄精良的釘金器，體重，可以作爲一件標準器，把大批同類型、一般帶宣德六字款的釘金器定爲十七世紀。帶宣德款的銅器絶大部份都是僞作，這大概是由於此朝代的銅器精良，十七世紀和十八世紀的銅器大多加上這個年號以便易於出售。展292是一個例外，它有宣德款，同時是真正宣德的產品。

最後，登記在目録的文房用具部份也有幾件有趣的金屬器物。它們包括一個印盒，上有鎏金的殘留和繁縟的錯銀紋飾（展品286），年代可能是十六世紀中期；一個帶「胡文明」款的香盒（展品289）。胡文明是晚明時一個著名的銅冶工人，活躍在萬曆年間。他的作品影响很大，十七世紀上半葉的冶鑄工人都仿效其風格，並衍生爲一派。有些產品還加上「胡文明」款，但質素大不相侔。這盒鎸刻精美，很可能是胡文明本人所造；此外，還有一件局部鎏金的水滴，以地鼠爲把，形似南瓜（展品290）；一件帶乾隆款的鎏金及釘金雙龍筆架（展品296）；一個三足香爐，上有大理石紋（案：像搞胎器一樣的紋飾），身黑色並經抛光（展品294）。展品296的筆架可能是一件御用的文房用具，因爲它帶四字乾隆款，而且造工精緻。展品294上的大理石紋似乎最早出現在十七世紀的高檔產品之上，但爲數極少。在日本也是出現在高檔的十九世紀金屬製品之上，並且頗爲受人歡迎。

除了前述的金製鄂爾多斯構件（展品298）以外，還有幾件晚期的金器（展品299至303），其中包括一套金帶飾（展品301）。與展品301形狀相似的帶飾似乎始自遼代，持續到明代。這套金帶飾的年代現定爲明代前期或較早。這是根據其中一件背後的木板，做過碳十四試驗，可能的年代是公元一五〇〇年，機率是68%。但由於運用碳十四對這個年代的文物的測試並非十分準確，我相信這套帶飾可能會是宋代或者最晚是元代的產品。除這套外，我並不知道有另外完整一套金帶飾的記載。

展覽中還有一件唐朝銀製浄水碗，身有捶壓凸紋和鎸刻花紋，包括三爪龍、魚、蟹、鴨和其他動物，圓圈形地紋；一件鎏銀銅小盒；一件填嵌硫合金的銀印盒，年代約是十三至十四世紀（展品304、305和306）；一個細工銀絲盒（展品307）。銀製浄水碗是盛唐（公元六八四年至七五六年）的一件佳作。鎏銀銅小盒（展品305）上有曲折回紋，在晚唐銀器上也有同樣花紋，此技法其後在南宋及金代（公元一一一五至公元一二三四年）的陶瓷上也有採用。特意使用較經濟的銅器以取代銀器的作法、牡丹的紋飾、圈足的存在——這一切都顯示這盒是在唐以後不久的時間裡所造，因此我認定它的年代是北宋（公元九六〇至公元一一二七年）。至於展品306，我還未見過另外一件年份像它那末早的同類產品。但它可以和同年代、形狀相似的庭園仕女紋漆盒相互比較。在此盒的圖案上一個婦女在彈奏一種像琵琶一類樂器。在唐朝，演奏者打直抱持琵琶，而在明朝則打横，這個婦女抱持的姿勢在横直之間，顯示其年代可能是介乎唐以後和明以前的時間。那異常精緻的蓮花池畔，蒼鷺擒魚的景象也可與同年代的藝術品互相比較。

嵌填硫合金一類銀器在中世紀早期的歐洲特別流行，早在公元一世紀羅馬帝國已有製造。展品269上紅銅與硫合金結合使用表明它是從西方傳入中國的少數裝飾技法的其中一種。展品304和306均有一個特點，值得我們注意，這便是它們的內層均留有清晰的鑿痕，這是由於工人在外層用捶鑿法形成紋飾的結果。Gyllensvard是一位有名的中國銀器專家。十年前，他告訴我只有元朝或以前的朝代有此特點，到明代已不復見到。但他補充說，在西藏製造的或是中國爲西藏製造的同類器物，在入明以後仍表現出此特色。根據我以往所見的中國古代銀器，我認爲他這兩個觀點均是正確的。十九世紀和二十世紀的仿唐銀器雖然也有此特色，但是委實太粗糙，與真品相較便很容易分別開來。展品304與306與西藏毫無關係。西藏製品或是中國爲西藏而造的銀器幾乎全部都有佛教或與佛教有關的紋飾。細工銀絲盒（展品307）是一件北京製造的佳作。據我所知，劣等的銀絲器物在四川成都也有製造。

除了金銀器之外，展覽中還有景泰藍和銅胎琺瑯器（展品308至315）。中國生產的工藝品中有小部份品種並非本土創製，以銅爲胎的景泰藍和琺瑯器便是其中兩類。根據元代文獻，景泰藍器被稱爲「大食窑」（阿拉伯窑），據此似乎可以確定這類器物是源自外國。日本奈良正倉院藏有一件琺瑯器，是該收藏中惟一的琺瑯器，清單稱爲中國景泰藍。根據其他器物的收藏歷史，這件琺瑯器的年代可定爲公元八世紀。除了這件以外，我們便再找不到另外一件年代確實比宣德（公元一四二六年至一四三五年）更早的景泰藍器。在以後的幾個世紀裏，景泰（公元一四五〇年至一四五七年）所產被公認是最佳的製品。很多帶有這個年款的景泰藍器大部份都是十七世紀和十八世紀所造。明朝景泰藍器的製作方法是在金屬的胎身上銲上用金屬綫圍成的「空間」，然後在「空間」中填入琺瑯。金屬胎身是由合金造成，包括銅約佔70%至80%，鋅佔20%至30%，小量的錫和鉛，各佔1%。這種金屬構成即爲紅銅，與現今的商業用銅接近，製成器物頗重。構成「空間」的金屬綫的露光部份都一定加以鎏金。隨着時間的推移，這些鎏金往往會被磨損。十七世紀以後景泰藍器的胎身不像前朝一樣用紅銅製造，而是用銅所造。這種胎身質料的改變似乎是自十七世紀開始。中國景泰藍器的底色幾乎一律是松石藍色。但在某段時期某些顏色的琺瑯會較其他顏色更爲常用。舉例來說，展品312是一件帶乾隆（公元一七三六至公元一七九五年）款的景泰藍器，其中的粉紅色是十八世紀早期以前未曾見到的。展品308是一個藥丸盒，胎身重，用紅銅製造，年代被定爲十五世紀。上有「景泰年製」陰刻四字款。根據最近出版的一本中國刊物，這種四字款是景泰一朝器物的正確款記，所以，展出的這一件有可能是景泰年間的產品。從紋飾及其「空間」中的琺瑯顏色看來，它的年份不可能在公元一五〇〇年之後。

最後一件景泰藍器帶「同治年器」（公元一八六二年至一八七四年）四字款。款字「空間」內填有琺瑯，這種形式的款字是必與器物本身同時所製，並不常見和有紀年價值。

除了幾件景泰藍器之外，展覽中還有四件琺瑯器。一件模仿安妮皇后時代銀製芥醬壺的小罌（展品311），是廣州琺瑯器的典型樣本。與北京宮廷所製的琺瑯器相較，廣州所產的琺瑯顏色互混，同時鎏金層較薄。展品310帶雍正（公元一七二三至一七三五年）款，是典型的北京宮廷作坊的產品。不同顏色並沒有相混，鎏金層厚。這件底色黃色，是北京御作坊產品上常見的色澤。帶乾隆款的碟子（展品313）地色橙黃，是仿效北京御作坊產品的一件精美的廣州產品；鎏金層薄，顏色相混，全然是廣州風格。第四件是帶紀年款的廣州琺瑯糖果盅和羹，是爲安南皇帝明明（統治期由公元一八二〇年至一八四〇年）所造，約造於公元一八三〇年。除了景泰藍和琺瑯器外，展覽中還有一件加上金色紋飾的錫器（展品293）。此類型作品的年代似乎是明末清初之間，造法是在頗軟的錫胎上，壓嵌以所需的薄金片圖案。

鎏金銅爐及硯盒（展品295）內有盛碳的盤子是另一件有趣的罕品。中國北方隆冬嚴寒，有需要把磨墨的水保暖以防結冰，這件文房用品便是這一特定環境的產物。展品297也是一件文房用具，表面拋光，錯銀，並有陰刻紋飾，帶紀年銘，相當於公元一八八一年。其上的銘文頗長，記載了工匠的名字和製造地點。

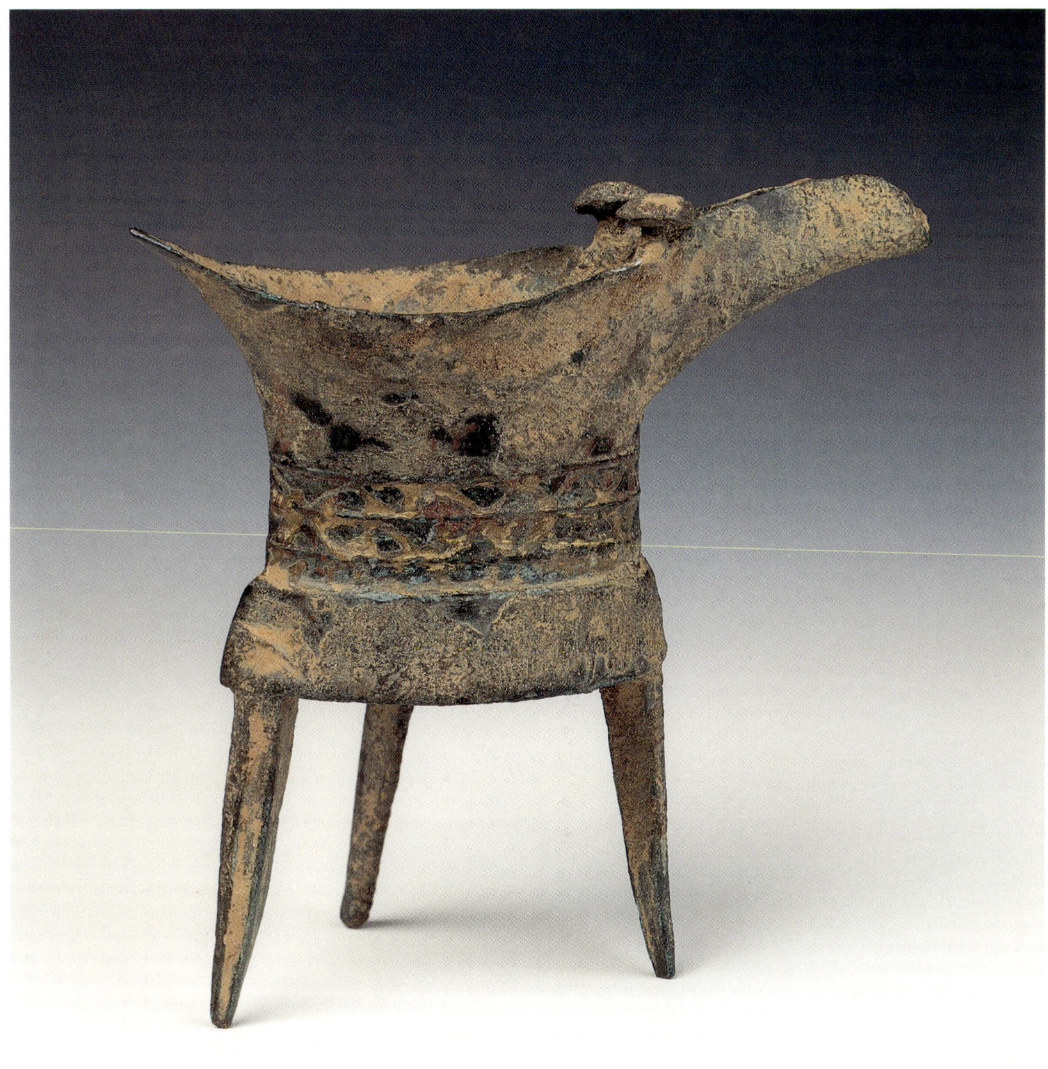

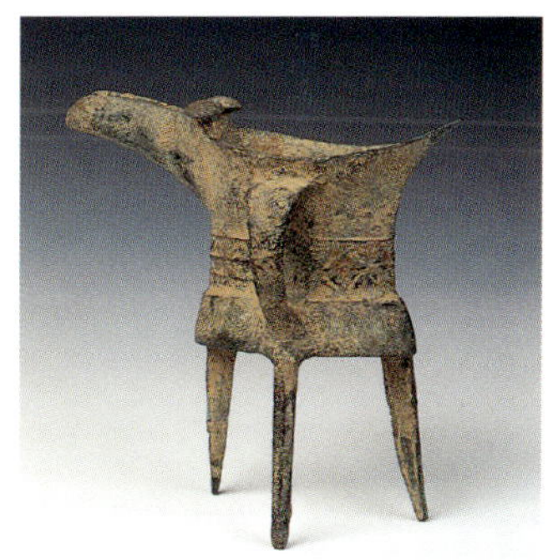

226

ERLITOU BRONZE FLAT-BOTTOMED *JUE*, ITS CENTRAL BAND OF THREAD DECORATION WITH TRACES OF GOLD SHEETING AFFIXED BY RED LACQUER TO THE BRONZE BODY

XIA/EARLY SHANG
(*circa* 1600 B.C.)
HEIGHT : 14.8 CM
LENGTH : 14.8 CM
DEPTH : 6 CM

An Erlitou bronze *jue*, flat bottomed as is typical of this period with long spout, stubby finials and plain handle, the body decorated with three raised concave bands embellished with gold sheet with cross hatching affixed to the bronze body by red lacquer.
The gold sheet embellishment, of which only part remains, is probably contemporary. A recent book on ancient chinese lacquer records a gold-sheet inlay on a red lacquer, wood based piece from this early period, though a bronze-based piece so embellished has not been hitherto recorded.

227

Bronze *jue* with traditional rounded base

Shang, Anyang period
(*circa* 12th century B.C.)
Height : 20.3 cm
Length : 17.5 cm
Width : 9.5 cm

This standard *jue* differs from the previous vessel in its more clearly articulated shape and rounded base. It is egg-shaped with a narrow vertical flange. The body stands on three narrow blade-shaped legs. A spout and a neat pointed rear balance the legs. The bowed handle has a small buffalo head at its top. The posts on the lip support roundels with intaglio spirals. The decoration consists of a *taotie* face on each side in dismembered form, the elements forming standing birds all against a neat *leiwen* ground. The elements of the faces also carry intaglio lines. The smooth surface is dark grey, with areas of rough and smooth green patina.

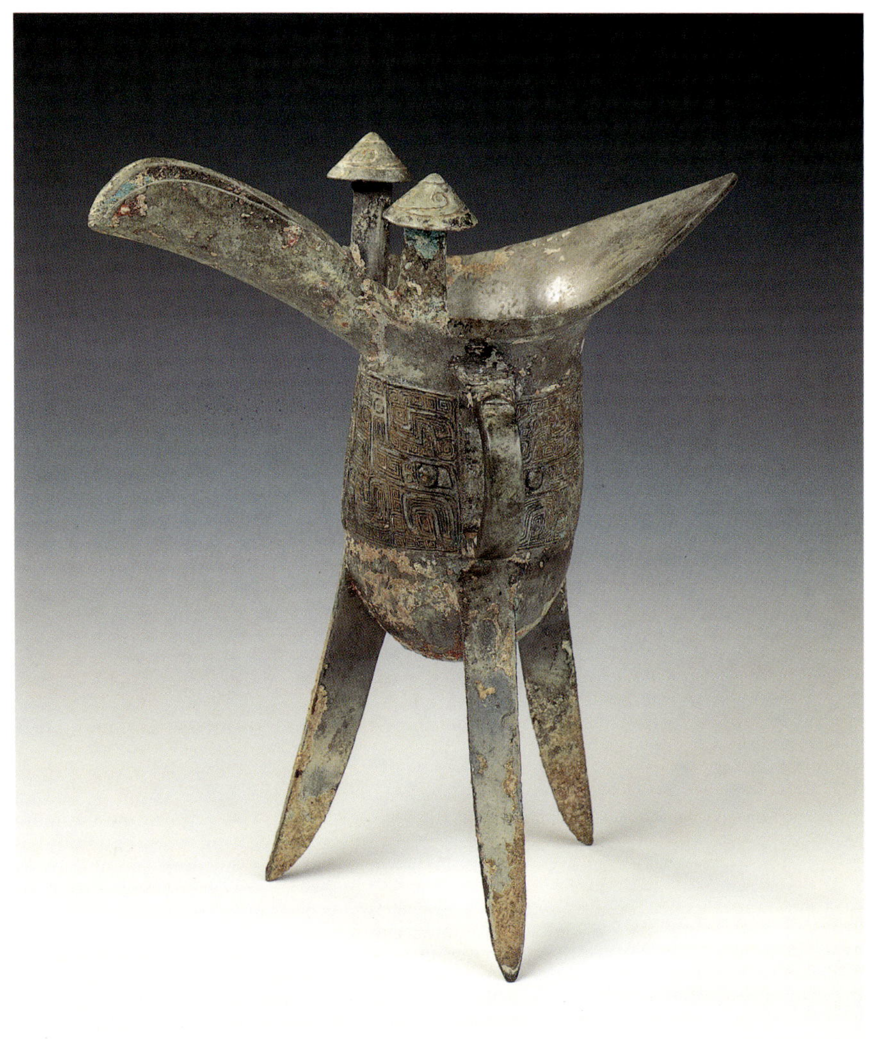

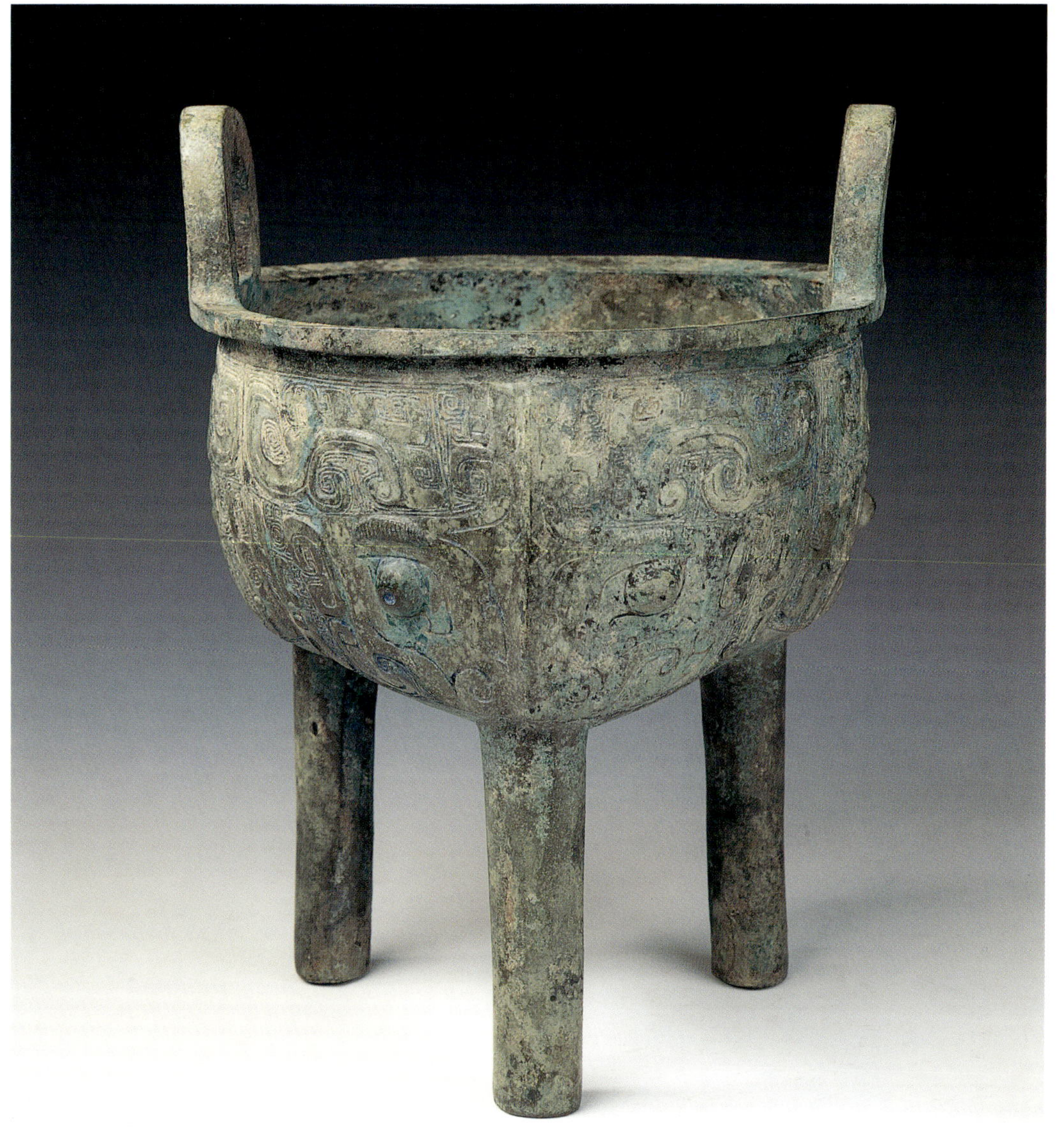

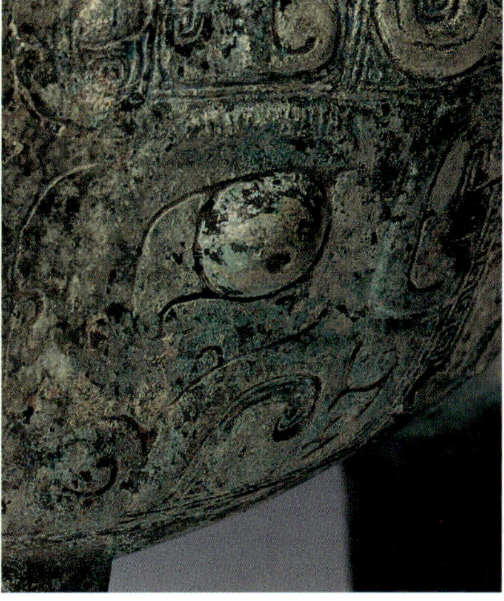

228

A RITUAL BRONZE CAULDRON *(DING)* SET ON A FLANGED RIM DECORATED WITH LARGE *TAOTIE* MASKS

EARLY WESTERN ZHOU
(*circa* 1050 B.C.)
HEIGHT : 24 CM
WIDTH : 18.5 CM

A ritual bronze cauldron *(ding)* with upright loop handles supported on three plain cylindrical legs and set on the flanged rim, the three lobes each cast with a large and elaborate *taotie* mask, whose two large hooked horns flank a crest rising from its ridged nose, the jaws with tight hooks, the eyebrows hatched and the eyes in higher relief, all on a ground of *leiwen* flanked by much simplified descending dragons, the patina a smooth grey-green and with areas of green and azurite encrustations. A virtually identical vessel has been found at the early western Zhou site of Liulihe where the inscribed bronzes mention the installation of the nephew of the first king of Zhou as Prince of Yan.

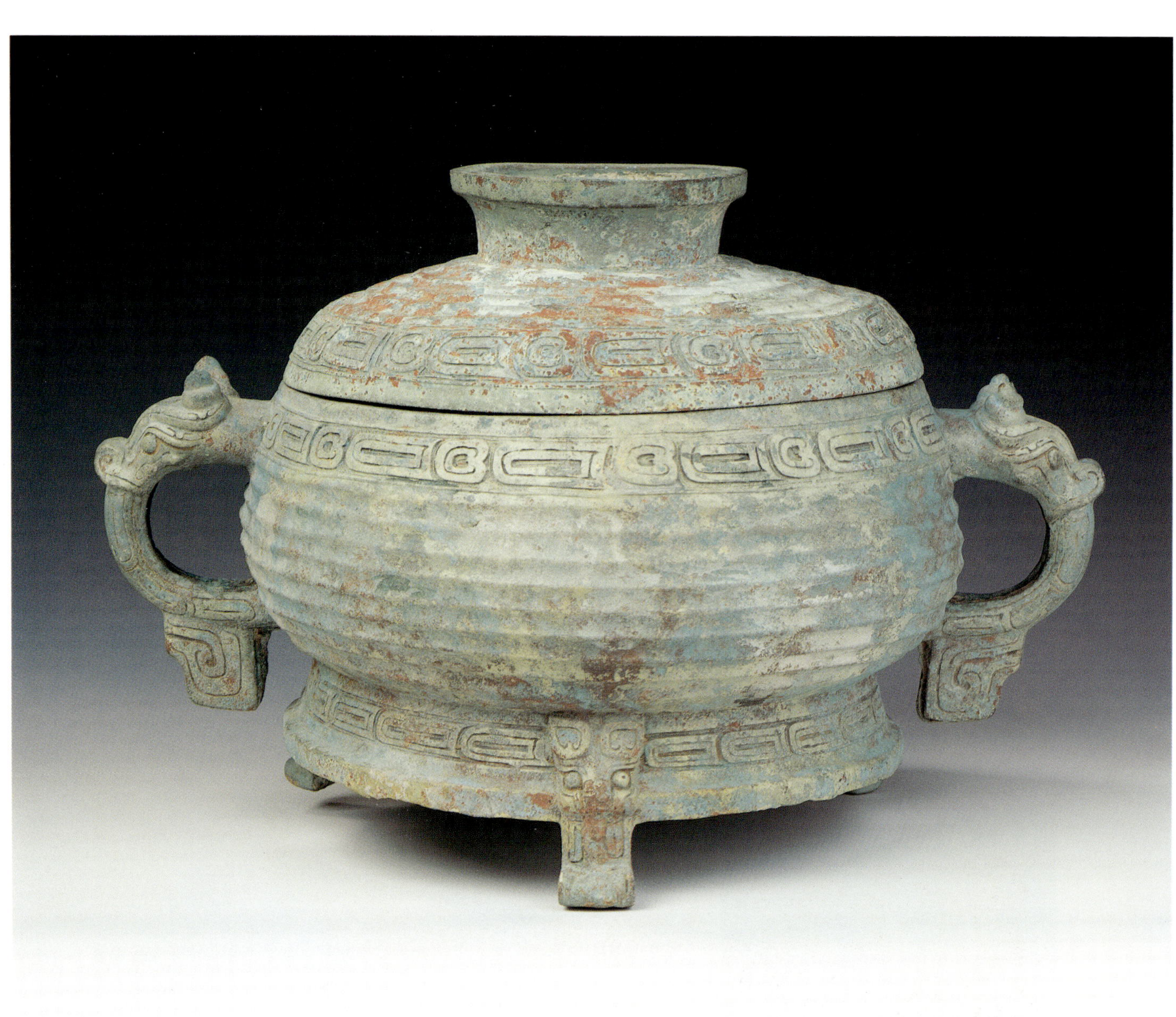

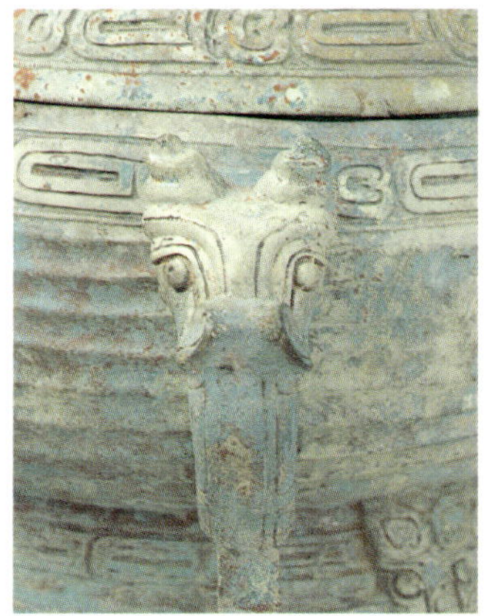

229

Gui WITH HORIZONTAL CONCAVE GROOVES BETWEEN BORDERS OF ALTERNATING LARGE AND SMALL SCALES, THE HANDLES TOPPED BY ANIMAL HEADS WITH COILED HORNS; INSCRIPTION OF 31 CHARACTERS

Late Western Zhou
(9th to 8th century B.C.)
Inscribed
Height : 25.2 cm
Width : 24 cm

The vessel shape curves inwards to include the lid in a rounded profile derived from a much earlier ceramic form. Decorated with horizontal grooves between borders of alternating large and small intaglio scales at the neck, on the lid and on the footring, which has three small feet. The lid has a circular flange as a handle, which probably served as a foot for the lid when it was inverted. Two U-shaped handles on each side are crowned by animal heads with coiled horns. The surface of the bronze is a rough grey-green with extensive red patches of cuprite. There is an inscription of 31 characters on both body and lid. Spacers are visible around the inscription on the body, but they are not evident on the lid. The inscription can be translated as follows : "Tai Shi Xiao Zi Shi made this honoured *gui* vessel for his august ancestor Shi to be used in prayer for a vigorous old age, peaceful and indulgent, with entreaties for generous blessing. May Shi's sons and grandsons forever value and employ (it) for a myriad years."
Sets of identical *gui* were used to indicate status during the late Western Zhou. Therefore, such *gui* as here were made in large numbers in a completely stereotyped form, which changed little from about 850 to 650 B.C. Its unchanging form may have been a prized attribute of the type. If such *gui* were to be clearly recognized as indicating a particular rank, perhaps by people who had relatively little experience of ritual, it was essential that the form remained the same.

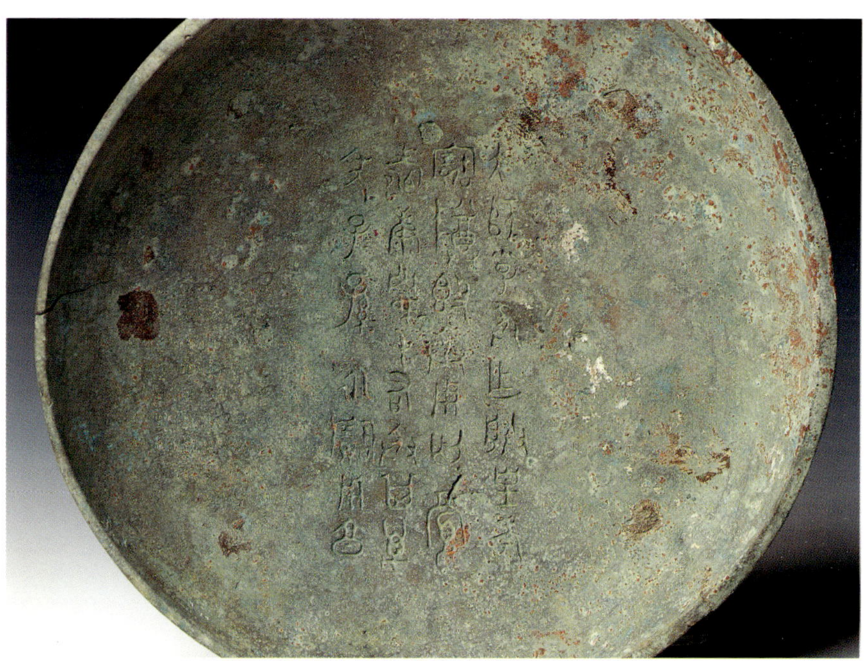

230

Bronze spearhead decorated with three *taotie* masks one on top of the other

Late Western Zhou to early Spring and Autumn period
(8th century B.C.)
Southwest China
Length : 29.8 cm
Width : 3.5 cm

A bronze spearhead, the blade section comparatively short with stubby point, the long handle section decorated on both sides with three *taotie* masks, one on top of the other, the topmost addorsed, the blunt end with a single band of pointed duo keyfret; the shaft on each side has a long wavy projection for affixation, typical of southwest China and particularly Sichuan.

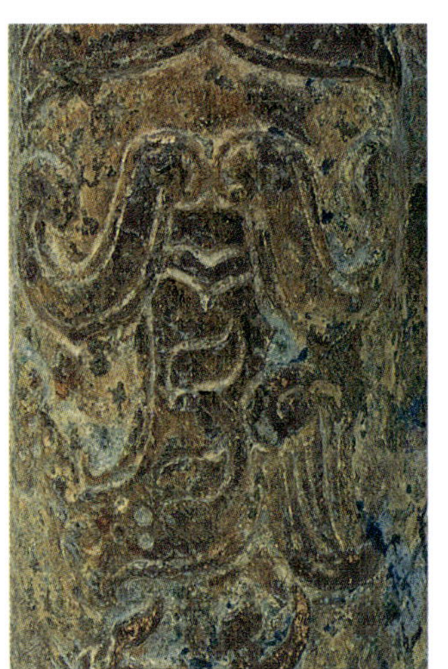

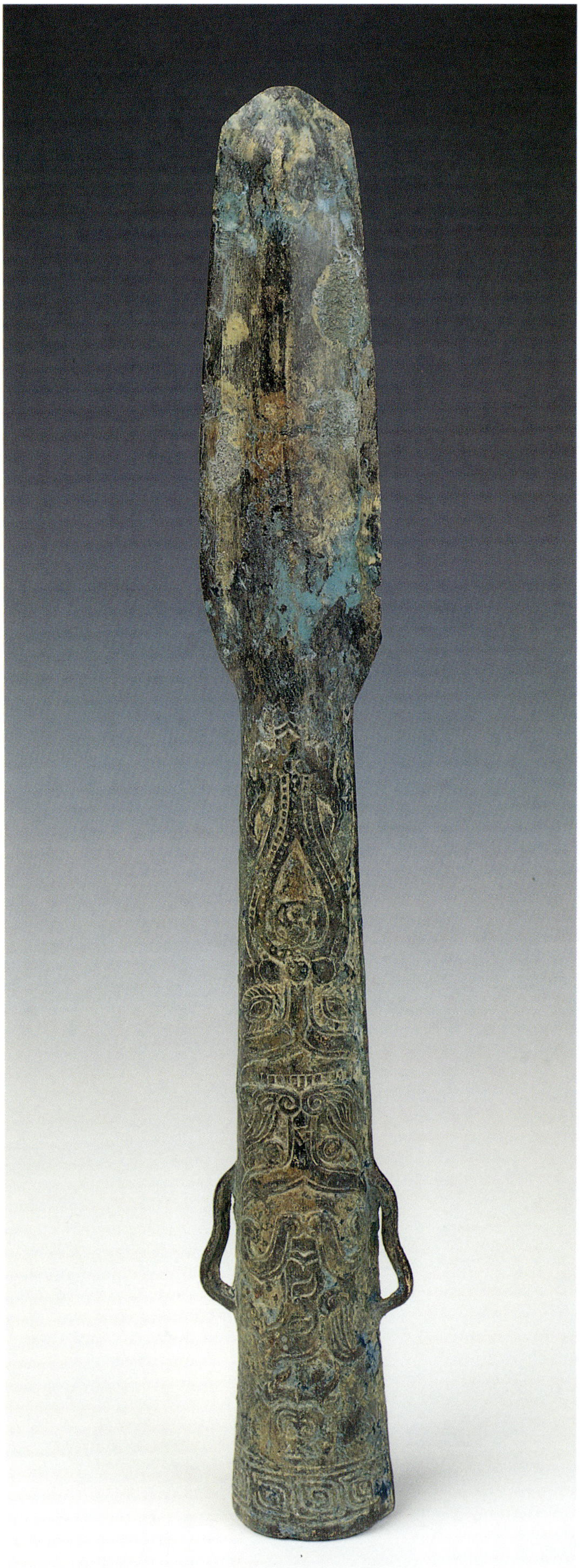

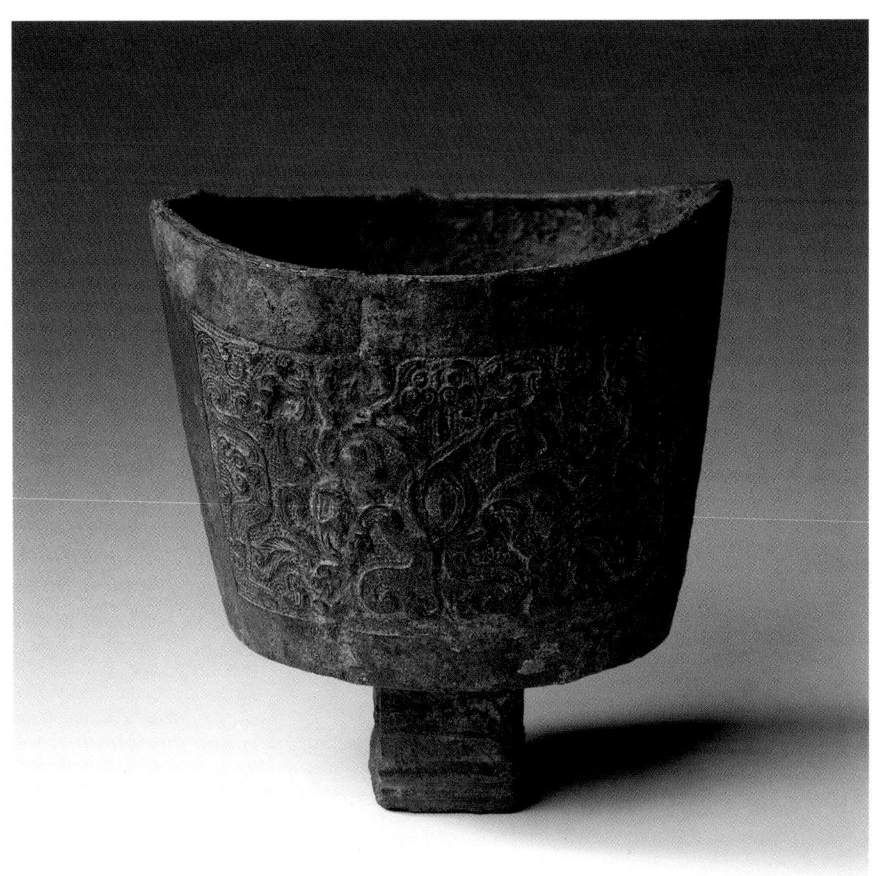

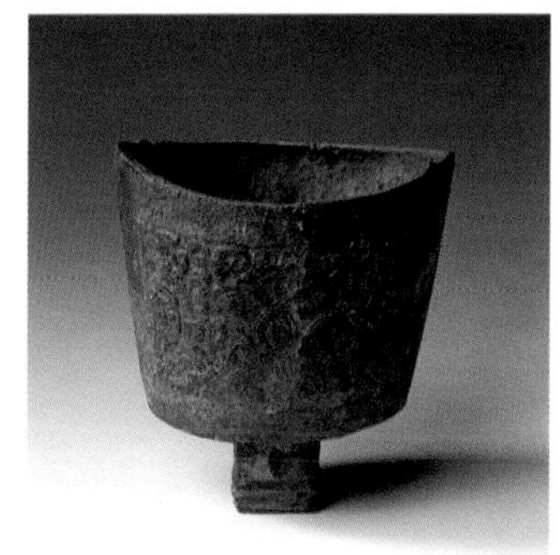

231

Bronze *duo* bell of characteristic form decorated with dragons

Late Spring and Autumn period
(6th to early 5th century B.C.)
Height : 8.2 cm
Width : 7.2 cm

Bronze *duo* bell of characteristic form with short squared handle with two raised bands round the mouth of the handle. Each side of the bell has a surface panel taking up most of the side in question with an elaborate decoration of two dragons with voluted and feathered bodies striding forward facing the handle with a baby dragon following each, another dragon between the striding dragons addorsed, all on a spotted ground; indecipherable two character inscription. From illustrations on Warring States bronzes it is believed that *duo* bells were played as follows : The *duo* bell was fixed at or near the top of a vertical stick, its mouth pointing upwards; balls hanging on a thread were fixed to the top of the stick. By twisting the stick the hanging balls struck the bell to create the desired sound. The decoration here is typical of the late Spring and Autumn period, which seems to make this *duo* bell the earliest example so far published.

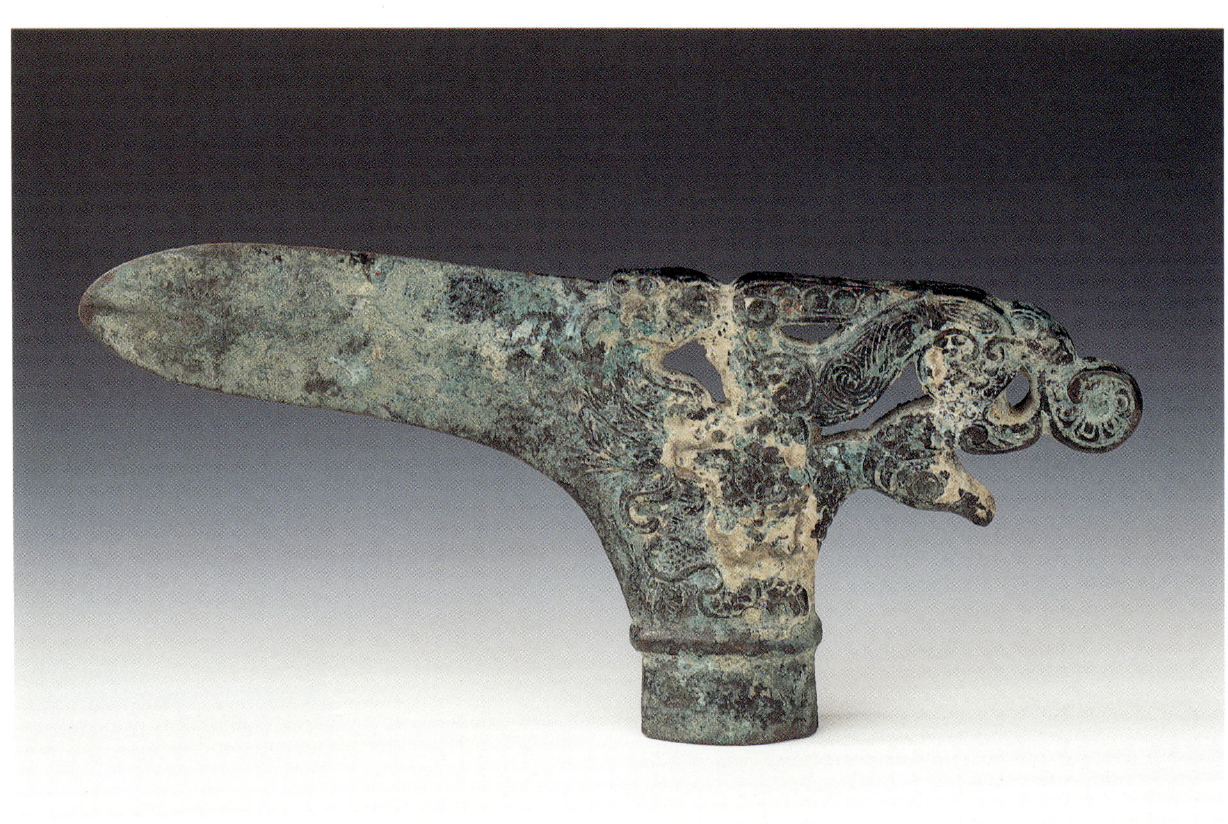

232

BRONZE DAGGER AXE WITH TIGER AND PHOENIX DESIGN

LATE SPRING AND AUTUMN PERIOD
(6TH TO 5TH CENTURY B.C.)
LENGTH : 14.2 CM
HEIGHT : 6.4 CM

A bronze dagger axe designed to fit on top of a wooden handle. The short and pointed blade is balanced by a tiger biting the top edge of the blade and holding in its talons the neck and rump of a phoenix squatting on the head of the shaft. The legs of the tiger are decorated with scales, its body with incised swirls.

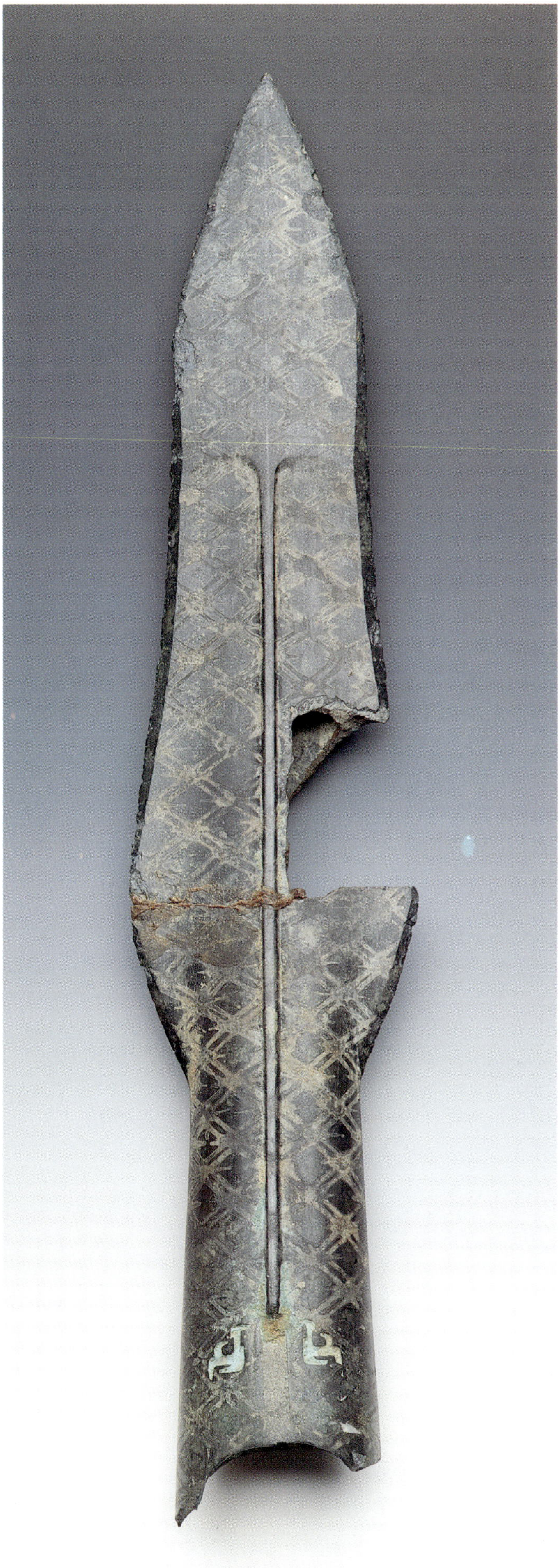

233

Spearhead with diamond diaper pattern

Late Spring and Autumn period
(6th to 5th century B.C.)
Length : 27.7 cm
Width : 5.5 cm

This spearhead has beautifully curved cutting edges. Down the centre is a ridge with two shallow depressions on either side. There are a pair of sunken decorative units near the shaft opening. The dark grey surface carries etched patterns of criss-cross lines, bisected by small diamonds.

This type of weapon is associated with the eastern States of Wu and Yue and is an example of the kind of prestige pieces that circulated between rulers of different states. The pattern is almost the same as that found on the famous sword of Goujian, King of Yue, who ruled from 496 - 465 B.C.

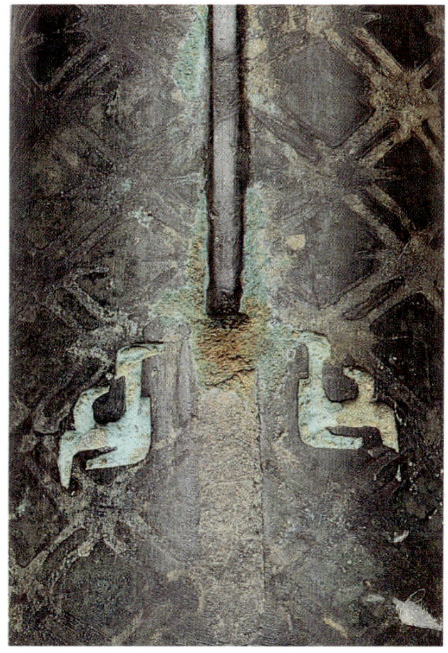

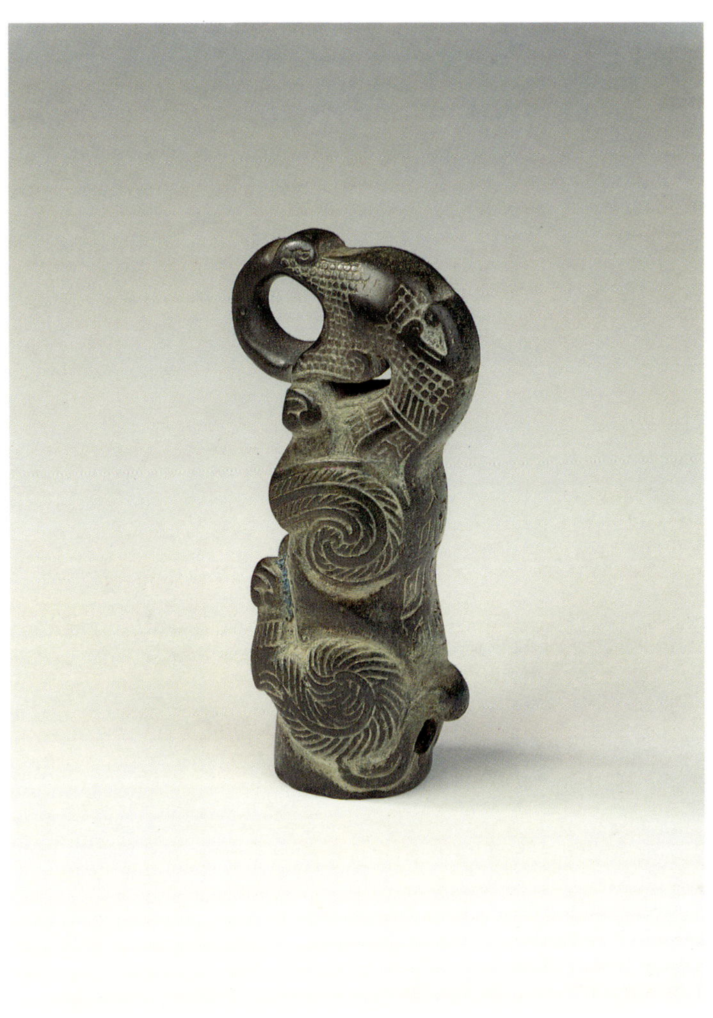

234

Small finial in the shape of an animal, its mouth forming a circular ring

Late Spring and Autumn period
(early 5th century B.C.)
Length : 5.6 cm
Height : 1.5 cm

Shaped like a crouching animal whose open mouth forms a circular ring, this bronze has a detailed surface, with small raised dots and furry striations to suggest the pelt, the back with intaglio mask decoration. This small finial fitted over a shaft and must have been intended to hold something in a circular ring. It was possibly part of a chariot parasol.

235

Bronze applique with design of tigers devouring boar

Late Spring and Autumn to Early Warring States period (5th century B.C.)
Diameter : 6.8 cm

A circular bronze applique with four ring holes at the rim. The centre is cast with a pierced design of two tigers, one of which is devouring a boar's head. The rim is decorated with cloud patterns. Probably originally a mirror back insert.

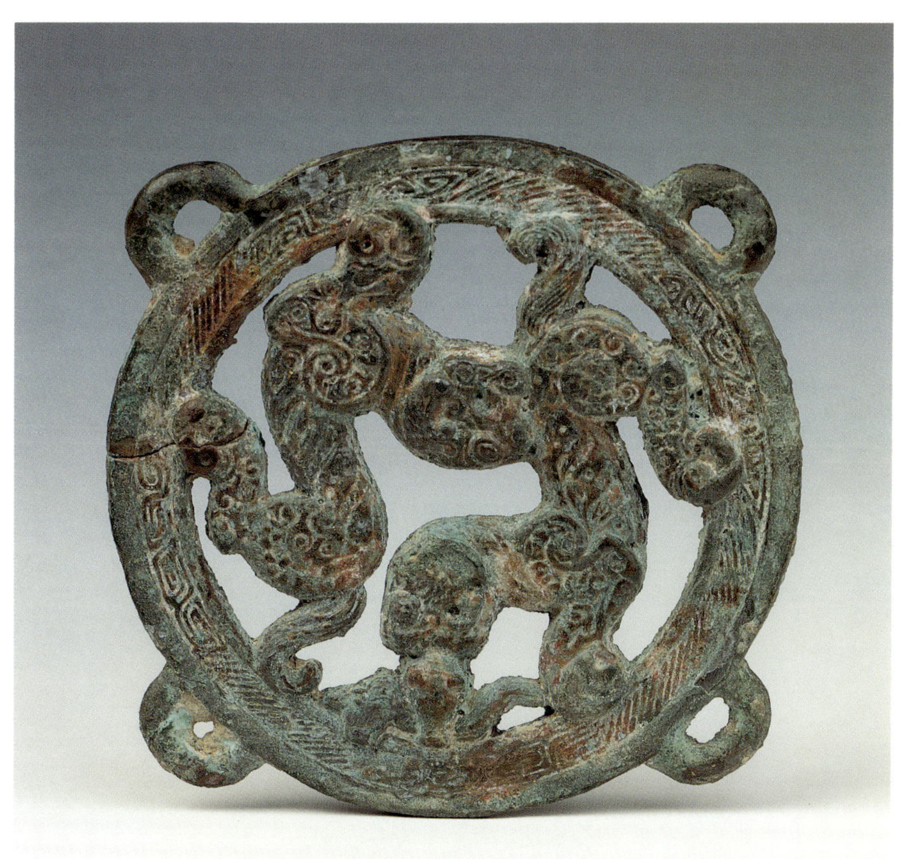

236

Ferrule decorated with a sphinx-like animal

Late Spring and Autumn to
Early Warring States p eriod
(5th century B.C.)
Height : 11.2 cm
Width : 5.0 cm

A bronze ferrule to cap the lower end of a weapon shaft. In place of the bird usually found at the junction of shaft and tip, there is a crouched creature, which looks somewhat sphinx-like, such as is found on Iranian metalwork and sculpture. The long neck carries striations as fur, and the legs have circular decorations reminiscent of patterns found on some early Ordos pieces, such as Exhibit 256. The design makes the shape rather wider than the more usual examples. The spare space is filled with small geometric patterns. There are cowrie patterns on the tail and crest. The cowrie motif, though found in the art of several states, was a motif particularly popular in the western State of Jin, which seems a probable provenance for this piece. The surface is a smooth grey-green.

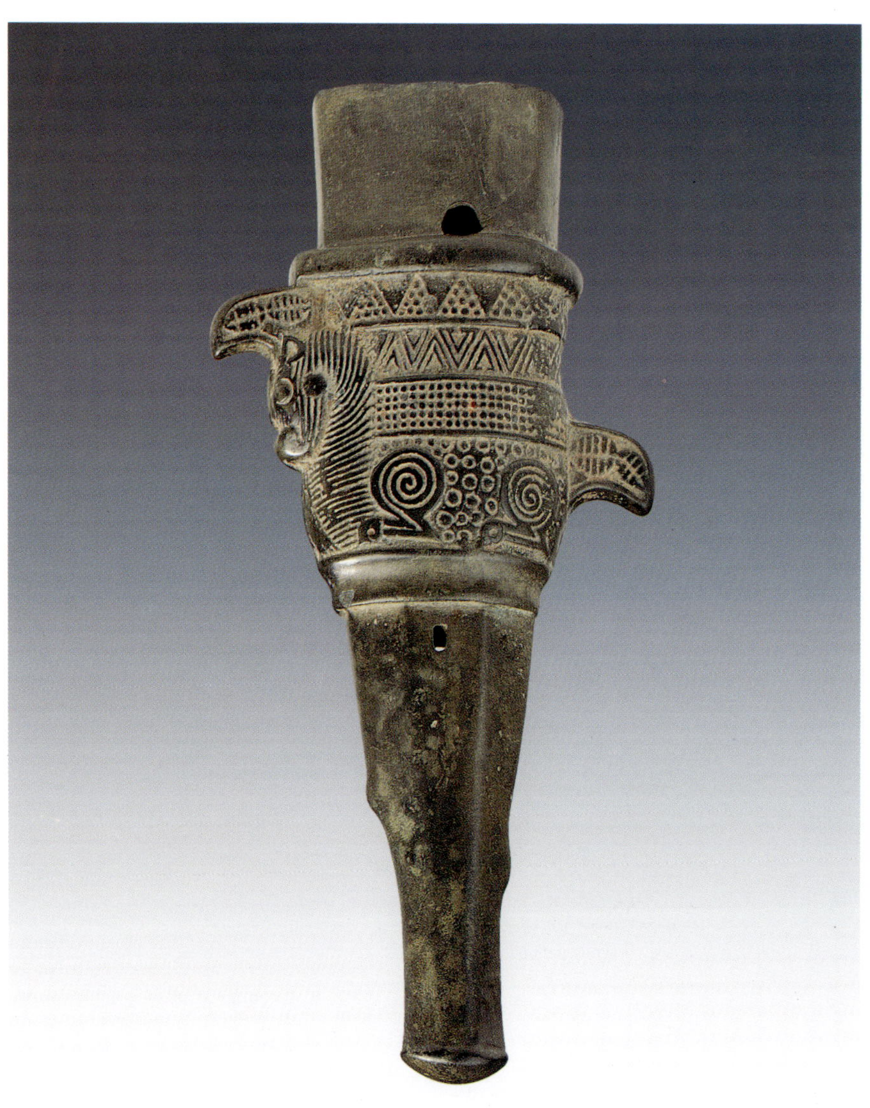

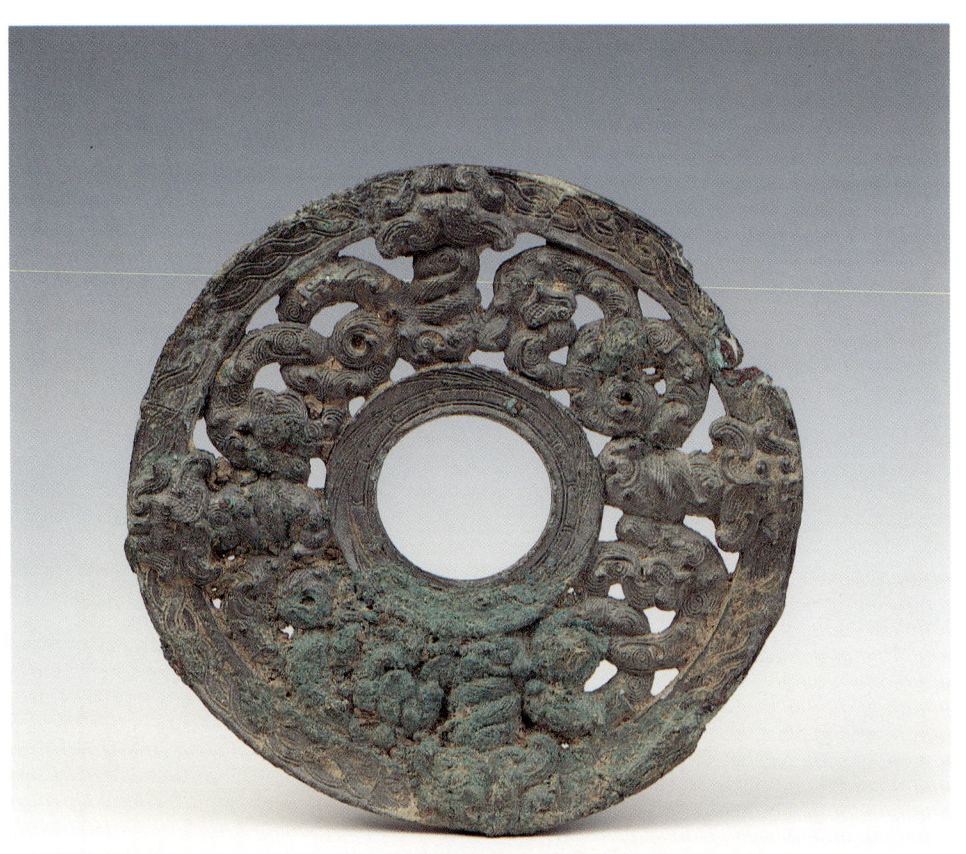

237

Bronze applique with coiled serpent design

Late Spring and Autumn to Early Warring States period (5th century B.C.)
Diameter : 7.3 cm

A circular bronze applique in the shape of two concentric circles. The space in between is decorated with four interlaced coiled serpents. Possibly for the back of a mirror. The very detailed casting here can only have been achieved by the lost wax method.

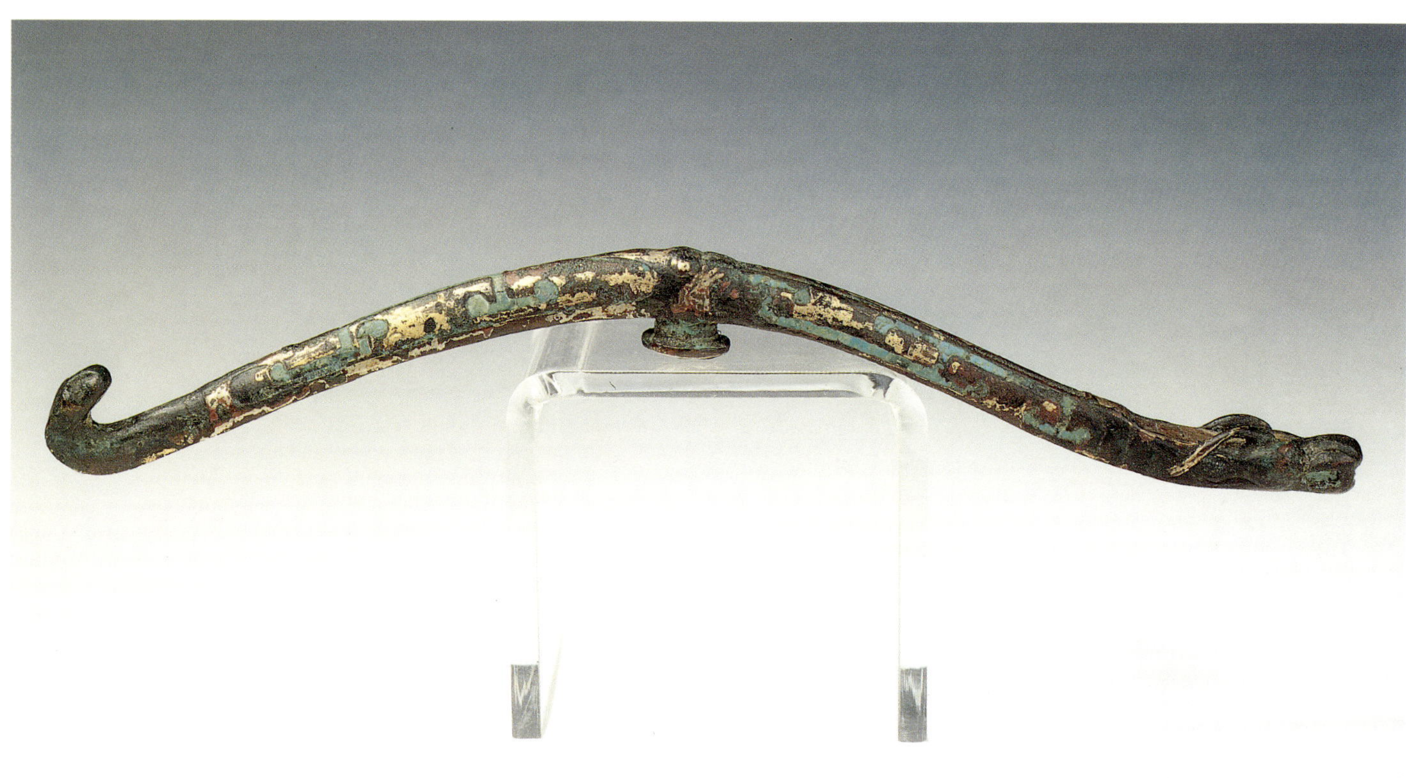

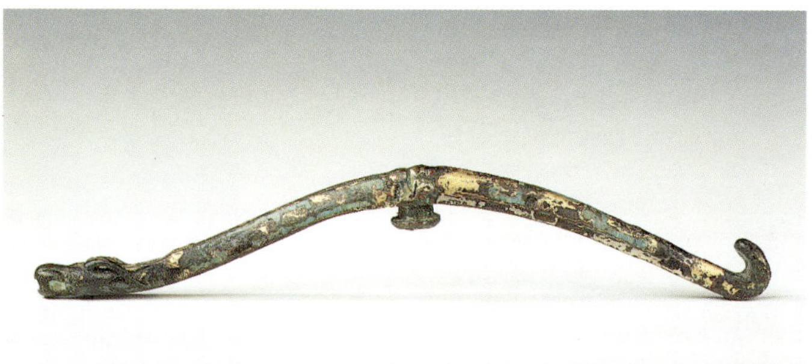

238

A large gilt bronze turquoise inlaid garment hook

Warring States period
(4th century B.C.)
Length : 20.9 cm
Height : 3.3 cm

A large gilt bronze turquoise inlaid garment hook bowed from a central stud, one end with a two horned dragon, the other with a snake's head.

239

Jade and turquoise inlaid gilt bronze garment hook

Warring States period
(4th century B.C.)
Length : 9.6 cm
Width : 4 cm
Height : 1.8 cm

Jade and turquoise inlaid gilt bronze garment hook with a flat pierced and carved D-shaped jade plaque at one end, set within a gilt bronze frame over the button, the plaque finely engraved and slightly calcified, the shaft issuing from an animal's head inlaid with turquoise highlighted in silver sheet terminating in an animal's head hook. Reported found at Jincun.

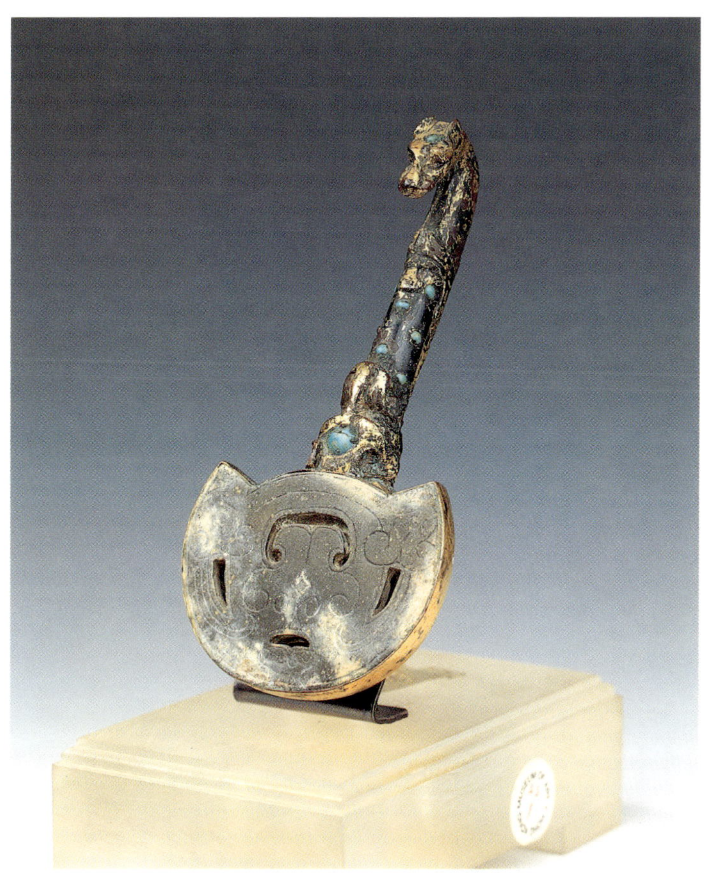

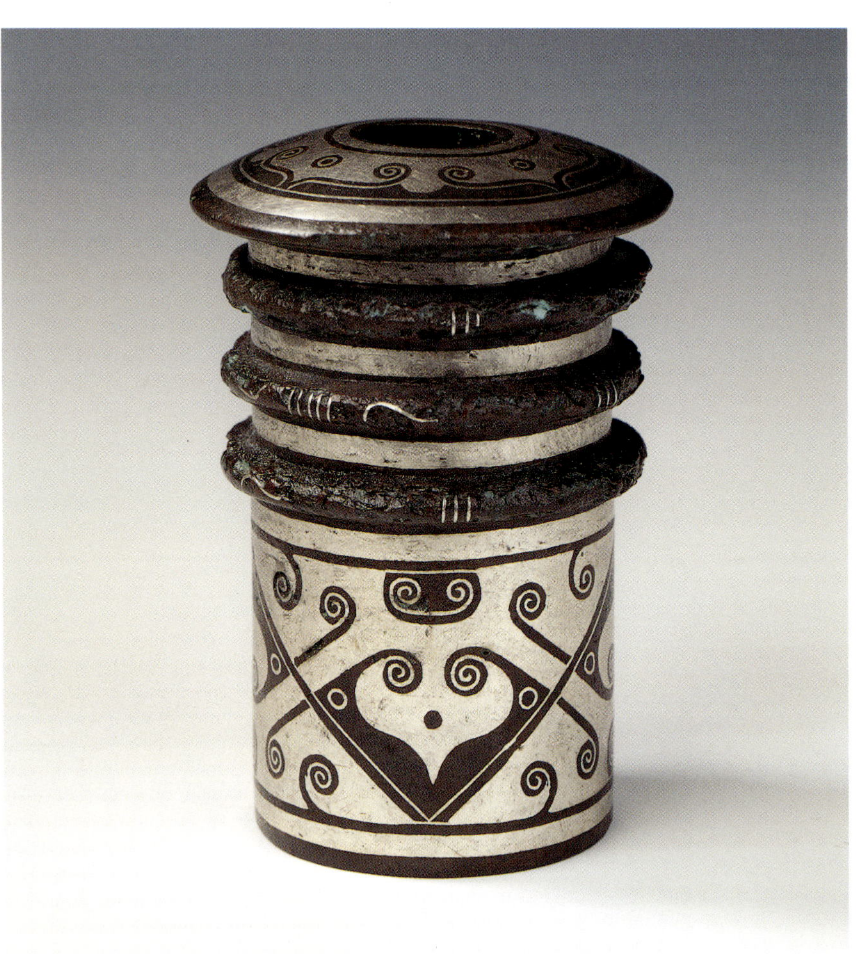

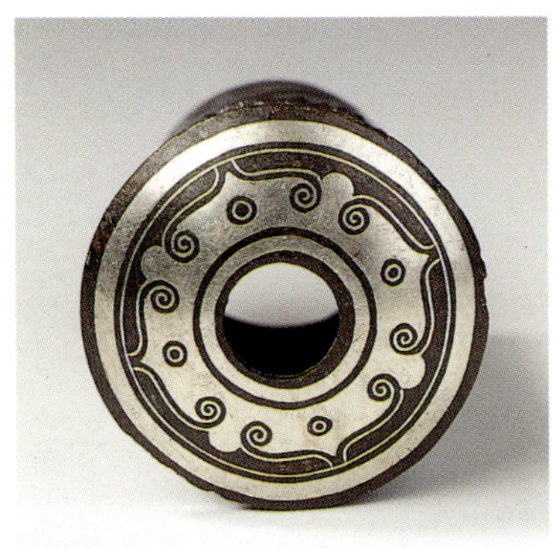

240

TUBULAR FITTING WITH THREE RAISED EDGE RINGS INLAID WITH SILVER, PROBABLY A CHARIOT AXLE CAP

WARRING STATES PERIOD
(4TH TO 3RD CENTURY B.C.)
HEIGHT : 7.5 CM
DIAMETER : 5.4 CM

This fitting is circular in cross-section with three raised rings and a slightly domed top with a hole in it. The top carries a silver inlay in the form of four broad pointed petals, the same motif of silver inlay appears around the shaft, alternating in direction and enclosed within diagonal frames. Small vertical threads of silver inlay around the raised rings as here are found on a number of Warring States inlaid bronzes, including similar chariot fittings.

241

Bronze sword decorated with leopard-like silvery spots

Warring States period
(4th to 3rd century B.C.)
State of Wu
Length : 46 cm
Width : 4 cm

This bronze short sword of typical Warring States form with bronze pommel and two ridges on the handle is decorated all over the blade by random silvery spots raised above the flat bronze surface. Such spots were found on expert examination of this sword to be of tin and to have been made by the masking of the unspotted surface of the sword during the tinning process. Such swords have been found in that part of China ruled by the State of Wu. This southern state was particularly famous for its fine swords and spears, which were treasured presentation items between the rulers of the various states during the Warring States period. This is one of the prestige swords made in the state of Wu during this period.

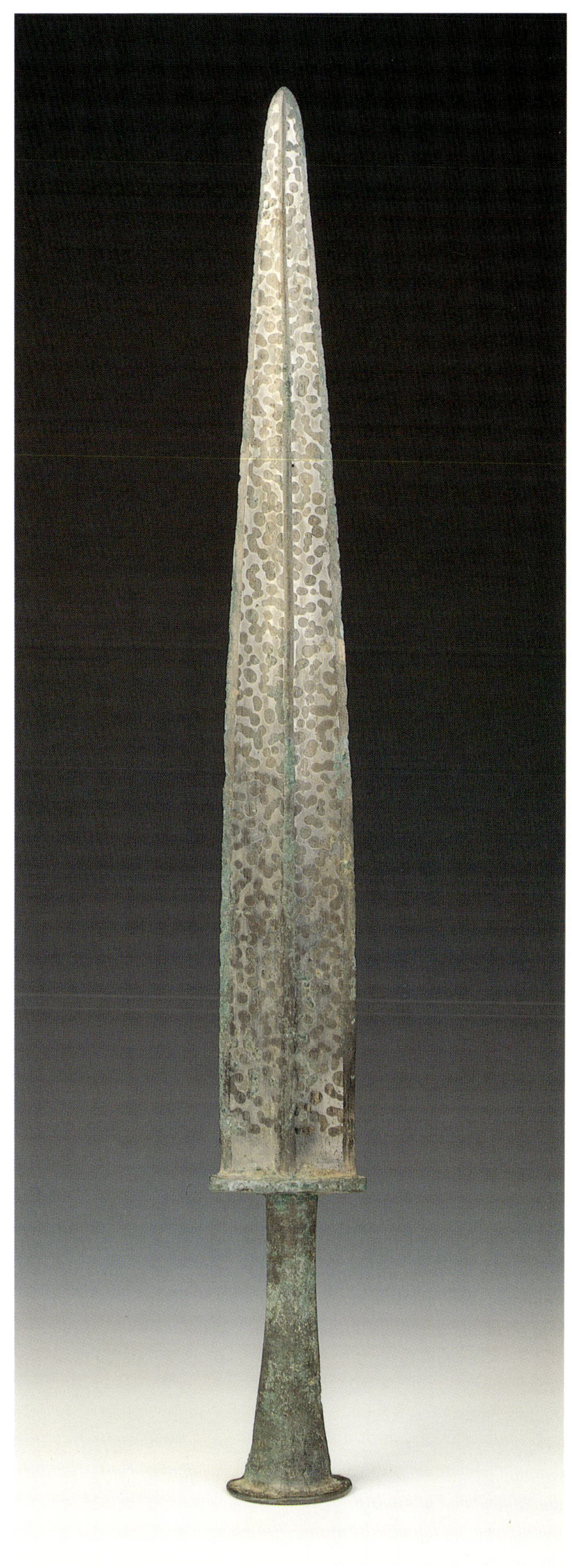

242

Cross-bow trigger mechanism, inlaid with gold

Warring States period
(3rd century B.C.)
Height : 14.5 cm
Length : 8.5 cm

China is credited with the invention of a release mechanism for firing a cross-bow. This example is small and finely cast. It seems to be complete, apart from a bolt to join the parts of the trigger together. The second bolt is in place. An unusual feature is the use of gold inlay in broad spirals on the upper surface. This decoration suggests that the trigger was part of a prestige piece rather than one for daily use, and was perhaps made for ceremonial purposes rather than for actual use.

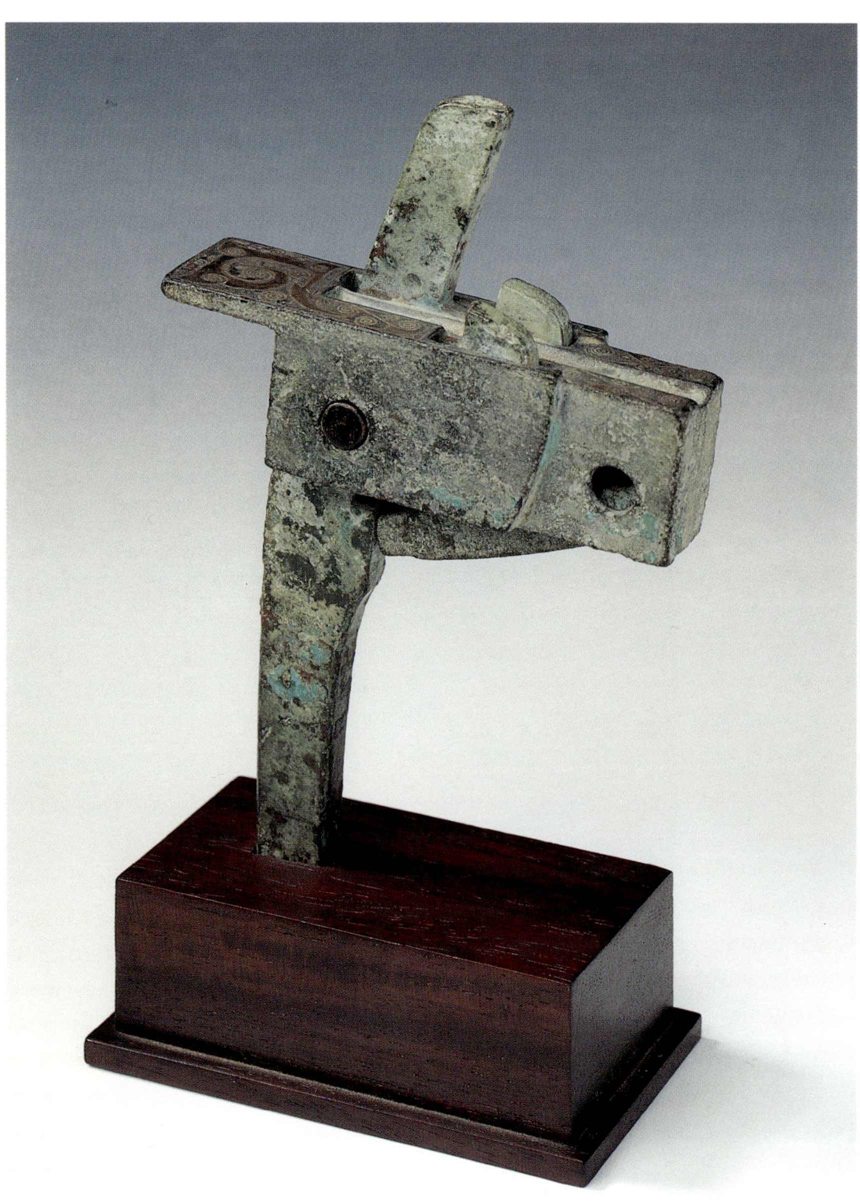

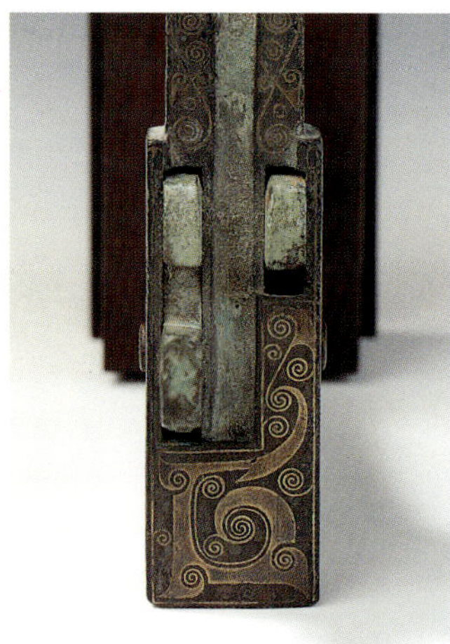

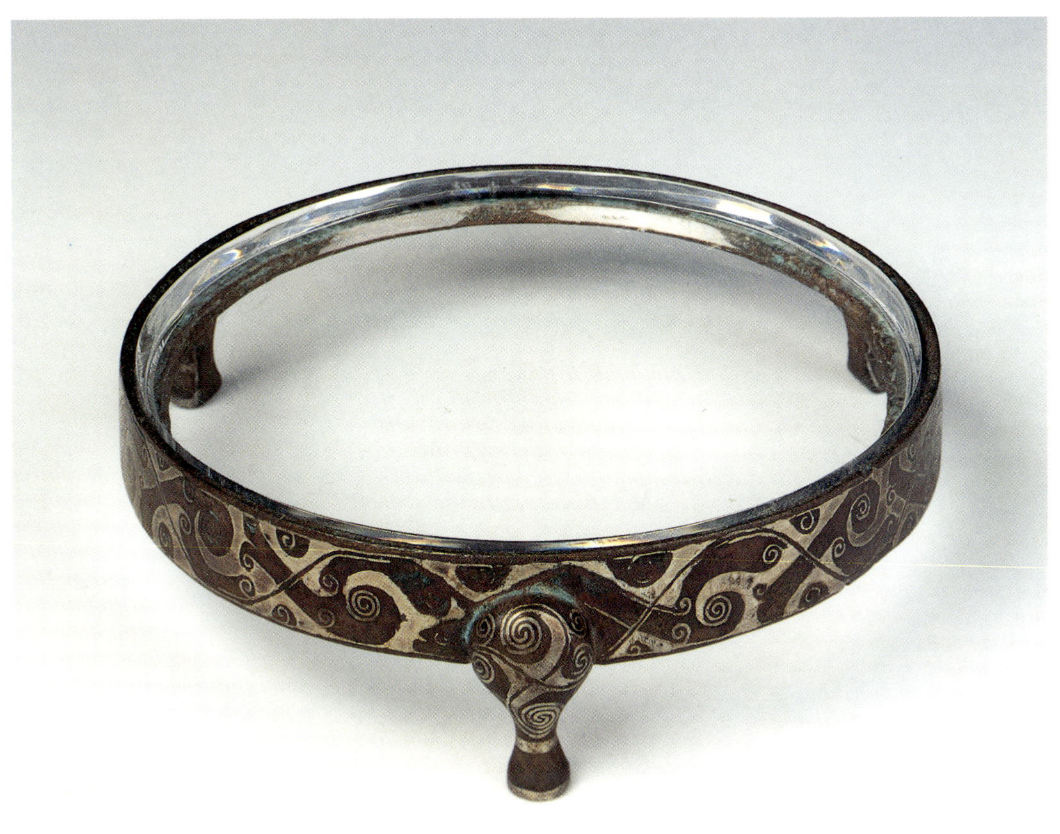

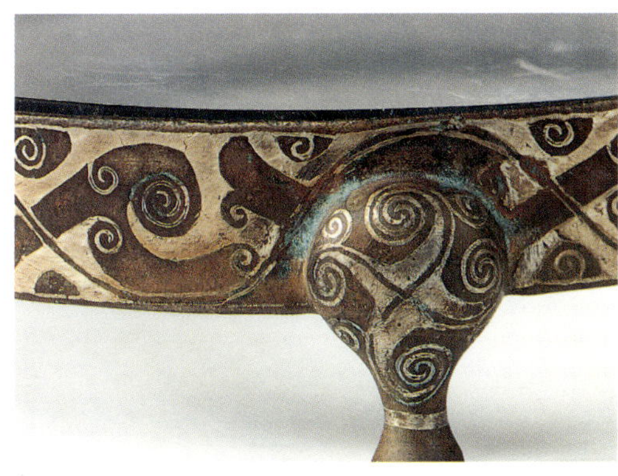

243

Binding from vessel with silver inlays of volutes

Warring States period
(3rd century B.C.)
Diameter : 11.5 cm
Height : 2 cm

This bronze binding has three small feet and would have encircled the lower part of a lacquer vessel, such as a *zun*. Similarly bound lacquer vessels are known from the 4th to 3rd century B.C. when they were popular, particularly in central and southern China. At first such cylindrical lacquer vessels were supplied with small bronze feet and handles directly applied to the lacquer surface. By the 3rd century, however, it was more usual to cast the feet as part of the bronze ring as here.

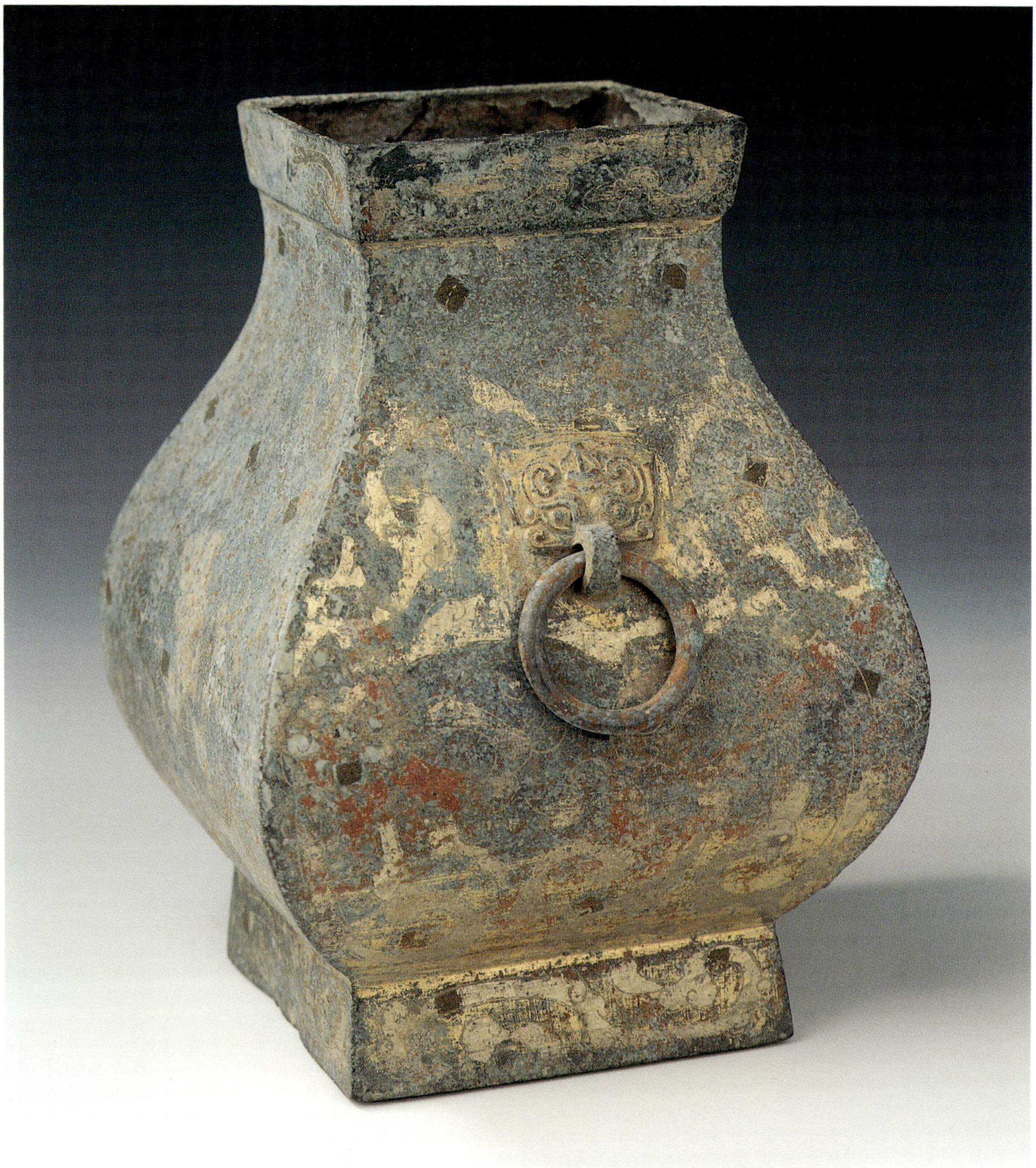

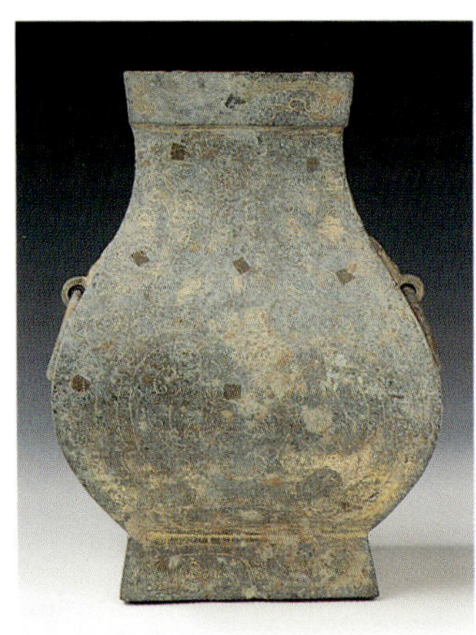

244

PARCEL-GILT BRONZE SQUARE *HU* VASE WITH RINGED *TAOTIE* HANDLES DECORATED WITH STYLISED DRAGON AND PHOENIXES, A LONG-TAILED LEOPARD AND A DEER

LATE WARRING STATES PERIOD TO EARLY WESTERN HAN
(3RD TO 2ND CENTURY B.C.)
HEIGHT : 13.5 CM
DEPTH : 6.1 CM
WIDTH : 5.8 CM

A small parcel-gilt square bronze *hu* (wine vessel) with square mouth and *taotie* ringed handles. The *hu* is covered all over with a parcel-gilt incised decoration of stylised dragons and phoenixes with a long-tailed leopard and a deer amid tracery on opposite sides of the *hu*.

245

Bronze lamp with warrior head and shoulders stand

Qin
(late 3rd century B.C.)
Height : 8.5 cm
Diameter : 6.7 cm

A bronze pricket lamp, the shallow tray on top of a short pillar issuing from the stand, which is in the shape of a warrior's torso with the head and dress ribboned in a style similar to some of the pottery warriors found near Qin Shihuangdi's tomb. The shoulders of the figure are pierced for affixing to furniture or a stand.

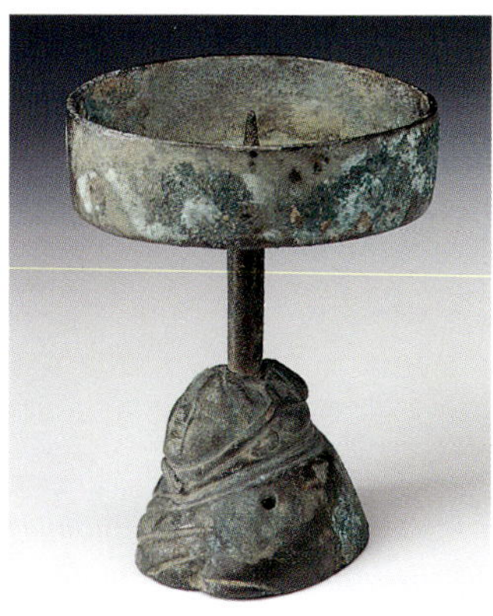

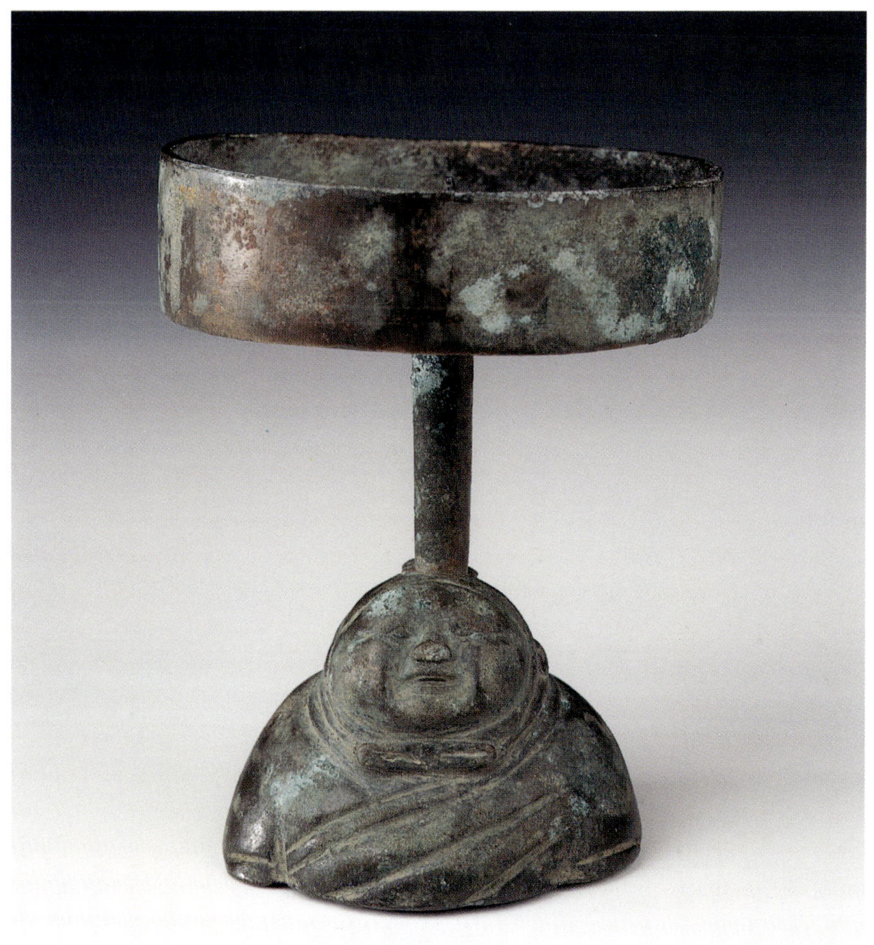

246

Bronze water basin painted with cloud scroll patterns

Early Western Han
(2nd century B.C.)
Diameter of mouth : 27 cm
Height : 11 cm

A painted bronze water basin with slightly everted rim. A slightly concave ridge surrounds the body about one-third down the exterior on which two *taotie* mask handles are superimposed. The basin is extensively painted inside and out with cloud scrolls similar to those found on lacquers from the Mawangdui tomb, dated *circa* 162 B.C.

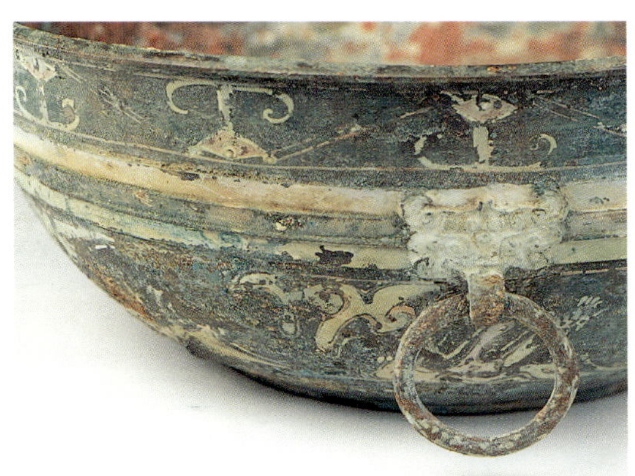

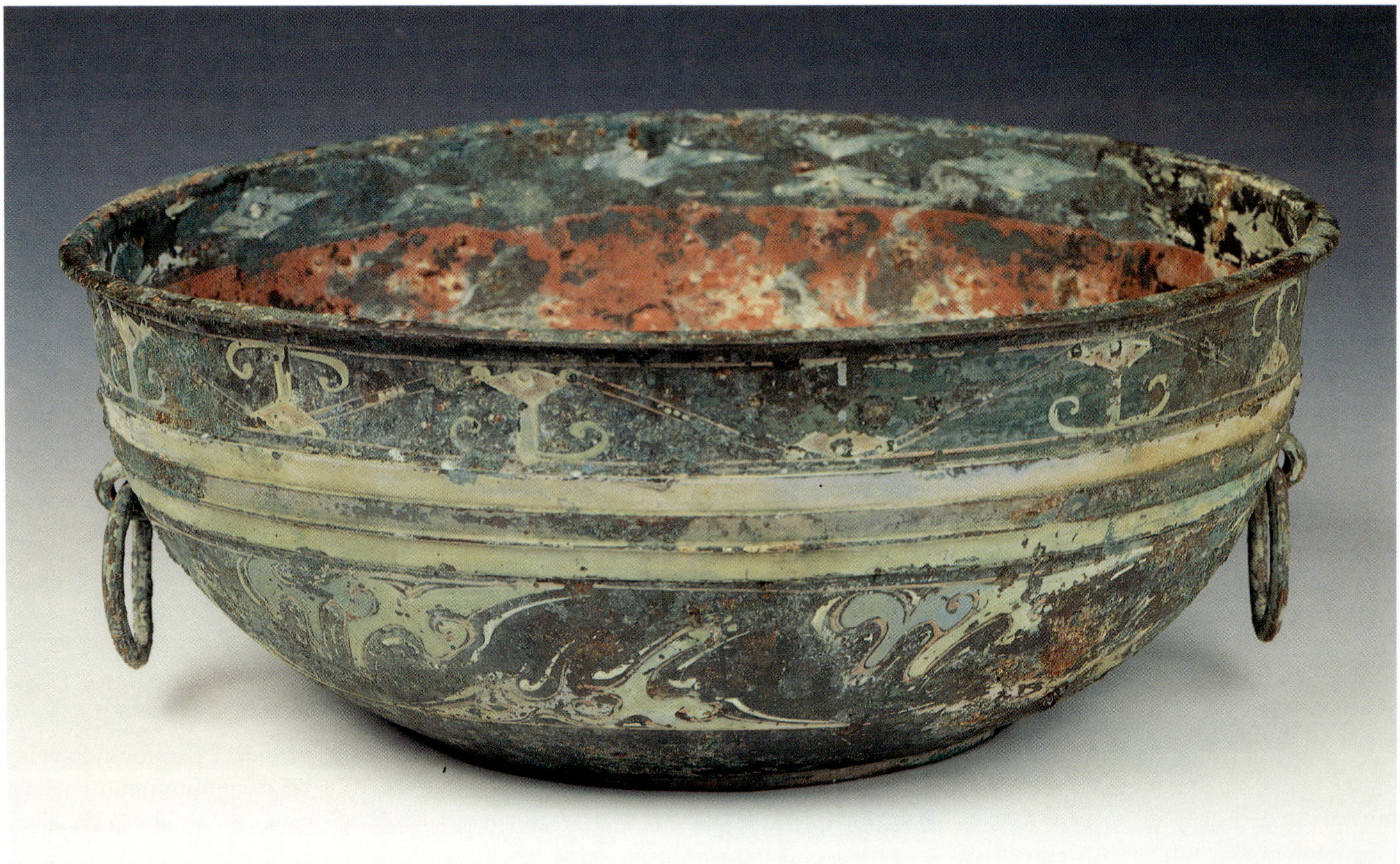

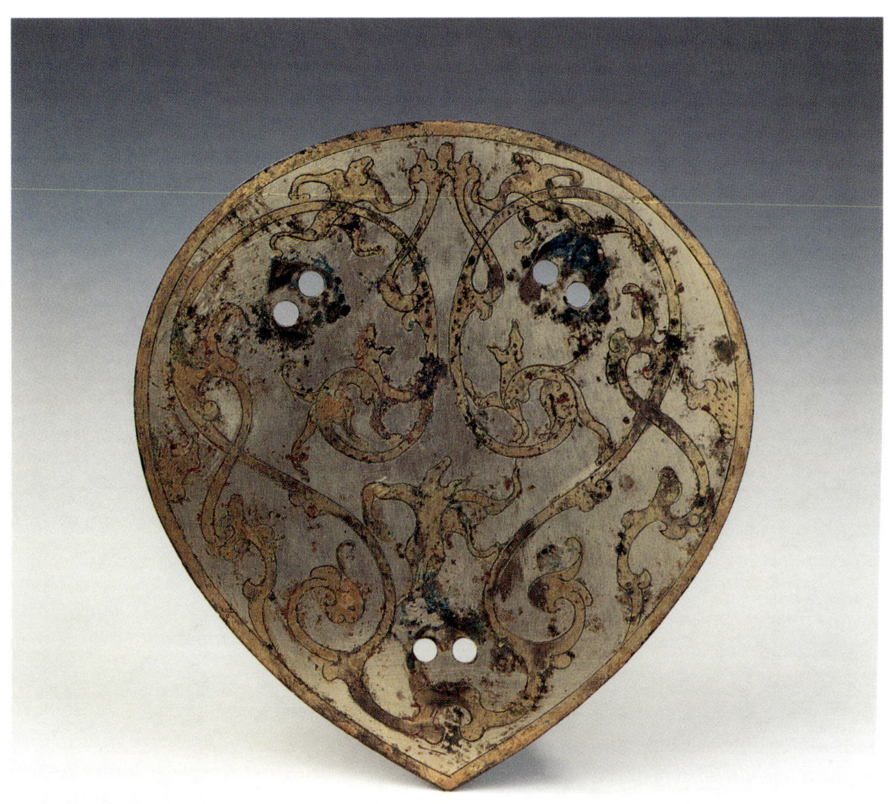

247

PARCEL-GILT BRONZE FITTING WITH DESIGN OF FABULOUS ANIMALS

WESTERN HAN
(2ND CENTURY B.C.)
HEIGHT : 11.5 CM
WIDTH : 10.5 CM

A parcel-gilt bronze petal-shaped fitting decorated in parcel-gilt with fabulous animals and birds arranged symmetrically. The six holes on the fitting are probably meant for fastening the fitting onto textile or leather. A similar fitting has been excavated in Liaoning Province. Probably used as a horse fitting by the Xiongnu or one of the other nomadic tribes active in the steppes.

248

A parcel-gilt bronze chamfron decorated with intertwined dragons, tortoise and peacock with tail displayed

Western Han
(late 2nd century B.C.)
Length : 16.5 cm
Width at widest point near the pointed end : 3.7 cm

A parcel-gilt bronze chamfron applique, one end pointed, the lower end rounded, decorated with two spindly intertwined dragons above a small tortoise at the rounded end, and at the pointed end a peacock standing with tail displayed, separated by brackets, the reverse with two pair of loops. The whole is a chamfron mount for leather or horse armour worn on the head and along the bridge of the nose. A similarly shaped parcel-gilt bronze piece with related decoration has been found *in situ* on a horse skeleton from a Western Han tomb in northern China.

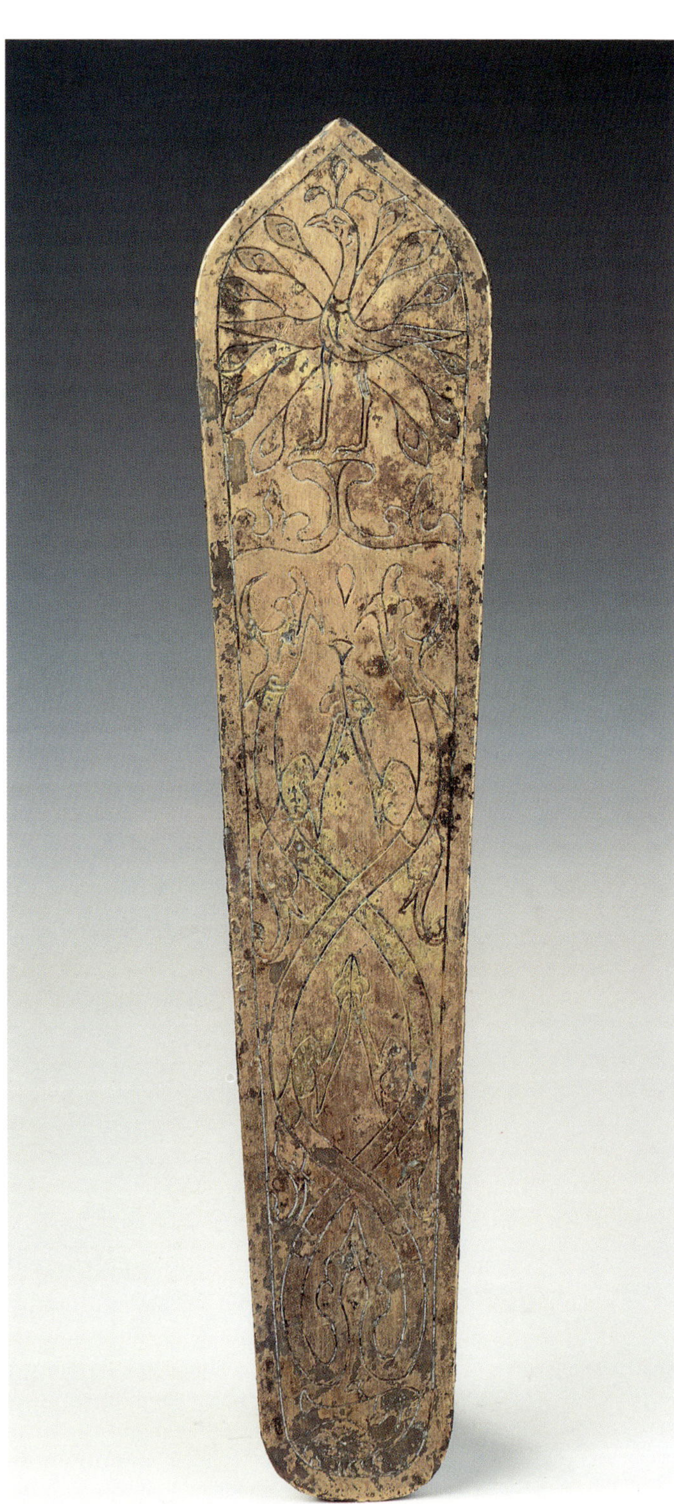

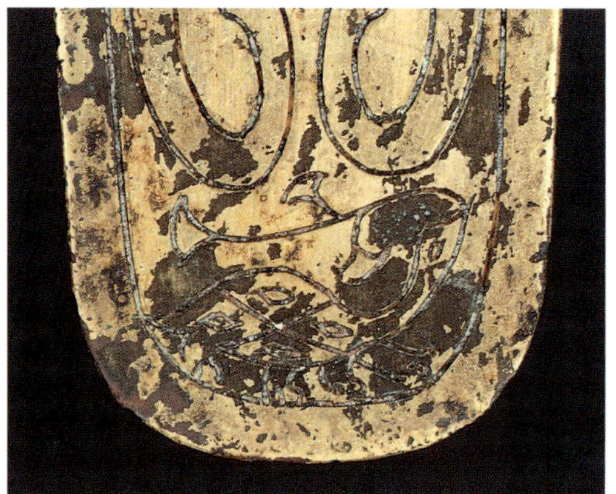

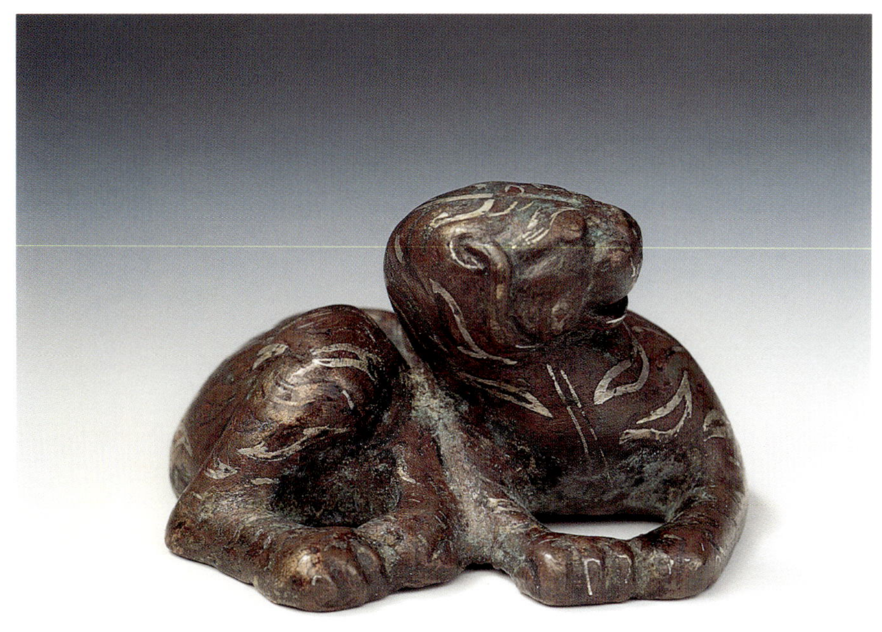

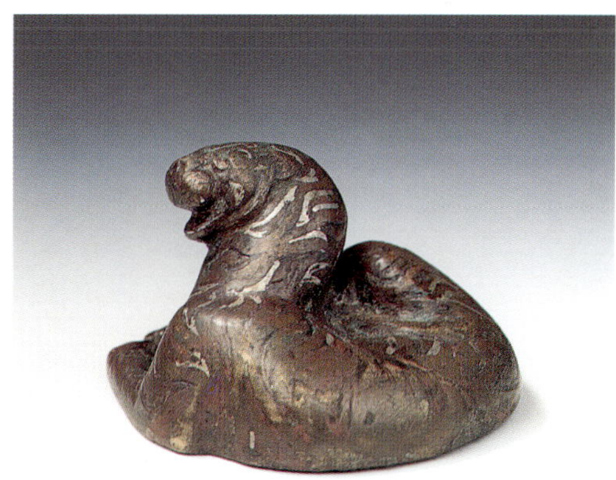

249

SILVER INLAID BRONZE
TIGER WEIGHT

WESTERN HAN
(LATE 2ND CENTURY B.C.)
LENGTH : 6.9 CM
HEIGHT : 4.1 CM

A silver-inlaid bronze tiger lying curled up with tail tucked between the rear legs and over the back, its raised head with mouth open, its neck long and coiled, the feet with prominent claws grouped together in two pairs; inlay of silver stripes, many missing. A pair of inlaid leopards in similar posture were found in the tomb of Princess Tou Wan at Mancheng, Hebei province dated to the late 2nd century B.C. Probably originally a shroud weight.

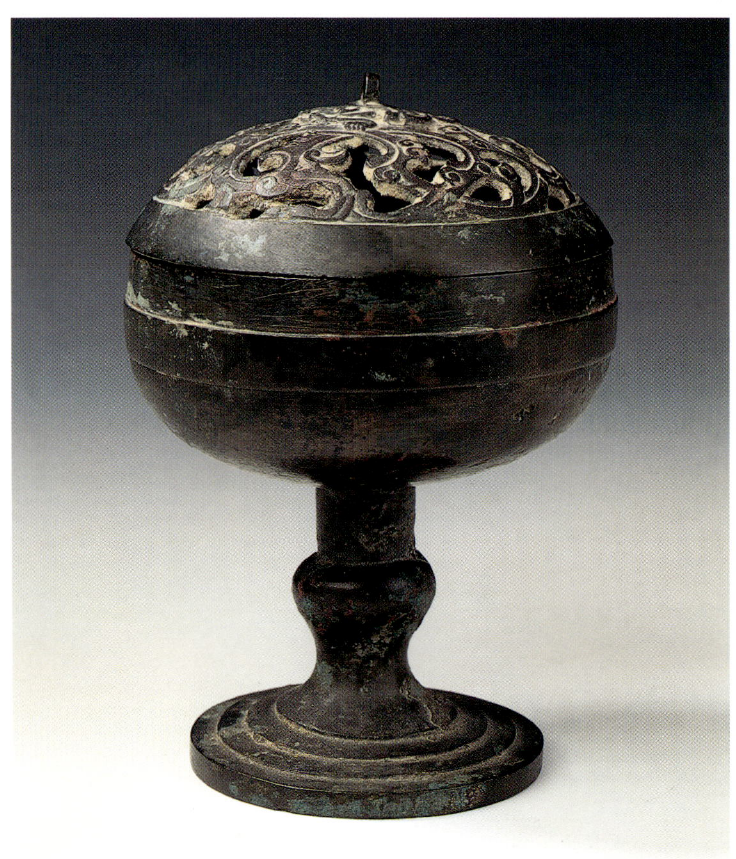

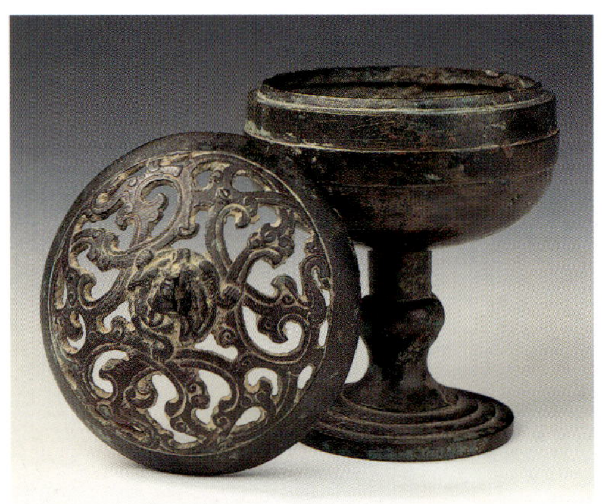

250

Incense burner

Western Han
(2nd to 1st century B.C.)
Height : 14.9 cm
Width : 10.3 cm

This incense burner consists of a bowl on a tall stem, with a pronounced bulge at the centre; there are also small steps on the ring foot. The bowl is hemispherical and has a raised band below the lip.

A vertical flange on the lid fits over the rim of the bowl. Within the central part of the lid is an openwork cloud scroll, in which a bear can be discerned. The bronze is a dark brownish-green with some areas of brighter corrosion.

Incense burners seem to have had a long history in southern China, particularly in the State of Chu, the earliest form known to date being an openwork beaker. Lamps in the shape of shallow *dou* were used somewhat later. The present incense burner seems to combine features from both these sources. Ceramic versions with a *dou*-body and an openwork lid have come from late Warring States tombs at Changsha in the State of Chu. The use of ceramic for burial suggests that bronze examples may have been used in everyday life. As Chu influence penetrated northwards and eastwards, Chu customs, such as the use of incense burners, also spread. Bronze examples similar to this have come from Shandong. These incense burners seem to precede the introduction of the Boshanlu hill censers such as Exhibit 252.

251

Yunnan bronze lamp in the shape of a dragon supported by three kneeling figures and bird on its tail

Western Han
(2nd to 1st century B.C.)
Length : 21.5 cm
Height : 10.8 cm

A circular Yunnan bronze lamp in the shape of a dragon. The shallow lamp tray with three prickets forms part of the body of the dragon and is supported by three kneeling figures wearing loin-cloths, one with clasped hands, one playing a flute and the third supporting two acrobats. The twin-horned dragon's head and plaited neck form the handle. The dragon's tail is in the form of a flap on which stands a bird with a flat tail and crested head turned to the rear.

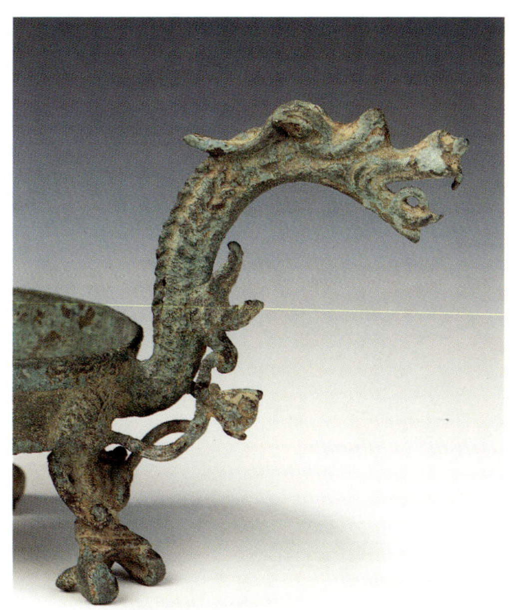

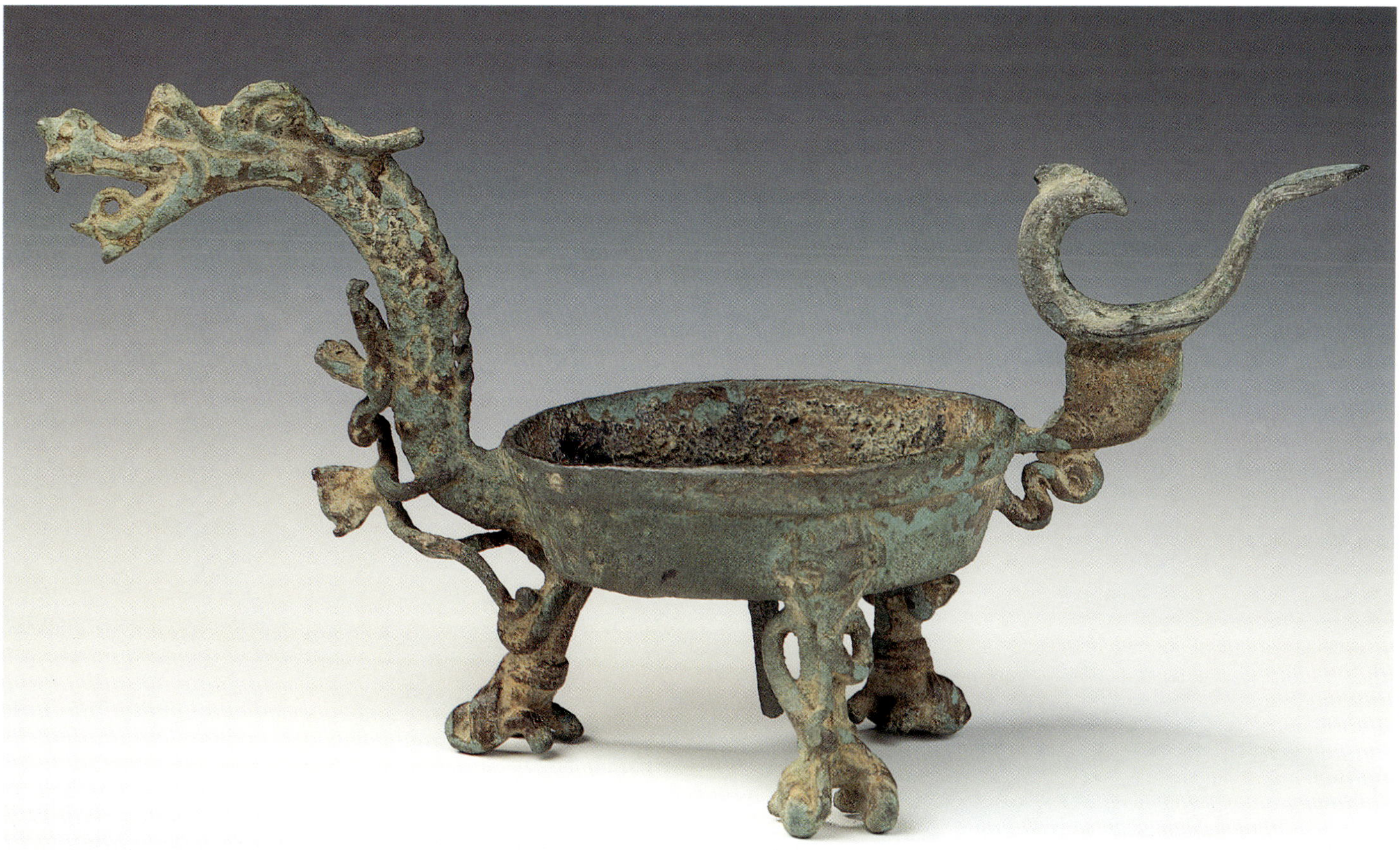

252

Boshanlu hill censer

Wang Mang Interregnum
(9 -25 A.D.)
Height : 22.5 cm
Diameter : 13 cm

A Boshanlu hill censer, the cover of which is in the shape of a mountain representing Mount Penglai, the central mountain in the Daoist paradise. The bowl is plain. However, the lower part of the stand is extensively decorated with a stylised *kui* dragon pattern. This Boshanlu is cast with an inscription which dates the piece to the reign of Wang Mang.

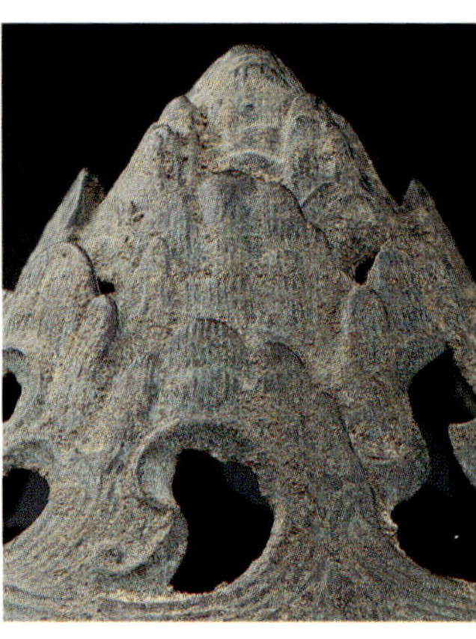

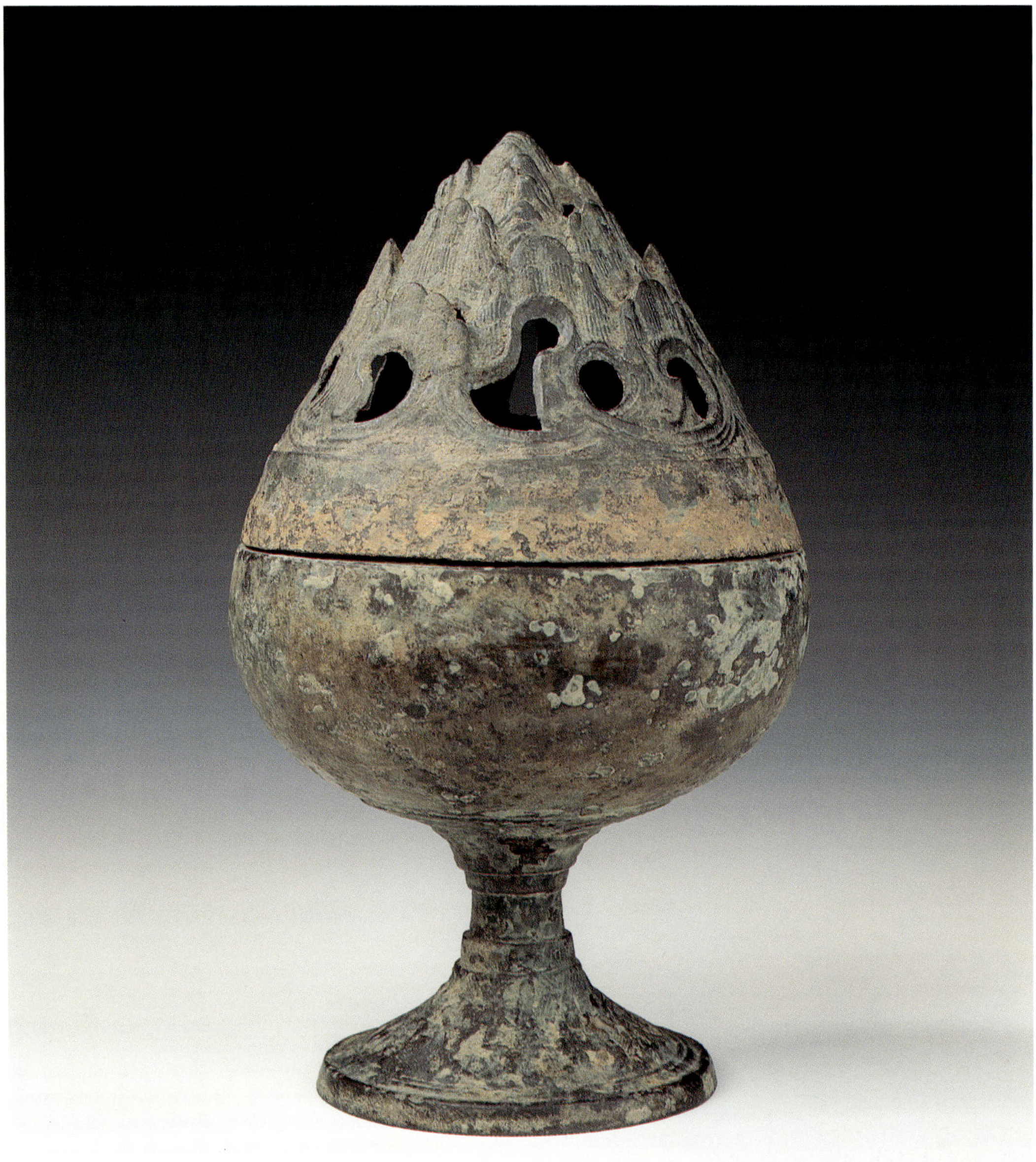

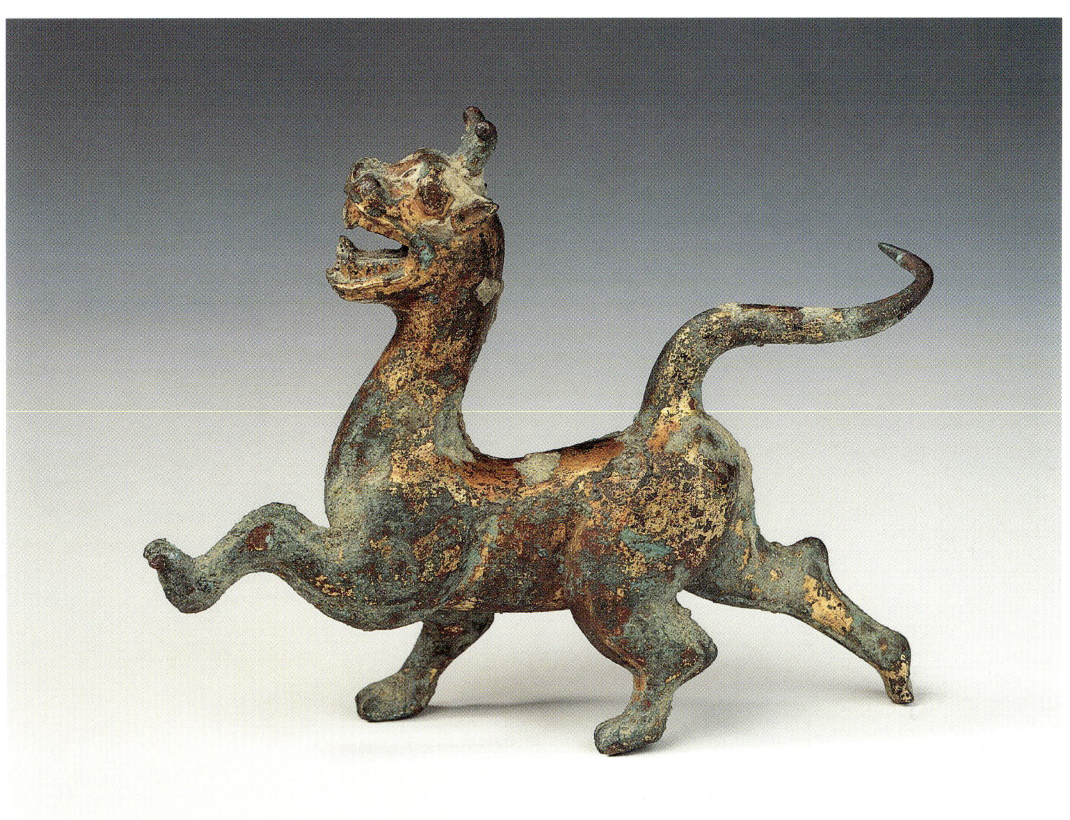

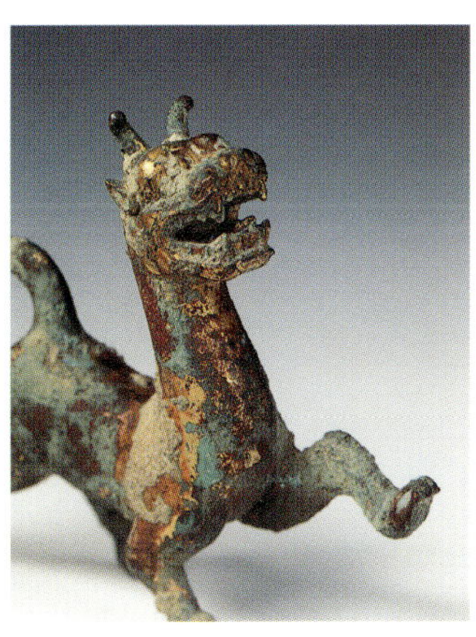

253

GILT BRONZE CHIMERA

LATE EASTERN HAN TO EARLY SIX DYNASTIES PERIOD
(3RD CENTURY A.D.)
LENGTH : 13 CM
HEIGHT : 10 CM

A gilt bronze chimera with two horns, small ears, long neck and long lashing tail. The chimera is modelled in motion with its mouth open. Its posture can be compared with Chinese sculptures of the same period.

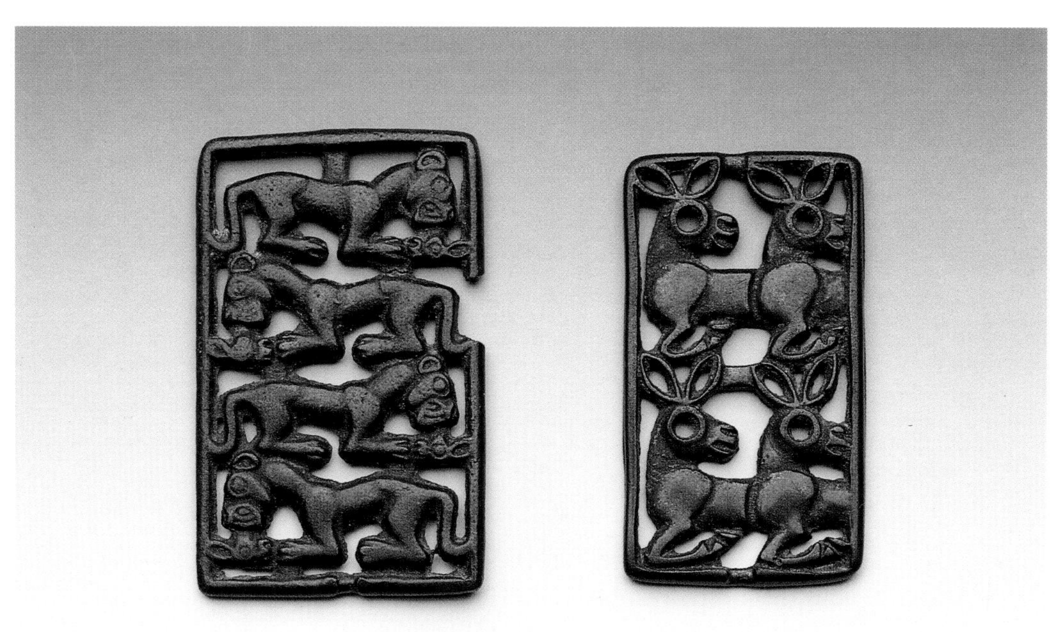

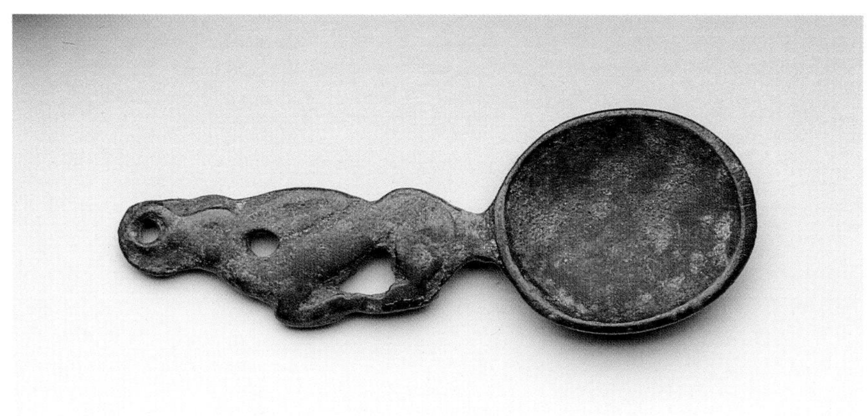

254

Group of three Ordos bronzes

Spring and Autumn period
(7th to 5th century B.C.)
South or western
Inner Mongolia
(i) Height : 5 cm; Width : 3.2 cm
(ii) Height : 4.7 cm; Width : 2.7 cm
(iii) Length : 7.1 cm; Width : 2.4 cm

The group consists of :

(i) An openwork plaque with four crouching leopards, each savaging the inverted head of a fawn within a rectangular frame. The leopards are arranged one above the other and face alternately right and left. The conventionalized eyes are each indicated by a round boss within a circular groove, and the ears are shown as depressions within a raised rim. The slightly open jaws reveal threatening fangs, and the paws each have three claws. The slightly concave back is without loops.
A rectangular openwork plaque with animals in profile facing alternately right and left in roughly the same style was excavated at Taohongbala in Hanggin Qi in western Inner Mongolia. A piece of wood from one tomb at this site has been dated 7th to 6th century B.C. by radio-carbon analysis.
A stylistically related plaque, which depicts the same type of leopard with three clawed paws, was discovered near Hohhot in south central Inner Mongolia. Many plaques similar to the one under discussion exist in collections around the world but none have been found in a controlled excavation. Until further archaeological discoveries prove otherwise, these plaques can be tentatively associated with south central Inner Mongolia.

(ii) Two pairs of wild ass protomes with folded front legs and heads turned 180 degrees are framed by a simple rectangle. The eye of each is a round hole surrounded by a circular ridge, the ears are oval holes, and the nostrils and mouths are indicated by slight depressions.
This plaque belongs to the same stylistic group as the previous example (i) above. The pose of the heads is not a natural one, but an artistic convention used much earlier in China's central plains, for example, on jades in the mid-Shang tomb of Fu Hao dated *circa* 1400 B.C.

(iii) A small oval spoon with a running female red deer handle pierced for suspension from a belt. Spring and Autumn period (6th to 5th Century B.C.). The size of the spoon here is too small for practical use and it was probably intended for ritual use.

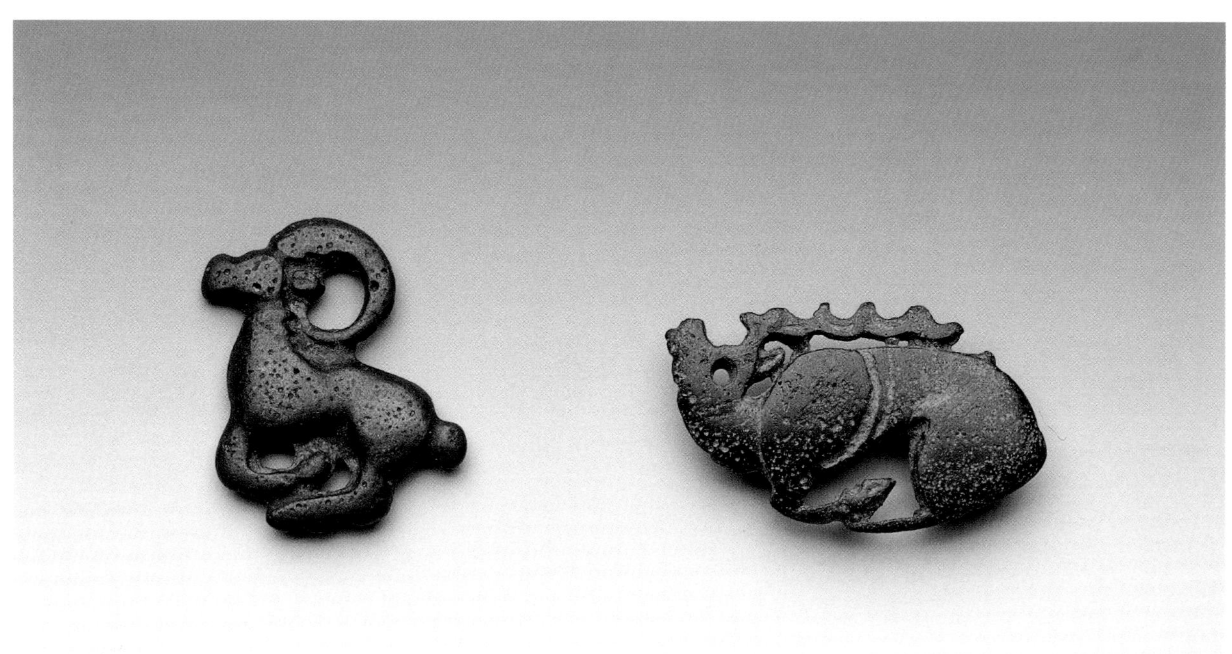

255

Group of two Ordos bronze animals in running style

Spring and Autumn period
(6th century B.C.)
South central Inner Mongolia
(i) Length 2.8 cm; Width 2.6 cm
(ii) Length 3.6 cm; Width 2 cm

This group consists of :

(i) A running ibex with its legs gathered underneath.
The running pose in these two pieces is very characteristic of the 6th century B.C. and was replaced in the 5th century B.C. by a more static posture, such as in Exhibit 257.

(ii) An ornamental plaque of a running red deer, the eye formed as a hole, the legs bunched together, the antlers laid back against the body and nose in the air

256

Group of two Ordos bronze tiger plaques

Spring and Autumn period
(6th to 5th century B.C.)
Northeast China or
south-east Inner Mongolia

(i) Height 2.8 cm ; Width 2.9 cm
(ii) Height 3 cm ; Width 3.5 cm

This group consists of two bronze tiger plaques; one with a single curled tiger and the other with two crouching tigers one on top of the other. In each case the face faces to the front with the eyes, mouths and feet stylistically drawn as circles. It has been suggested this very characteristic stylisation of the animal is attributable to the Shanrong tribes, who were active in the Ordos region at the time in question. It should also be noted that the circular decoration on the tigers in the double plaque is paralleled on the bronze ferrule from central China in this exhibition (Exhibit 236).

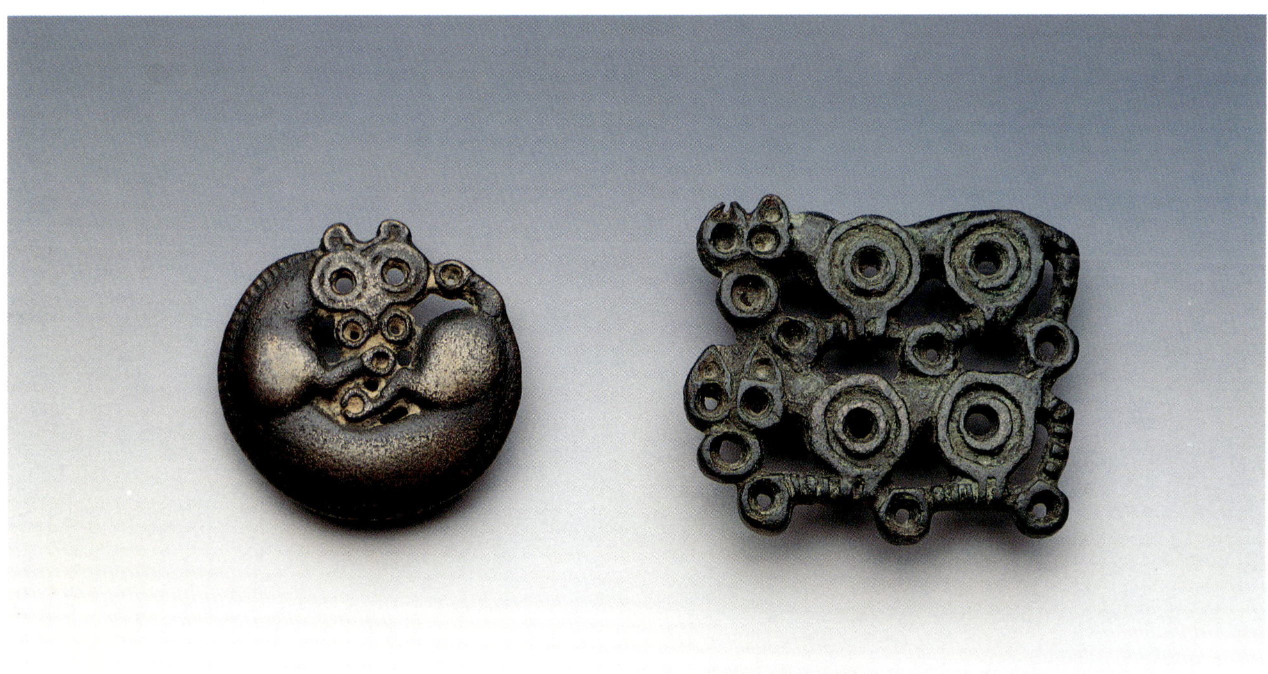

257

ORDOS STANDING DEER

WARRING STATES PERIOD
(5TH TO 4TH CENTURY B.C.)
WESTERN INNER MONGOLIA
LENGTH : 5.5 CM
HEIGHT : 5.3 CM
WIDTH : 1.5 CM

A hollow bronze Ordos doe in the round standing on a baseline which consists of two bars, one under the hooves on each side. The animal's distinctive conformation - the hind legs longer than the front legs - suggests the musk deer, which has inhabited Siberia and East Asia from antiquity. Mould marks bisect the body lengthwise. Similar standing deer with baseline runners dating to the 5th to 4th century B.C. have been excavated at Sujigou, Jungar Qi in Western Inner Mongolia and at Yushougou, Yongdeng in Gansu province.

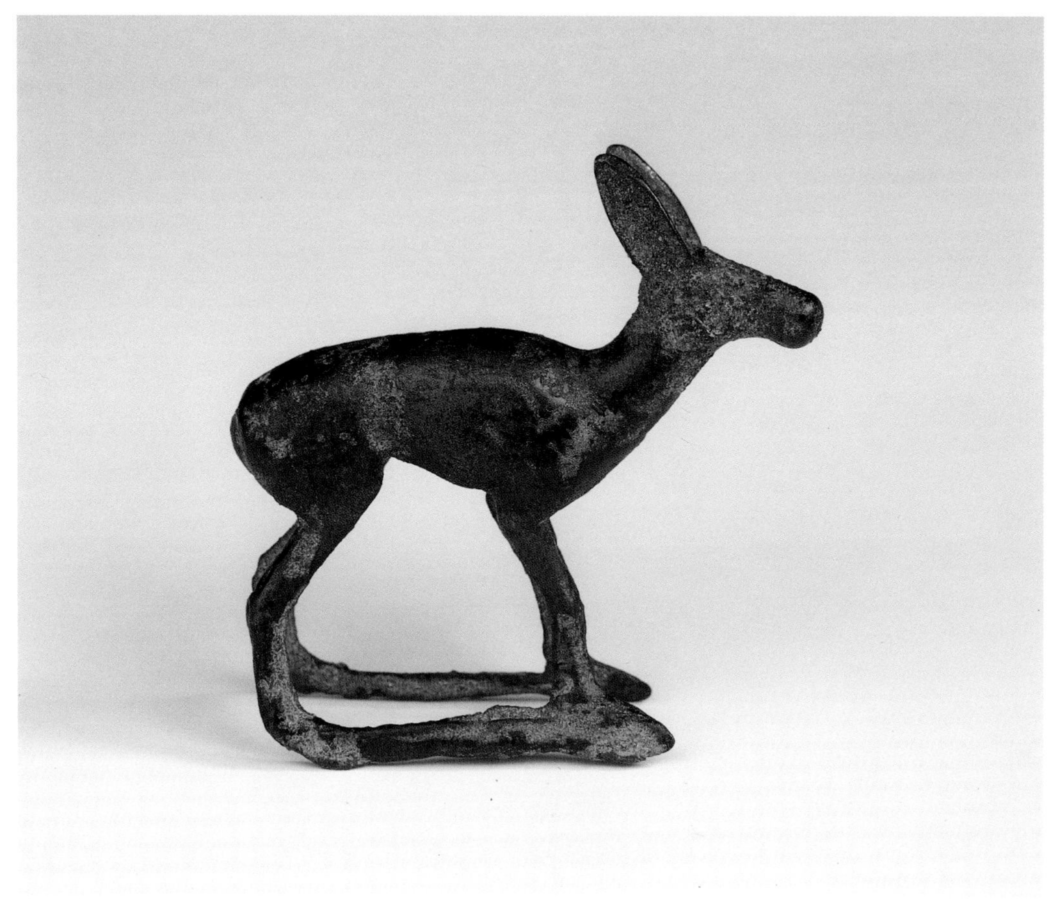

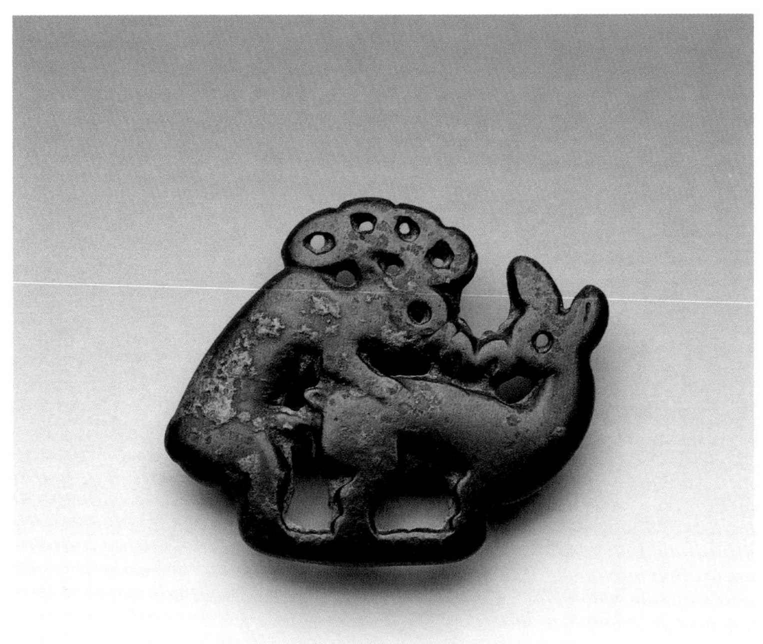

258

Ordos bronze of stag and doe copulating

Warring States period
(4th century B.C.)
South central Inner Mongolia
Length : 3.8 cm
Width : 3 cm

An openwork plaque of a stag with stylised antlers and a highly visible penis mounting a standing doe, with ring for attachment at the back. Such subjects were popular with the Mongolian pastoral tribes, to whom the increase of wildlife was of immense economic importance. Similar plaques have been found near Hohhot in Inner Mongolia.

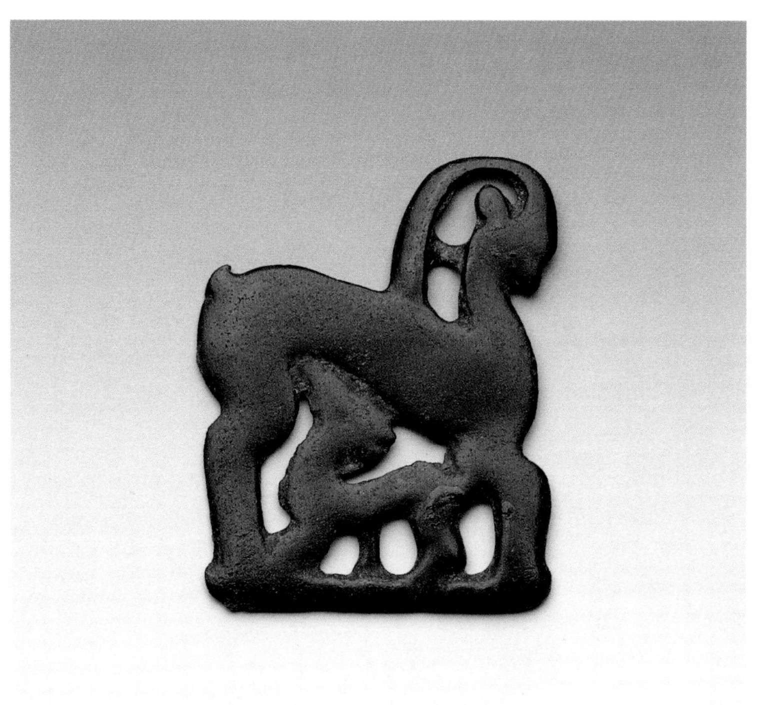

259

ORDOS PLAQUE OF SHE-GOAT WITH SUCKLING KID

WARRING STATES PERIOD
(4TH CENTURY B.C.)
SOUTH CENTRAL INNER MONGOLIA
HEIGHT : 3.8 CM
LENGTH : 3.3 CM

This Ordos plaque without attachment is another example showing the Mongolian pastoral tribes' interest in the increase of their herds.

 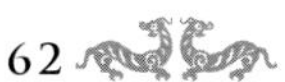

260

Two Ordos bronze bridle ornaments, one a lynx mask with stylised bird form, the other a recumbent argali ram

Warring States period
(3rd century B.C.)
Western Inner Mongolia
(i) Height : 2.5 cm; Width : 3 cm
(ii) Height : 4.5 cm; Width : 2 cm

(i) A bridle ornament in the form of a recumbent argali ram resting with its head turned back against its hindquarters and legs curled up. The back with a ring for attachment. This design here can be traced back to Scythian examples of the 5th century B.C. in the region of the Black Sea. A similar plaque of the late 4th to early 3rd century B.C. has been excavated in northern Shaanxi.

(ii) A bridle ornament in the form of a lynx mask with stylised bird form hanging from its jaws. Ring for attachment at back. Similar examples in silver are known dating from the 3rd century B.C.

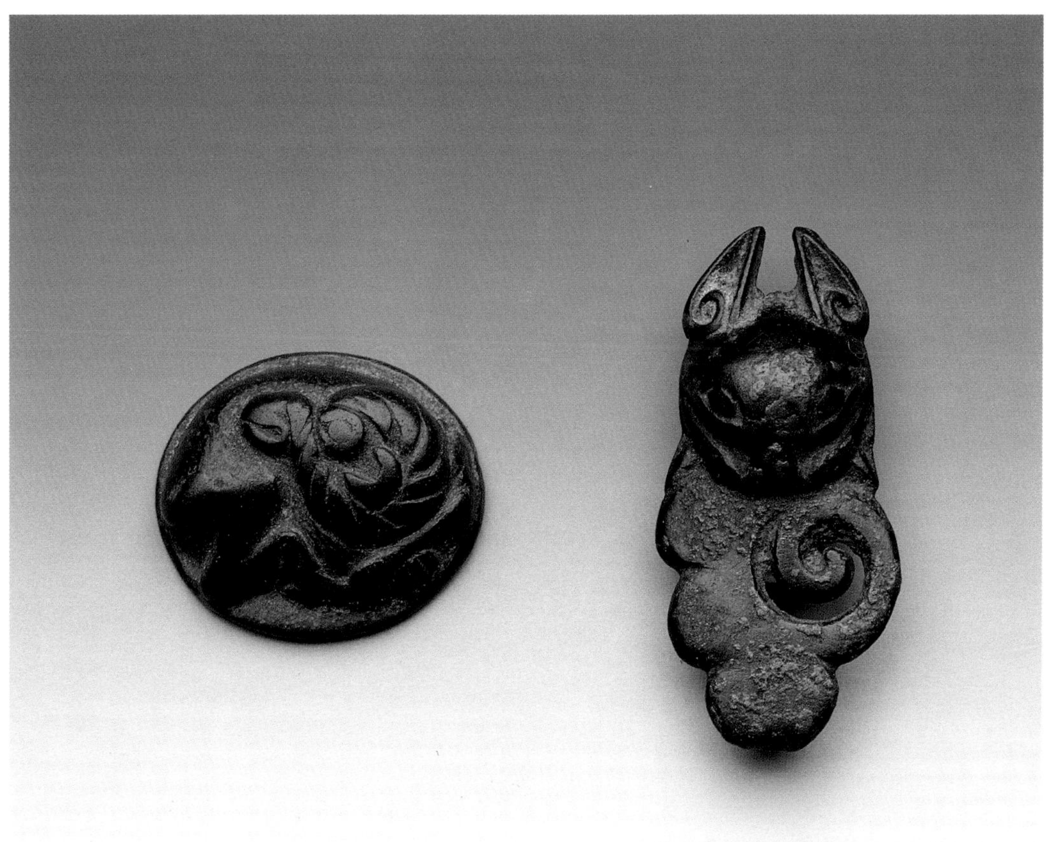

261

Group of four Ordos bronze belt or garment hooks

Warring States to Western Han period
(4th to 2nd century B.C.)
Northwest China or south
central Inner Mongolia
(i) Length : 3.4 cm; Width : 3.2 cm
(ii) Length : 6.5 cm; Width : 2 cm
(iii) Length : 6.5 cm; Width : 2.1 cm
(iv) Length : 3.4 cm; Width : 1.5 cm

Consisting of :

(i) A belt hook made of two joined birds.

(ii) A belt hook with bird head hook and a feline at the other end covering the stud.

(iii) A tiger belt hook formed by two half tigers each ending in an almost rectangular section which interlock making one complete tiger.

(iv) Garment hook in the form of a duck, the neck and beak forming the hook, with a stud under the body for attachment to the garment.

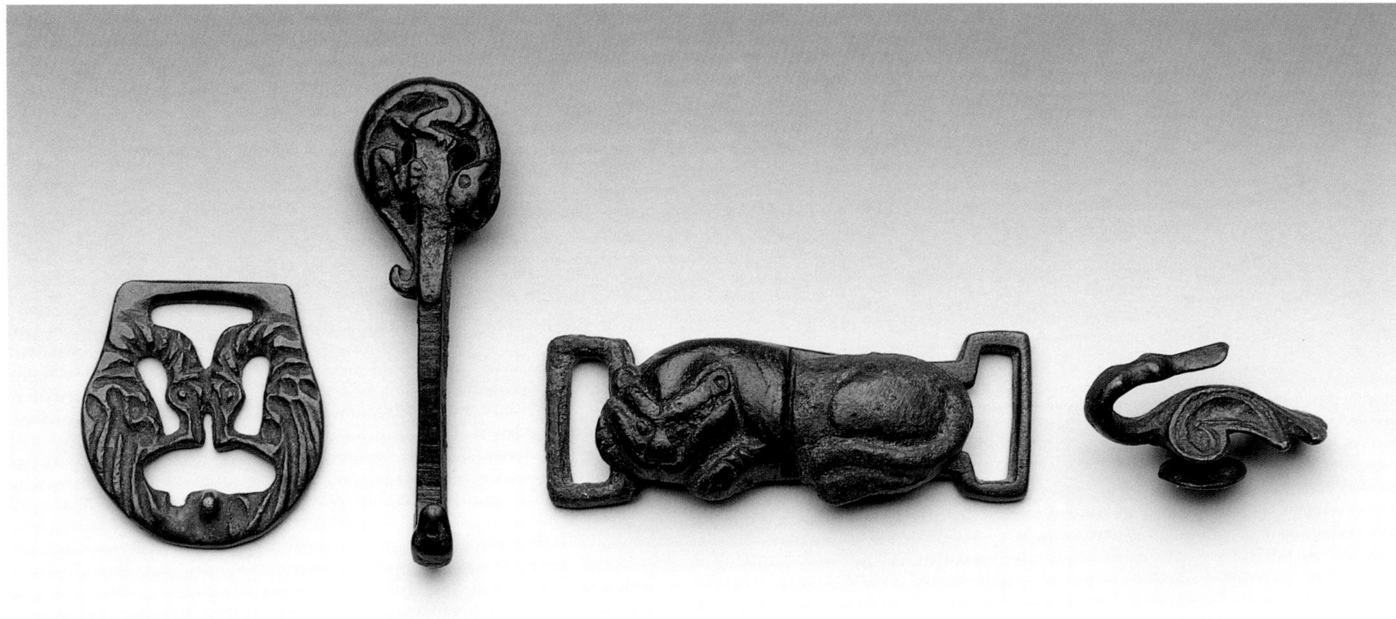

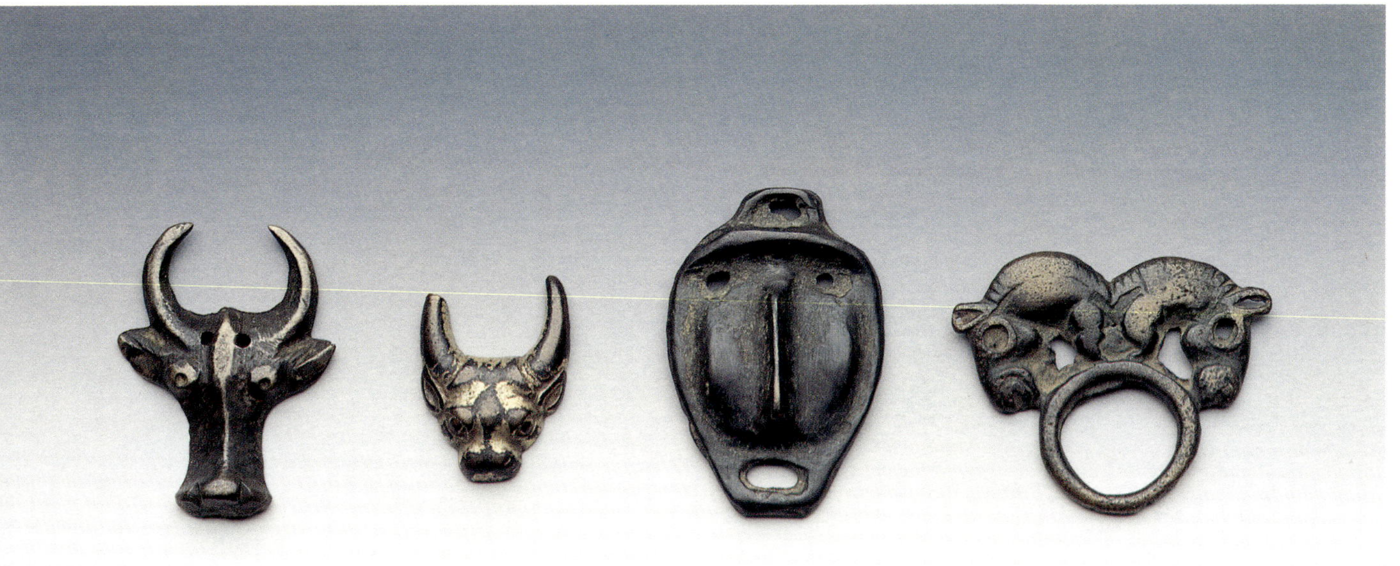

262

GROUP OF FOUR ORDOS BRONZES DEPICTING COWS' HEADS, HORSES' HEADS AND A STYLISED HUMAN MASK

WARRING STATES PERIOD TO
WESTERN HAN
(3RD TO 2ND CENTURY B.C.)
INNER MONGOLIA
(i) LENGTH : 4 CM; WIDTH : 2.4 CM
(ii) LENGTH : 2.8 CM; WIDTH : 2 CM
(iii) HEIGHT : 4.5 CM; WIDTH : 3 CM
(iv) HEIGHT : 3.6 CM; WIDTH : 4.5 CM

Consisting of :

(i) A bronze cow-head plaque.

(ii) A bronze cow-head plaque with silver and gilt.

(iii) A stylised human mask.

(iv) A ring topped by two horses' heads facing in opposite directions.

263

Group of two Ordos bronze plaques depicting a wolf and a buck ibex

Late Warring States period
to Western Han
(late 3rd to 2nd century B.C.)
Northwest China or
south Inner Mongolia
(i) Width : 5.7 cm; Height : 3.5 cm
(ii) Width : 4.0 cm; Height : 2.9 cm

Flat openwork plaques with no ring for attachment depicting:

(i) A crouching wolf.

(ii) A grazing buck ibex.
The feet on both animals have small teardrop depressions typical of the area and period.

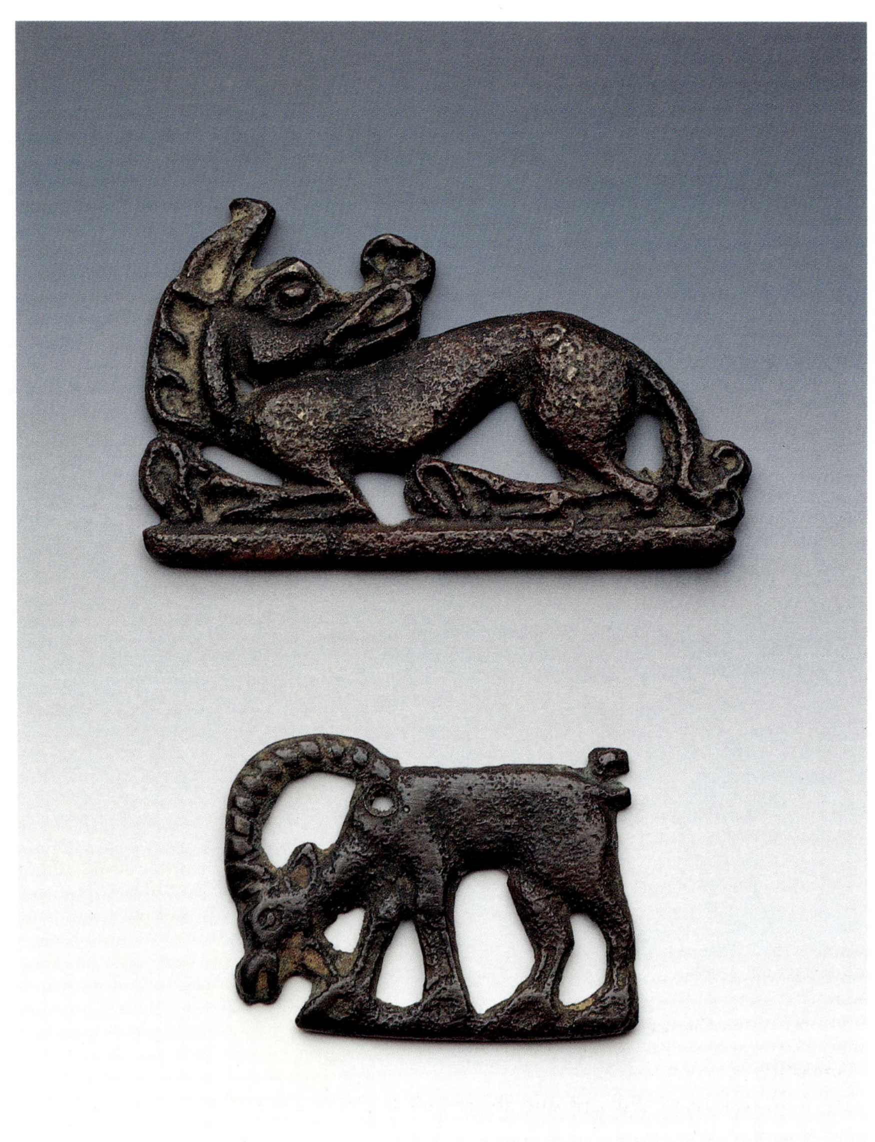

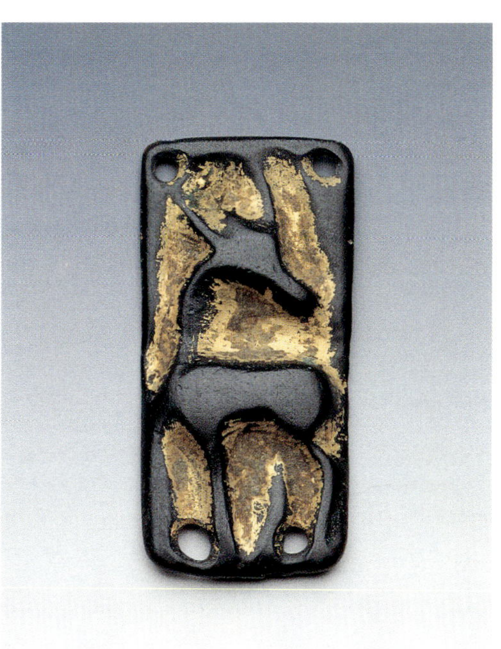

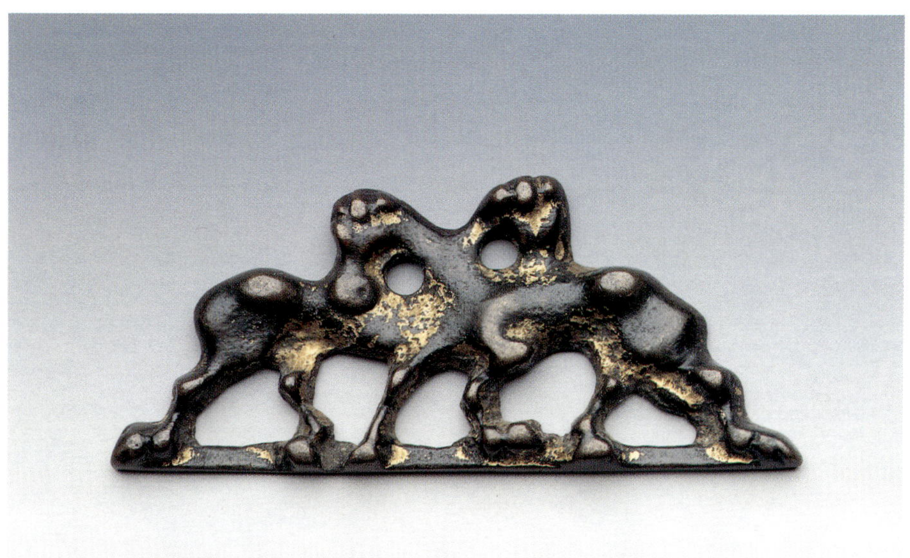

264

Two gilt bronze Ordos plaques

Eastern Han
(1st century A.D.)
Northeast Inner Mongolia
(i) Height : 4 cm; Width : 1.9 cm
(ii) Width : 6.5 cm; Height : 2.5 cm

Consisting of :

(i) A vertical rectangular plaque, the rounded corners pierced for attachment, cast as a single stag, its head turned over the back and gilded. A similar plaque has been found in a 1st century A.D. burial near the Korean border.

(ii) A pair of fighting horses with traces of gilding.

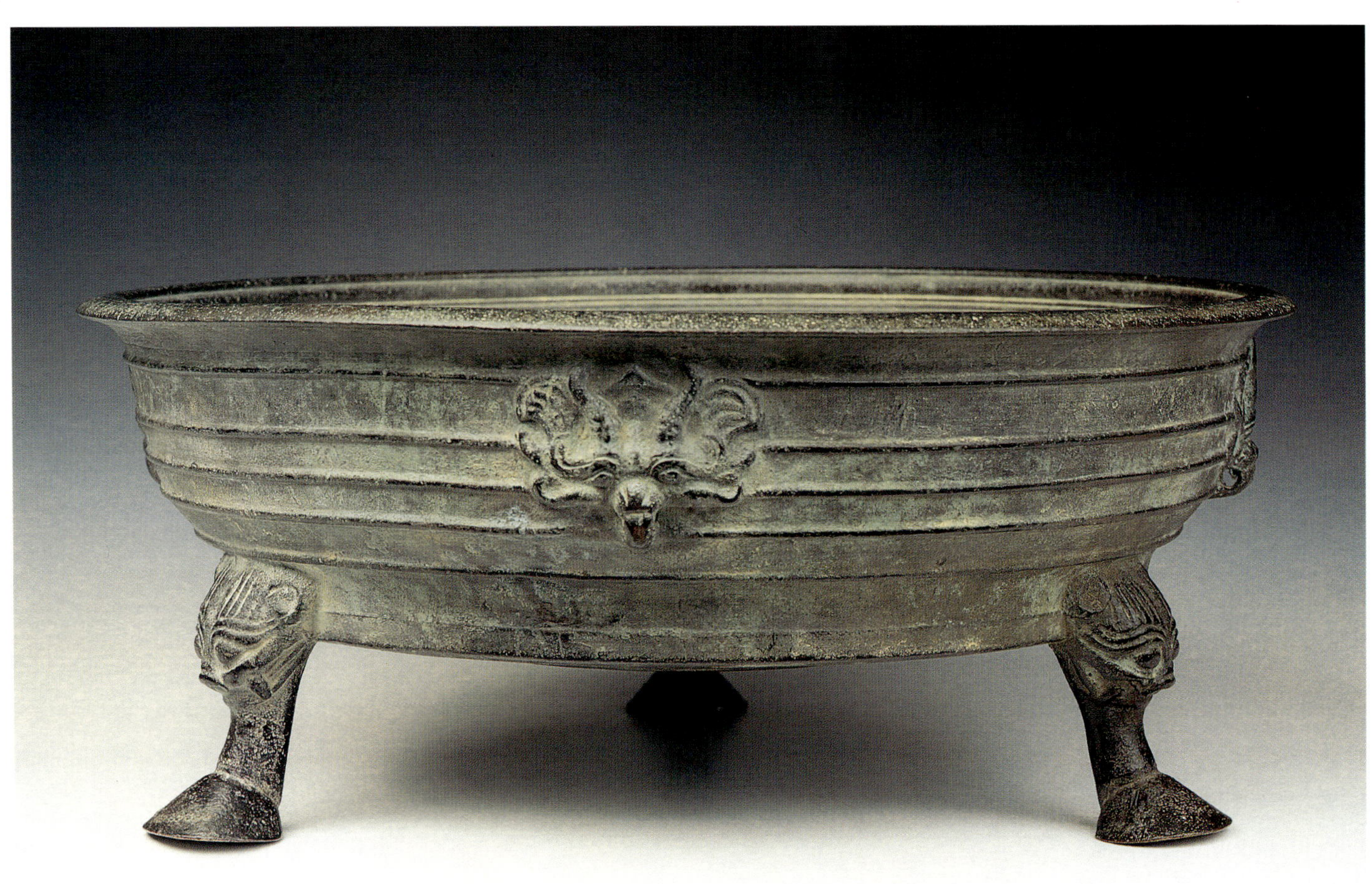

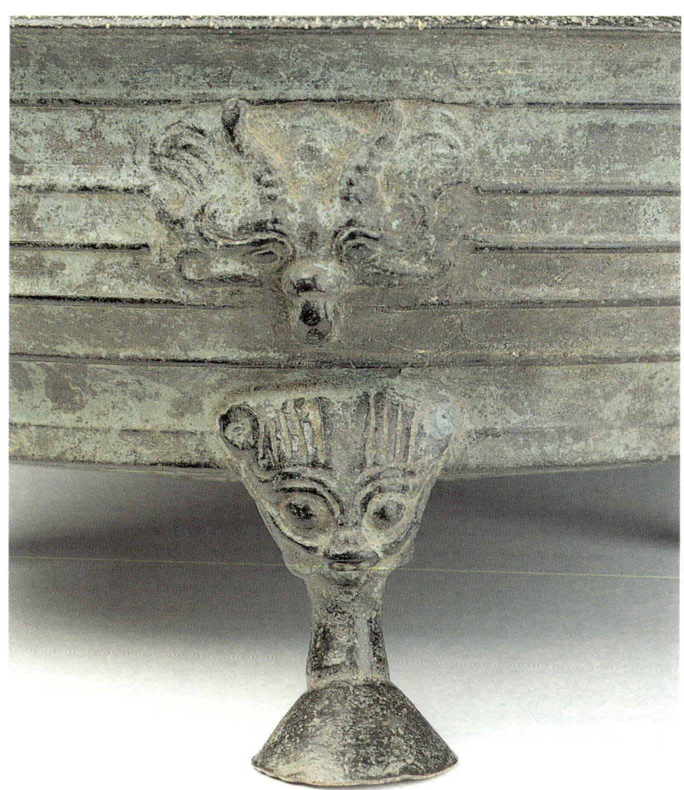

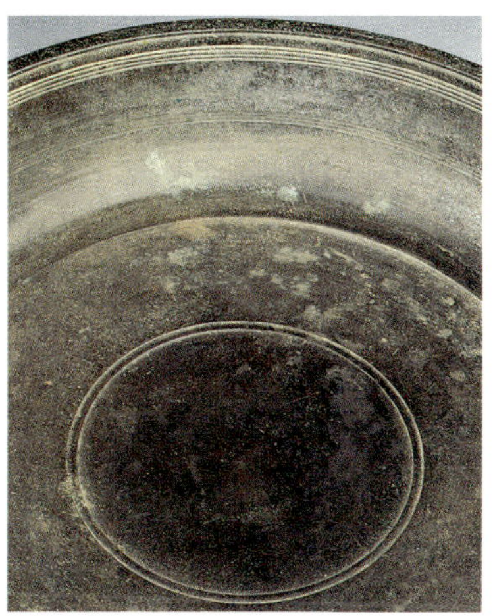

265

BRONZE CIRCULAR TRIPOD BASIN DECORATED WITH RAISED BANDS AND FOUR LONG-HORNED *TAOTIE* MASKS, ITS THREE HOOF-LIKE FEET ISSUING FROM STYLISED FELINE HEADS

EARLY SIX DYNASTIES PERIOD
(3RD OR 4TH CENTURY)
DIAMETER : 42.5 CM
HEIGHT : 17.8 CM

A heavy bronze circular tripod basin, the bottom flat with the central section slightly sagging, the interior plain save for a double circle in the centre of the base, the sides of ogee form showing bands in the interior, the exterior with five raised bands accentuating the shape. The three splayed legs issue from stylised feline heads and end in hoof-like feet, the body with four *taotie* masks each with two long horns. The thick rim is everted. The hoofed feet issuing from stylised feline heads can be compared with examples of Yue celadon from the same period.

266

GILT BRONZE WATER DROPPER IN THE SHAPE OF A TORTOISE HOLDING AN EARED CUP

SIX DYNASTIES
(4TH OR 5TH CENTURY A.D.)
LENGTH : 11.5 CM
HEIGHT : 5 CM

A gilt bronze water dropper in the shape of a tortoise holding a winged cup with extensive traces of gilding throughout the body, which is connected to the cup by a hole in the tortoise's mouth. There is a ring on each side of the body, probably meant for suspension.

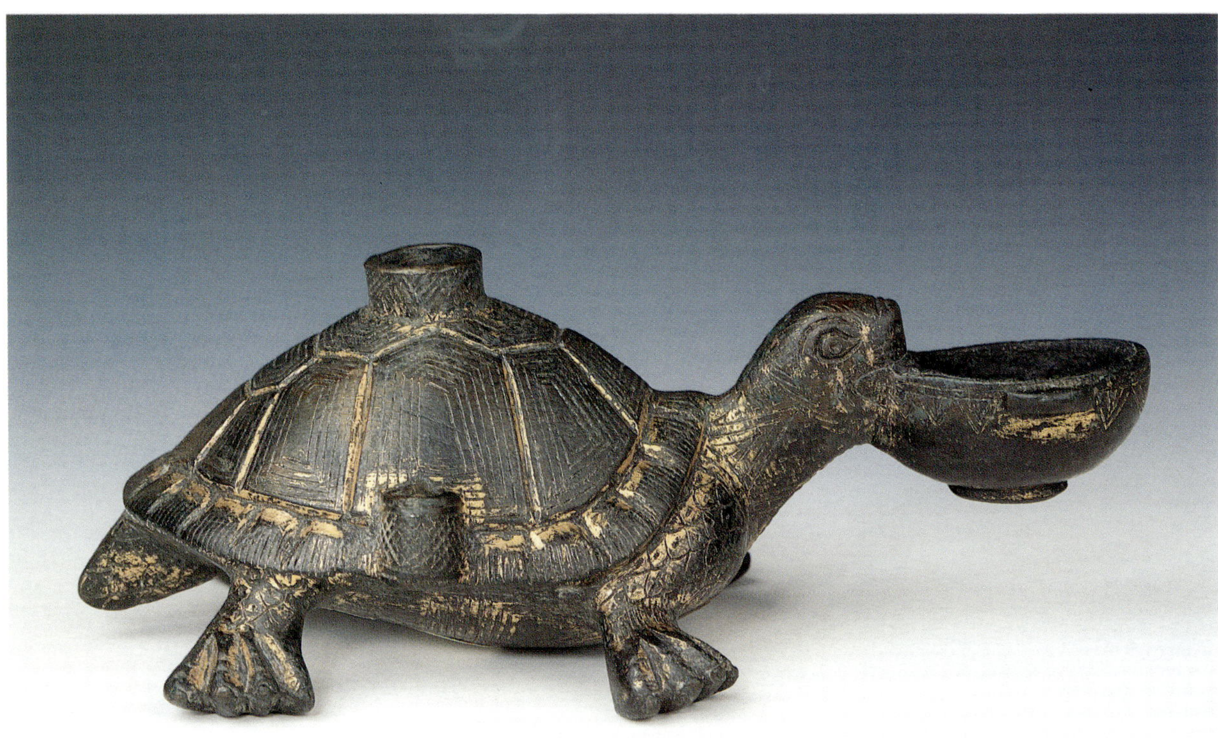

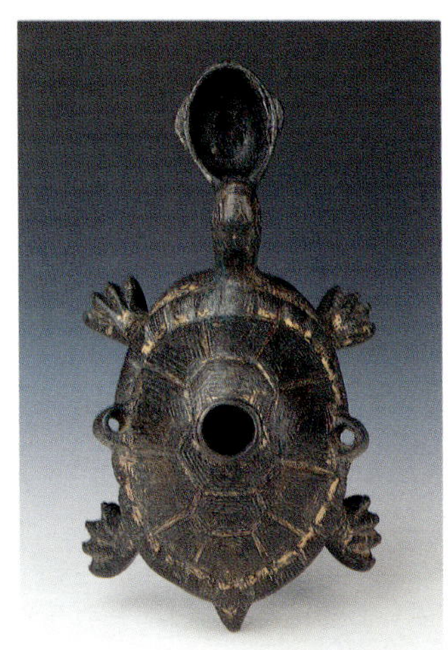

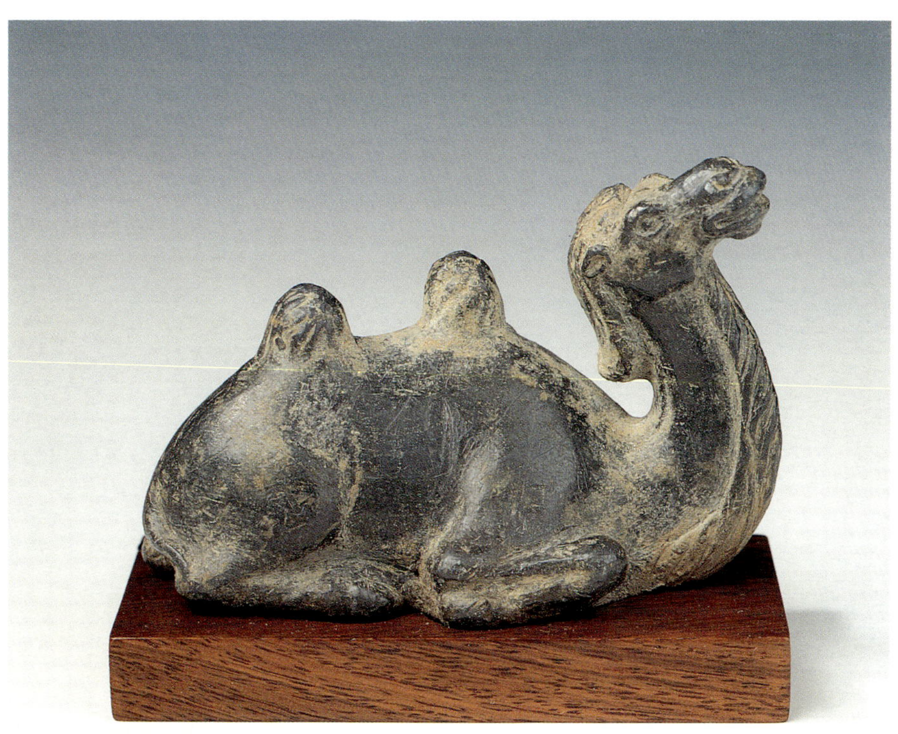

267

LEAD TWO-HUMPED CAMEL

SUI TO EARLY TANG DYNASTY
(LATE 6TH OR 7TH CENTURY)
LENGTH : 8.5 CM
HEIGHT : 6.3 CM

Lead two-humped camel, the head thrown back and to one side. The camel is lying down with legs underneath, one protruding, a shaggy mane and details; the base with a circular plug. Such camels have been known to decorate Buddhist lead shrines of this period and the circular plug here renders such a use likely for this example.

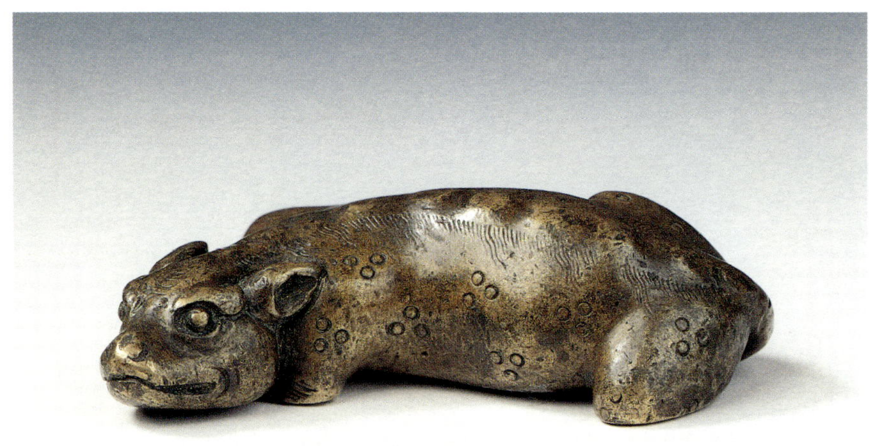

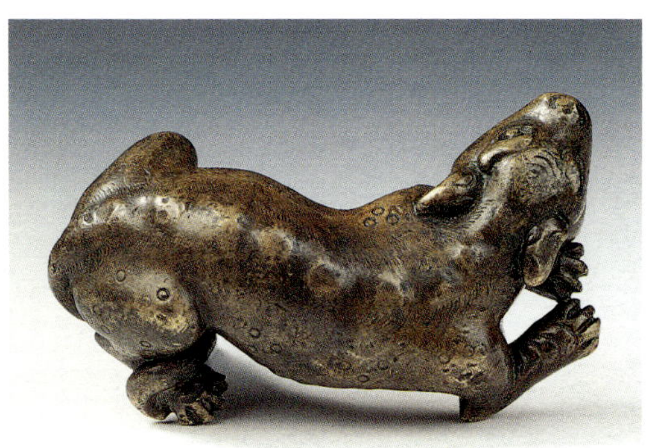

268

Bronze spotted dog-like animal

Tang dynasty
(618 - 906) or earlier
Length : 6.9 cm
Height : 1.6 cm

Bronze spotted dog-like animal, the head resting on one paw and slightly turned to the left, the eyes well defined under beetling brows, the back legs, one under the body, the other to one side with the tail looped over it. The paws are well defined, and the curving backbone knobbly with clusters of fine incised hairs on each side of the spine. The body is decorated with groups of three incised round dots. Such fine incised hairs are found on some Han and Six Dynasties jades and it is possible this bronze is somewhat earlier than Tang. Its relaxed but strong sculptured posture can, however, also be compared to some Tang animal sculptures.

269

A NIELLO-INLAID, RED BRASS ALMS-BOWL SHAPED CIRCULAR CONTAINER DECORATED WITH ROWS OF FOUR-PETALLED FLOWERS

HIGH TANG PERIOD
(684 - 756)
HEIGHT : 10.3 CM
DIAMETER : 15.1 CM
DIAMETER OF THE MOUTH: 9.6CM

A niello-inlaid red brass alms-bowl shaped circular container; the mouth inverted and surrounded by a narrow band of red brass, the red brass body cast with nine rows of red brass four petalled flowers, each petal has a square niello inset. The body is otherwise covered by a thick niello inlay and the base has a slightly raised undecorated section. The interior has a small hidden loop possibly for a chain to attach a lid. Expert investigation of this apparently unique piece found that the body material is red brass, in which 20% zinc is added to the normal bronze mixture, the same body compound on which early cloisonné was built, and that the inlay is niello of 42 % lead, 35% copper and 23% sulphur, close to the ideal proportions for such a niello mix.

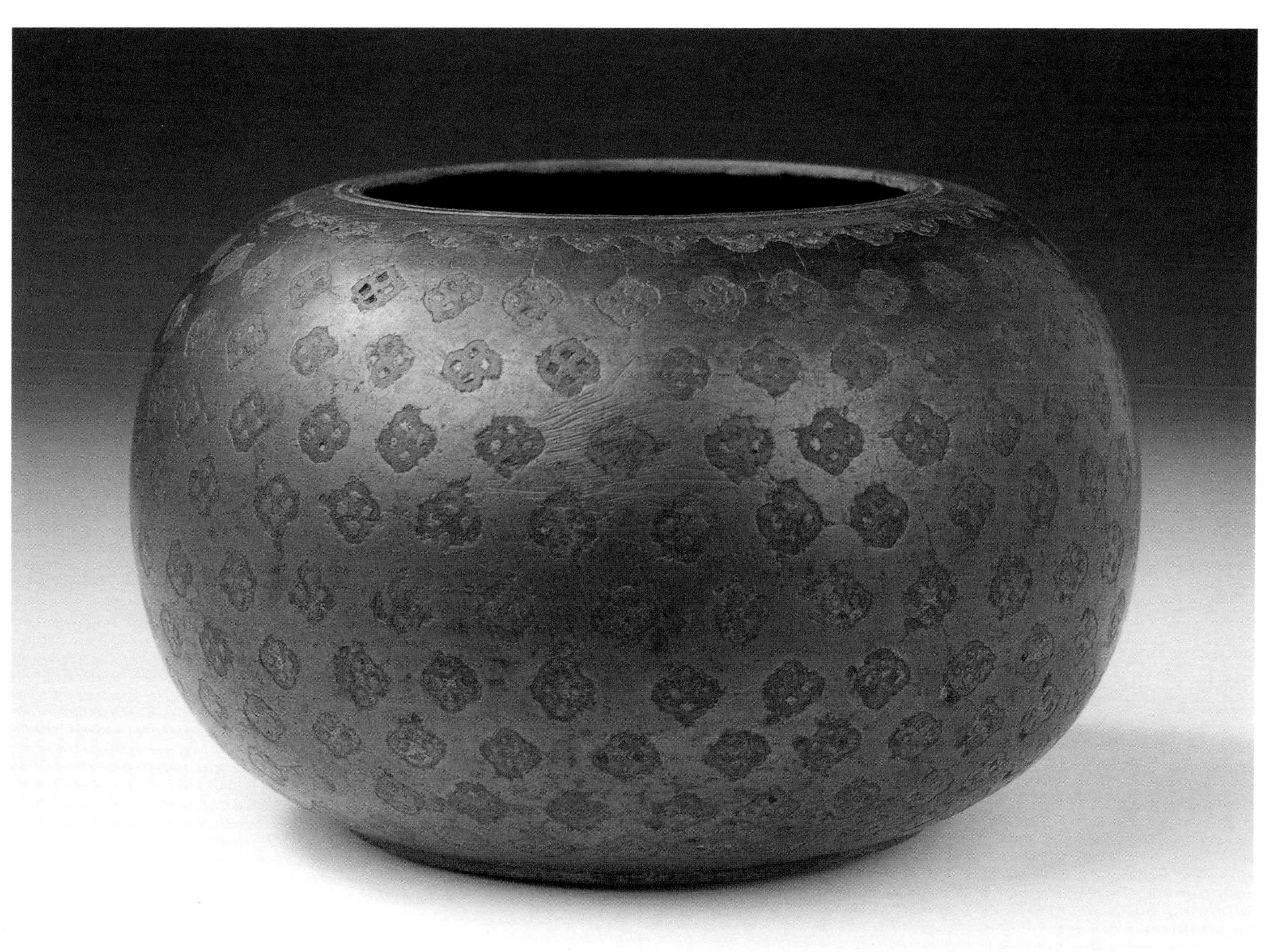

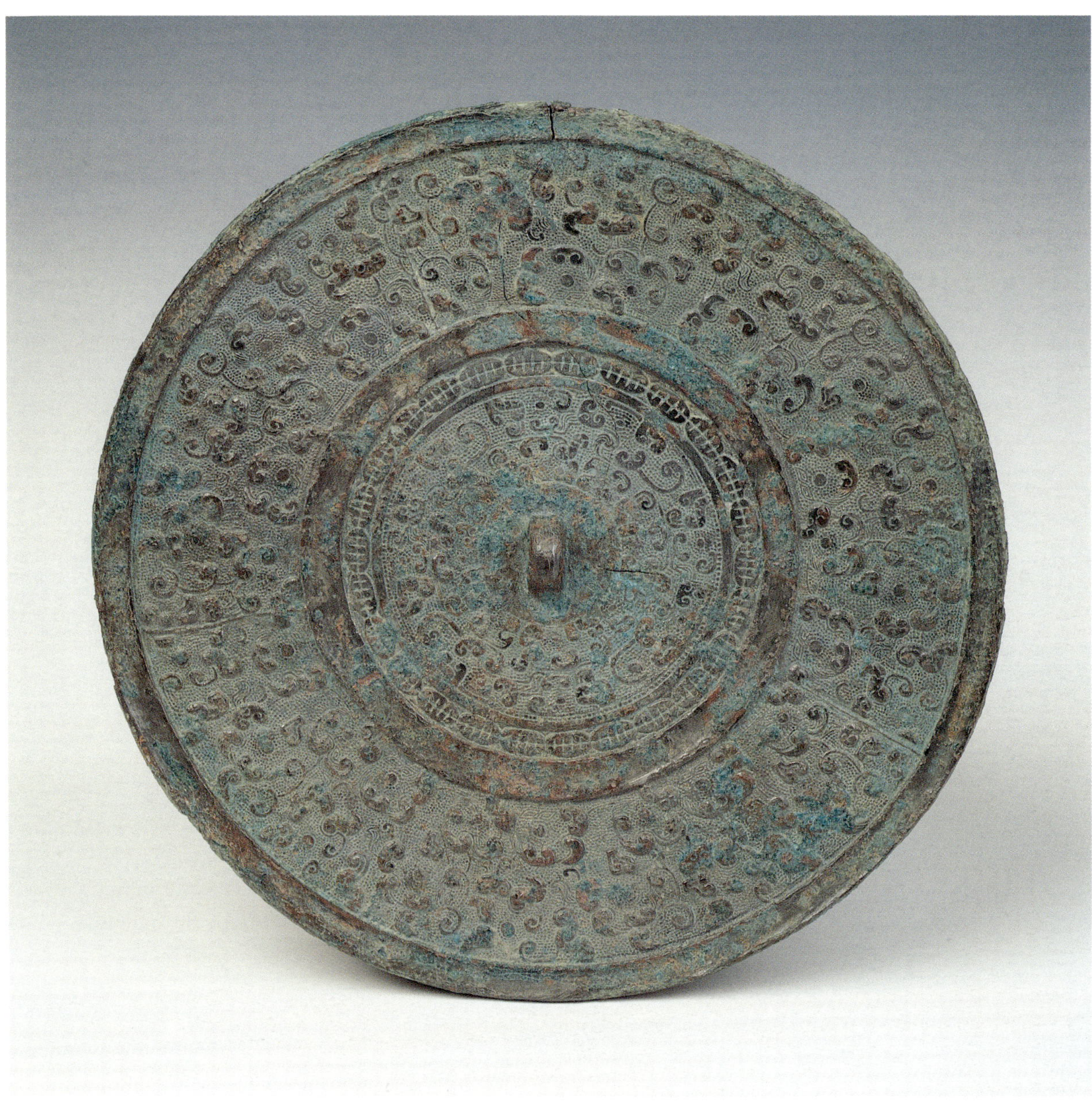

270

Mirror with bronze pattern of relief dragon heads

Spring and Autumn period
(6th to 5th century B.C.)
Diameter : 12 cm

Mirrors on which the decoration matches the ornamentation of contemporary bronze vessels are rare. On this example, the motifs resemble the designs current in the Jin state and cast on bronzes at the foundry at Houma, where a large number of moulds and pattern blocks have been found. The handle is a plain, thick, convex arch. The surface is covered with small relief dragon heads delineated by commas on a granulated ground. This field of raised commas resembles jade patterns of the same period. Identical designs are found on bells and vessels from Shanxi and Henan provinces. There is a narrow border of cowrie shell decor midway between the central knob and the rim. These cowrie shell patterns are also familiar from other bronzes from the Jin state. An almost identical mirror has been found at Luoyang.

271

Bronze mirror with *kui* dragon pattern

Western Han dynasty
(2nd century B.C.)
Diameter : 11.5 cm

A bronze mirror with a flat surface and a slightly raised plain rim. The space between the rim and the body is decorated with stylised interlaced *kui* dragons in low relief against a background of cloud and thunder patterns. The handle is a strap with three concave sections.

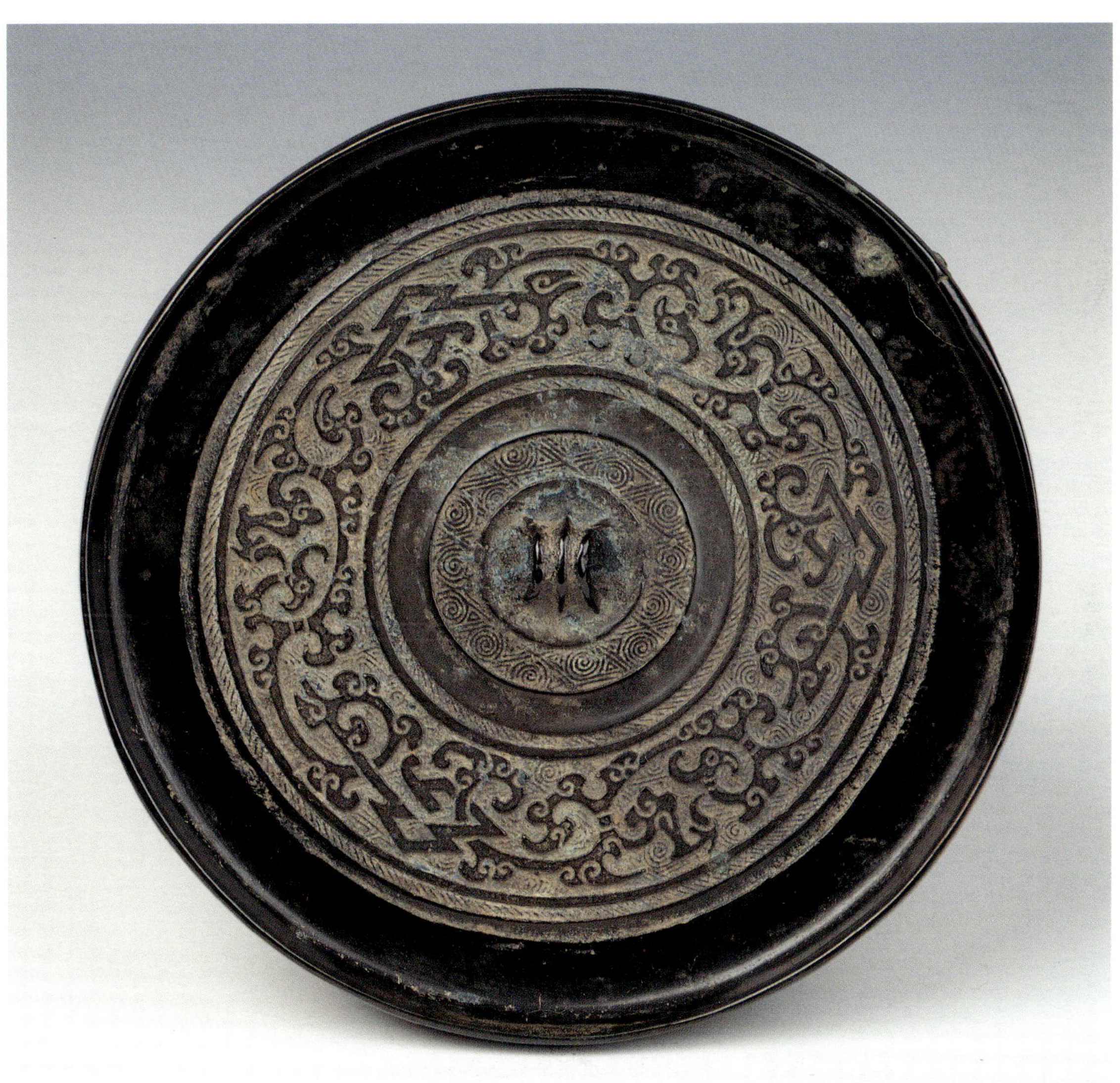

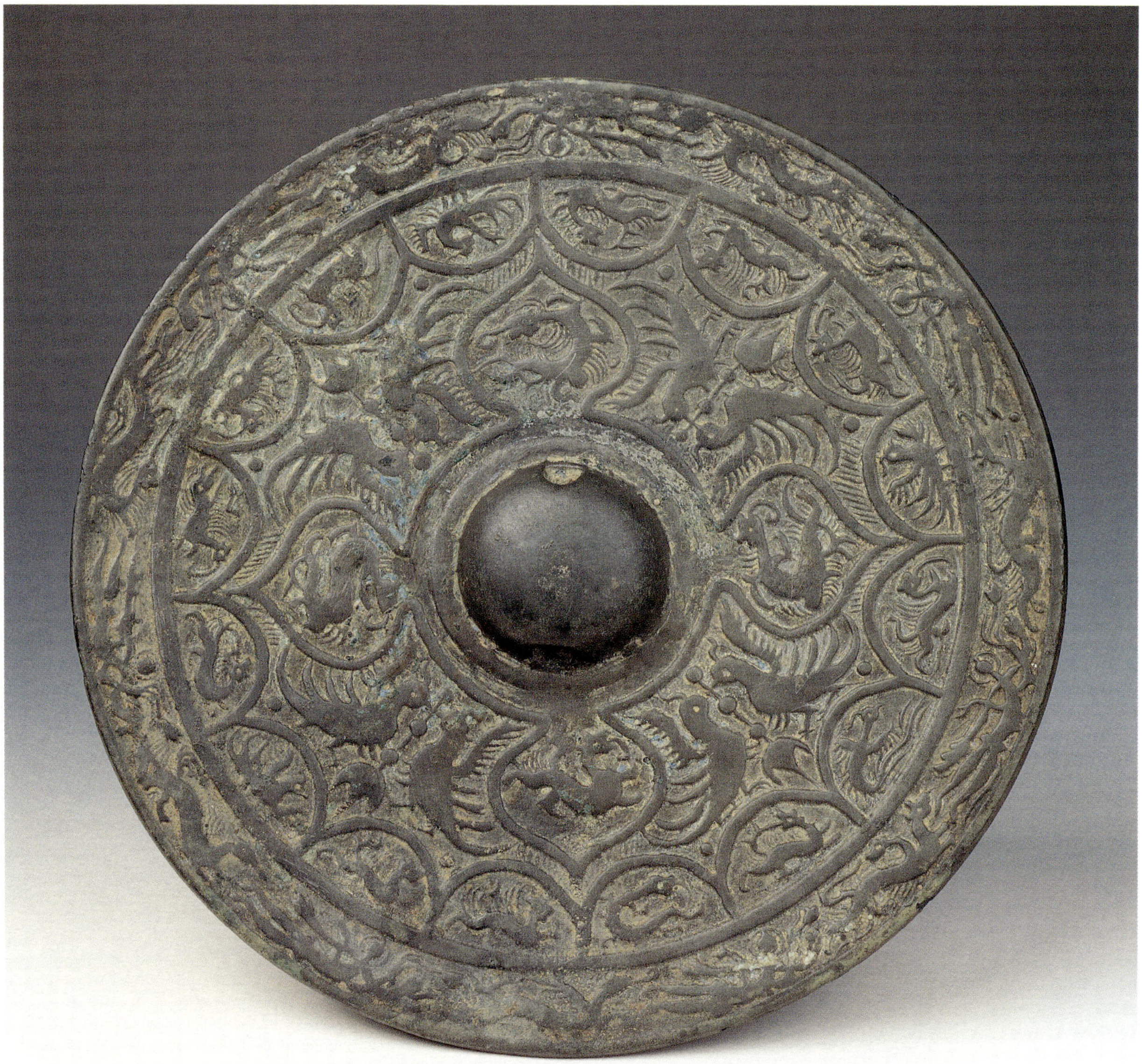

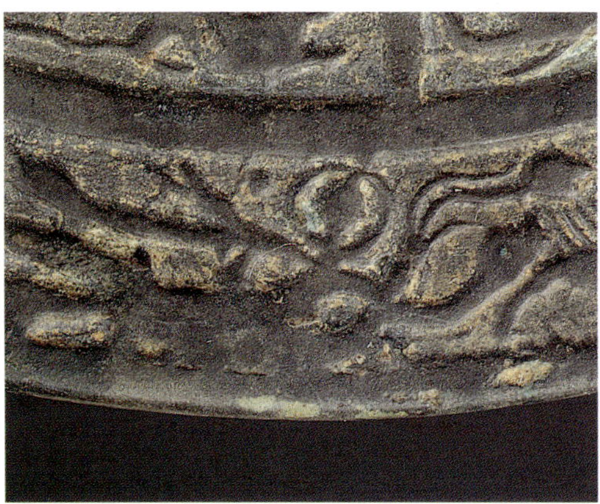

272

BRONZE MIRROR OF DRAGON AND PHOENIX DESIGN WITH LARGE FLAT BOSS HANDLE CAST IN LOW RELIEF

Early Six Dynasties
(mid 3rd century)
Wu Kingdom
Diameter : 17.8 cm

A bronze mirror with a large flat boss cast in low relief with a thin outer band of dragons and flying spirit figures between line borders, the broad inner band bordered with semi-circles enclosing dragons, *apsara* with halo, phoenixes and tigers, the boss handle imposed on a quatrefoil pattern enclosing fabulous animals separating four pairs of phoenixes holding up a standard in the broad band. Such dragon and phoenix mirrors are sometimes known as *kuifeng* mirrors and similar examples of mid-3rd century date have been found at Echeng, Hubei province. The inclusion of an *apsara* with a halo, a Buddhist motif, at this early period marks this as one of the earliest objects with a Buddhist related decoration.

273

Bronze mirror decorated with scene of the lunar palace and four supernatural beings

Tang dynasty
(8th century)
Diameter : 14.7 cm

A circular bronze mirror, the central boss of which is a toad, the main decoration being a tree with the moon goddess and a hare pounding the elixir of immortality above a mountain top. The four quarters in the outer band are cast with the four supernatural beings, namely, the Green Dragon, the White Tiger, the Scarlet Bird and the Sombre Warrior, which symbolize the four quadrants of the world, separated by clouds.

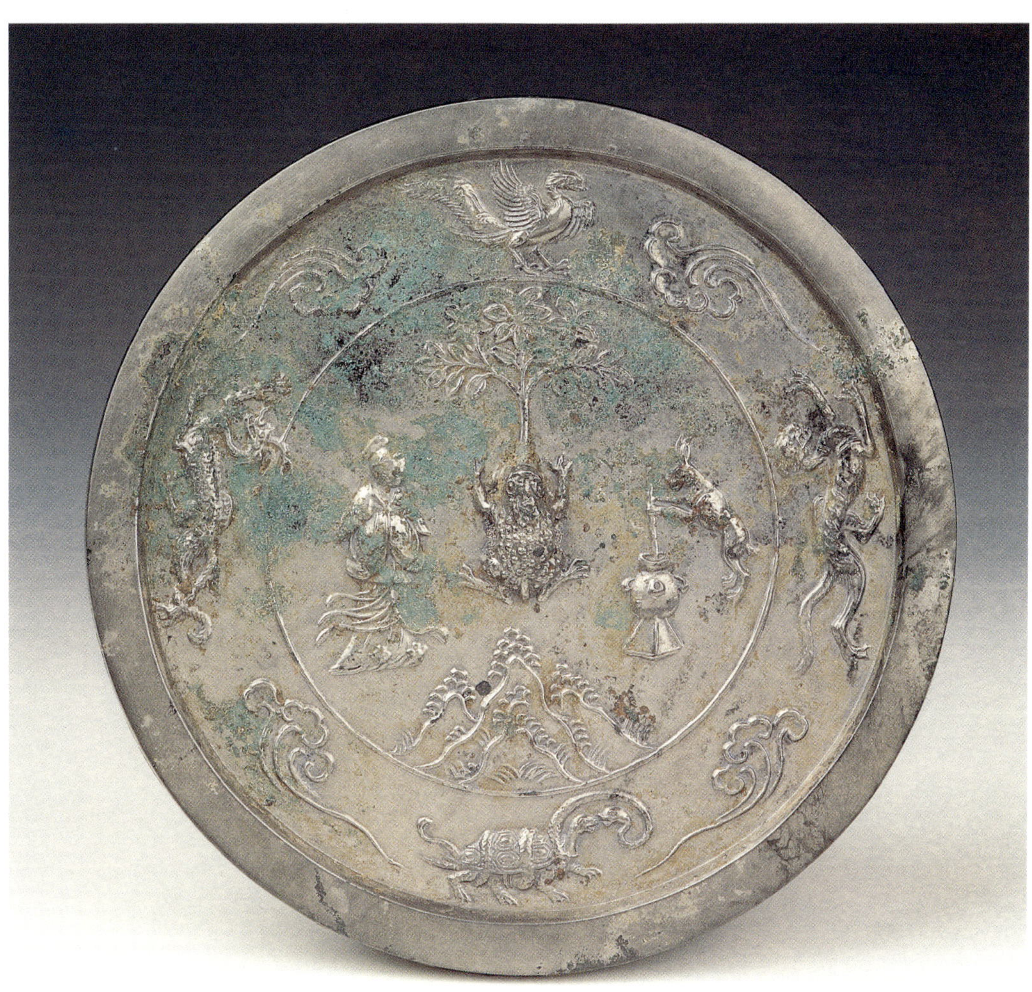

274

Bronze mirror of four-lobed shape decorated with a phoenix and a stork in flight and peonies

Northern Song
(11th century)
Diameter : 17 cm

Bronze mirror of four-lobed shape decorated with a phoenix and stork in flight diagonally to the upper left and lower right of the central knob, which is small and cast on top of a six petalled flower, the upper right and lower left are cast with clusters of peonies.

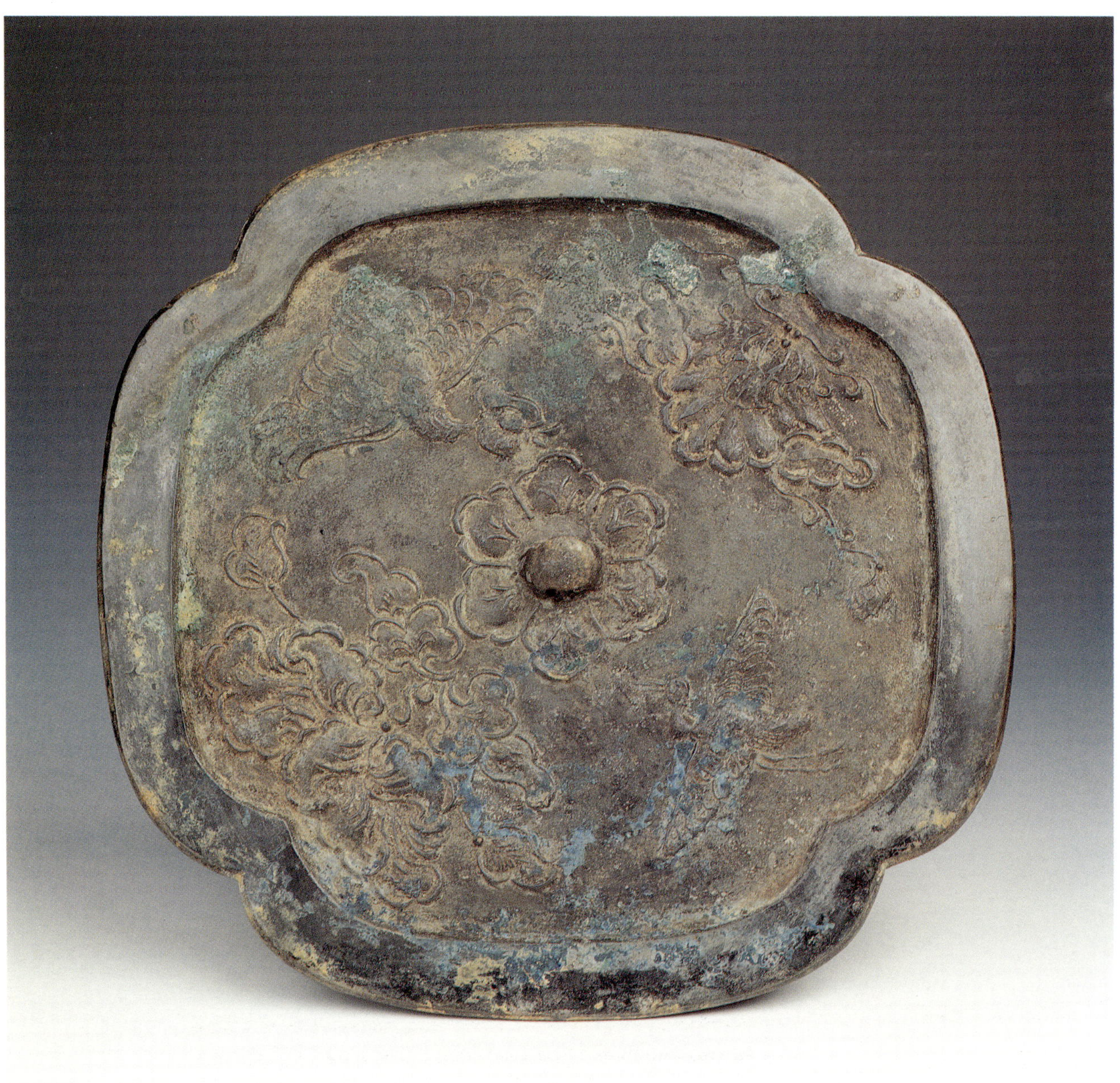

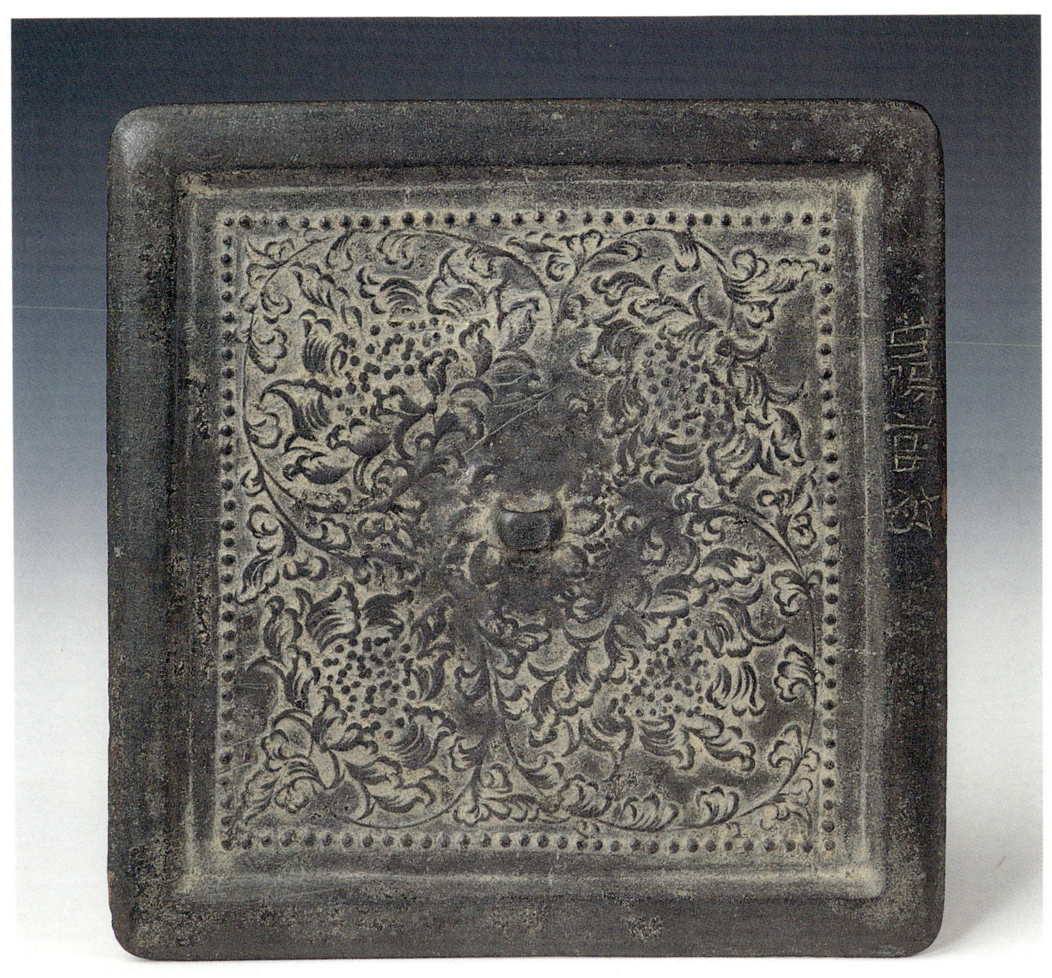

275

Bronze square mirror with scrolling peonies and inscription

Southern Song dynasty
(12th century)
Diameter : 12.5 cm

A square bronze mirror with rounded corners and a broad flat rim incised with three Chinese characters. The surface is decorated with four peony blossoms joined by tendrils confined within a continuous nibble border. The inscription is probably the official permission for the export of the mirror from the south to Jin occupied northern China.

276

Bronze mirror with the reflecting surface incised, with multi-armed Avalokitesvara and Tibetan characters

Yuan dynasty
(late 13th to mid 14th century)
Diameter : 11.5 cm

A circular bronze mirror with a flat surface and a raised plain rim. The space between the rim and the body is decorated with a band of stylised phoenixes in four pairs separated by studs or flower heads. A small raised character enclosed in a small medallion is cast on the head of one phoenix. The reflecting surface of the mirror is unusual in being finely etched with Avalokitesvara with fourteen of his sixteen hands holding different ritual objects. The *bodhisattva* is surrounded by incised, outlined Tibetan characters.

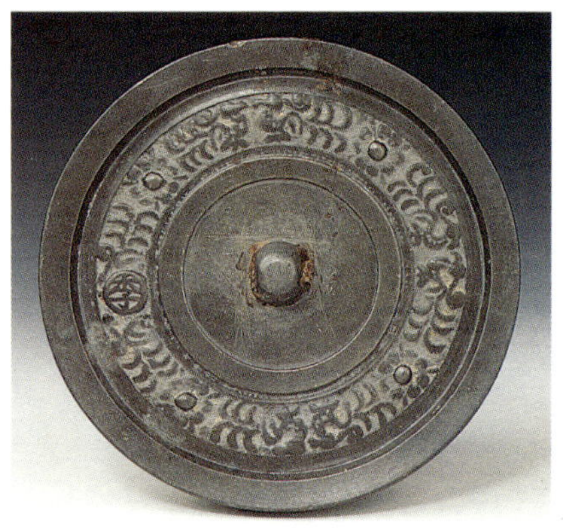

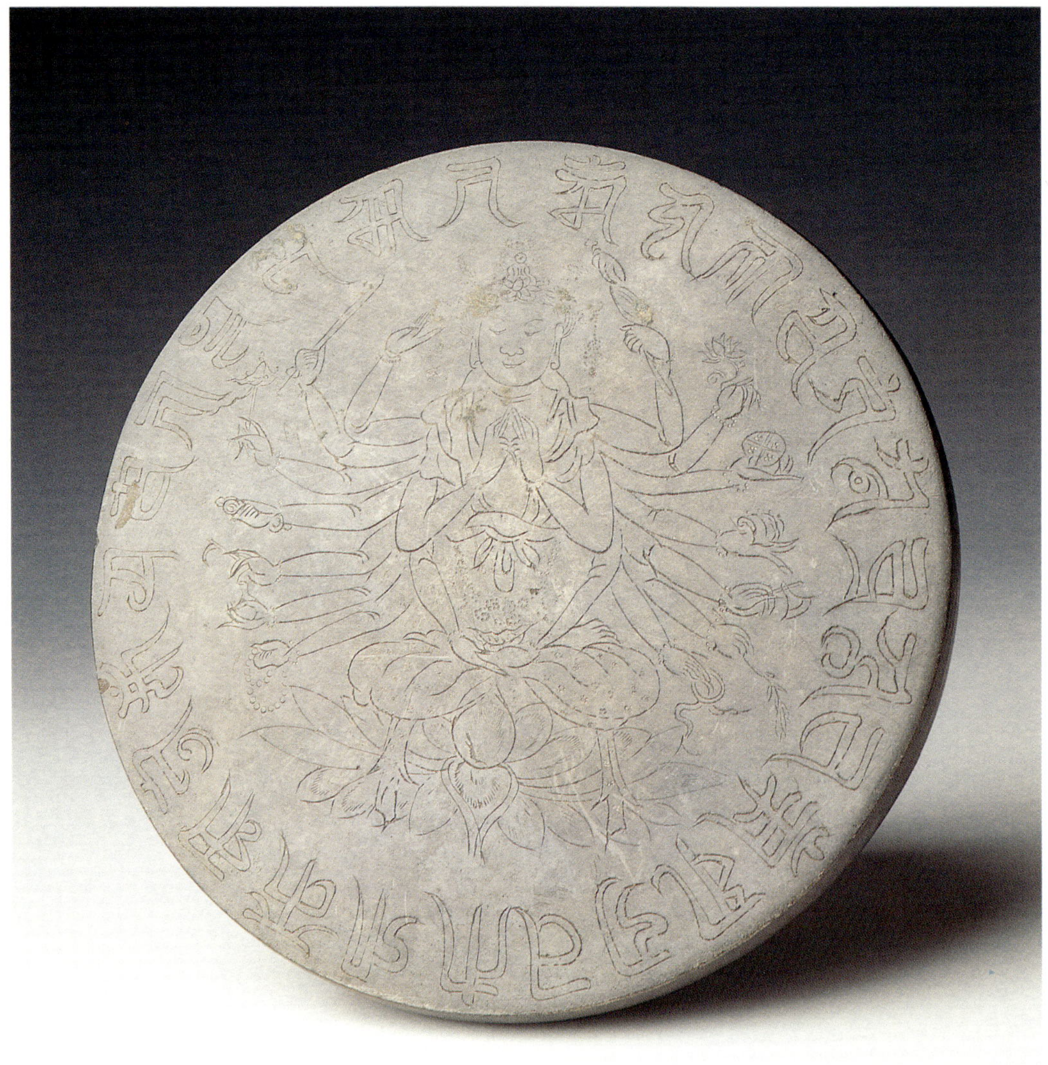

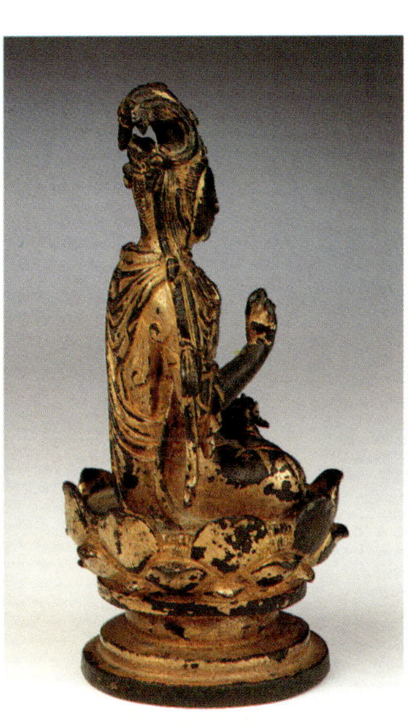

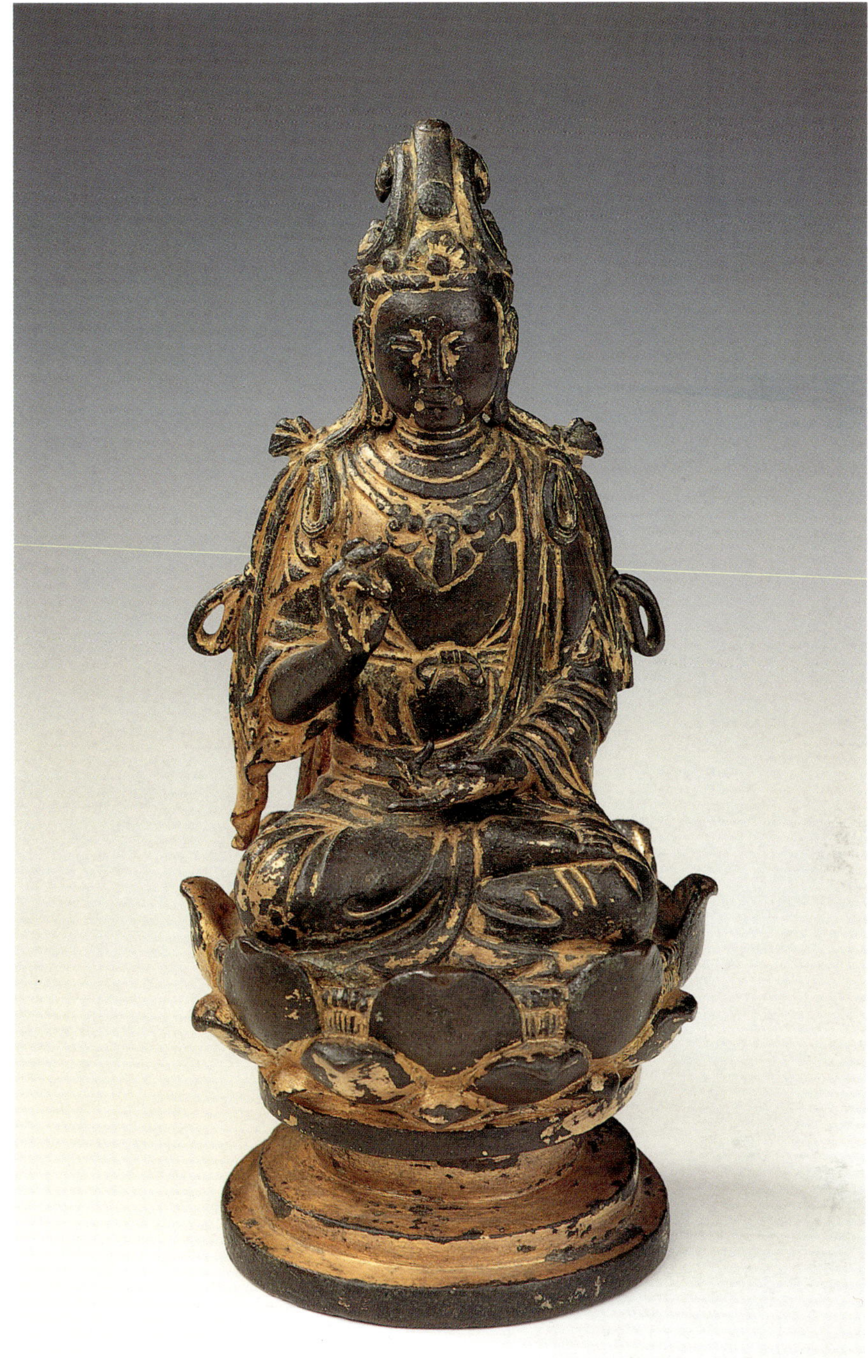

277

A GILT BRONZE *BODHISATTVA* WITH HIGH PIERCED HEADDRESS ON HIGH PLINTH WITH LOTUS PETALS

LIAO DYNASTY
(MID 11TH CENTURY)
OVERALL HEIGHT : 15.8 CM
WIDTH : 6.5 CM

A gilt bronze *bodhisattva*, sitting in the meditation posture with one hand raised in the gesture of blessing, on a lotus plinth with some everted petals, the headdress of characteristic Liao form swept up and over, and the gilding extensively worn.

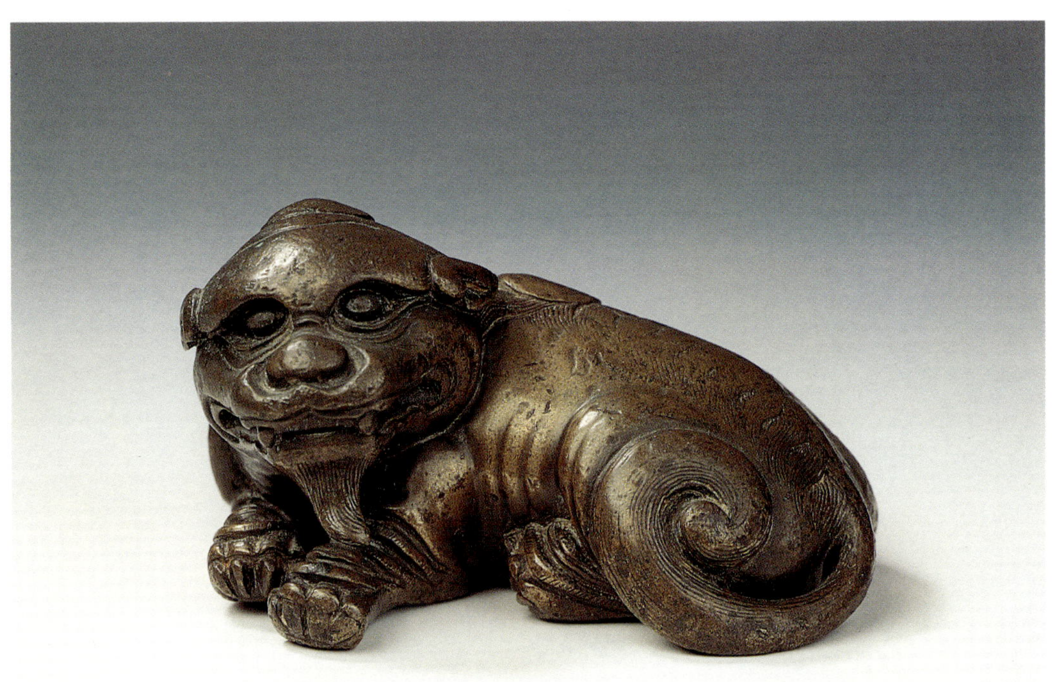

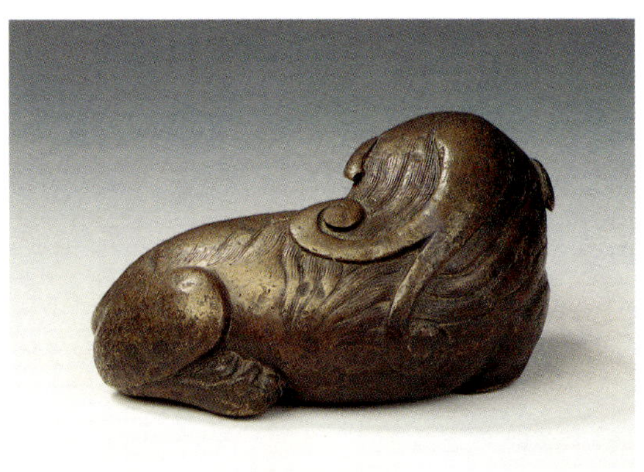

278

Bronze mythical animal strongly sculptured with a long horn dividing in two, the hair carefully incised

Song dynasty
(960 - 1279) or earlier
Length : 7.5 cm
Height : 2.5 cm

A strongly sculptured bronze animal, its head and front feet turned to one side, the tail curled and finely incised, the back also incised to indicate fur. The long horn, under which there is a long-haired mane, divides in two. This animal has beetle brows and a beard, two prominent fangs, and prominent claws.

279

A so-called Nestorian cross

Probably first millenium A.D.
Length : 5 cm
Width : 5 cm

A so-called Nestorian cross with a swastika design in the middle and a bird to one side. The use of these crosses is currently disputed as is their dating and their possible association with the Ongut Mongols, who were Nestorian Christians. They have been found near the belt in some nomadic burials and may be personal seals. The diversity of the forms found seems to militate against attributing to them a religious significance.

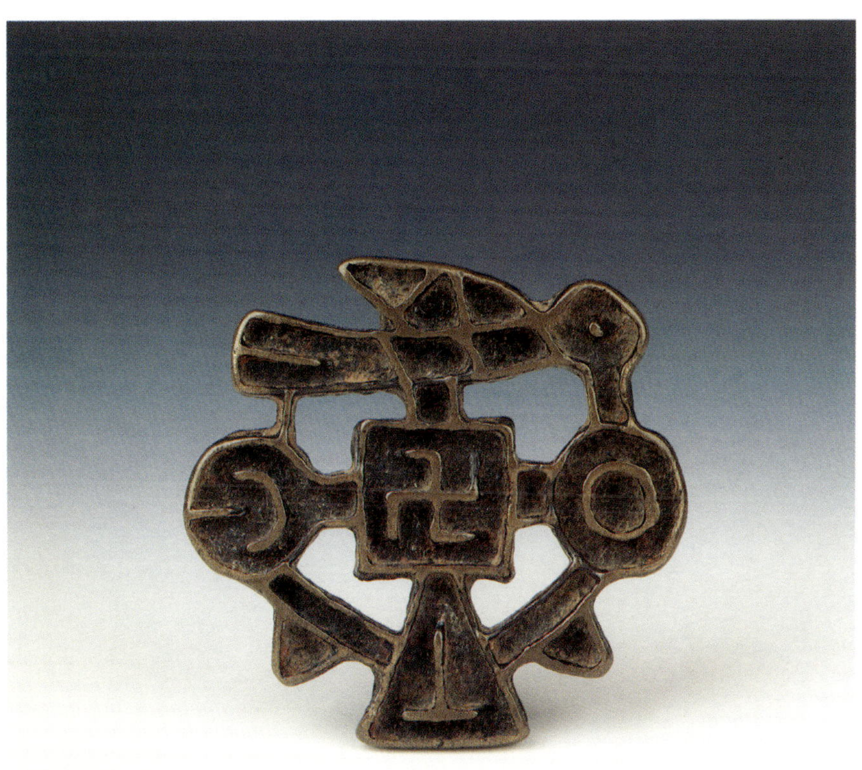

280

Gilt bronze statue of a standing monk with begging bowl

Yuan dynasty
(14th century)
Height : 19.9 cm
Diameter : 5.5 cm

Gilt bronze statue of a standing monk holding in one hand a begging bowl, the other raised in the teaching *mudra*, standing on a deeply carved lotus throne, the head with black lacquer hair, the body with a slightly undulating stance. This figure is comparable with illustrations of similar monk figures from the early 14th century.

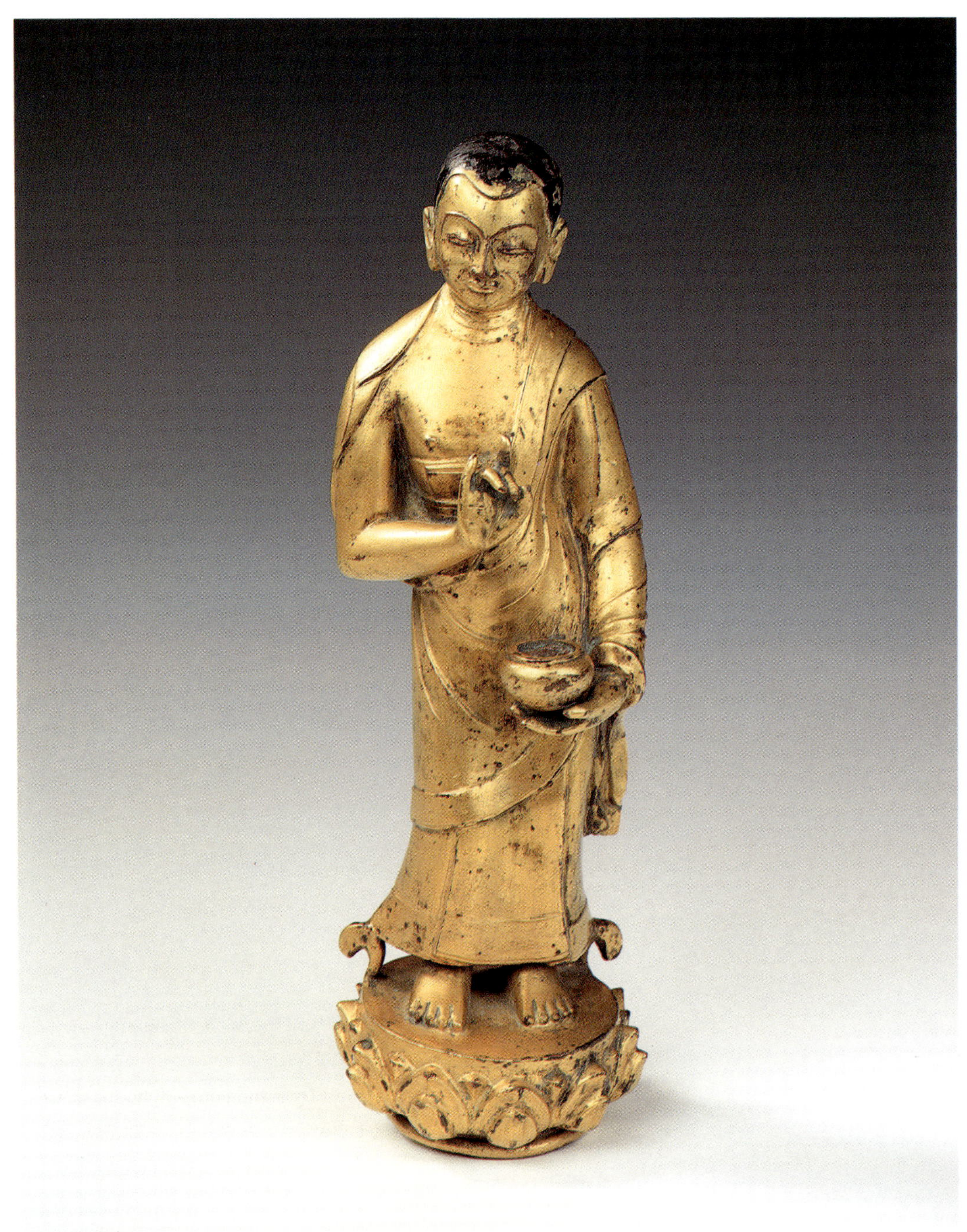

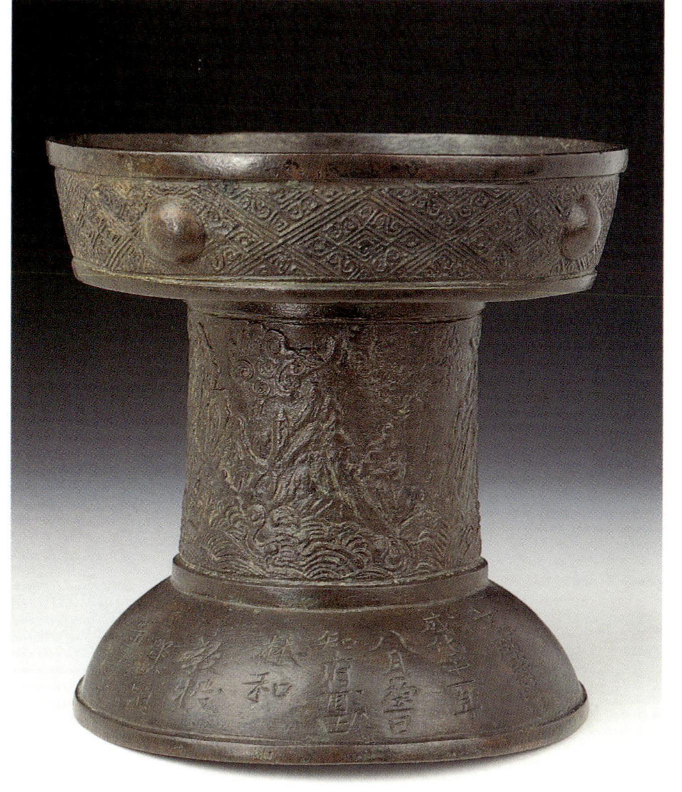

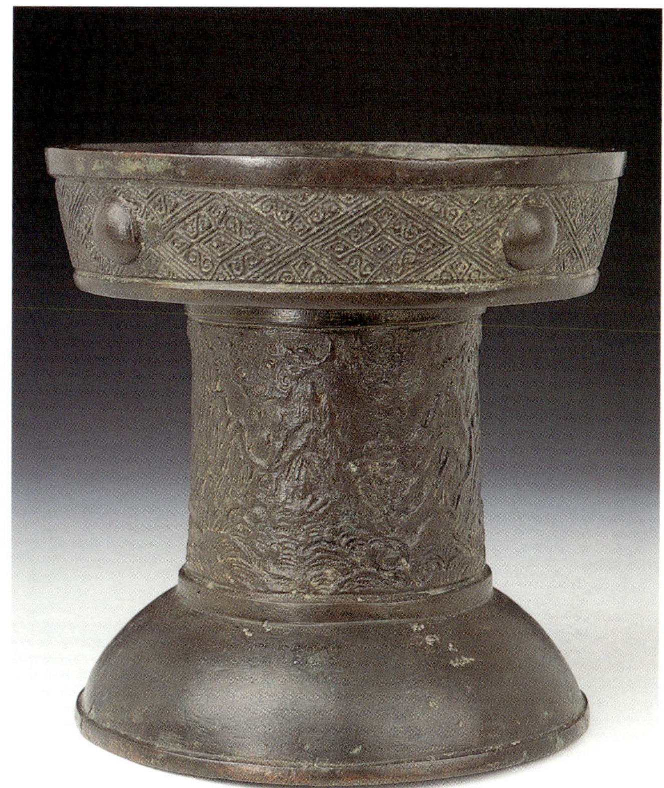

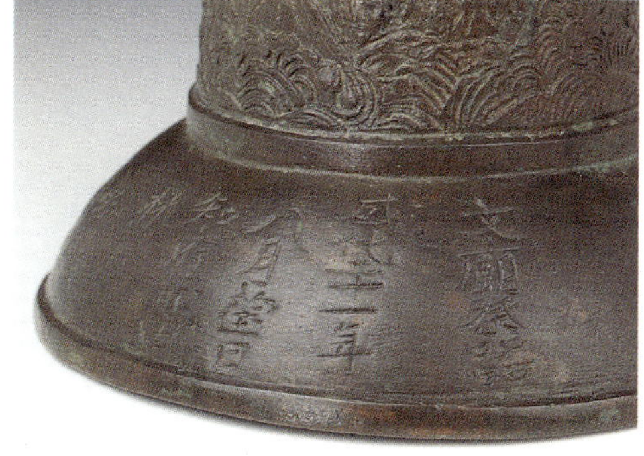

281

Bronze offertory stand with landscape design and dated inscription

Ming dynasty Chenghua period (1485)
Height : 16.3 cm
Diameter : 16.2 cm

A bronze offertory stand with a cylindrical body cast with a continuous mountain landscape. The rim is decorated with a foliated lozenge diaper interrupted by four bosses. According to the inscriptions cast on the foot of the vessel, this stand was originally made in the twenty-first year of Chenghua (1485), Ming dynasty, for use in a Confucian temple.

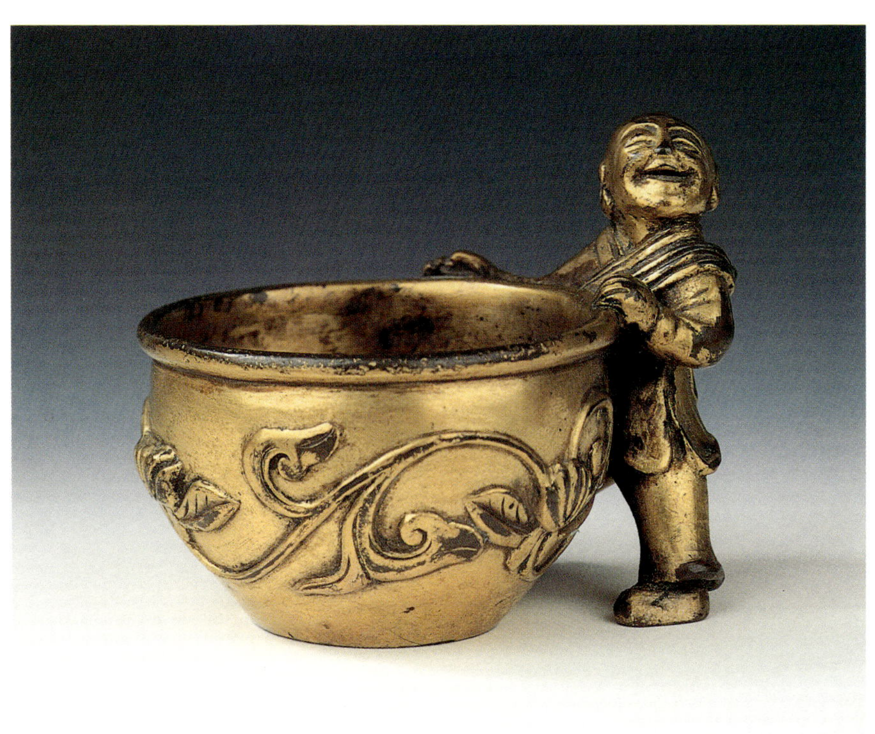

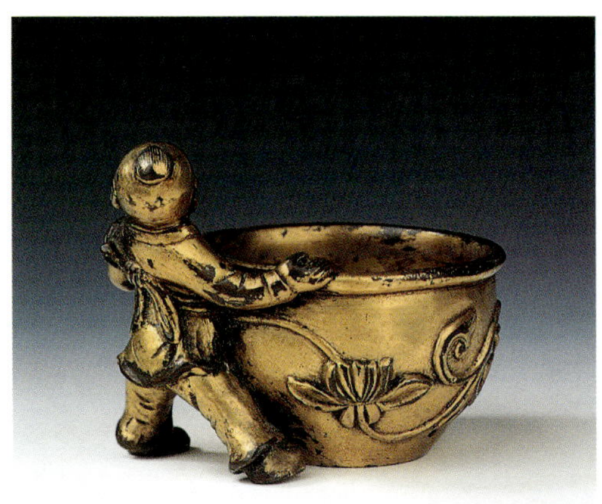

282

GILT BRONZE WATER CONTAINER WITH BOY HOLDING THE RIM

16TH CENTURY OR EARLIER
WIDTH : 7.5 CM
HEIGHT : 6.2 CM

A small but heavy gilt bronze water container in the form of a fishbowl with a standing boy looking upwards holding the thickened rim. The fish bowl has a continuous lotus scroll decoration in relief and the base is slightly recessed. This style of decoration is reminiscent of late 15th/early 16th century *fahua* wares.

283

GILT BRONZE ONE-HORNED *KUI* DRAGON

MING OR EARLIER
(16TH CENTURY OR EARLIER)
LENGTH : 17.1 CM
HEIGHT : 3 CM

Gilt bronze one-horned *kui* dragon, its left front leg stretched out, its left rear leg stretched back over the tail, the head turned right towards the rear looking up slightly. The posture is similar to that found on some Song dragons, particularly the way the back leg and the tail intertwine.

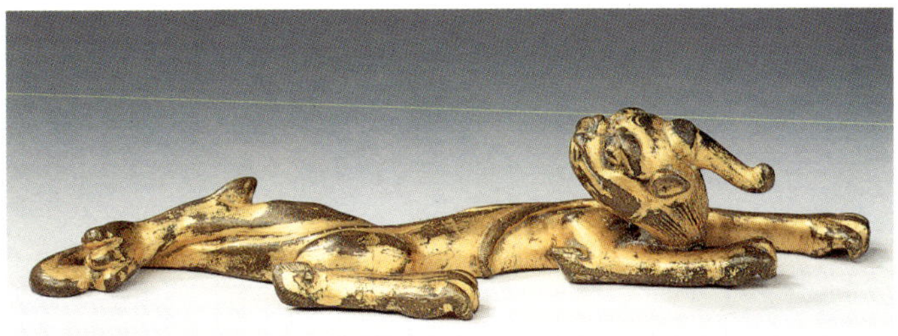

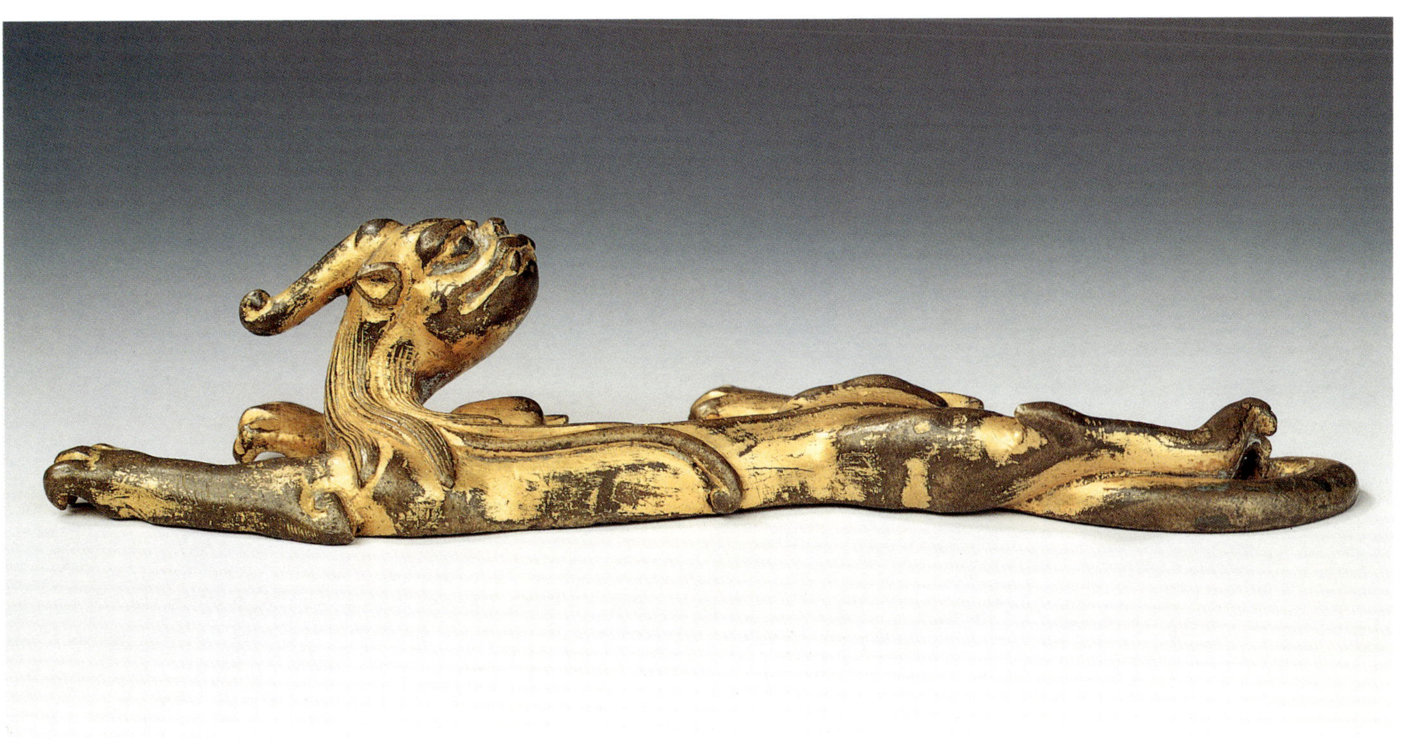

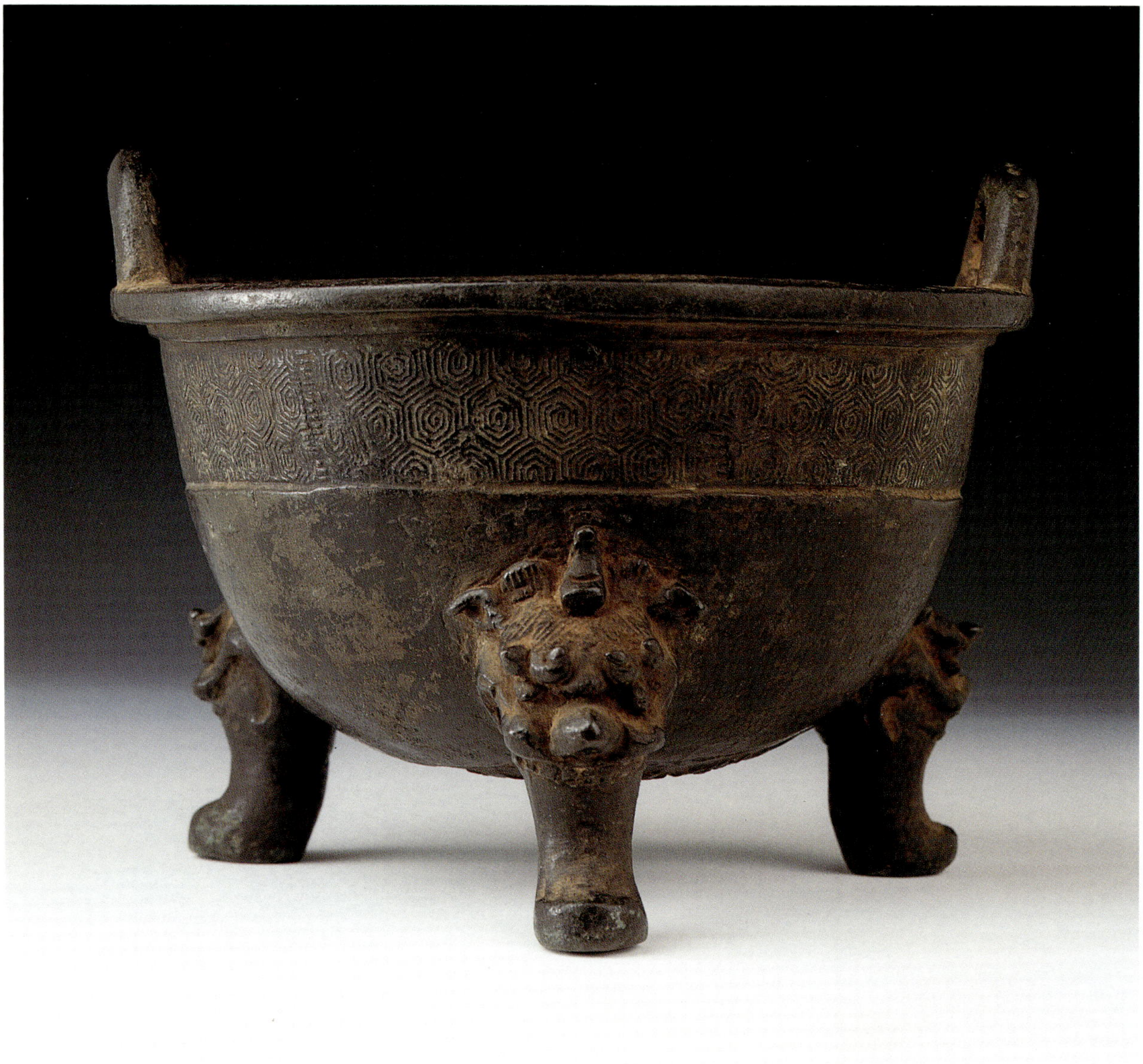

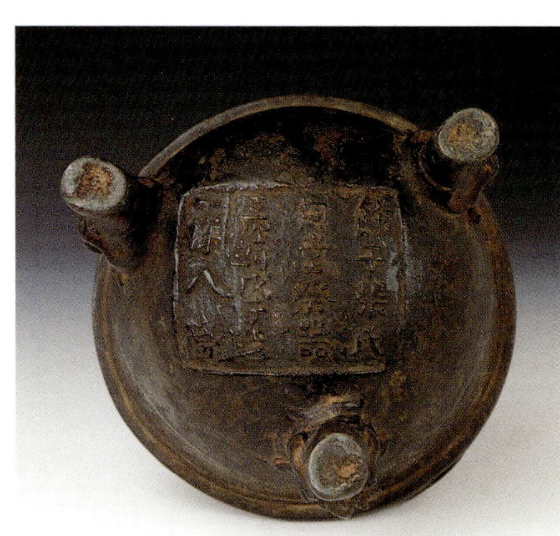

284

Dated bronze *ding* with tortoise-shell diaper pattern

Ming, Jiajing period (1528)
Diameter : 14.8 cm
Height : 10 cm

A bronze *ding* with a wide mouth standing on three solid legs issuing from one-horned monster mouths. The mouth rim is everted and has two U-shaped handles. The next zone is decorated with a band of tortoise-shell diaper pattern. The lengthy inscription cast on the base dates the piece to the Maozi year of Jiajing (1528).

285

A BRONZE BRUSH REST OF THREE TREE STUMPS AND A DRAGON CHASING A PEARL AMID CLOUDS AND WAVES

MING
(16TH CENTURY OR EARLIER)
LENGTH : 13 CM
HEIGHT : 4.3 CM

A bronze brush rest in the form of three tree stumps, the middle one with a circular hole with a two-horned three-clawed dragon chasing a pearl amid clouds and curling waves, a tall rock and bamboo by one stump. The base is incised with a four character Xuande mark.

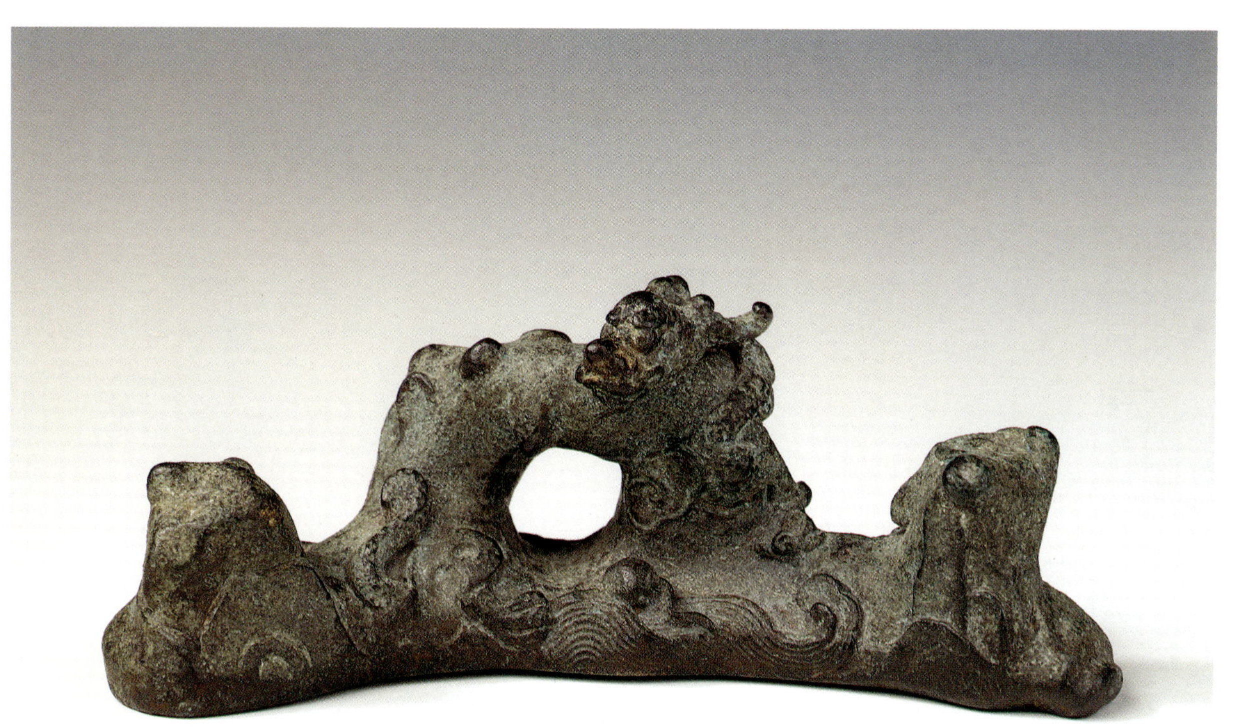

286

Silver inlaid bronze square seal paste box with rebus decoration

Ming
(16th century)
Diameter : 8 cm
Height : 3.8 cm

Silver inlaid bronze square seal paste box, the top decorated with a rebus of a monkey in a peach tree, deer, magpie and bees, a rebus meaning to "May you become a marquis", in a square bordered cartouche surrounded by elaborate silver swastika diaper inlay ground confined within a key fret border, the sides also with silver swastika diaper inlay, each side with silver inlaid rectangular pictures with indented corners conveying other wishes for good fortune as follows: (i) a heron and a duck in a lotus pond, (ii) two peacocks on a peony, (iii) a hawk in a pine tree with a bird in flight above a hound, (iv) two birds in a prunus tree.

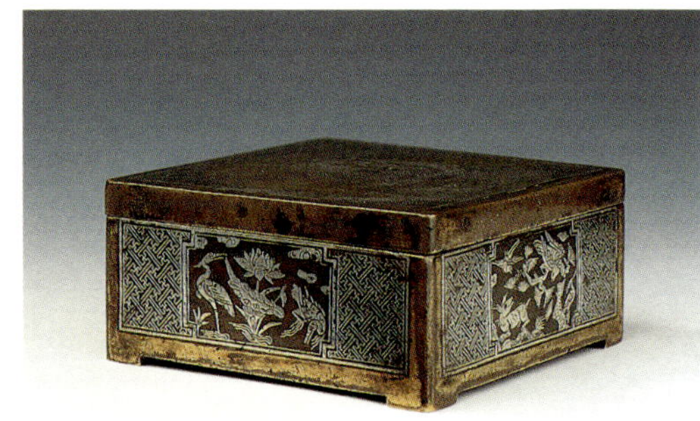

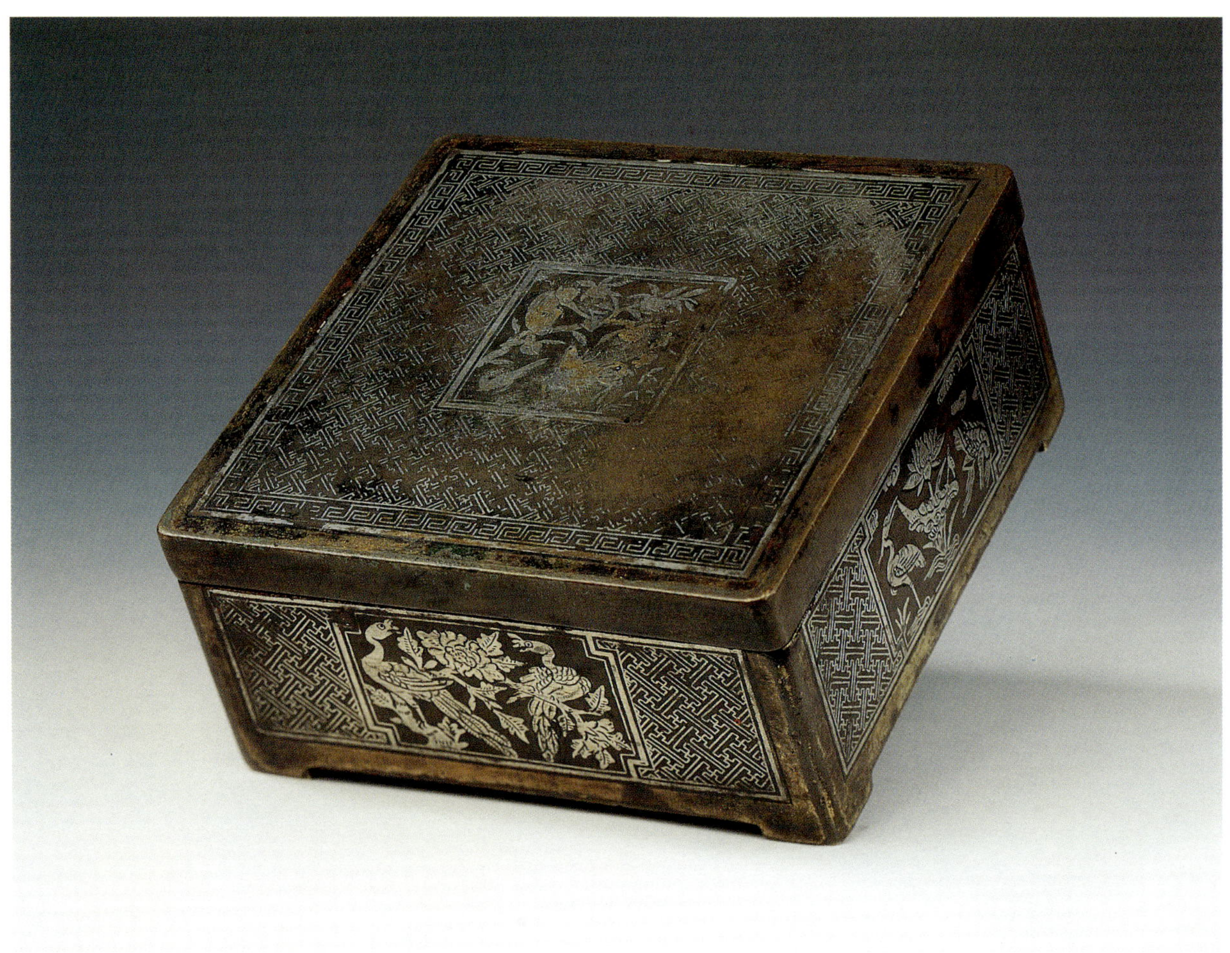

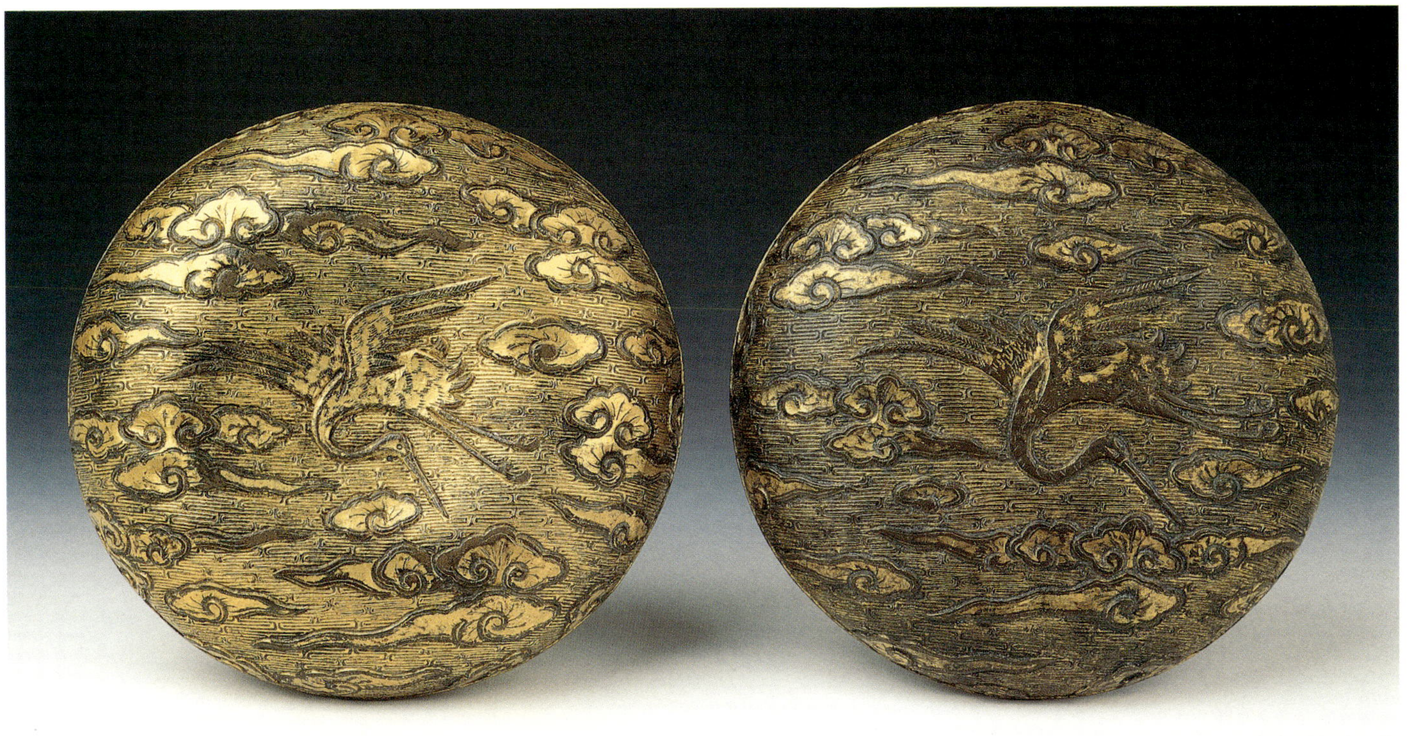

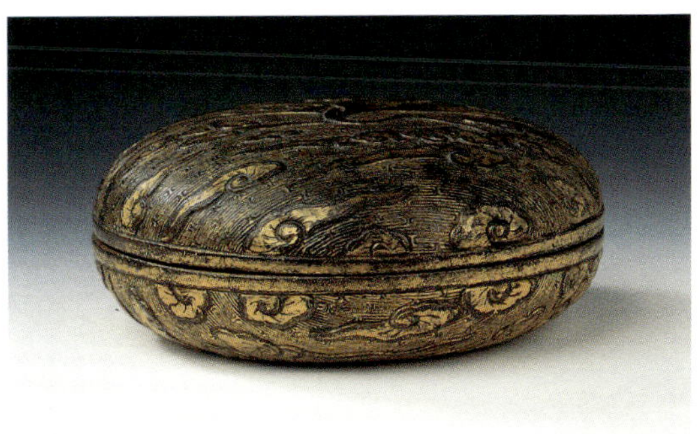

287

GILT BRONZE COVERED BOX WITH DESIGN OF A CRANE AMID CLOUDS

MING, JIAJING/WANLI PERIOD
(SECOND HALF 16TH CENTURY)
DIAMETER : 8 CM
HEIGHT : 4 CM

A gilt bronze covered seal paste box with slightly concave base decorated on both top and bottom with a single crane amid cloud scrolls on a background simulating a lacquer box; the interior also gilded.

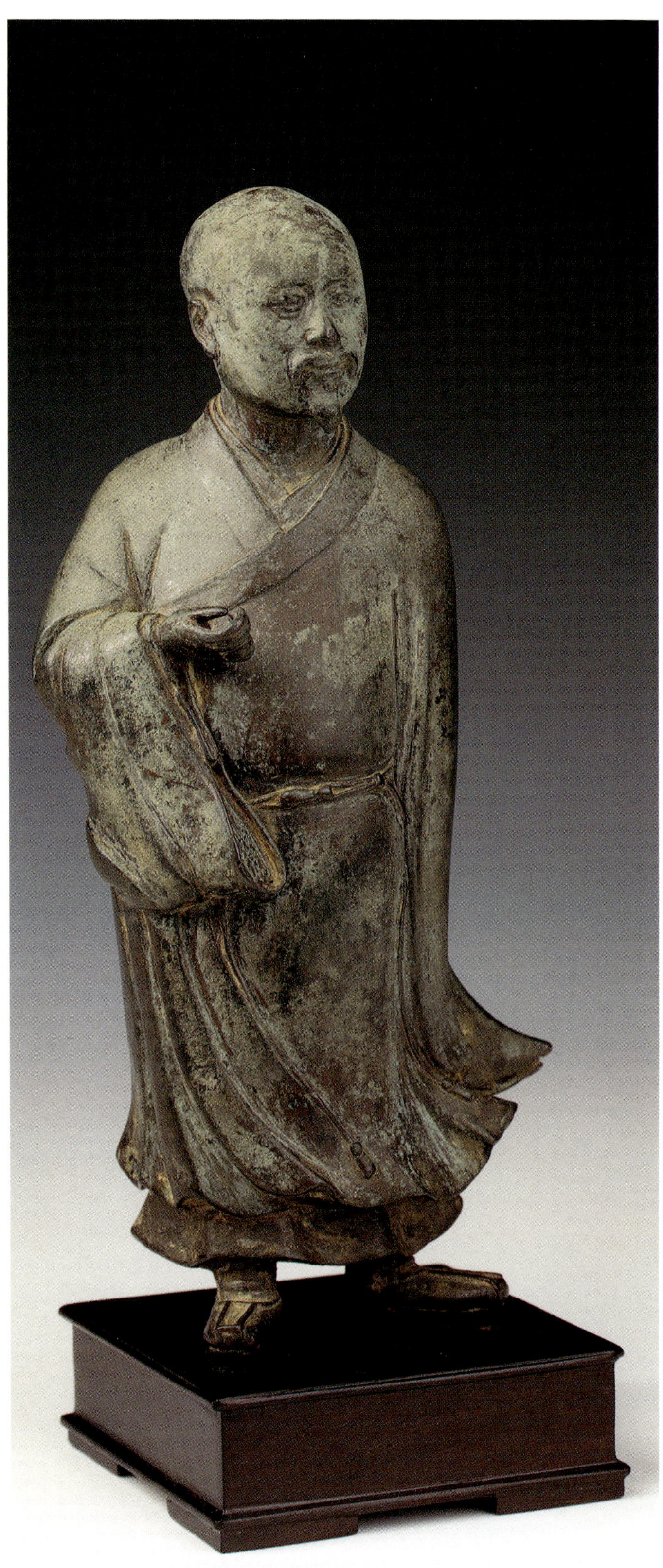

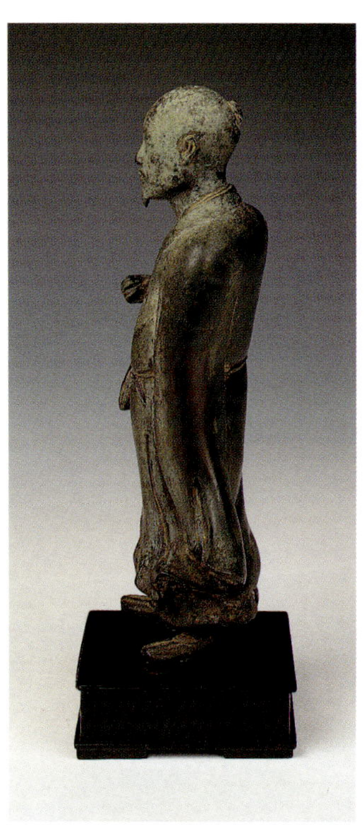

288

Bronze sculpture of an official

Ming
(second half of the 16th century)
Height : 21.9 cm
Width : 7.5 cm

A bronze sculpture of an official with a small beard and moustache, his hair confined in a topknot, his robe tied by a belt with long tassels, the robe with deep sleeves tied in the middle, the shoes squared and a greenish patina. Secular bronze sculptures are rare. This one can be compared with ivory figures of the 16th century. The cloth topknot covering is common for scholars in Ming paintings from the 16th century to the end of the dynasty.

289

Hu Wenming bronze incense box decorated with a design of magnolia with gilding

Ming, Wanli period
(1573 - 1620)
Diameter : 7.5 cm
Height : 3.2 cm

A bronze circular incense box. The cover is decorated in gilded relief with a magnolia branch on a diaper ground. The exterior of the sides is also decorated with gilded lotus and prunus sprays in relief. The base has the mark of Hu Wenming in a gilt square cartouche. Hu was one of China's most celebrated bronze casters and his pieces are dated to the Wanli period. The quality of the casting makes it likely that this piece is by the master. The bottom half of this box has an extended rim in-bent to keep the incense from blowing away.

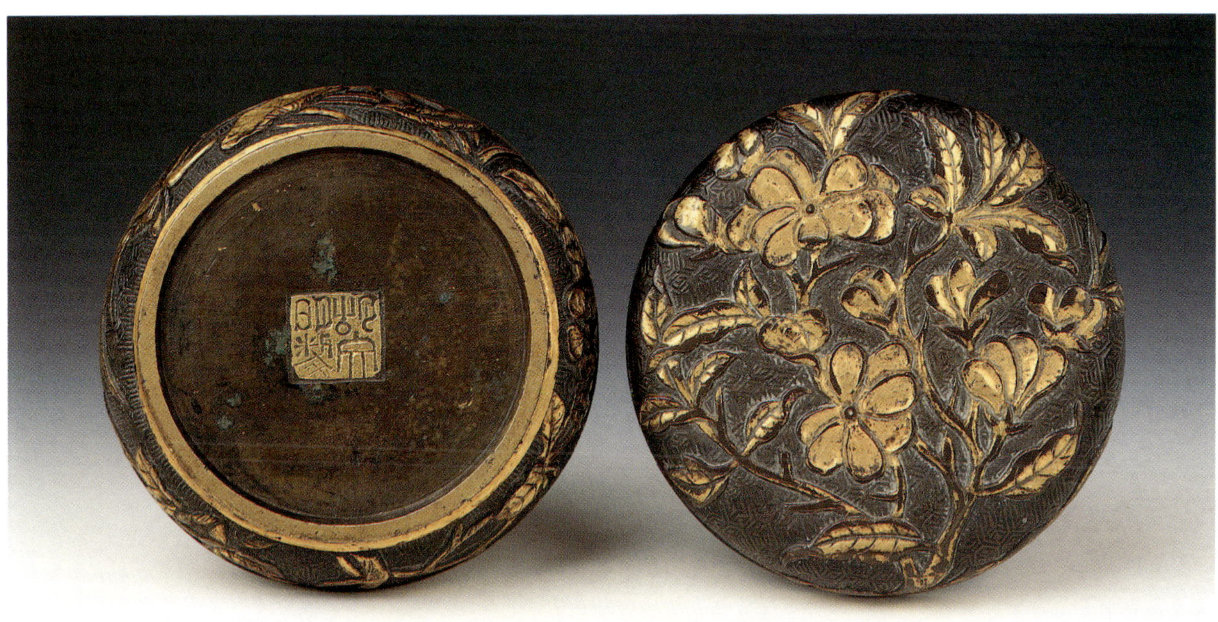

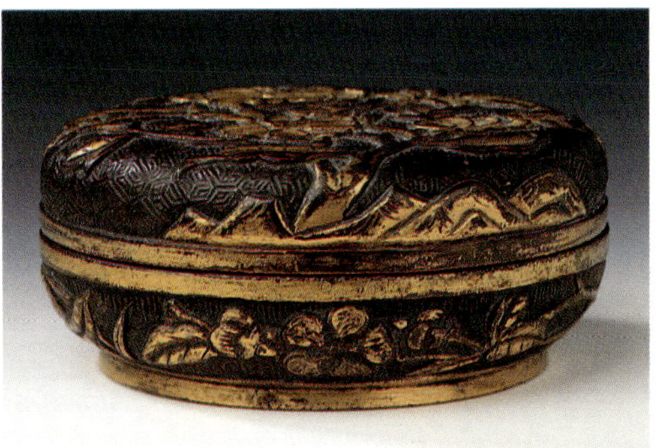

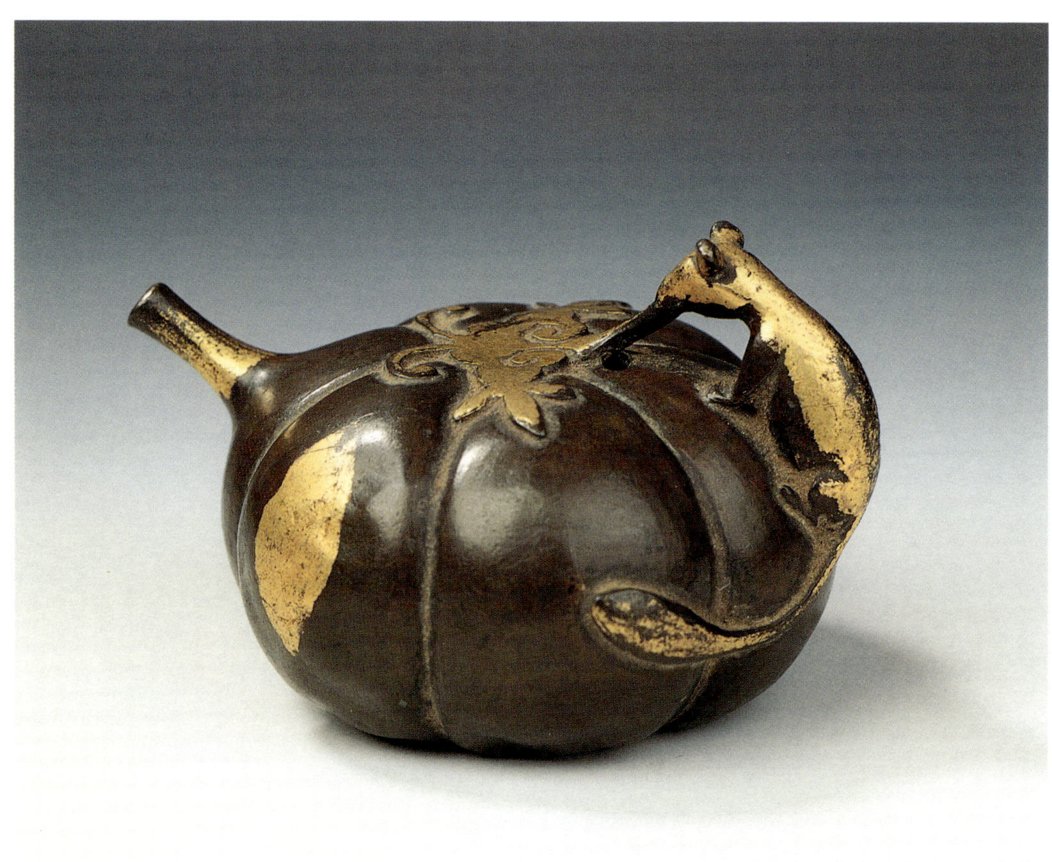

290

Gold and gilt enriched bronze water dropper in the form of a pumpkin with tree-shrew handle

Late Ming
(1600 - 1644)
Length : 7.5 cm
Width : 5.5 cm
Height : 4.8 cm

Gold and gilt enriched bronze water dropper in the form of a pumpkin of six segments, the handle a gilded tree-shrew or squirrel holding in its mouth a gilded fungus covering the air hole, a short gilded spout opposite the handle.

291

Gilded bronze statue of an emaciated *lohan* on a circular rush mat

Late Ming
(1600 - 1644)
Height : 6.9 cm
Length : 6.4 cm
Width : 5.4 cm

A bronze statue of an emaciated *lohan* seated on a rush mat, his hands one on top of the other resting on his left knee, with traces of gilding on red lacquer affixature, the same gilding method as employed on Exhibit 226.

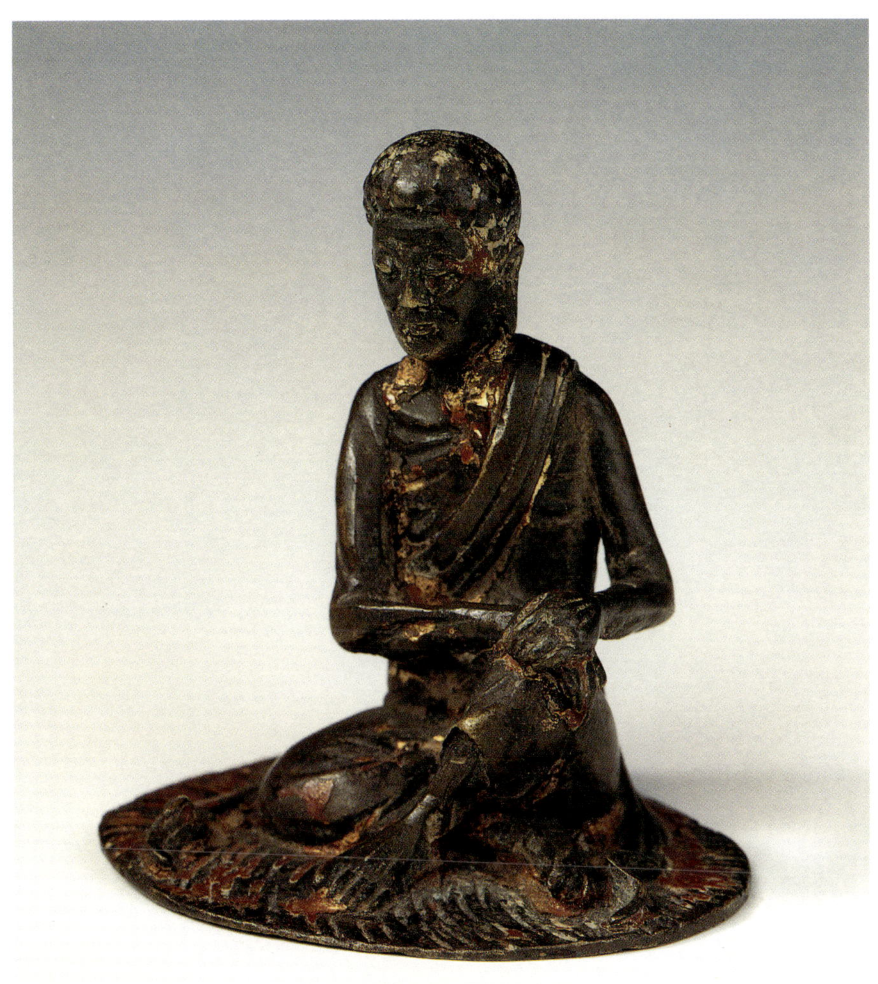

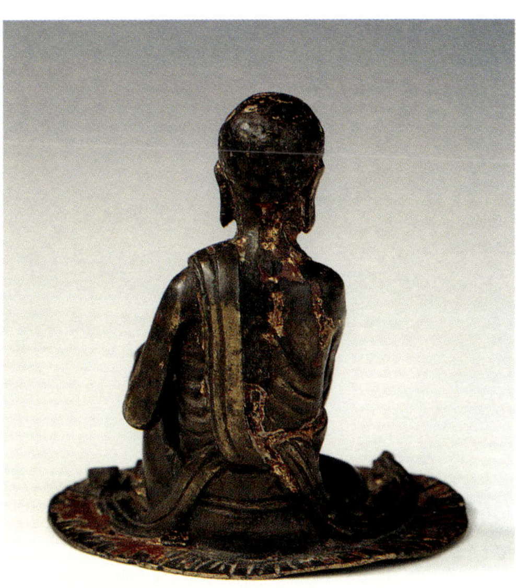

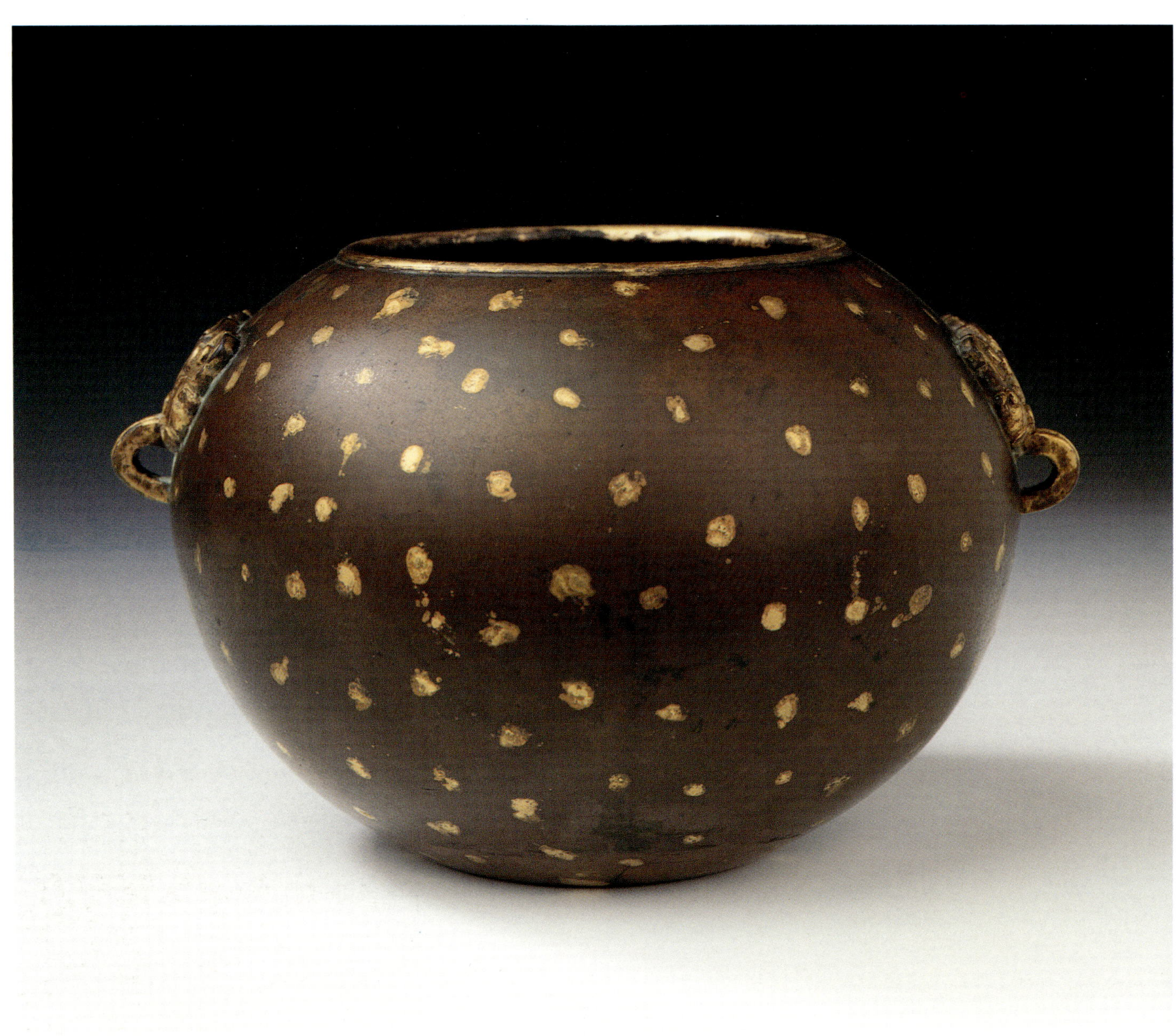

292

Gold encrusted bronze censer with *taotie* mask handles

Ming dynasty Chongzhen period
(1628 - 1644)
Height : 10 cm
Diameter of mouth : 7.7 cm

A bronze censer with a globular body and a wide gilt edge to the mouth, decorated on the shoulders with two gilt *taotie* mask handles. The body is decorated on the exterior with extensive gold encrustations. The six character mark of Chongzhen in gold splashed relief is in a rectangular inset on the base.

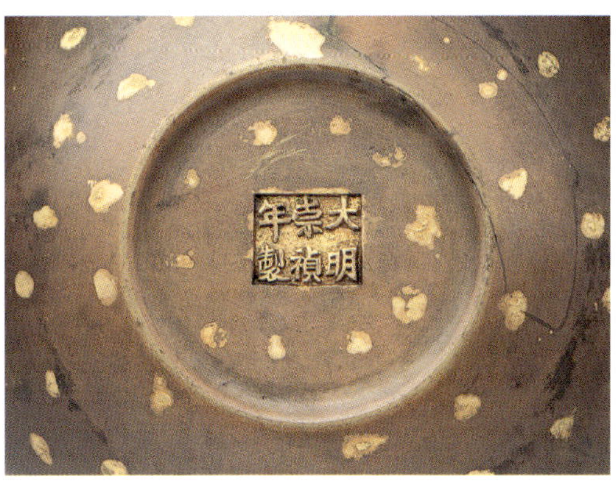

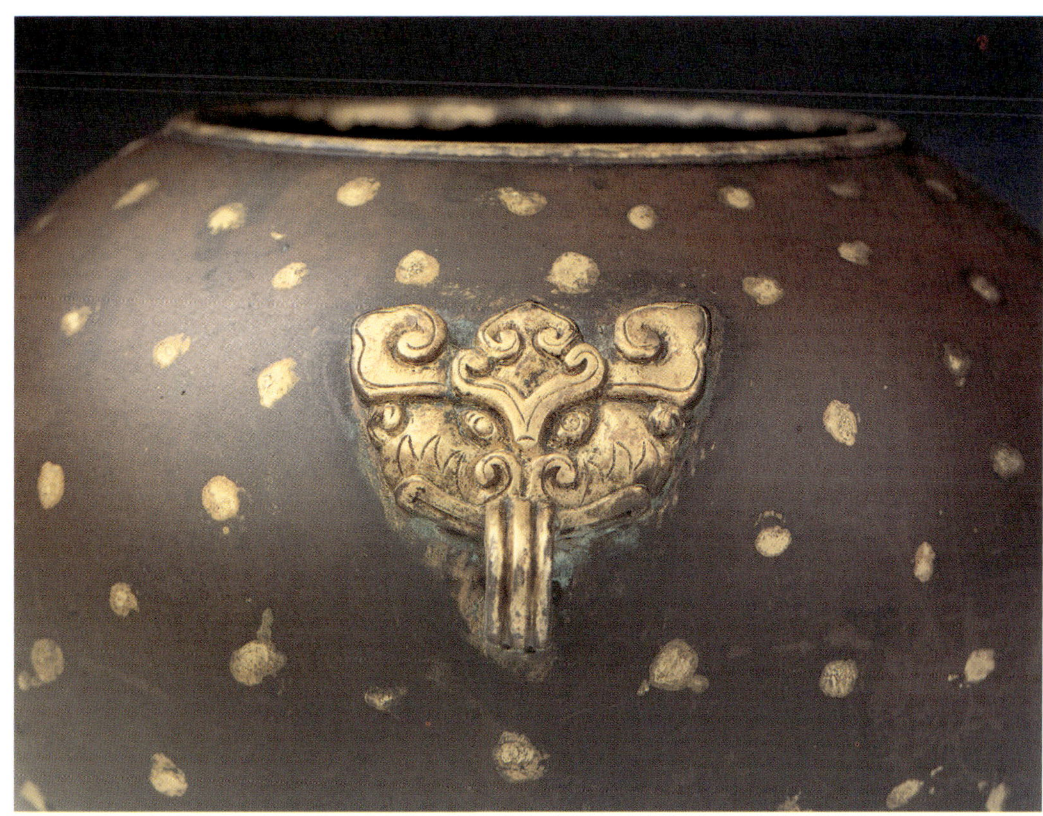

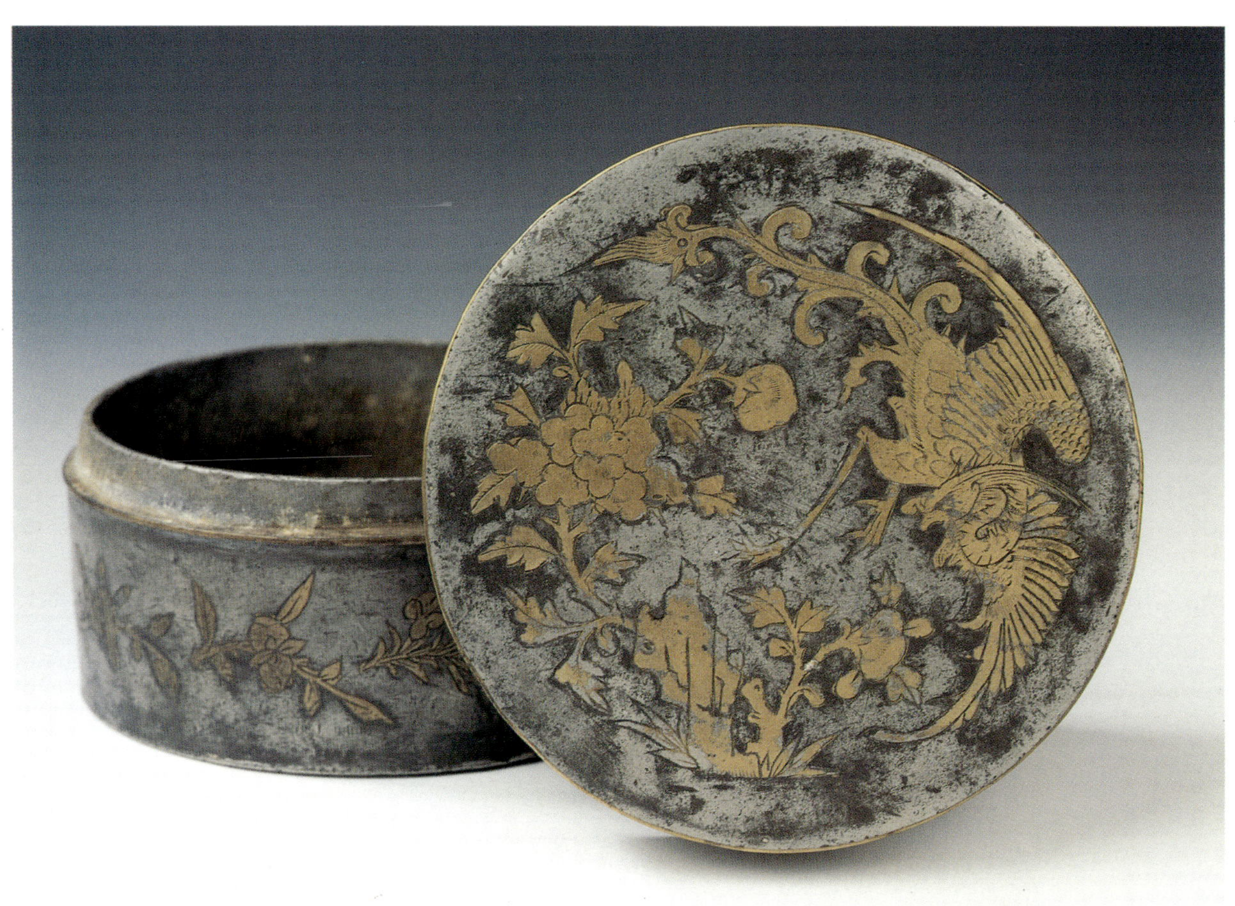

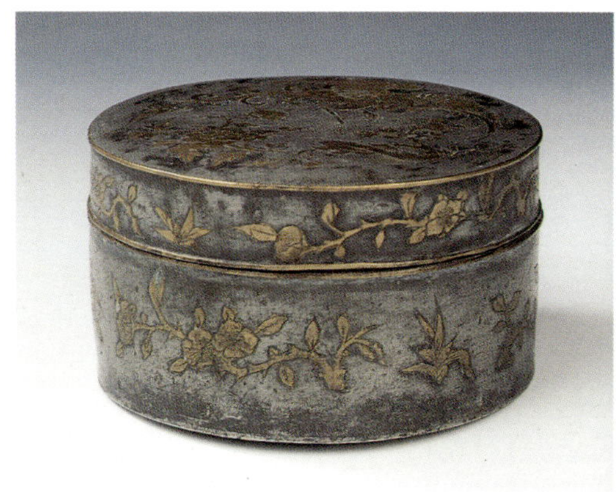

293

Gold enriched pewter covered box with phoenix, rock and floral designs

Early Qing dynasty
(1650 - 1720)
Diameter : 10.5 cm
Height : 5.7 cm

A circular pewter box, its rim bound with brass. The top of the cover is decorated with a thin gold inlay of a rock, peonies and a flying phoenix, the sides with gold inlays of prunus sprays, bees and birds.

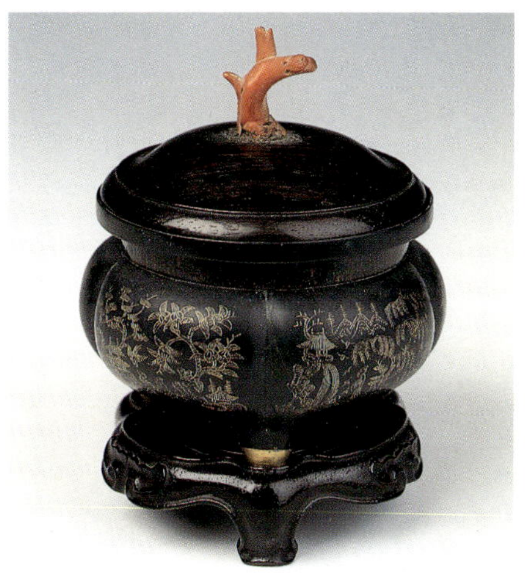

294

A BRONZE AND MARBLED METAL TRIPOD INCENSE BURNER WITH INCISED GOLD-FILLED DECORATION

QING DYNASTY
(LATE 17TH OR 18TH CENTURY)
DIAMETER : 9.6 CM
HEIGHT : 6 CM

A bronze tripod incense burner of five-lobed form, the inside and ends of the legs gilded, the body incised and gold filled with pictures in each lobe as follows : (i) sage under a willow by a waterfall and pagoda, (ii) a pine, temple, peach tree and two scholars, (iii) tiger, prunus and birds, (vi) pheasant, peach tree and two sages, (v) lion dog, peonies and birds. The collar is of marbled metal, which seems confined to pieces of high quality. Its use seems to have started in the late 17th century and was to influence Japanese 19th century metalwork on which it was used extensively.

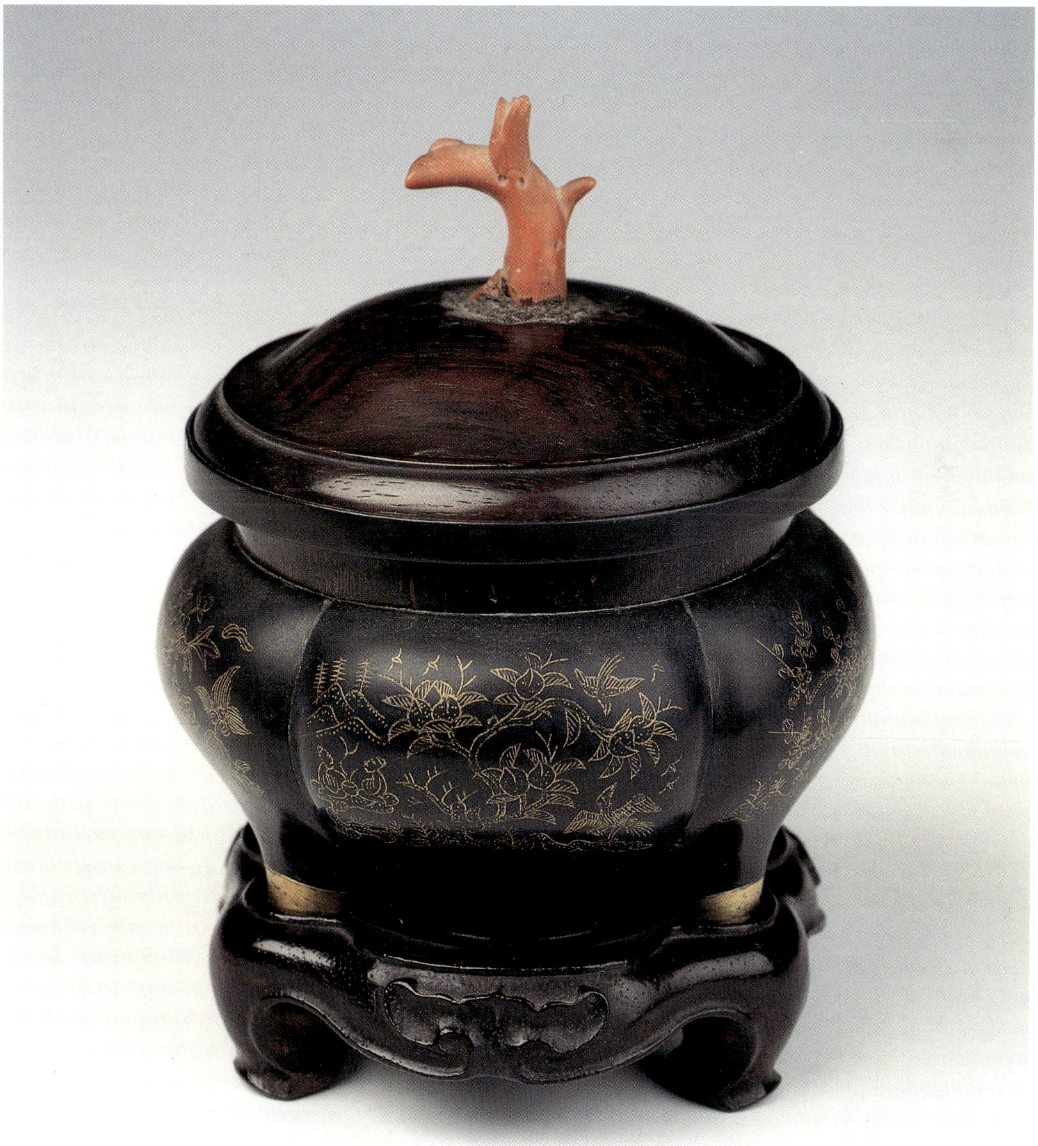

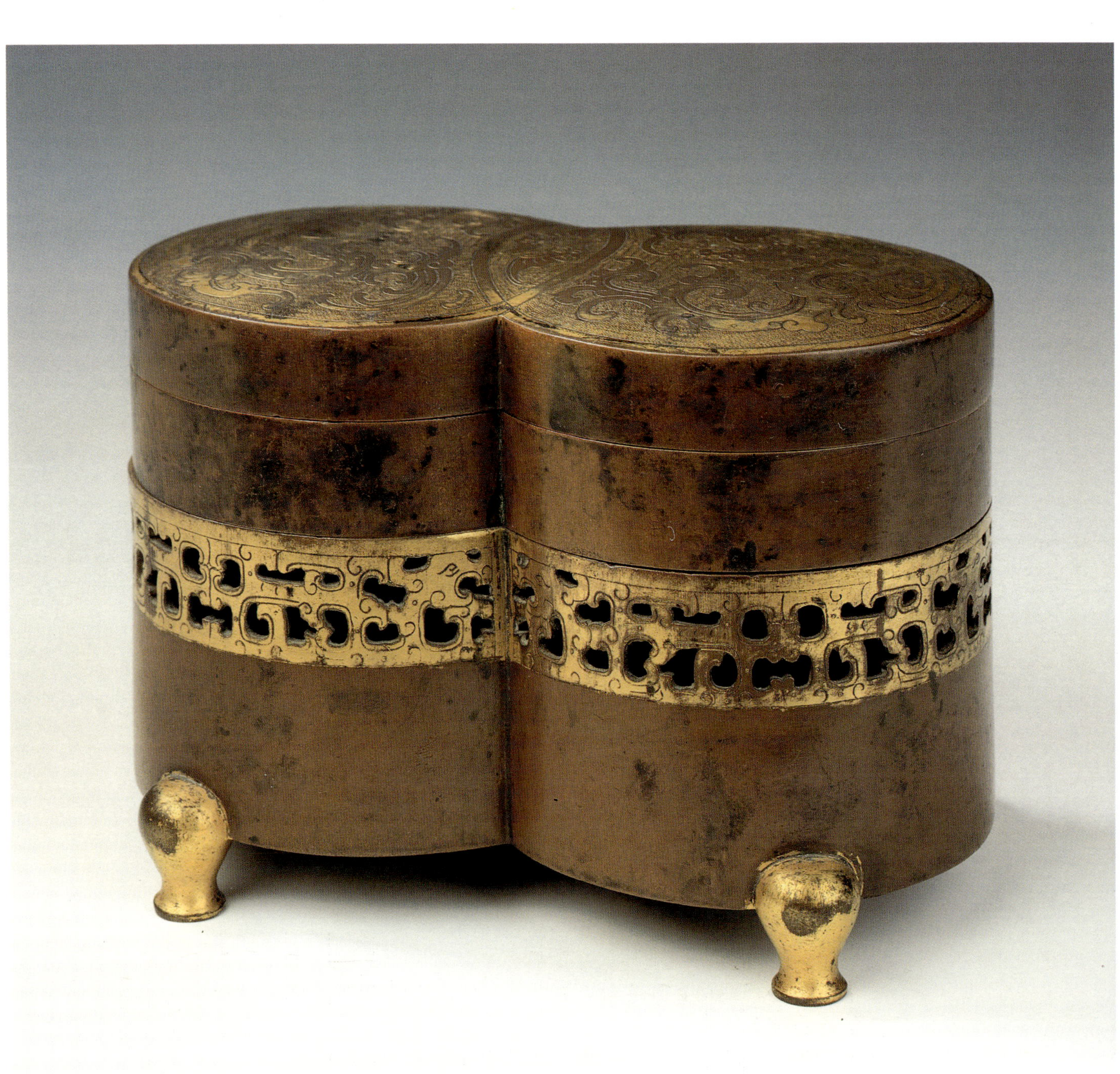

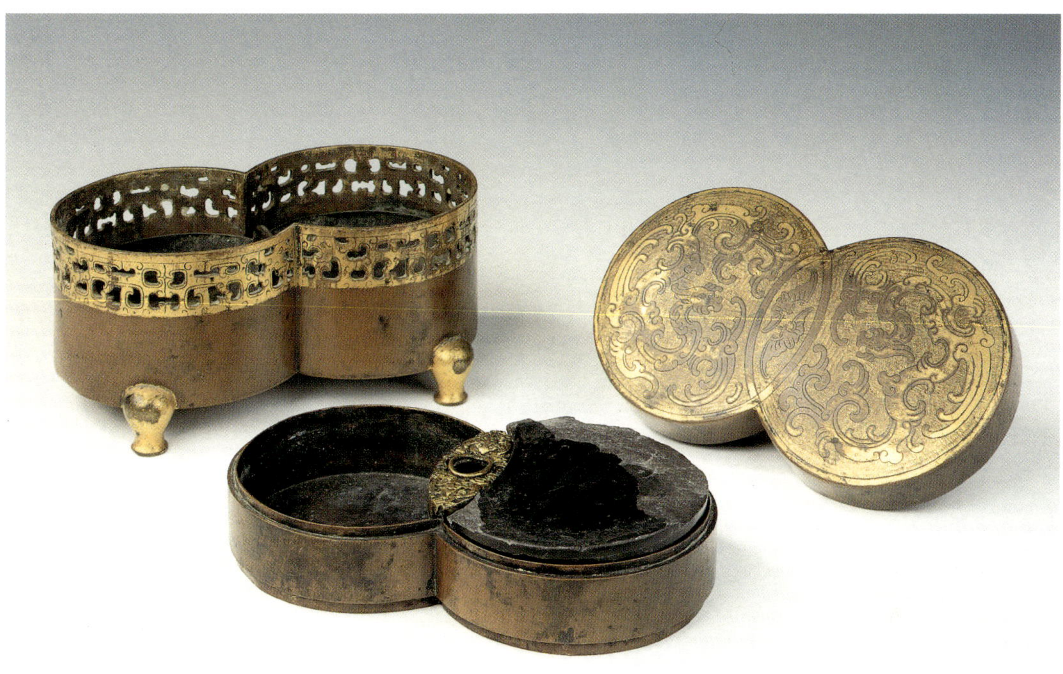

295

Gilded copper combined ink-slab, water container and brazier of interlocking circles form for a scholar's studio, decorated with stylised *kui* dragons

Qing dynasty
(first half 18th century)
Length : 16.4 cm
Height : 11 cm
Width : 9.6 cm

Gilded copper container of interlocking circles form combining an ink-slab, water container and brazier, the top decorated with two stylised *kui* dragons, the interior ink-slab and water container separated by a gilded section flanked by bats made to hold the brush. The top third lifts off, the central section is plain, the bottom third has a pierced fringe of *kui* dragon heads near the top, the feet of bulbous shape and gilded. The bottom section is probably for a tray to hold burning charcoal used to keep the water in the water container from freezing in the depths of the northern Chinese winter.

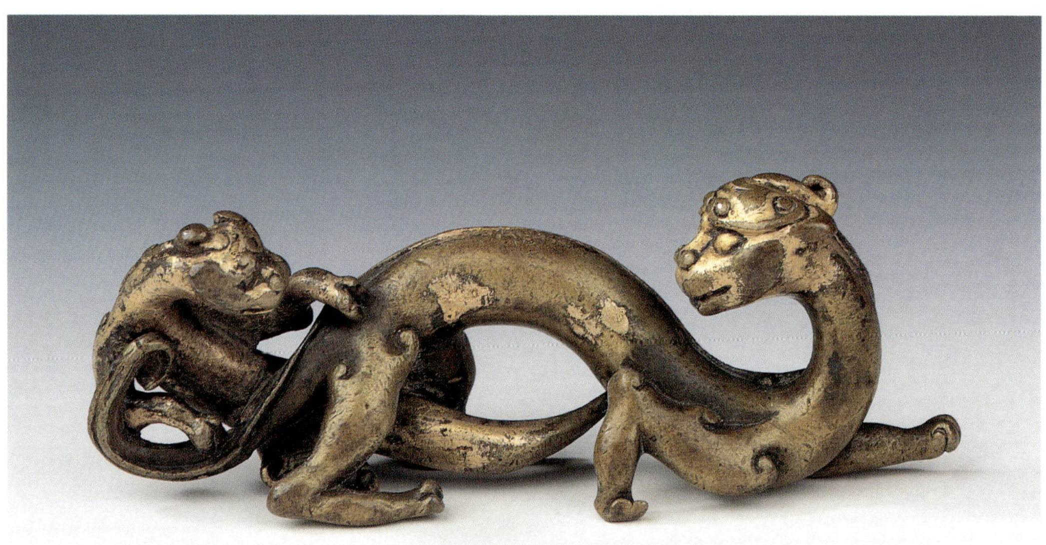

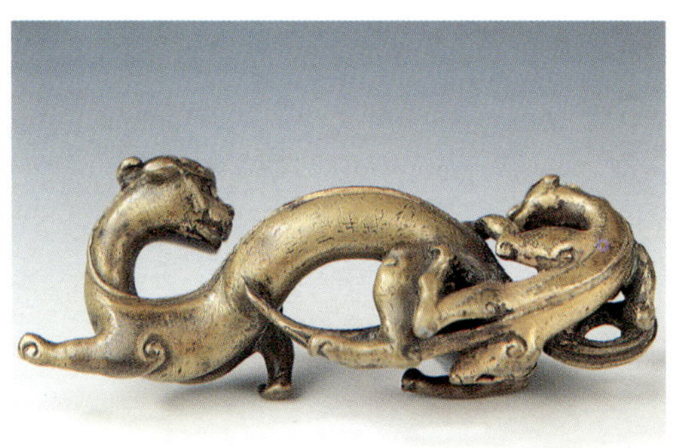

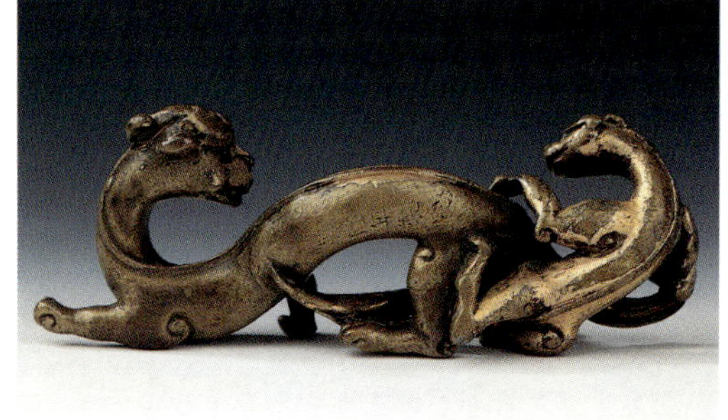

296

Gold encrusted and gilt bronze brush rest in the form of two *kui* dragons at play

Qing dynasty, Qianlong period
(1736 - 1795)
Length : 7.3 cm
Height : 2.5 cm

A gold splashed and gilt bronze brush rest in the shape of an adult and a young *kui* dragon at play. The smaller dragon gilt, the larger with gold encrustations. A four character Qianlong mark is incised on the body of the adult *kui* dragon. The sophisticated technique and the use of the four character mark probably indicate an imperial provenance.

297

Dated and signed silver inlaid copper box of oval shape, the sides with gold etched landscape decoration and a poem

Dated 1881
Length : 8 cm
Width : 6 cm
Height : 3.8cm

A silver inlaid copper box of oval shape, the top decorated with silver characters and key fret border, the sides with etched gold decoration of a pine tree, bamboo by pavilions, a resting man and a poem. The inscription on the top documents it as having been made by the year 1881 at a studio within the compound of an official in the town of Yuanyang; mark of the Yue Zhongxing workshop.

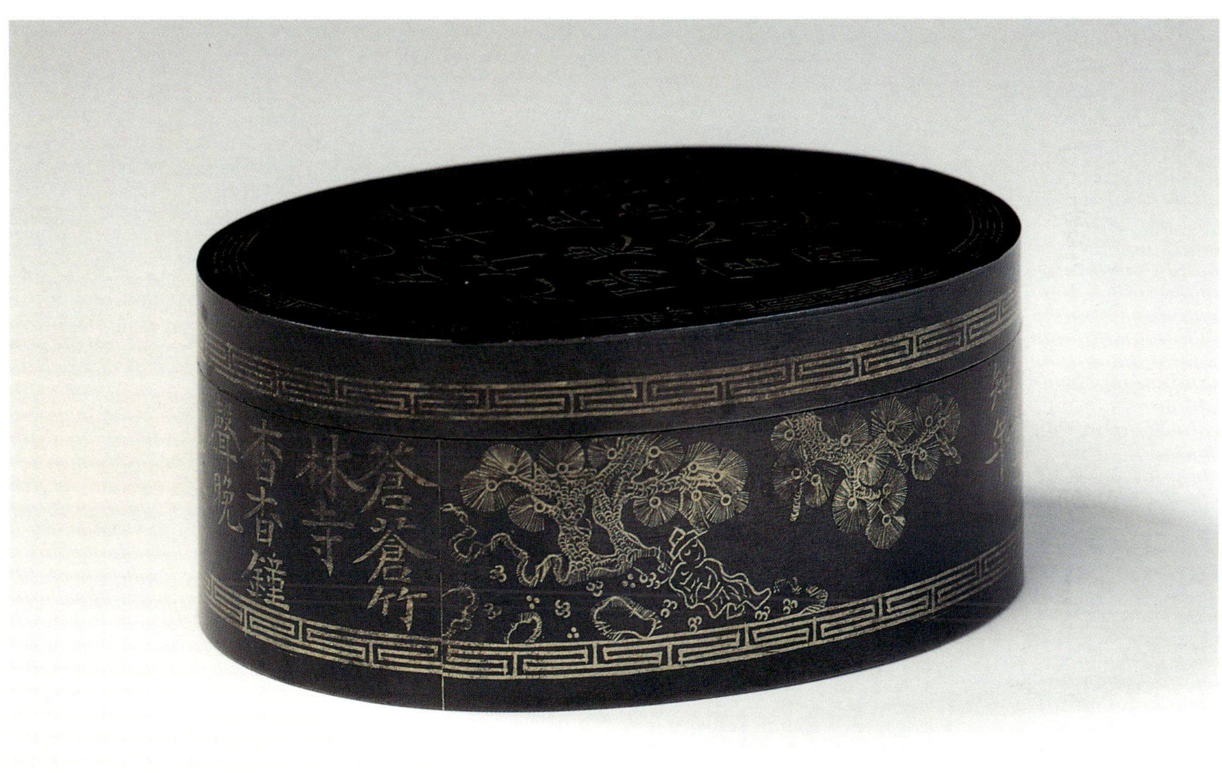

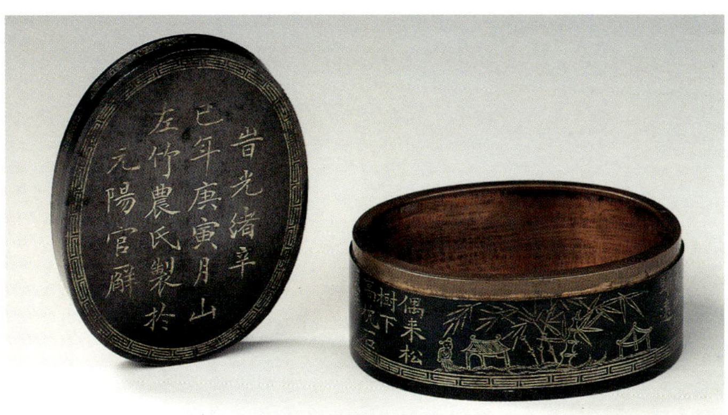

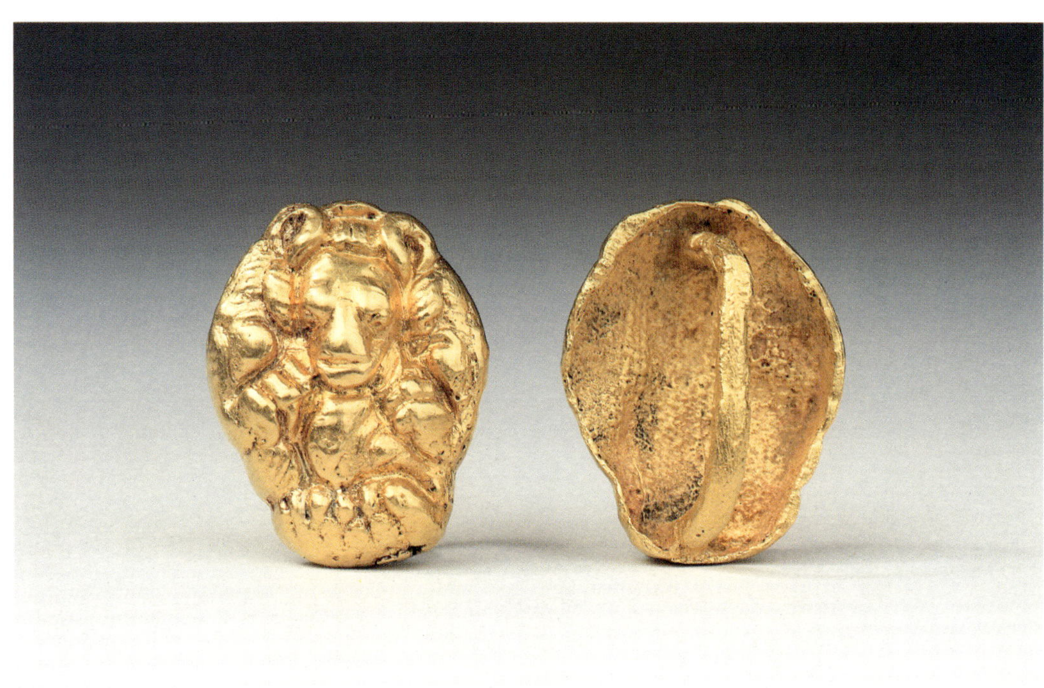

298

ORDOS GOLD
BEAR BELT OR HORSE BRIDLE FITTING, THE BEAR WITH PROMINENT RUFF, EARS AND CLAWS WITH LOOP AT REVERSE FOR ATTACHMENT

LATE WARRING STATES
(3RD CENTURY B.C.)
HEIGHT : 3.1 CM
WIDTH : 2.1 CM

A gold fitting of a bear shown frontally with prominent ruff, ears and claws, with a loop at reverse for attachment. The reverse showing the positive textile impression of the casting is typical of some Ordos gold pieces made for the nomads of the Mongolian steppe. Such important pieces were probably made at Yanxiadu, the southern capital of the State of Yan from 311 to 222 B.C. during the late Warring States period. Ceramic moulds showing such textile traces have recently been excavated from the ruins of this city.

299

Gold openwork escutcheon plaque with stylised cicada

Six Dynasties period, probably Northern Wei
(5th to 6th century A.D.)
Height : 5 cm
Width : 4 cm

A small openwork plaque in gold with granular work, shaped as an inverted escutcheon with openwork representation of a stylised cicada, the design of which is accentuated by granular lines.
The eyes and edges were probably originally inlaid with turquoise. On present evidence such granular work, common in Etruscan and Hellenistic art from a much earlier date (at least 7th and 4th centuries B.C. respectively), was not used in Chinese gold work before the Eastern Han. Similar plaques are thought to be badges of some sort and to date from the Northern Wei period.

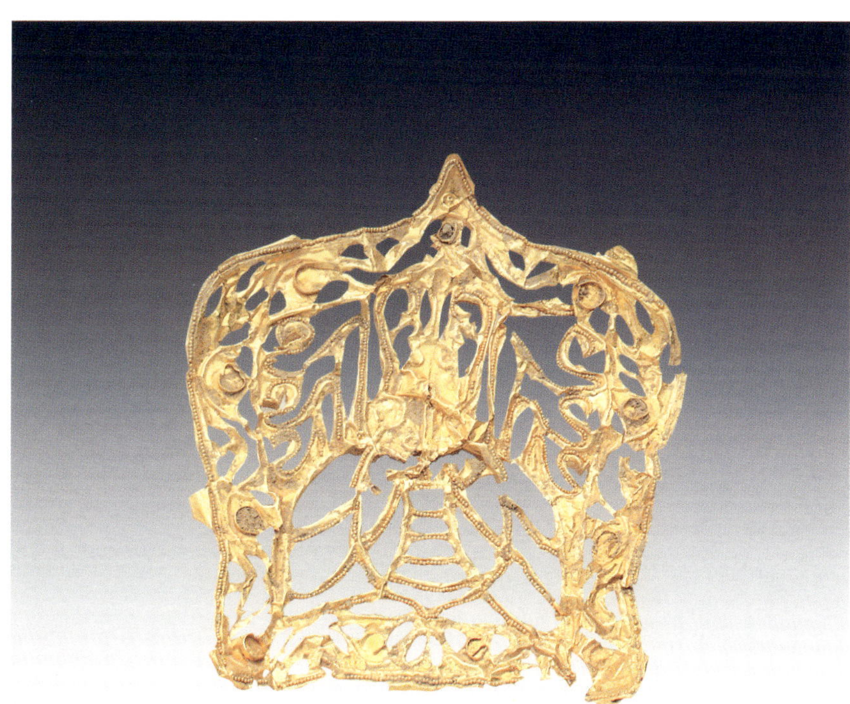

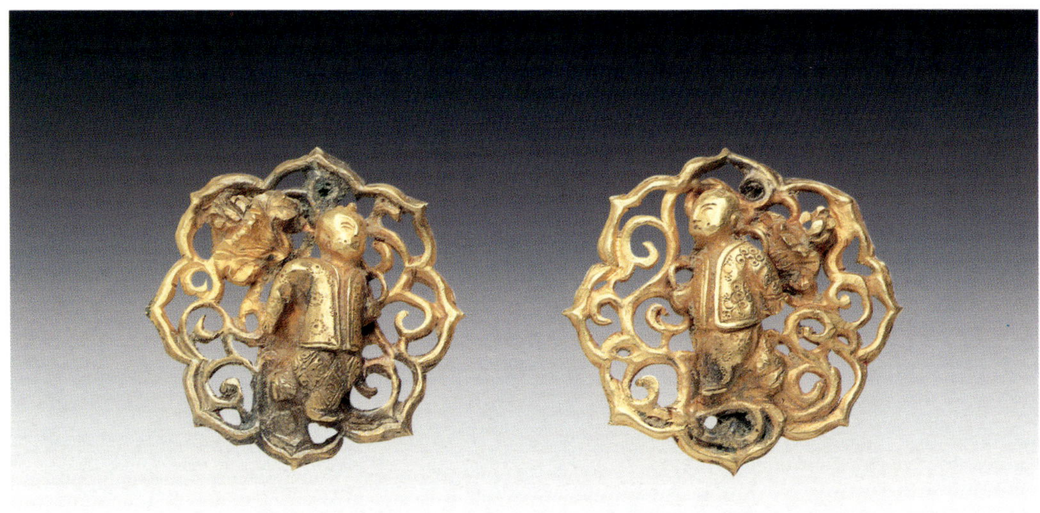

300

Pair of gold buckles in the form of a rosette with boy holding a lotus spray in high relief on a classic scroll ground

Southern Song to Jin dynasty
(13th century)
Diameter : 2.5 cm

A pair of small gold buckles with bronze bar fitting, shaped as an eight-sectioned foliated rosette with pierced classic scroll tracery, decorated in high relief in the centre with a boy holding a lotus spray over his shoulder. A boy holding a lotus was a popular design in the 13th century. It is recorded that at that time boys holding a lotus leaf paraded round on the festival held on the 7th day of the 7th month.

301

Set of fourteen gold belt plaques of varying shapes and sizes decorated with floral motifs in repoussé work and chased

Early Ming dynasty
(*circa* 1500) or earlier
(i) Length : 4.5 cm; Width : 3.8 cm
(ii) Length : 3.9 cm; Width : 2.3 cm
(iii) Length : 12 cm; Width : 4.1 cm
(iv) Length : 6.3 cm; Width : 3.8 cm

A set of fourteen gold belt plaques of varying shapes and sizes, (i) four of teardrop shape (one still backed by desiccated wood with traces of textile with which all these plaques would originally have been backed), (ii) two of small vertical rectangular shape, (iii) two of extra large rectangular shape rounded at one end, (iv) six of rectangular shape, all decorated with various floral motifs such as lotus and chrysanthemum, all made in similar manner; the decorative element, a gold sheet in high relief repoussé work and chased against a rough ground, held in place by a plain gold strip bent at right angles with a single line of beading at the bottom edge of the sides. Several flaps hold the decorative sheet and original wood filling in place. Belt plaques of the shape seen here are known in jade and other material from the Liao dynasty to the Ming. Carbon 14 testing of the wood backing suggests a Ming dating for this set but at least one expert has suggested a Liao date.

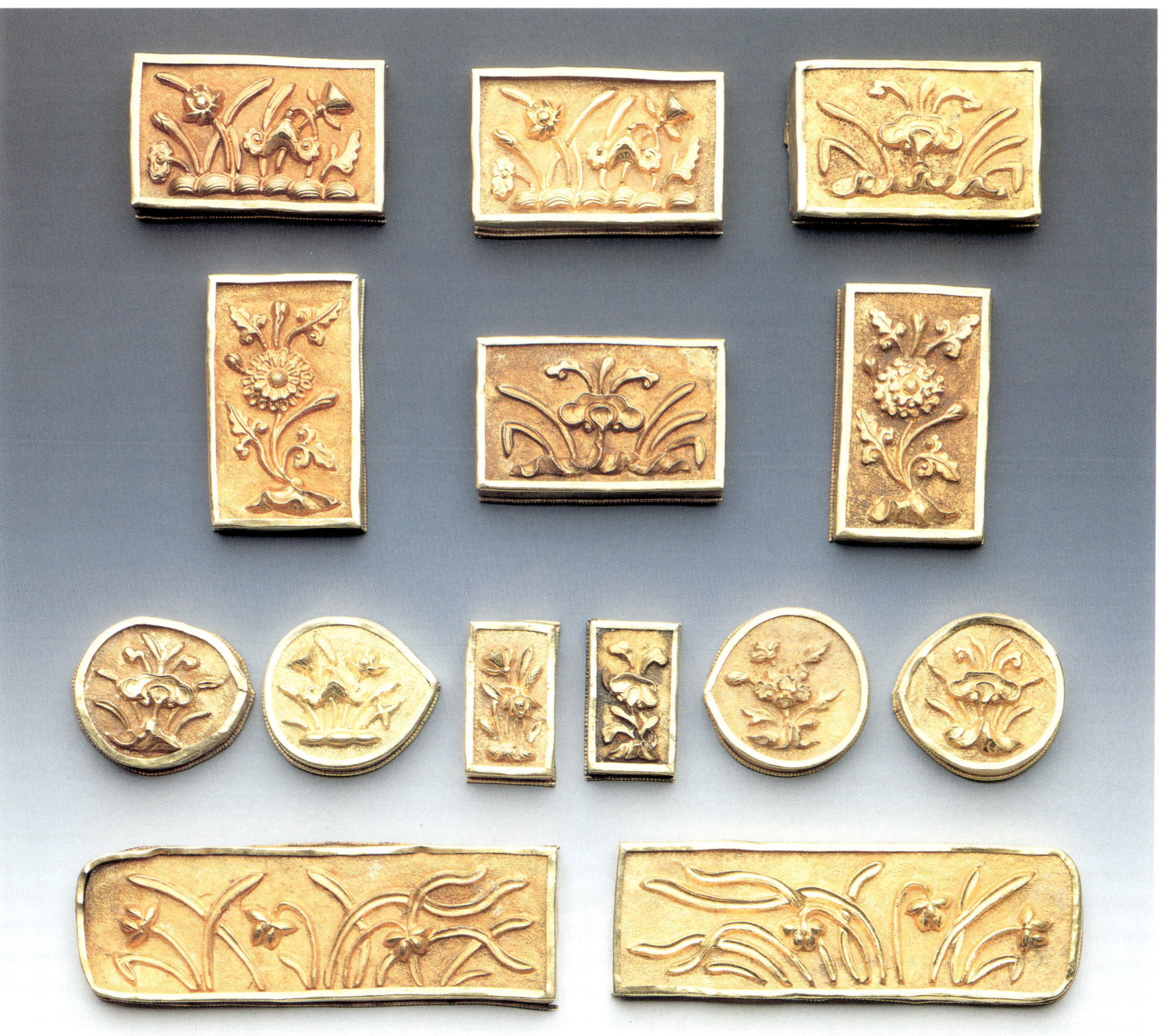

302

Gold filigree headdress fitting in the shape of a phoenix with ruby inlay

Ming dynasty or earlier
(1368-1644)
Height : 5.8 cm
Width : 3.4 cm

A gold filigree fitting for a noblewoman's headdress in the shape of a phoenix, its head on a long neck resting against the body. The head of the phoenix, which has a crest, is inlaid with a ruby. Such phoenix fittings with only minor variations were produced over a long period from about 1000 to 1500 A.D. This one seems to relate closest to Song examples of *circa* 1200 A.D.

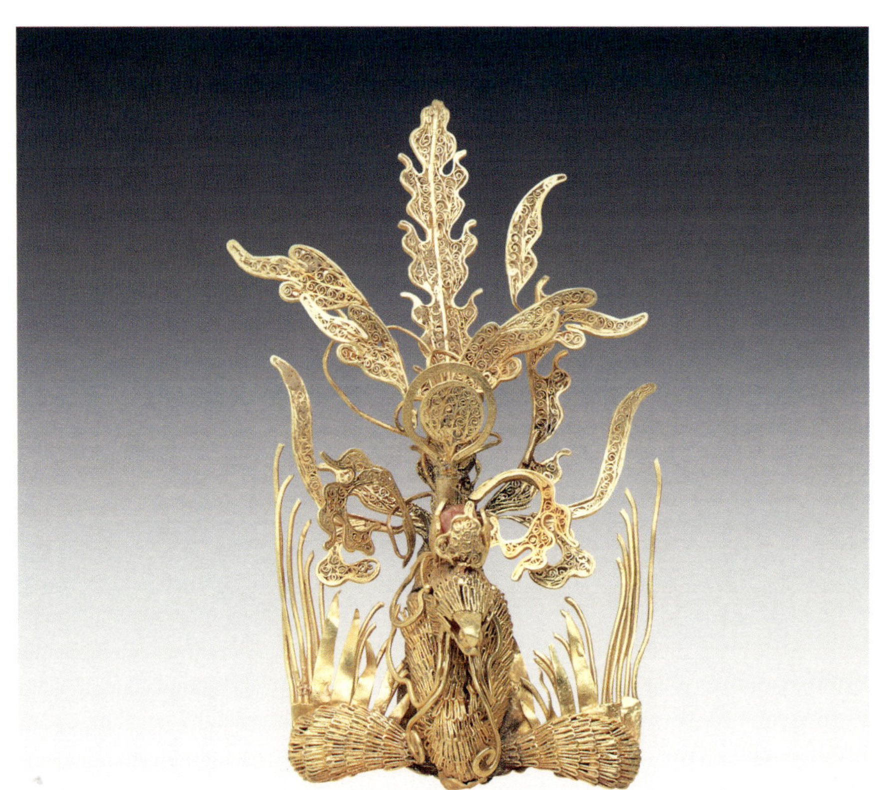

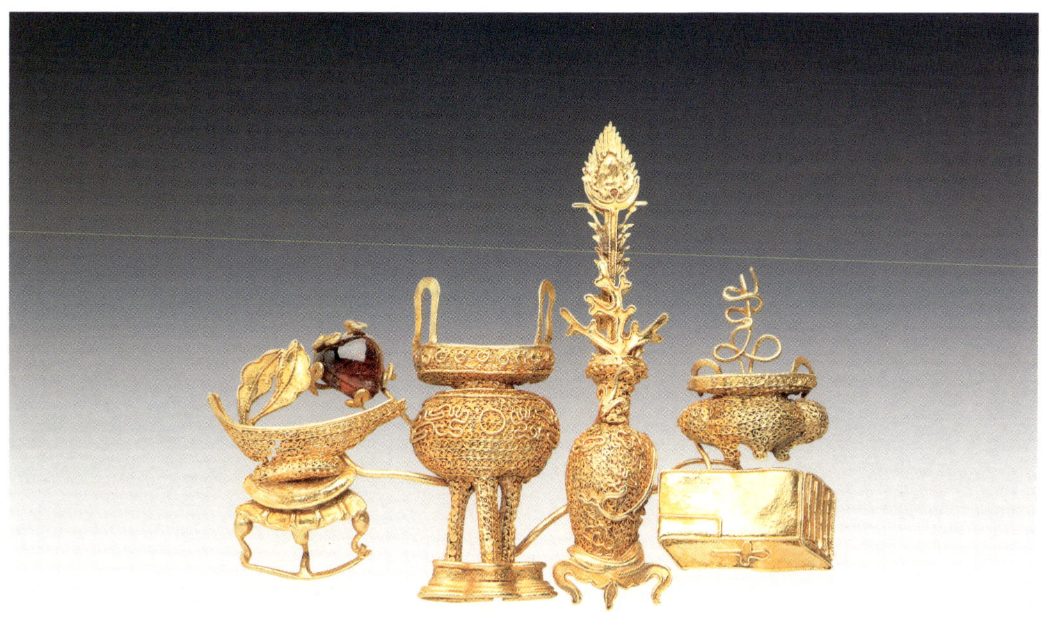

303

GOLD FILIGREE HEADDRESS FITTING IN THE SHAPE OF AN INCENSE ALTAR SET WITH GARNET ATTACHMENT

LATE MING DYNASTY
(*circa* 1600)
WIDTH : 5.5 CM
HEIGHT : 4 CM

A gold filigree fitting for a noblewoman's headdress in the shape of an incense altar set with garnet attachment.

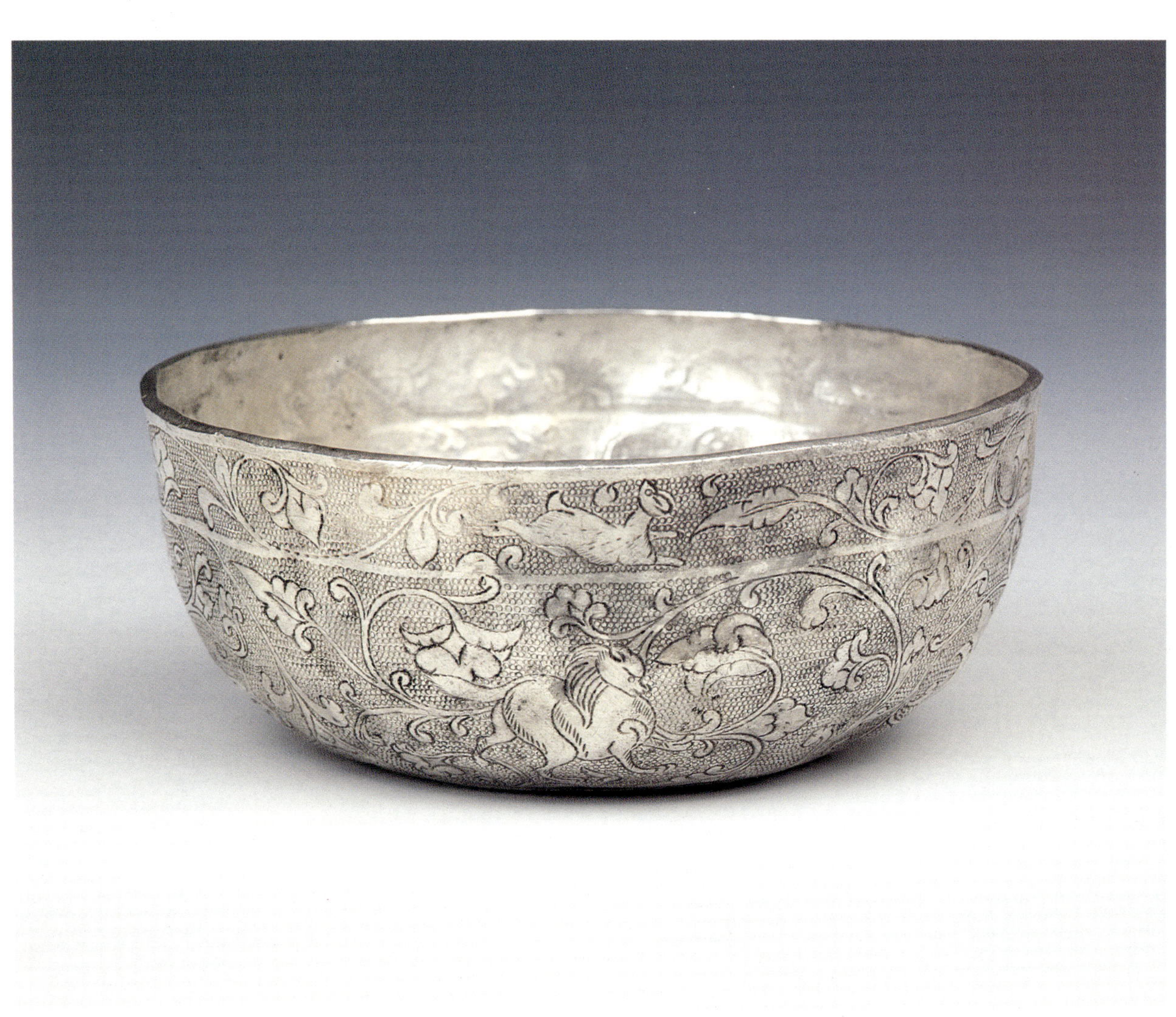

304*

SILVER LUSTRAL BOWL OF SHALLOW U-SHAPE DECORATED WITH CHASED MYTHICAL ANIMALS, DUCKS, GEESE AND RUNNING DOE AMID FOLIAGE ON A RING PUNCHED GROUND, WITH REPOUSSÉ DRAGON, CRAB AND FISH IN CENTRE OF INTERIOR

TANG DYNASTY, HIGH TANG PERIOD (8TH CENTURY)
DIAMETER : 8 CM
HEIGHT : 3.5 CM

Silver lustral bowl of shallow U-shape, chased in the main panel with a pair of mythical animals separated by a standing mandarin duck amid floral scrolls with a narrow chased border of a running doe and two geese amid floral scrolls all on a ring punched ground. The centre of the interior with a three-clawed dragon, crab and fish in a pearl bordered medallion in repoussé technique. The small crab seems a somewhat odd inclusion in the decoration but compares with a series of high quality bowls of the same shape, some of which have a small turtle replacing the crab. It seems likely that the crab here was the personal mark of the craftsman who made the piece or the personal mark of the noble who commissioned it.

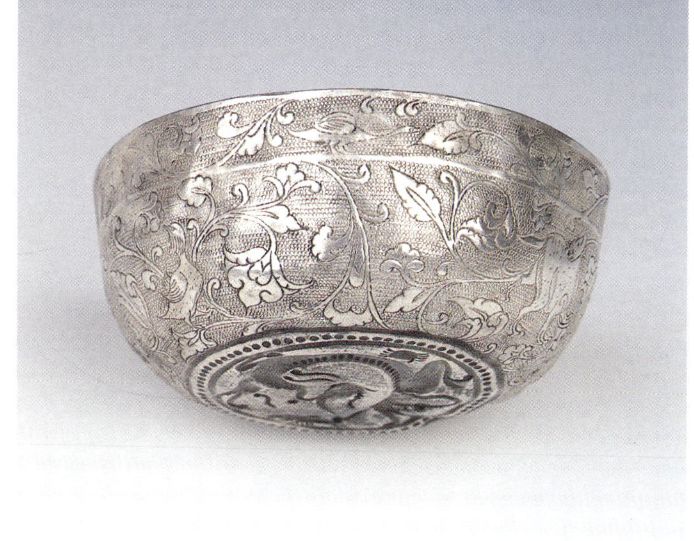

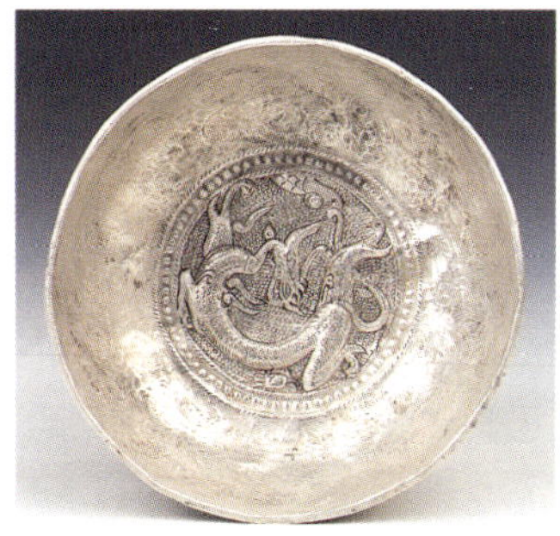

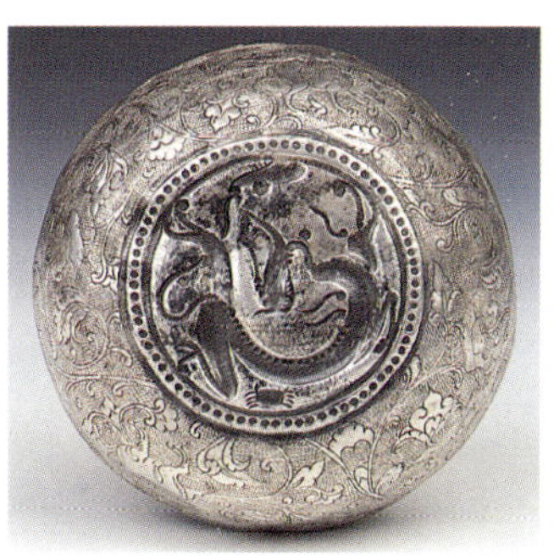

305

Circular silvered bronze box with peony decoration and angular key fret

Late Tang to Northern Song
(10th to 11th century)
Diameter : 3.8 cm
Depth : 2.7 cm

Small circular silvered bronze box with small foot decorated on the top with an open peony flower spray with leaves in a medallion, all on a circular ring punched ground, a band of angular key fret surrounding the medallion. The base section with a band of narrow incised pointed petals round the foot ring with incised highlights on a plain background.

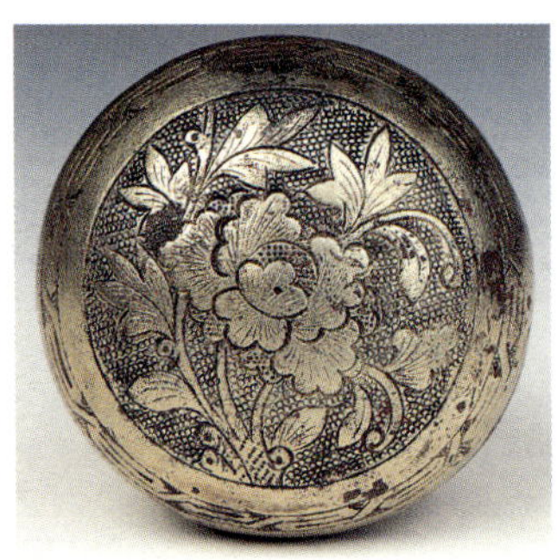

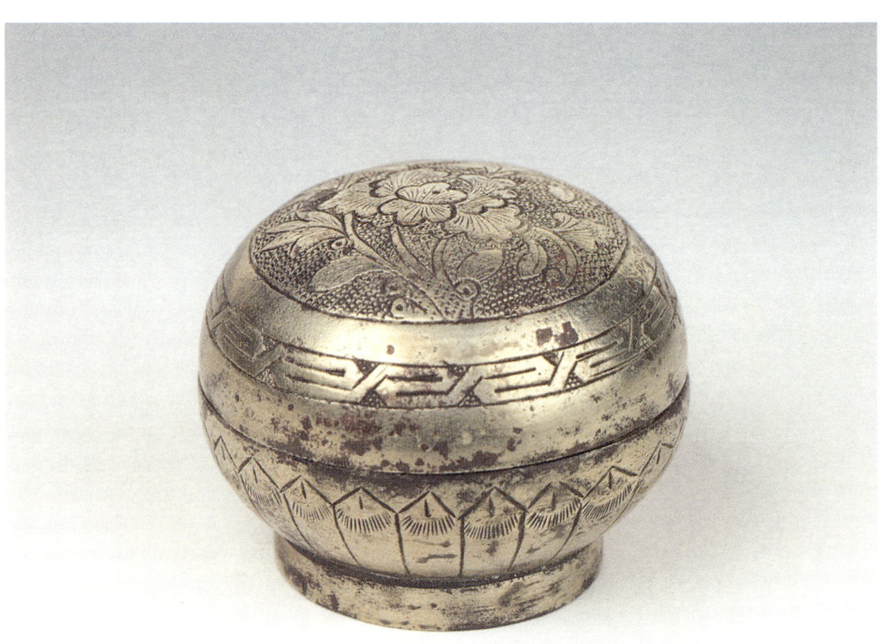

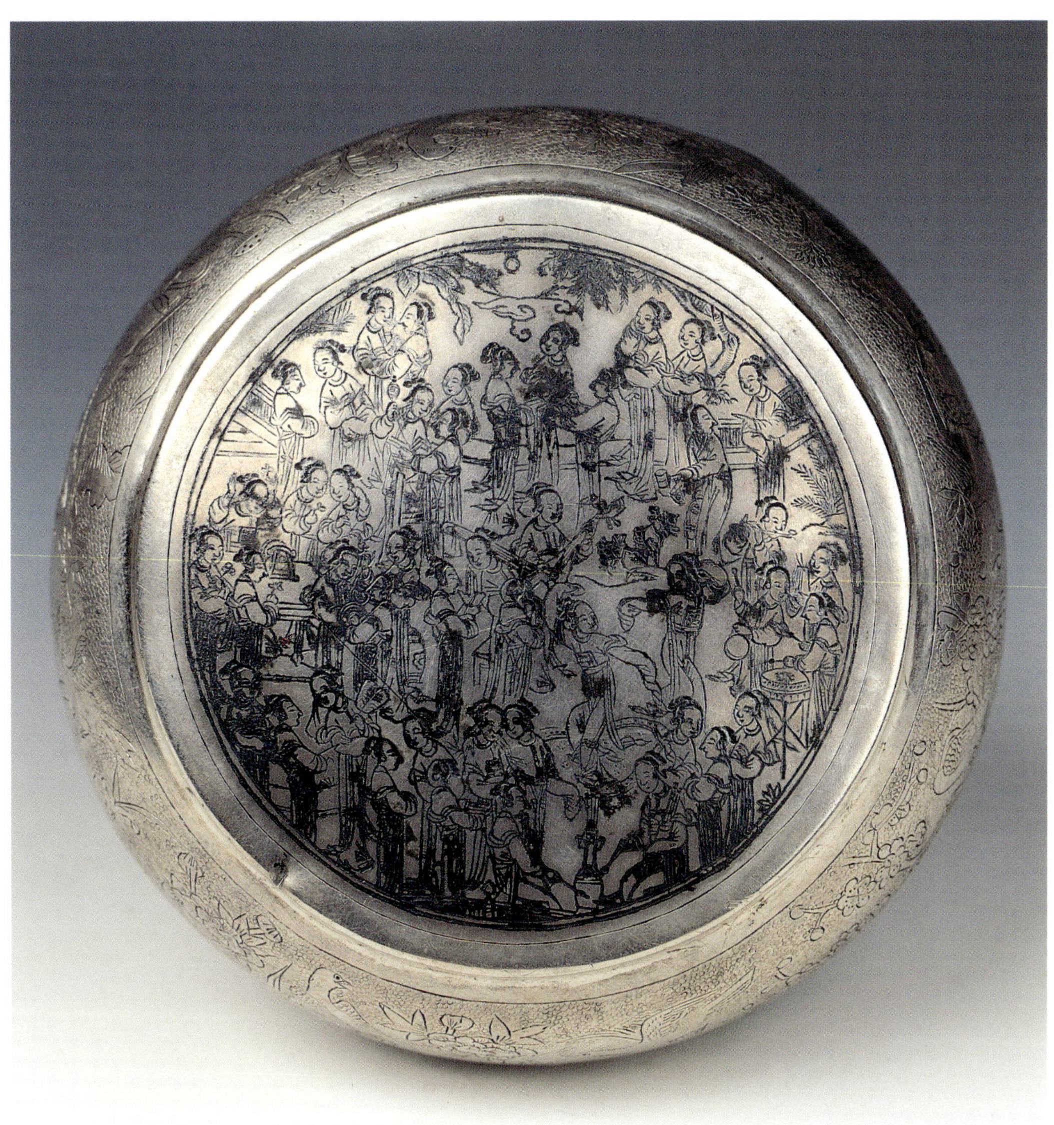

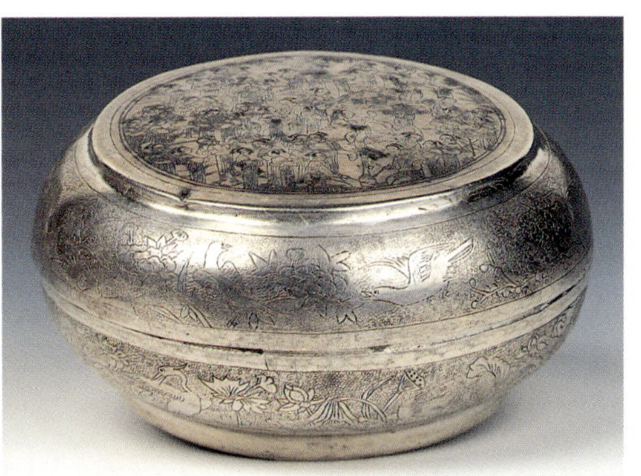

306

A CIRCULAR CHASED SILVER, NIELLO-ENRICHED COVERED BOX DECORATED ON THE TOP WITH LADIES AND ATTENDANTS ENGAGED IN VARIOUS PURSUITS, THE SHOULDERS WITH BIRD AND FLOWER DECORATION AND THE BASE SECTION WITH HERONS IN OR BY A LOTUS POND, ALL ON A CLOSELY RING PUNCHED GROUND

SOUTHERN SONG TO YUAN
(13TH CENTURY)
DIAMETER : 7.3 CM
HEIGHT : 4.1 CM

A circular, chased silver covered box of Song to early Ming lacquer shape with circular, slightly raised section on the top, the base without a foot rim. Decorated on the top with numerous ladies and attendants engaged in various pursuits in a garden setting, their hair accentuated with silver sulphide niello. The curved sides with birds amid prunus, chrysanthemum and other flowers, the base section with herons in a lotus pond in various positions chasing fish.One of the ladies is playing a *pipa* held half-way between the vertical and horizontal positions. By the Ming dynasty the *pipa* was played in the horizontal position. In the Tang it was played vertically.

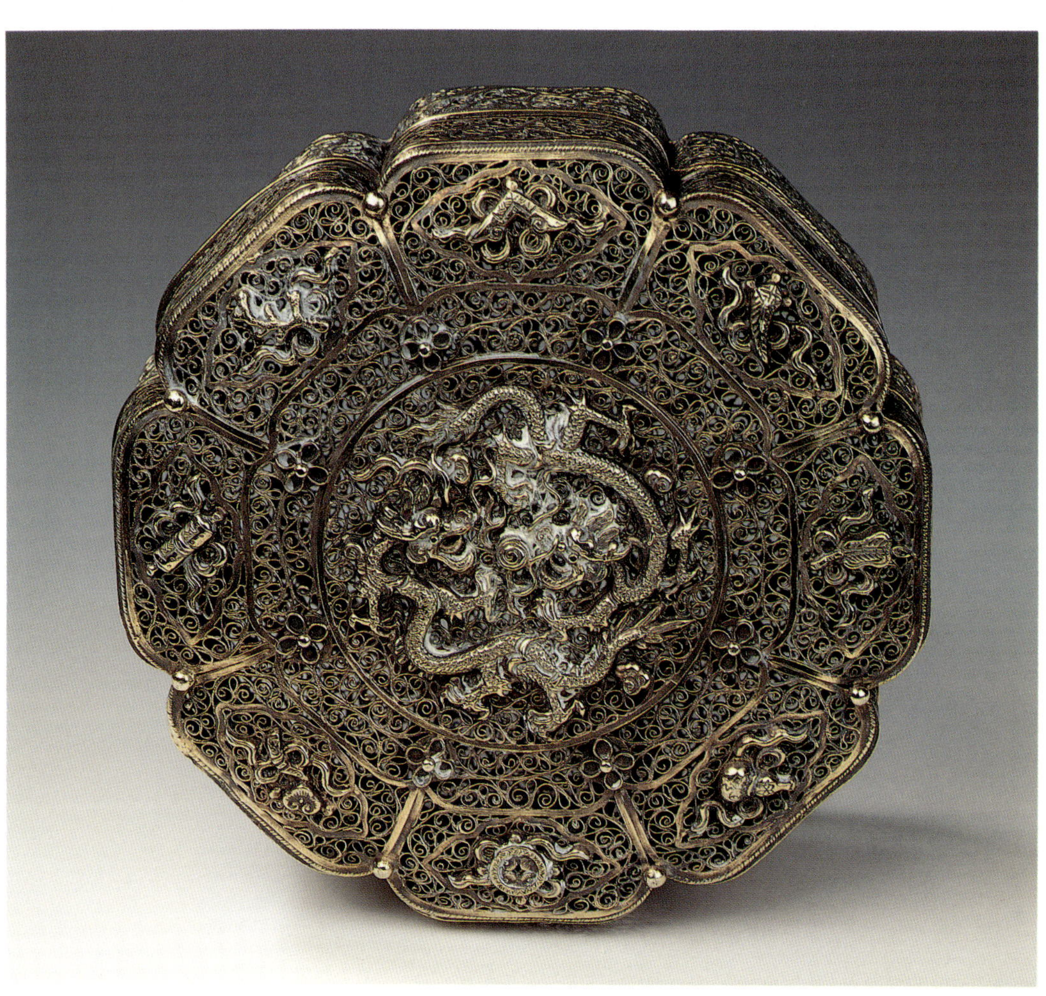

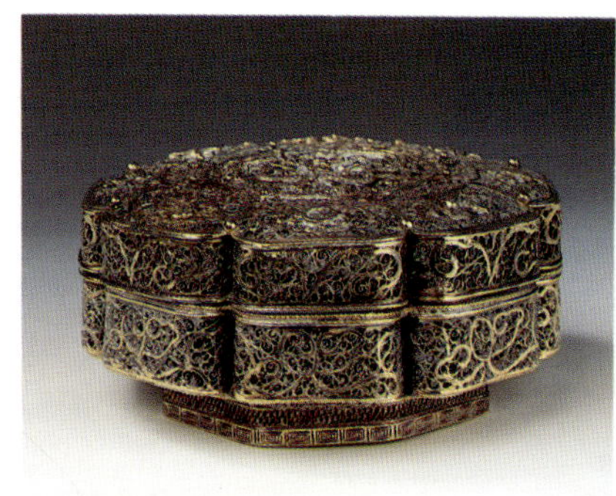

307

EIGHT-LOBED PETAL SHAPED SILVER FILIGREE BOX

LATE 18TH TO EARLY 19TH CENTURY
DIAMETER : 10.3 CM
HEIGHT : 4.5 CM

Eight-lobed petal shaped silver filigree box, the top with two four -clawed dragons chasing a flaming pearl in the centre, surrounded in the outer panel with the eight precious emblems in high relief, the sides and base with filigree work of delicate thin and thick silver wires. Probably Beijing work, late 18th to early 19th century.

308

Cloisonné enamel covered box with design of scrolling lotus. Four character incised Jingtai mark (1450 - 1457)

Ming dynasty
(second half of the 15th century)
Diameter : 4.5 cm
Height : 2 cm

A small, round red brass cloisonné pill box, the top of which is decorated with a lotus head and leaves in red, green, white and yellow enamels on a turquoise ground. The sides are decorated with floral scrolls. There is an incised four character Jingtai mark on the base.

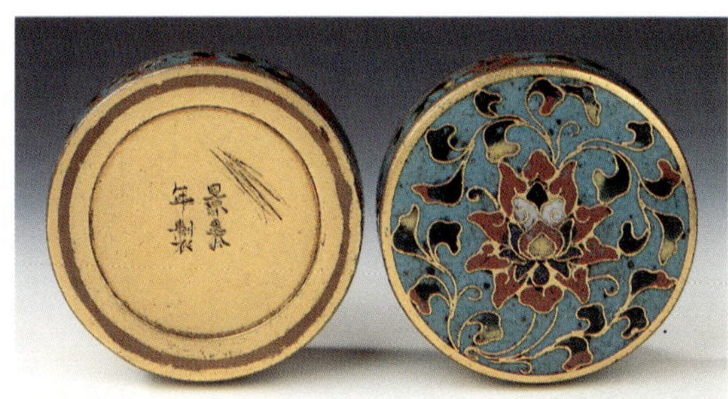

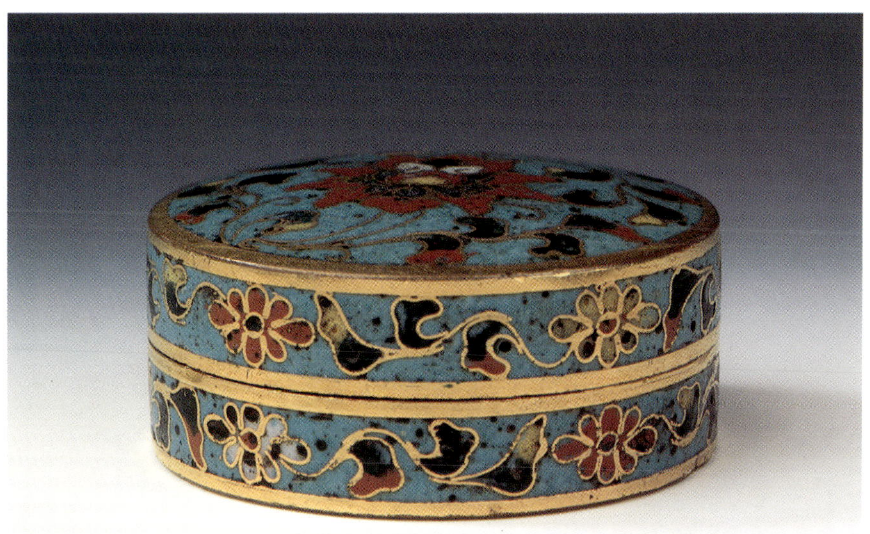

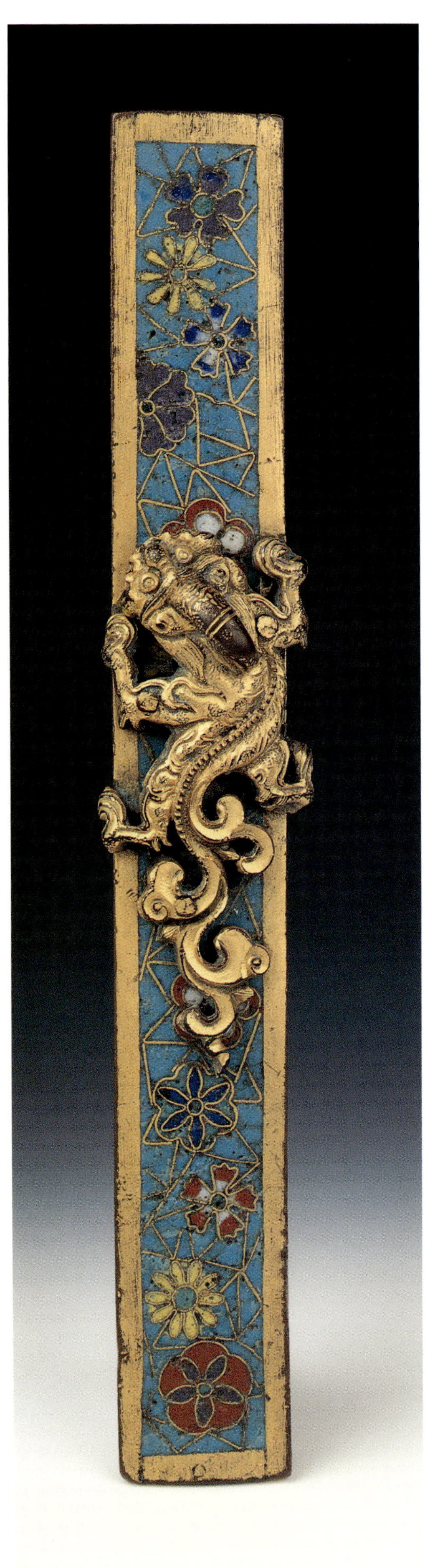

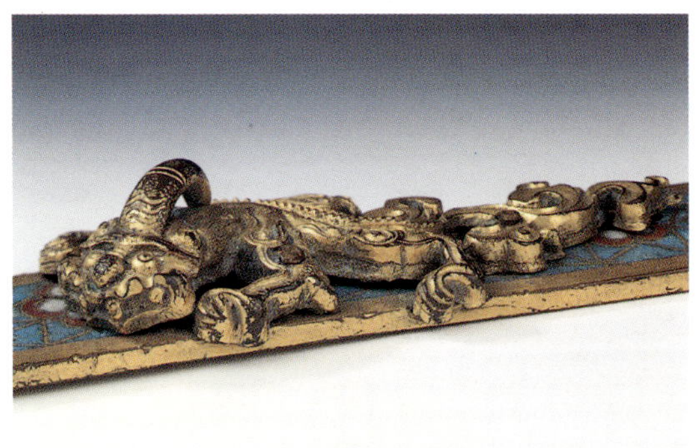

309

Cloisonné enamel paper-weight decorated with flower heads on cracked-ice turquoise ground with gilt bronze *kui* dragon appliqué

Late Ming dynasty
(*circa* 1600)
Length : 20 cm
Width : 2.5 cm

A cloisonné paperweight in the shape of a ruler, the surface of which is decorated with various flower blossoms in yellow, red, blue and aubergine on a so-called cracked-ice turquoise ground. The top of the paperweight has atttached a gilt bronze *kui* dragon with foliated tail, pronounced claws and a snarling mouth.

310

Beijing enamel incense stick holder in the shape of a flower with pierced bronze cover

Qing dynasty
Yongzheng mark and period
(1723 - 35)
Diameter : 10 cm
Height : 4.5 cm

A small Beijing enamel incense stick holder with a pierced bronze cover with lotus scrolls carved in openwork. The foliated flanged rim of the shallow bowl of the censer is divided into twelve lobes each painted with a lotus blossom in pink enamel while the body of the bowl is decorated with lotus scrolls in pink and red enamels with green leaves all on a lemon-yellow enamel ground. The interior of the bowl is covered with blue enamel with a cylindrical incense stick holder in the centre. The edges of the censer are covered with thick gilding. The white enamelled base has a four character mark of Yongzheng in blue enamel in a square cartouche. The use of the four character mark, the yellow ground and thick gilding identify this piece as a product of the Beijing imperial workshop.

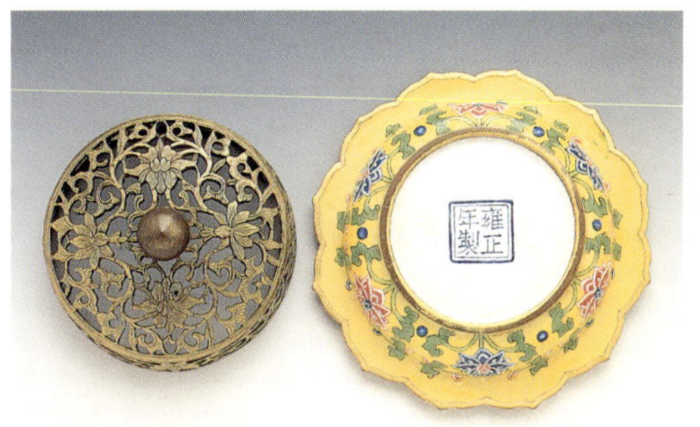

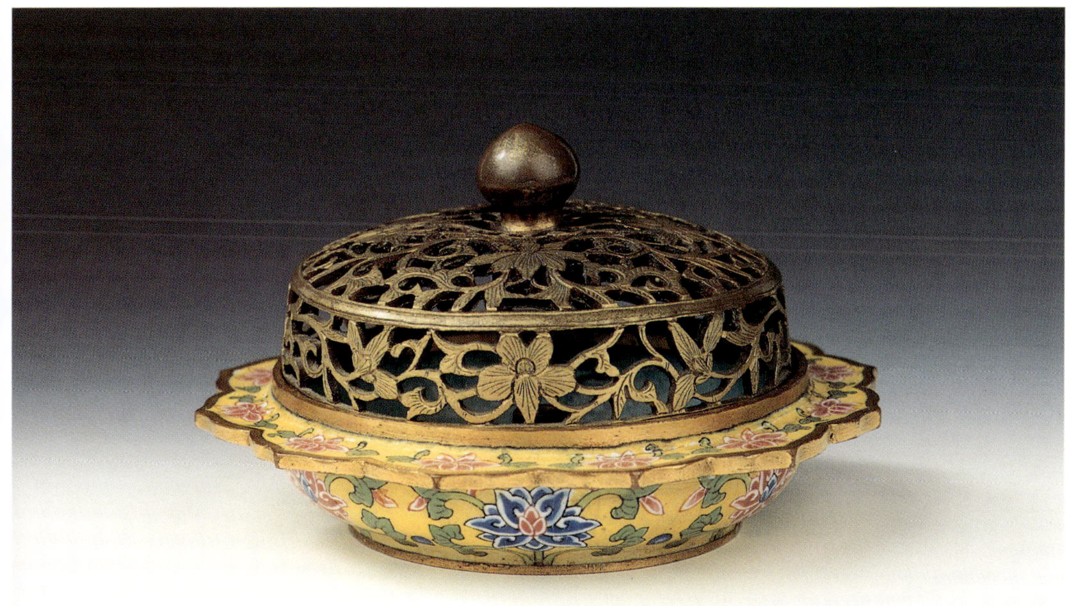

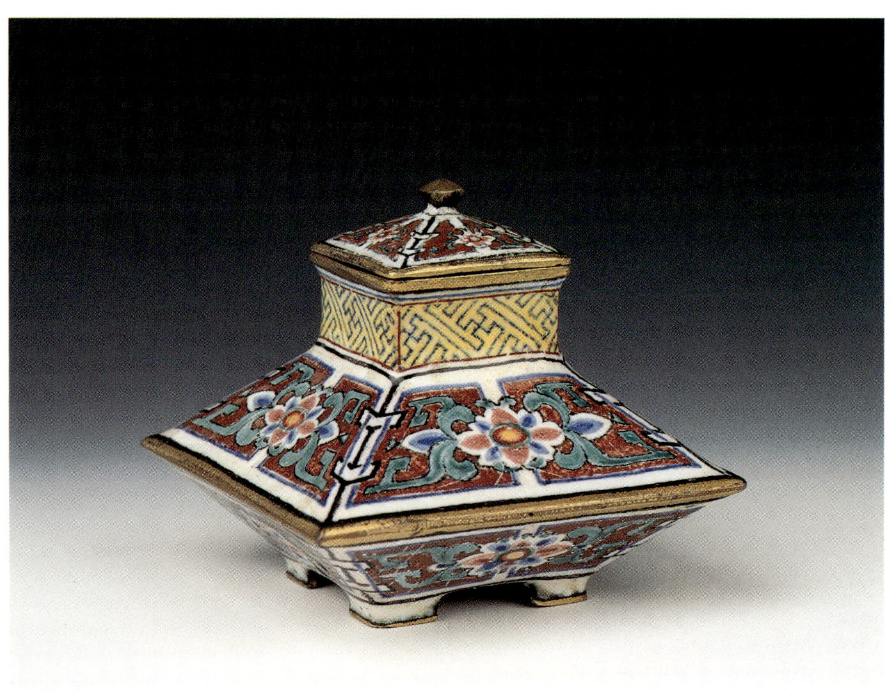

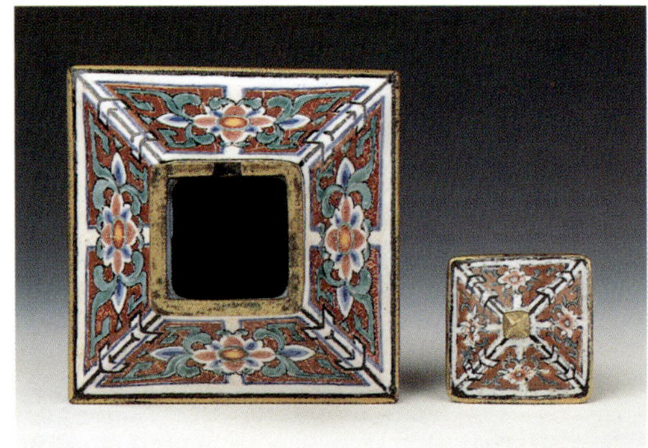

311

Covered square enamel condiment container with floral design

Qing dynasty
Yongzheng/early Qianlong period
(1723 - 1750)
Diameter : 4.5 cm
Height : 4 cm

A covered square Canton enamel condiment container in Queen Anne English silver shape, the lid indented to take a spoon. The lid and body are each divided into four sections decorated with eight-petalled flowers in red, yellow and blue enamels surrounded by green tendrils all on a white bordered, plum-coloured ground. The base shows a stylised peony in plum, blue and yellow enamels, while the neck is decorated with a swastika key fret on a yellow ground. The copying of the English silver shape and thinner gilding than on the Beijing example (Exhibit 310) identify this piece as probably having been produced in Canton for export .

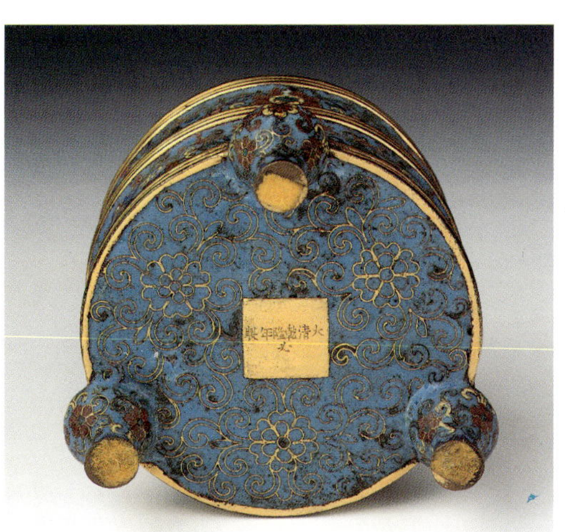

312

Cloisonné enamel tripod censer with floral patterns

Qing dynasty
Qianlong mark and period
(1736 - 1795)
Diameter : 9 cm
Height : 8 cm

A three legged, circular cloisonné censer on a copper body with three thickly gilded fluted horizontal bands separating two panels of lotus scrolls in red, yellow, pink and green enamels on a turquoise ground. The bulbous legs are also decorated with yellow and red florettes on a similar ground, while the base has gilt floral scrolls on a turquoise enamel ground. The six character mark of Qianlong has the additional character *bi* incised on a square gold plaque attached to the bottom of the censer.

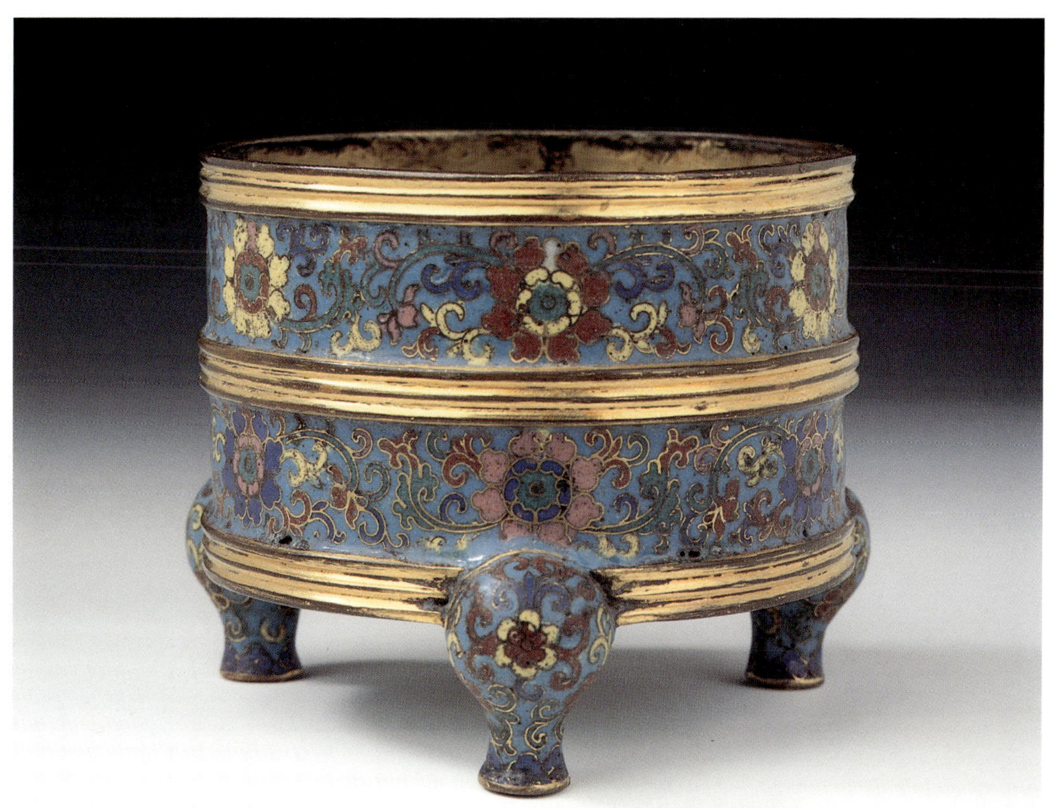

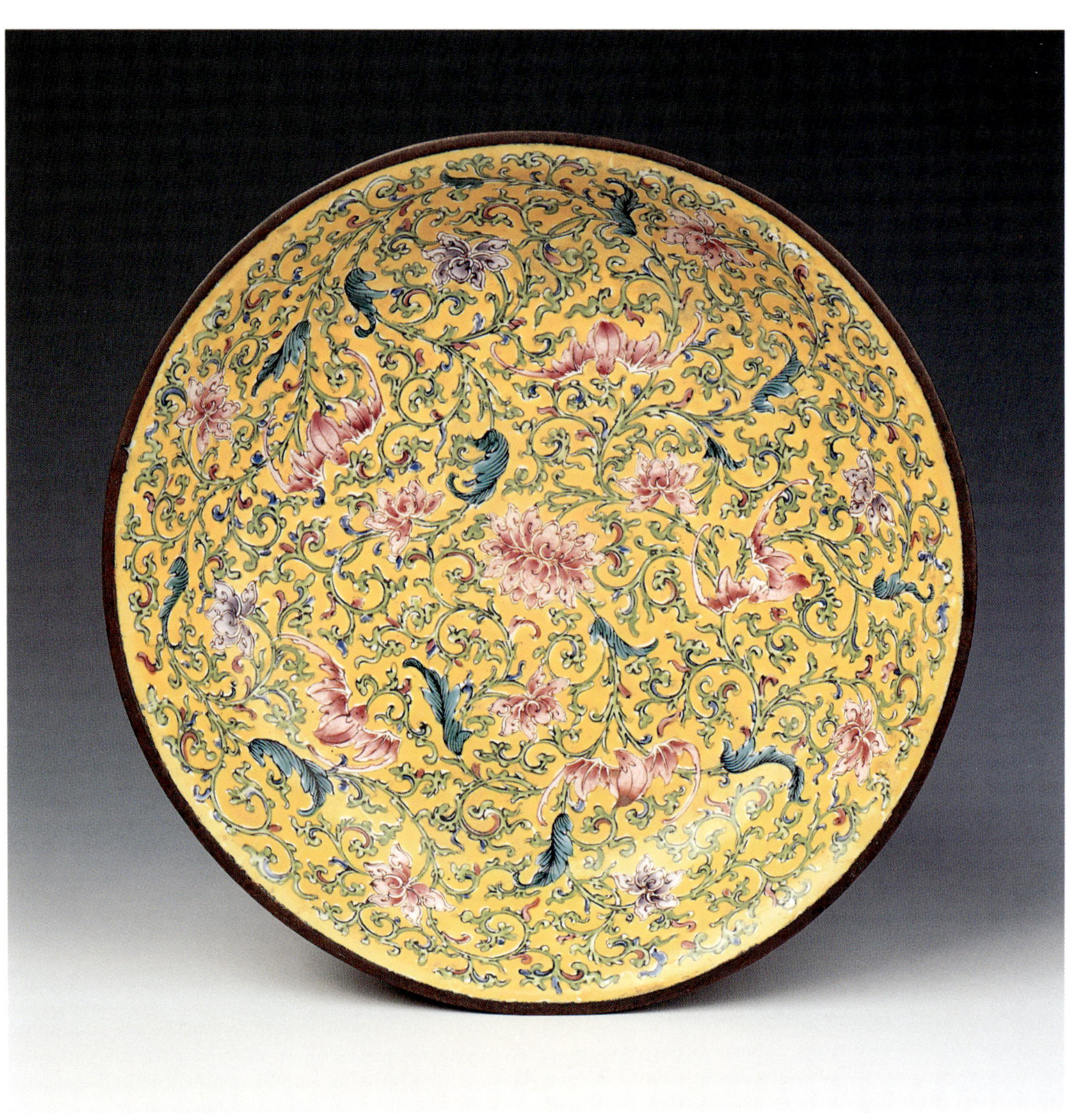

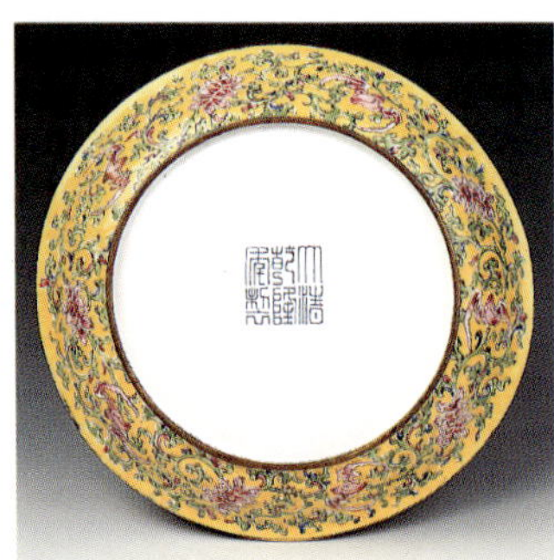

313

Canton enamel saucer dish with pink bats amid scrolling foliage on an orange-yellow ground

Qianlong mark and period (1736 - 1795)
Diameter : 15.5cm

A Canton enamel saucer dish decorated both inside and out with five pink bats amid light and dark green scrolling foliage all on an orange-yellow ground, the white enamel base with a six character blue enamel Qianlong seal mark.

314*

Dated yellow-ground Canton enamel miniature covered condiment jar and spoon made for the Annamese court

The spoon dated 1830
The jar with reign mark of the period 1820-40
Width : 8 cm
Height : 7 cm

A yellow-ground Canton enamel miniature covered condiment jar and spoon, probably a mustard pot made in Canton for the Annamese court. Of slightly compressed globular form, decorated in bright *famille rose* enamels with alternating stylisations of lotus amid foliage, the cover with a single lotus bloom around a small gilt spherical knob. The base is painted in brown enamel on a white ground with the reign mark "Ming mingnian zao", "made in the years of the Ming ming period", "Annam 1820 - 1840". The small spoon inscribed on one side "Ming ming shiyi nian zao", " made in the 11th year of Ming ming" i.e. 1830, and on the other side "bai jin zhong er fen", "white gold weight two fen."

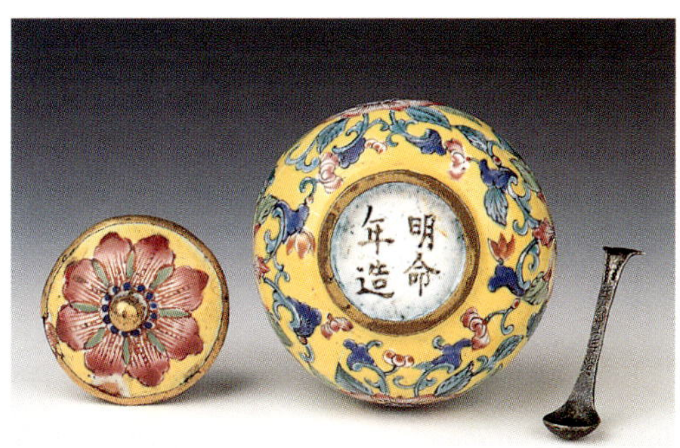

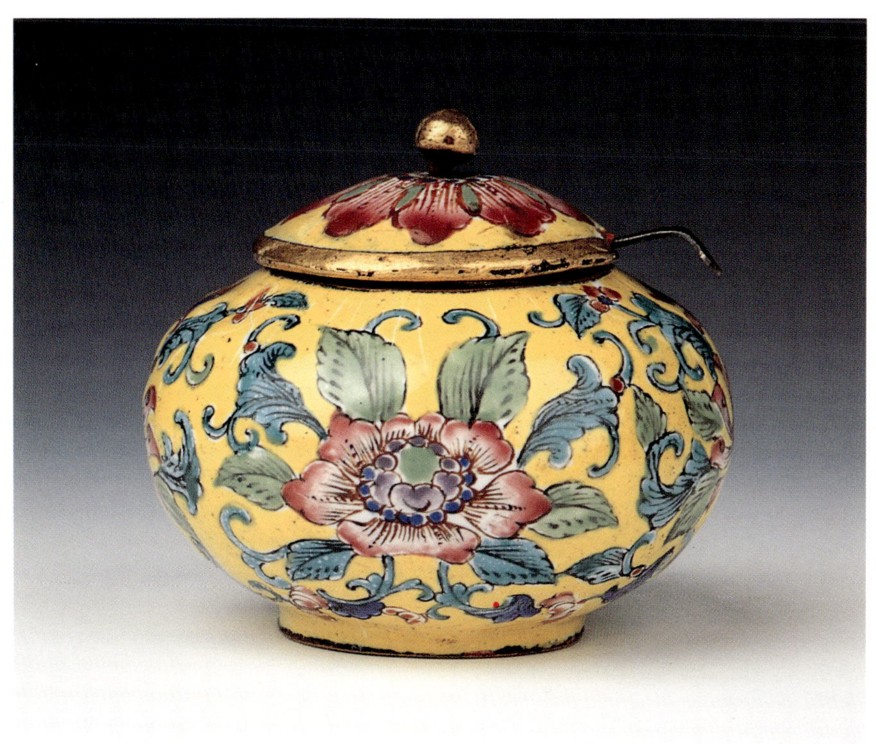

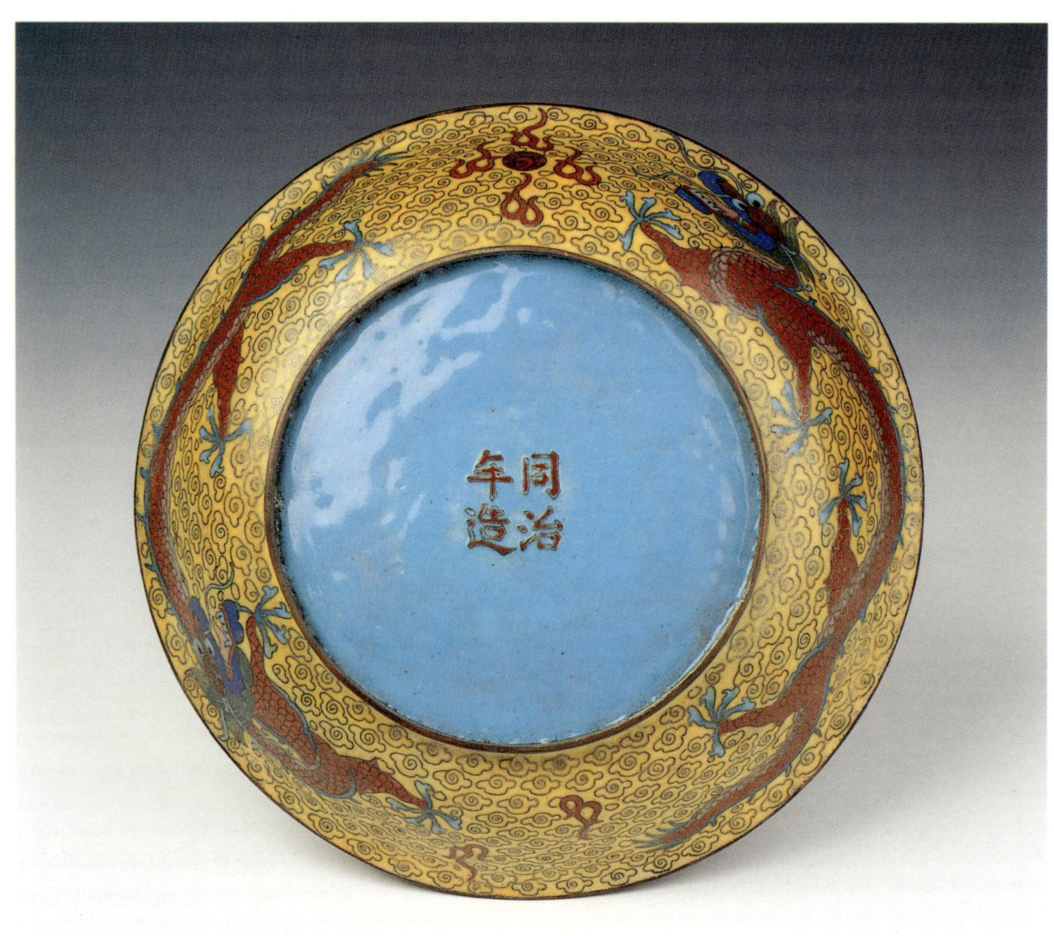

315

Pair of shallow cloisonné bowls with everted rim, the interior with plain imperial yellow enamel, the exterior with two five-clawed dragons chasing pearls in cloisonné on imperial yellow ground

Tongzhi mark and period
(1862 - 1874)
Diameter : 19.2 cm

Pair of shallow bowls with everted rims, the exterior of cloisonné, the interior covered overall with imperial yellow enamel, the exterior with two five-clawed dragons chasing a flaming pearl, one facing towards the pearl, the other with head turned back towards the pearl, the dragons of dark red colour with cerise belly and turquoise claws, spine and outline, the mane green, the base dark blue, the whole on a yellow ground with curled cloissons. The base of turquoise colour with four character red enamel Tongzhi mark in cloisons and of the period. Enamelled cloisonné marks as opposed to incised marks are very rare and only a handful are known. In contrast to incised or merely enamelled marks, which might have been added later, cloisonné marks must be contemporary with the piece.

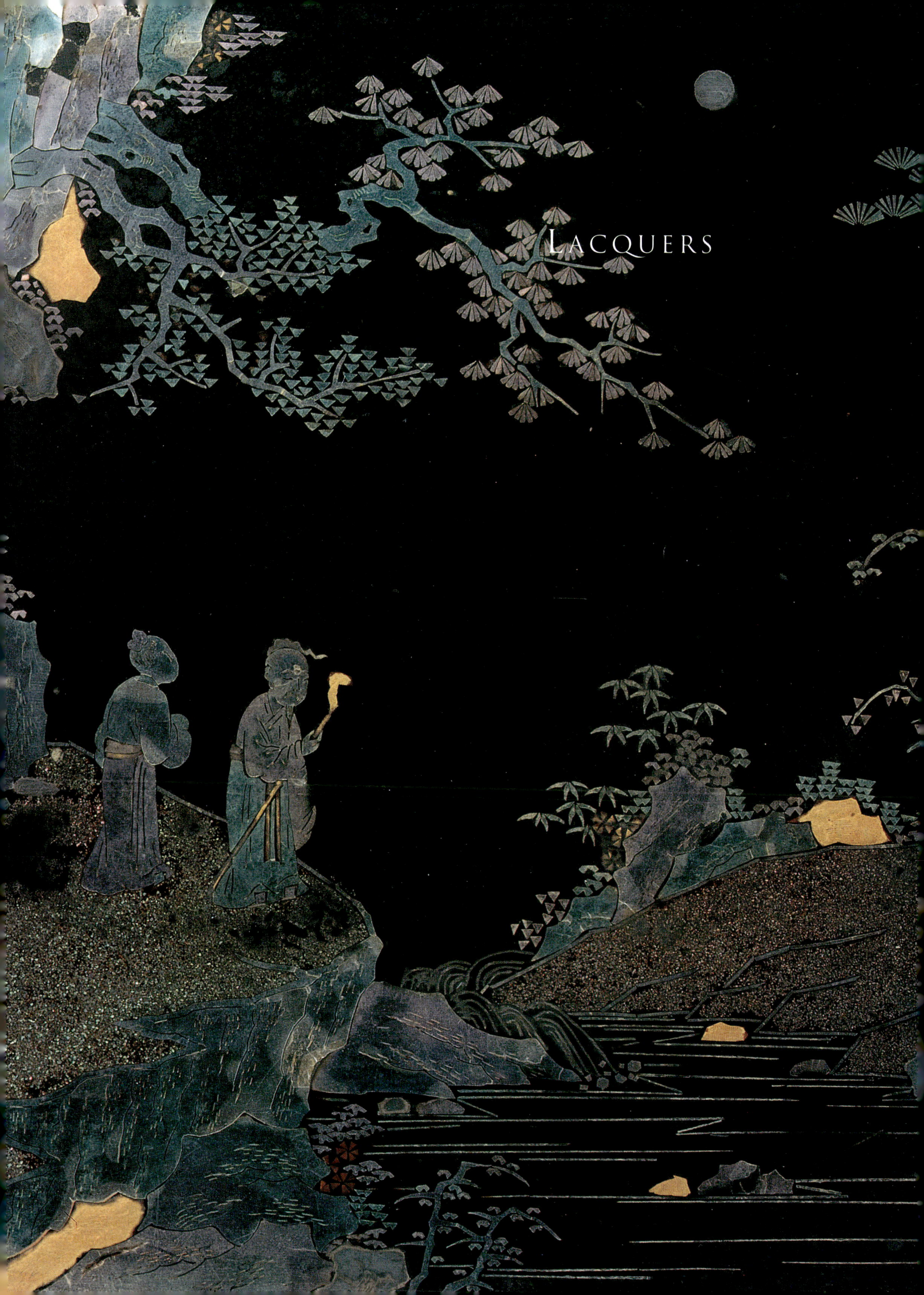

Lacquers

Lacquers

Included in the exhibition are thirteen pieces of Chinese lacquer in various techniques ranging in date from the early 16th century to the early 19th century. Lacquer has been used in China since prehistoric times, and has been found in the well-known excavations at Hemudu, dated to approximately 5000 B.C.. The lacquer used in China all seems to have come from the sap of the lacquer tree *Rhus verniciflua*, which is widely distributed south of the Yangzi River. It is possible, however, that a closely related tree, *Rhus succedanea* may also have been used in China for making lacquer on the borders of Vietnam. It is known that there are other species of trees suitable for the manufacture of lacquer, which were used for the purpose in Japan, the Ryuku Islands and Formosa. The sap of the tree, from which the lacquer is made, is taken in a similar way to rubber by tapping the tree. Once the lacquer dries it is almost indestructible and is not affected by alkali, salt, water or most other substances. Before it dries, however, lacquer can cause a bad rash in the same way as poison ivy, and since it cannot dry without being exposed to oxygen, before use it is kept in an airtight container much like paint is today.

Lacquer objects normally have a core of other material such as wood, bamboo, cloth, ceramic or bronze but it has also been asserted that some Song lacquers had a core of precious metal. All the early lacquers seem to have a core of wood or cloth and, as a result of desiccation of the core over time, are frequently subject to crinkling. For this same reason early lacquers are rare and also distinguished by being very light in weight. The alleged core of precious metal has also been given as a reason for the rarity of surviving Song lacquers, but Song lacquers with cores of precious metal have not been found in any controlled excavation and the assertion of the use of precious metal at that time seems to be apocryphal.

Carved lacquer, where many layers of lacquer are left to dry one on top of the other and then carved, was a Chinese speciality from at least the Yuan dynasty onwards. This is in contrast to the position in Japan where lacquer of other types such as *maki-e* (gold-sprinkled) was much preferred. Four such carved pieces are included in the exhibition dating from the 16th, 17th and 18th centuries.

The earliest carved lacquer included in this exhibition is a small circular box dating from the first half of the 16th century in black carved lacquer on a red ground (Exhibit 316). Similar boxes are well-known and are fairly common. The dragon dish dating from the first few years of the Wanli reign period (1573 - 1620) is decorated in the imperial style normally associated with the reign of Jiajing (1523 - 1566) (Exhibit 317). This piece has the usual diaper ground and the gold filed mark inscribed vertically down the centre of the base associated with the imperial pieces of Jiajing. Wanli pieces normally lack the diaper ground and the usual position of the mark is round the edge of the level base near the foot-rim. This piece, which I purchased from a shop in Florence where it was being used as an ashtray, also shows the removal of the fifth claw of the dragon at some time in the past (no doubt to hide its imperial origin) and there are several old repairs to the lacquer. There are no more than half a dozen such dishes known with the

Wanli mark written in the way it is here, and on the above evidence it must date from early in Wanli's reign.

The carved lacquers of the 17th century are represented by a cup with a silvered bronze lining carved on the outside with a pair of chattering birds amid branches under a key fret border (Exhibit 321). Similarly positioned birds are frequently found on Transitional period (1620-1683) pieces in other media.

The Qianlong red lacquer box exhibited (Exhibit 326) is sharply carved in the style of the time with horses amid waves. The Ming carved lacquers are in contrast much less sharply carved. This box is a good example of one of the 80 or so lacquer designs commissioned by the imperial palace at the time, to which the Emperor Qianlong (1736-1795) gave names.

In addition to the carved lacquers, there are also two *lac burgaute* pieces included in the exhibition. In *lac burgaute*, mother-of-pearl pieces are inlaid in black, brown or red lacquer to create the picture required. Occasionally thin gold sections are added to highlight parts of the design. Mother-of-pearl inlaid lacquers have a long history and have been produced in the Hangzhou region since at least the Tang dynasty. In the late 17th and 18th century in particular, use was also made of the various colours and the lustre which are occasionally present in the mother-of-pearl to add very rich and colourful tones to the decoration. The two pieces of *lac burgaute* which are included in the exhibition date from the Wanli (1573-1620) and Kangxi (1662-1722) periods respectively (Exhibits 318 and 322). The tray with ducks by a lotus pond and overhanging peonies and narcissi can be paralleled in the non-imperial blue and white kraak wares from the late 16th century. The Buddhist lions chasing reticulated balls appearing in the border panels of this tray can also be dated to the same century in ceramics. The tray is an interesting example of *lac burgaute* from the Wanli period. The Kangxi example has some gold sheet highlights added to the mother-of-pearl inlay . Such use of gold highlights seems to have become popular during the Kangxi period, and the use of gold, but only on high quality pieces, continued into the Yongzheng period (1723-1735). This small tray has decoration which is typical of the second half of the 17th century. The later versions of similar square trays with cut off corners seem to be coarser and to lose the gold sheeting highlights. I have seen *lac burgaute* bowls decorated in similar fashion to these later trays without the gold highlights but with a core of porcelain, the bases of which bore the underglaze blue mark of the Ming emperor Chenghua (1465-1487) written in a way typical of the last few years of the Kangxi period. Such pieces can thus be dated to approximately 1720. The square tray (Exhibit 322) probably dates from 1680 - 1700.

During the 17th and early 18th century screens inlaid with lacquer panels enriched with jade, cornelian, soapstone, mother-of-pearl and other materials were popular. Two interesting screens of this type are included in the exhibition (Exhibits 323 and 324).

Lacquers in other techniques are also included, the earliest is a circular bead box decorated with *kui* dragons in various colours on a red ground, the technique dating from the late Ming (Exhibit 320). At this time, painted lacquers also become popular in south China as a folk art; the pair of dishes painted with designs of birds and flowers are good examples of such art (Exhibit 319).

From the Qing dynasty are two further pieces, the first a marbled lacquer cup with silvered bronze lining. This lacquer technique seems to have been invented in the Tang dynasty, but is rare. This cup (Exhibit 325), moreover, bears the mark normally used by Lu Yingzhi, the first of a famous family of Qing lacquerers from the town of Yangzhou and is a good and rare example of his work. Lu Yingzhi was the grandfather of Lu Dong alias Lu Kuisheng (ante 1780 - 1850) who was the most famous lacquerer of this particular family (Note 1). Lu Dong's exact birth date is not known but he is known to have died in 1850 at the age of at least 70 years. In view of his grandson's dates, Lu Yingzhi must have worked in the mid 18th century. There is an interesting story that records how Lu Yingzhi purchased an ink-slab in the market of Yangzhou, which had been made in the Song reign of Xuanhe (1119-1125) in the Song imperial workshops. The ink slab in question resembled a type of ink slab known as *dengni* (this type of ink slab involved the use of the finest clay and molding to achieve the desired shape) and was so light that it would not even sink in water. Lu Yingzhi experimented and ascertained that the slab he had found was made from lacquer sand which he was able to duplicate in his workshop. As a result he commenced using lacquer sand to make pieces for the scholar's table. He became famous for making such pieces and for his engravings of landscapes, flowers and bird design. His son Lu Shenzhi is known to have followed Lu Yingzhi as a Yangzhou lacquer maker but little is known about him. Lu Yingzhi's grandson, Lu Dong , however, became the most famous of his family and probably the most famous lacquerer of the entire Qing dynasty. Lu Dong also frequently built up his pieces from a core of enamelled Yixing pottery. Exhibit 327 is just such a piece decorated with a prunus spray and signed with his usual personal seal mark "Kuisheng". It is a good example of his work, which is rare.

Note 1 : For further information on this artist see *Wenwu* 1957 vol. 7

漆器

展覽中有十二件中國漆器，以不同技法製成，年代自十六世紀初至十九世紀初。漆在中國的歷史可上溯至史前時代，在有名的河姆渡遺址（約公元前伍仟年）中便發掘到一些漆器。在中國使用的漆似乎是來自一種學名叫 *Rhus Verniciflua* 的漆樹的汁液，這種漆樹分佈甚廣，幾乎遍及整個中國，長江以南的地區。有一種學名叫 *Rhus Succedanea* 的漆樹，與前述的一種漆樹非常相似，生長在越南邊界的地方，中國人也用以製造漆器。除以上兩種外，還有些其他種類的樹可以製漆，日本、硫球群島和台灣便出產這些樹。提取漆樹液汁與提取橡膠的方法相同，是在樹身作切口讓液汁流出。製成的漆幾乎具有不能破壞的特性：一旦乾了以後，即使是接觸到鹼、鹽、水或其他物質也不會被侵蝕。在乾之前，漆可以令人發疹，一如接觸到有毒的常春藤一樣；漆需要暴露在氧氣中才可以乾，所以在使用前，必須放在密封的容器中，正如現今所用的油漆一樣。

漆器一般有胎。作胎的材料有木、竹、布、瓷和銅。傳說宋代漆器是用貴重的金屬做胎，但此說可能是不確的。所有的早期漆器似乎都有用木或布做的胎，由於年代久遠，胎身變得乾燥，因而捲縮。基於同樣理由，古代漆器的重量很輕，而且非常難得。傳聞宋漆以貴重金屬爲胎，或許是宋漆留傳極少的原因。而在監管下發掘的宋代遺址中從未發現過這一類漆器，所以此說法似乎未可置信。

剔紅的製法是罩上多層薄漆，待乾後鎸刻圖案。這工藝至少自元代起便成爲中國特有。而這是與日本相對而言。日本人比較喜歡其他類型的漆器如「蒔繪」（即洒金）漆器。展覽中有四件剔紅器，年代是十六、十七和十八世紀。

年代最早的一件剔紅是一個十六世紀上半葉的紅底黑漆小盒（展品316）。這種類型的盒頗爲普遍。龍碟的年份可定爲萬曆（公元一五七三年至一六二〇年）的最初幾年，其裝飾表現御製風格，與嘉靖（公元一五二二年至一五六六年）接近（展品317）。地紋是常見的菱紋，碟底正中陰刻填金一行六字款也與嘉靖御製一類剔紅器相似。萬曆器通常沒有菱紋的地紋，款字則是在平底上沿圈足彎形擺放。我在意大利佛洛倫斯買得這碟，當時是被作烟灰碟，上有幾處舊的修補，龍的第五隻爪已被除去（顯然是舊日掩飾御製的特有風格）。已知帶這種一行六字金款的萬曆剔紅器存世不多，不會超過六件。基於以上論據，這一件應是萬曆早年的件品。

展覽中有一件十七世紀的剔紅器。這是一件內有銀裡，外面刻有蹲在枝頭呢喃的雙鳥，上部近口沿飾以回文邊飾（展品321）。用其他質料製造的明末清初（公元一六二〇年至一六八三年）器上也可見到類似的鳥紋。

乾隆剔紅盒（展品326）飾以深刻的海馬紋，是當時流行的紋飾。與明代產品相較，後者便顯得刻工較淺。此盒是八十多件由乾隆皇帝（公元一七三六年至一七九五年）依照紋飾定名的漆盒中的一個，是由宮廷定製。

除剔紅外，展覽中還有兩件螺鈿漆器。這一類漆器是以螺鈿嵌在黑、褐或紅漆上，構成圖案，偶或加入金片以加强部份花紋的裝飾效果。螺鈿漆器歷史悠久，遠在唐代時杭州已有生產。特別是在十七世紀末和十八世紀，匠人們利用螺鈿片的顏色和光澤以潤飾花紋。展覽中兩件螺鈿器，一件是萬曆，一件是康熙（公元一六六二至公元一七二二年）（展品318和322）。漆盤的牡丹和水仙花下蓮池游鴨紋可與十六世紀晚期民窑的加櫓瓷相互比較；而邊上的開光獅子滚球也可與同時代的陶瓷相互印證。此物是萬曆年間一件有趣的螺鈿漆器。康熙的一件螺鈿器加有金片，以加强其藝術效果。這種技法似乎只用於精美的螺鈿器，自康熙起流行，持續到雍正年間（公元一七二三至一七三五年）。這個小碟的紋飾是典型十七世紀下半葉的風格。其後的同類型方碟通常是委角，一般較粗，沒有加上金片裝飾。嘗見以瓷器爲胎的螺鈿碗，紋飾風格與這些後期的小碟相同，底鈐釉下青花「大明成化年製」（公元一四六五年至一四八七年）款，書體與康熙朝最後幾年的寫款樣式相同，因此這些瓷胎螺鈿漆碗的年份可以定爲約在公元一七二〇年。方碟（展品322）的年代可能是公元一六八〇年至一七〇〇年。

十七世紀末至十八世紀初流行鑲玉、瑪瑙、粉石、文武壳和其他雜寶的漆屏。展覽中便有兩件這一類的漆屏（展品323和324）。

展覽中也有用其他技法製造的漆器。最早的一件是圓形的珠串盒，在紅底上飾以不同顏色的夔龍紋，技法是「填彩漆」，年代約是晚明（展品320）。與此同時，中國南方流行彩繪漆器，在民間通用。這裡展出的一對彩繪花鳥紋漆碟正是此類民間藝術的例子（展品319）。

展覽中還有兩件清朝漆器。第一件是「犀皮」漆杯，內有鎏銀銅裡。這種技法似乎是唐代首創，但極爲罕見。此杯（展品325）還帶有「煐之」款，屬揚州名工楊氏的第一代盧映之的款記。盧映之是葵生祖父。盧葵生是盧氏家族中最負盛名的漆工。其準確的出生年份不明，但已知他死於公元一八五〇年，年齡超過七十歲。由此推算，盧葵生的生卒年代是公元一七八〇年以前至一八五〇年。因此，我們可推斷盧映之的活躍時間一定是十八世紀中葉。據文獻記載，盧映之在揚州市內買得一個墨硯，是宋朝宣和年間（公元一一一九年至一一二五年）御作坊所製。該硯似澄泥硯，體極輕，輕至不沉於水。盧映之實驗證明該硯爲漆砂所製，並在其工場仿製。自後遂開始用漆砂製造文房用具，一技成名，尤其以刻山水、花鳥著名。兒子盧慎之承其業爲揚州漆工，但生平資料甚少。孫兒盧棟字葵生（註1）是家族中最出色的一員，可能是清代最出色的漆工。盧葵生往往在蘸有白釉的宜興胎身加漆。展品327便是這一類作品，飾以梅枝，並加上他常用的簽款「葵生」，此物爲盧氏作品的一個好的範例。

註1：有關盧葵生資料，參閱文物1957年7月號9-17頁。

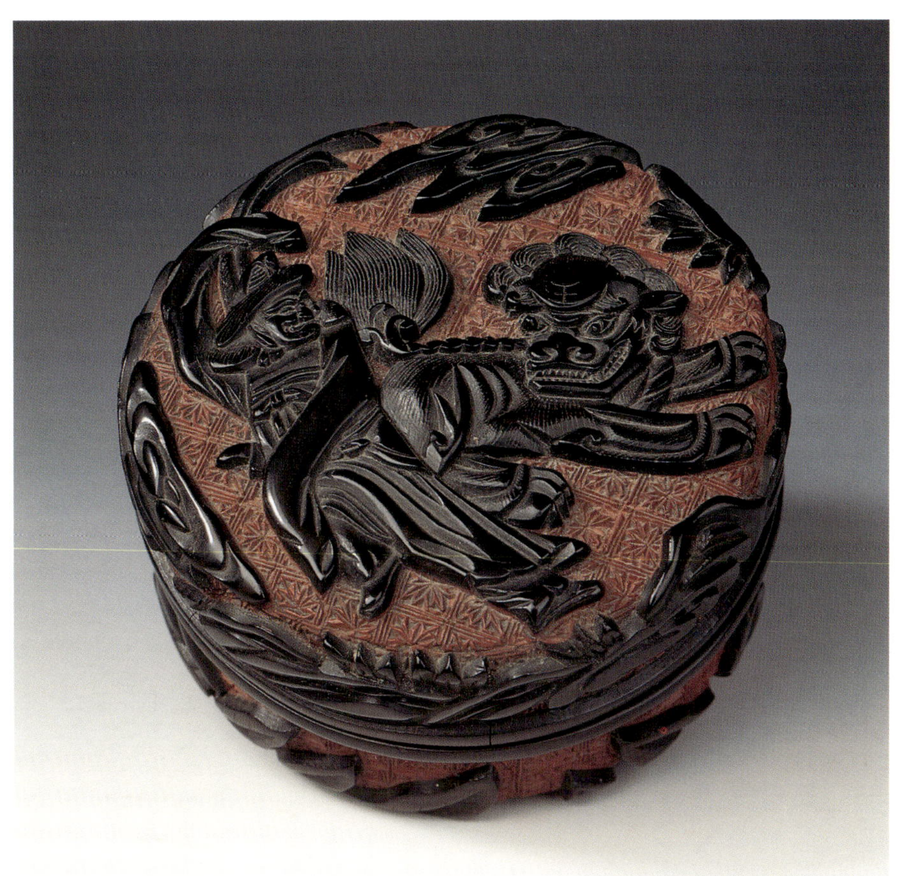

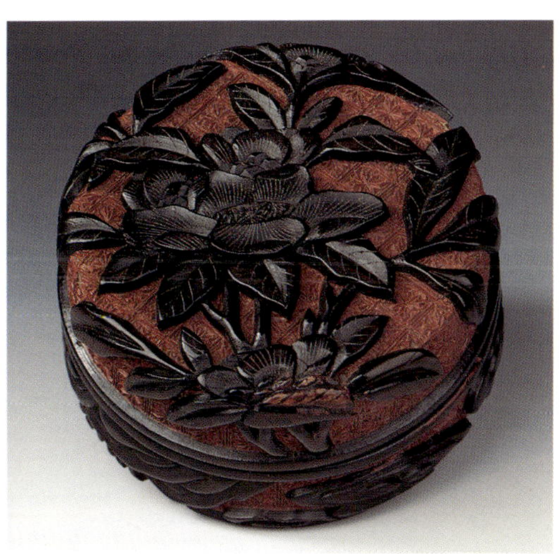

316

A CIRCULAR LACQUER BOX AND COVER CARVED ON THE TOP WITH A WESTERN ASIATIC MAN AND *QILIN* IN BLACK LACQUER ON RED LAND DIAPER GROUND, THE BASE WITH DESIGN OF FLOWERING CAMELLIA IN BLACK LACQUER ON RED LAND DIAPER GROUND

LATE 15TH TO EARLY 16TH CENTURY
DIAMETER : 7 CM
HEIGHT : 4 CM

A circular lacquer box and cover carved on the cover with a man of west Asiatic type dancing with a *qilin*, the man wearing a wide-brimmed pointed cap and a robe with long sleeves, the lower part fringed with rocks, the upper part with clouds, the base carved with a design of flowering camellia, the whole in black lacquer on a red land diaper ground, the interior lacquered black.

317

Carved red lacquer circular saucer with design of five-clawed dragon amid clouds chasing a flaming pearl, with peony scroll border

Ming, early Wanli period (1573 - 1580)
Diameter : 15.5 cm

A red lacquer saucer dish carved in its central medallion with a five-clawed dragon amid clouds chasing a flaming pearl against a stylised wave background. The fifth claw on each foot has been deliberately removed at some time in the past. The border and exterior are decorated with a band of continuous peony scrolls. The piece is inscribed vertically on the reverse in a straight line down the centre of the black lacquered base with a six character mark of Wanli, which is infilled in gold. The stylised background of the design and the vertical central placing of the mark, both common in the earlier reign of Jiajing, are unusual in the Wanli period, when the mark was usually inscribed in an arc near the footrim, and indicate a date for this piece very early in the reign.

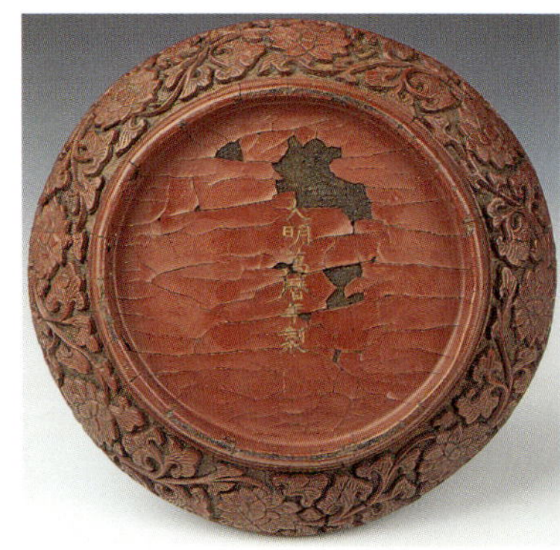

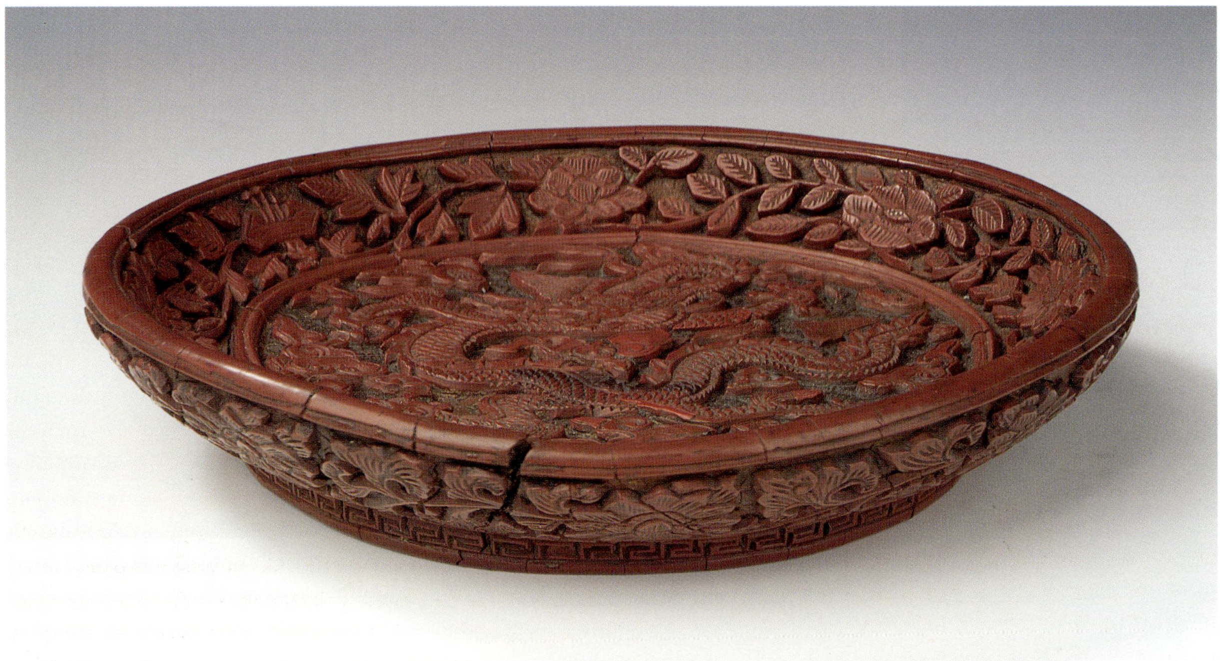

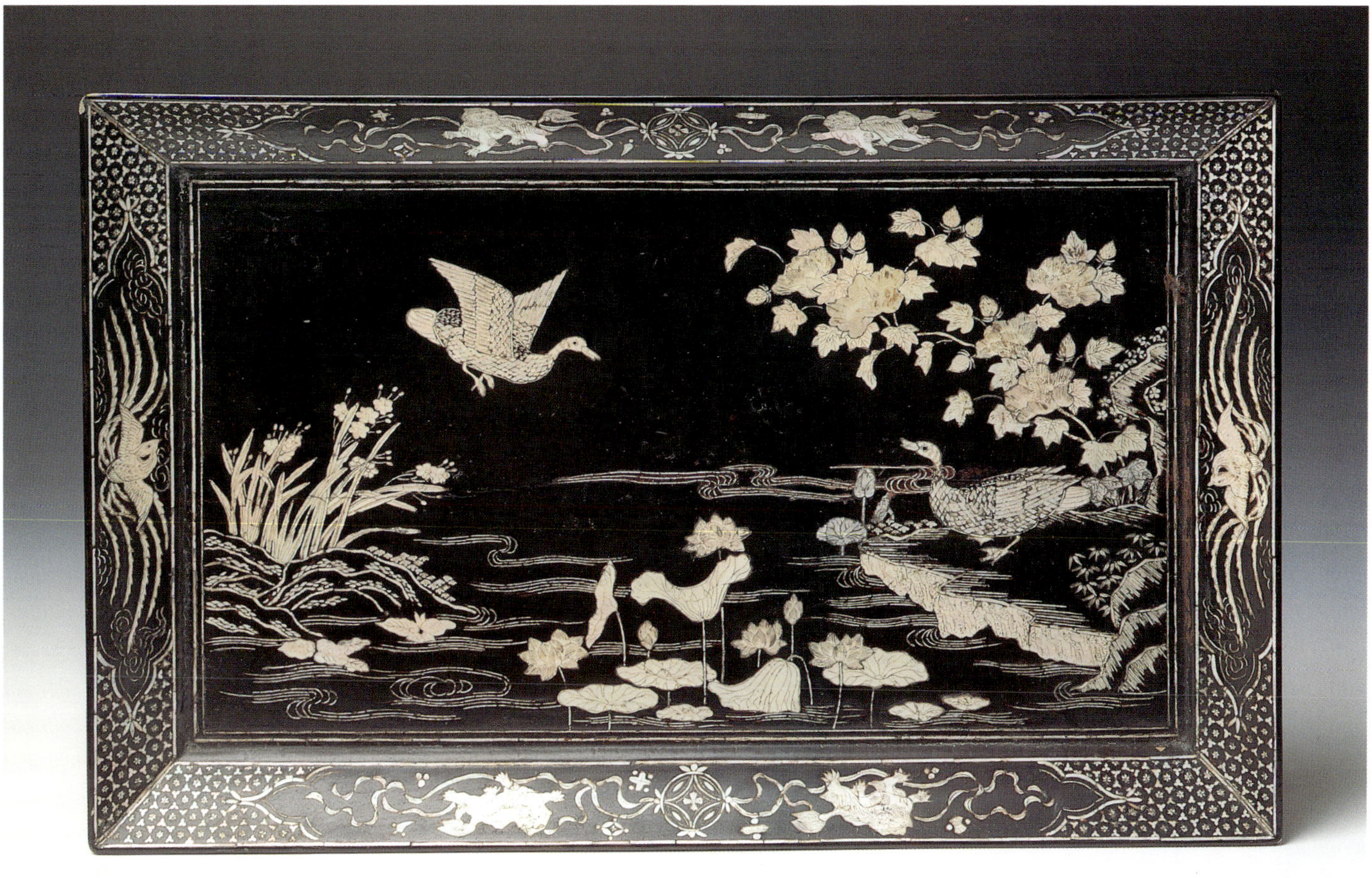

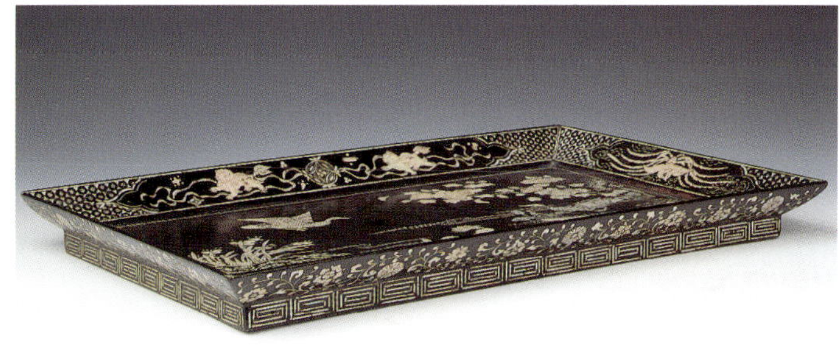

318

Lac burgaute rectangular tray with inlaid mother-of-pearl design of ducks by a lotus pond

Ming dynasty
(second half of 16th century)
Length : 40 cm
Width : 20.6 cm
Height : 3.5 cm

A rectangular black *lac burgaute* tray decorated with mother-of-pearl inlays of two ducks by a lotus pond beside narcissi and peony trees. The sloping sides are decorated with Buddhist lions with brocaded balls and precious emblems on the long sides and two phoenixes in flight on the shorter sides separated at the corners with diaper pattern. The similarity of the main design to that found on some early kraak porcelains is striking.

319

A pair of painted lacquer dishes decorated with birds and floral sprays

Ming dynasty Wanli period
(1573 - 1620)
Diameter : 13.5 cm
Height : 1.5 cm

A pair of painted lacquer dishes with everted rims, one of which is painted with two cranes among prunus and peony sprays and the other with two birds amid prunus and peach sprays. Both dishes are covered with brownish lacquer. The outline on one of the dishes is highlighted in gold.

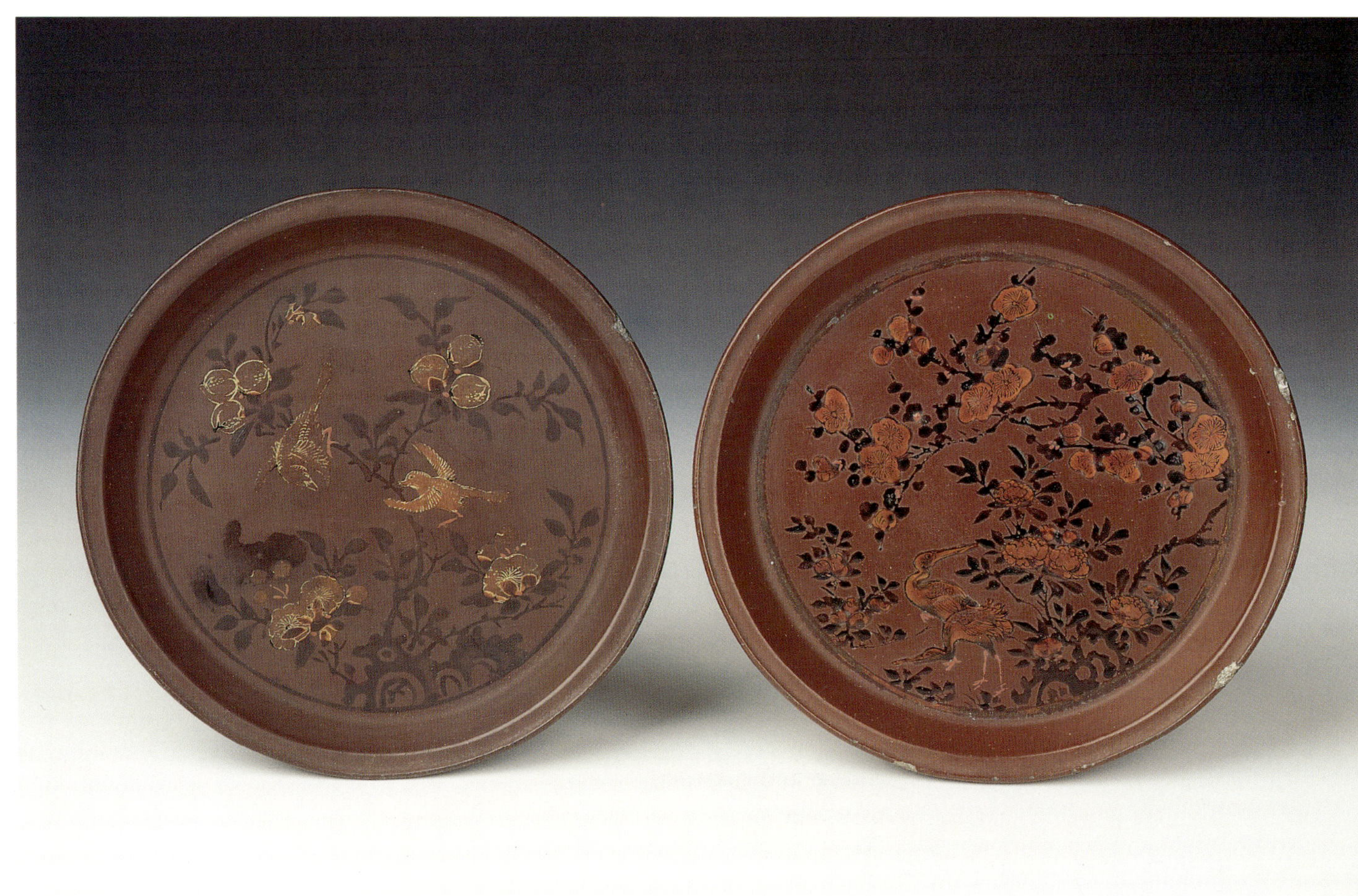

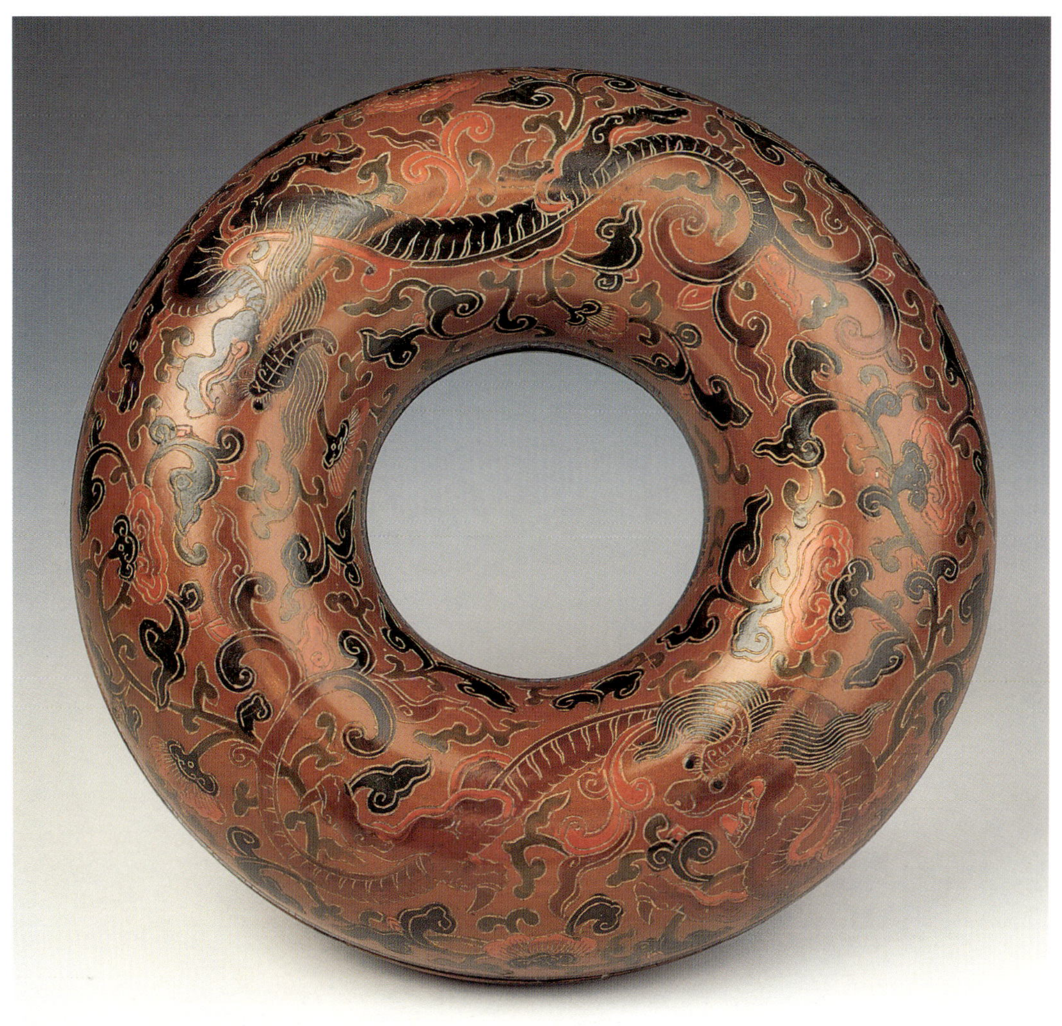

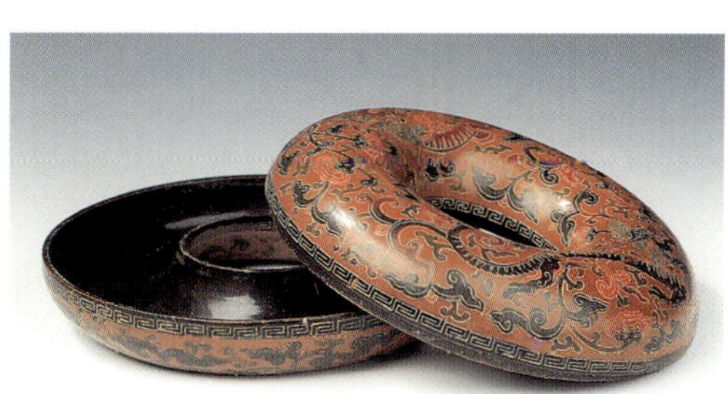

320

LACQUER BEAD BOX OF CIRCULAR TUBE-LIKE SECTION, THE TOP AND BOTTOM OF EQUAL SIZE, EACH SECTION DECORATED IN INLAID LACQUER TECHNIQUE WITH TWO INCISED *KUI* DRAGONS AND FUNGI AMID FOLIAGE, THE COLOURS OF THE DESIGN ARE RED, DARK BROWN AND GREEN AGAINST A BRICK-RED GROUND

1ST HALF 17TH CENTURY
DIAMETER : 19.2 CM
HEIGHT : 6.5 CM

Painted red lacquer bead box of circular tube-like section, the top and bottom halves of the box of equal size, both decorated in inlaid lacquer technique with two *kui* dragons and red fungi amid green foliage. The *kui* dragons each with one claw of reddish brown colour, the dragons being dark brown and red brown respectively, both with green gilded manes all on a brick-red ground, each section edged with key fret picked out in gold on a narrow black lacquer band, the whole design with traces of gold edging; the interior lacquered black.

321

Carved red lacquer bowl with design of peonies and birds

Late Ming dynasty
(first half of 17th century)
Diameter : 11.4 cm
Height : 6.2 cm

A carved red lacquer bowl with decoration of two birds amid peonies above a slanting petal border; the lip and base rim are each carved with a band of key fret. The interior of the bowl is lined with silvered sheet bronze. The positioning of the two birds in relation to each other is as commonly found on ceramics of the period.

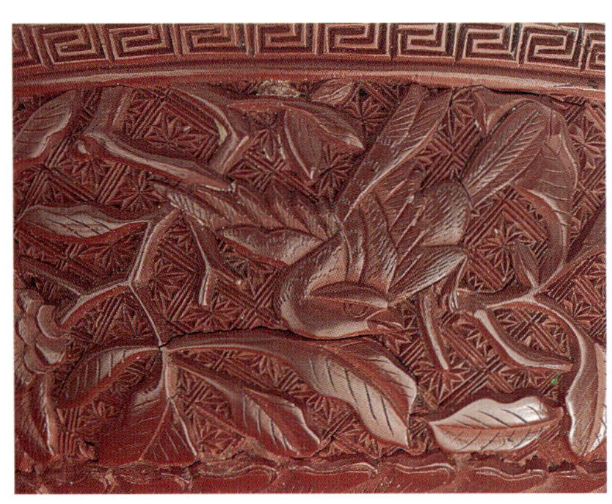

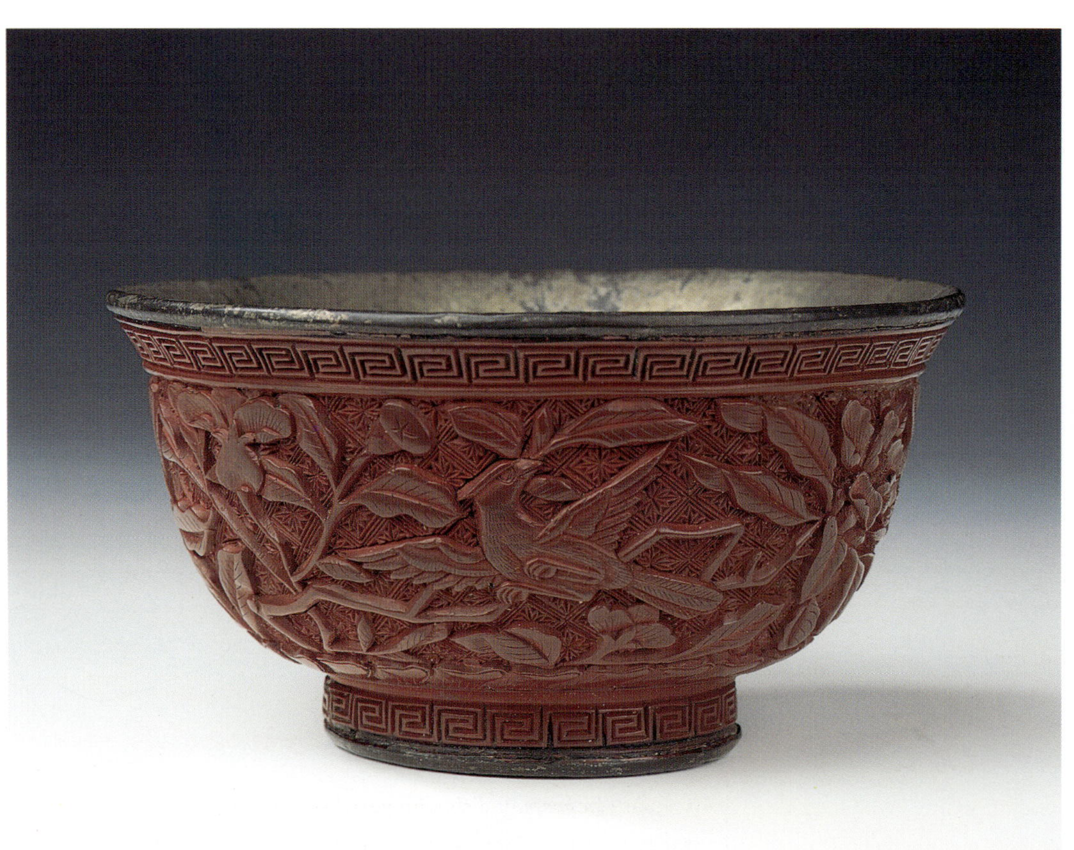

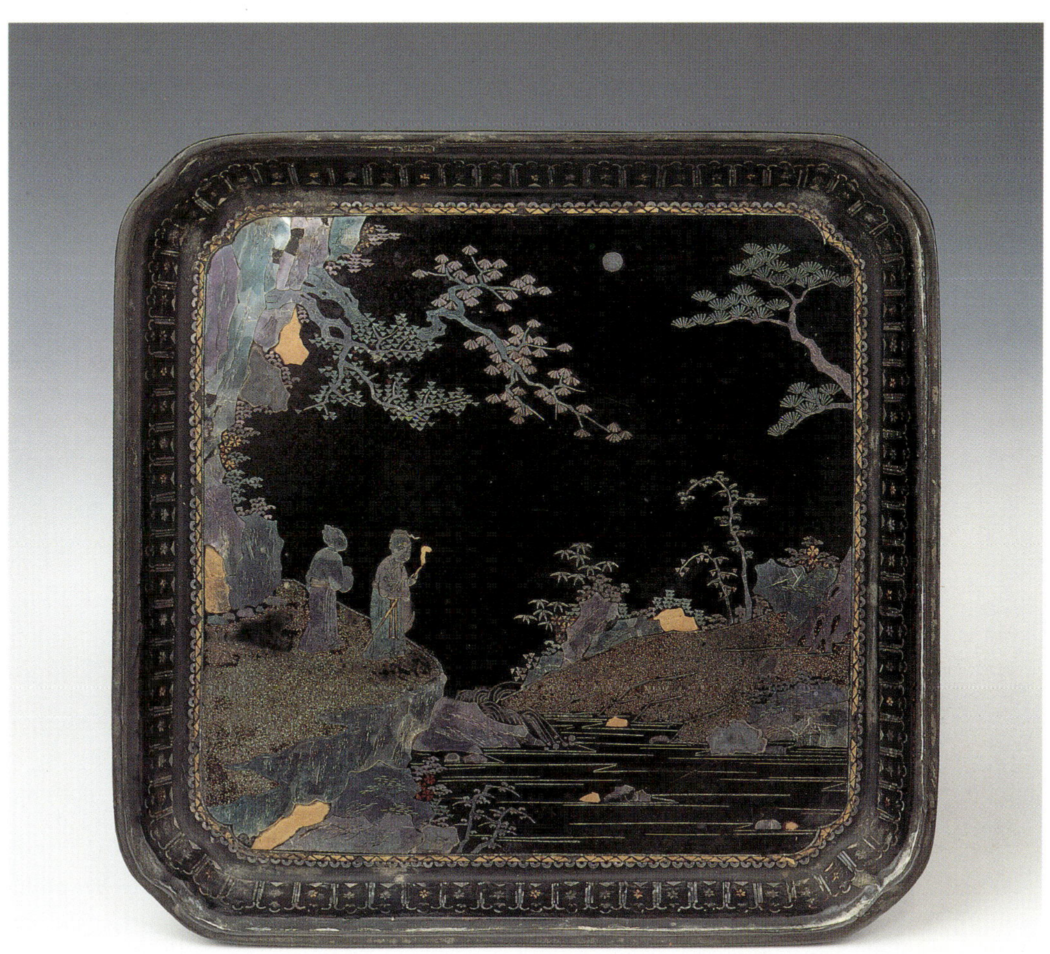

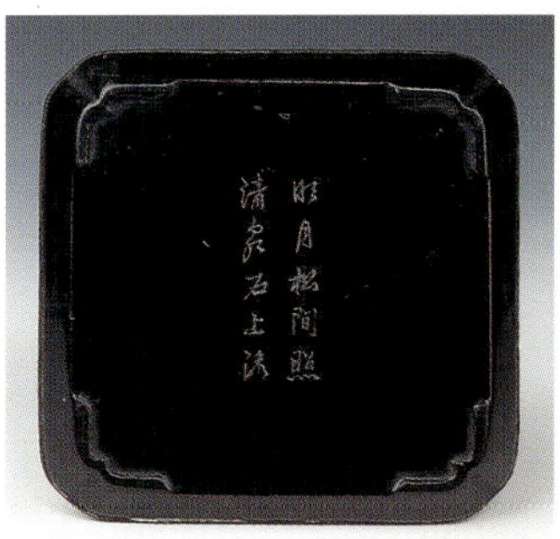

322

LAC BURGAUTE DISH WITH INLAID MOTHER-OF-PEARL AND GOLD SHEET HIGHLIGHTS IN A DESIGN OF A SCHOLAR AND AN ATTENDANT IN A LANDSCAPE

QING, KANGXI PERIOD (1662 - 1722),
BUT PROBABLY 1680-1700
LENGTH : 10.7 CM
WIDTH : 10.7 CM

A square *lac burgaute* dish with pared corners. The mother-of-pearl and gold sheet inlays depict a scholar with his attendant watching a winding stream under a rocky cliff with three protruding branches in the moon-light. The borders are decorated with diapers and the reverse has a mother-of-pearl inlay of two stanzas of a poem by the Tang poet Wang Wei.

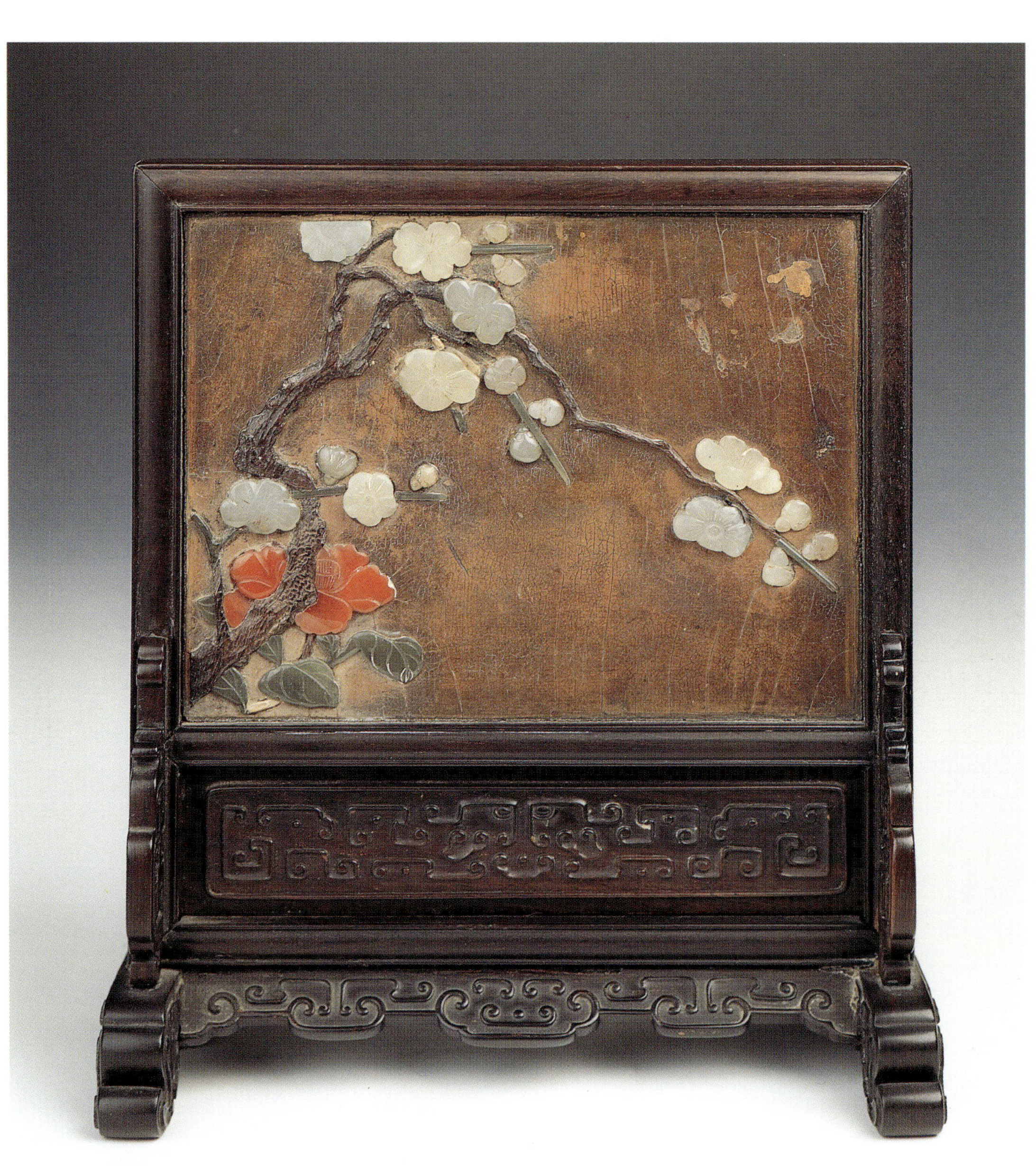

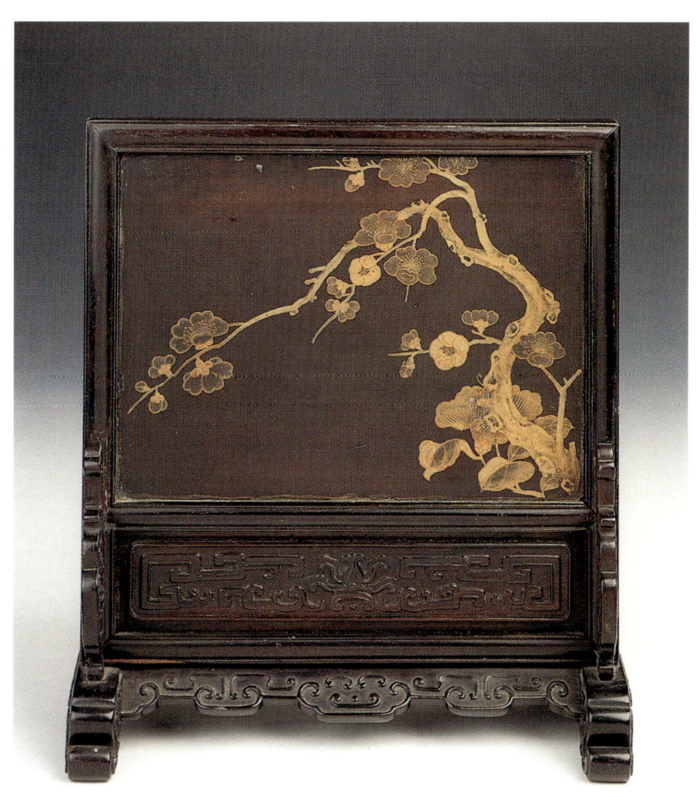

323

Lacquer plaque with inlays of jade and cornelian in carved wood table screen

17th century
Height : 24 cm
Width : 18 cm

Lacquered wood plaque mounted as a table screen with a frame and stand carved of fine blackwood, the lacquered wood with inlays of a prunus tree in various colours of jade and cornelian; the reverse with lacquered panel decorated with gold prunus spray similar to the front against a dark brown ground. The different treatment of the prunus branch on the front, where the new growth is indicated by celadon-green jade inlay, in contrast to the brown lacquer of the old growth should be noted.

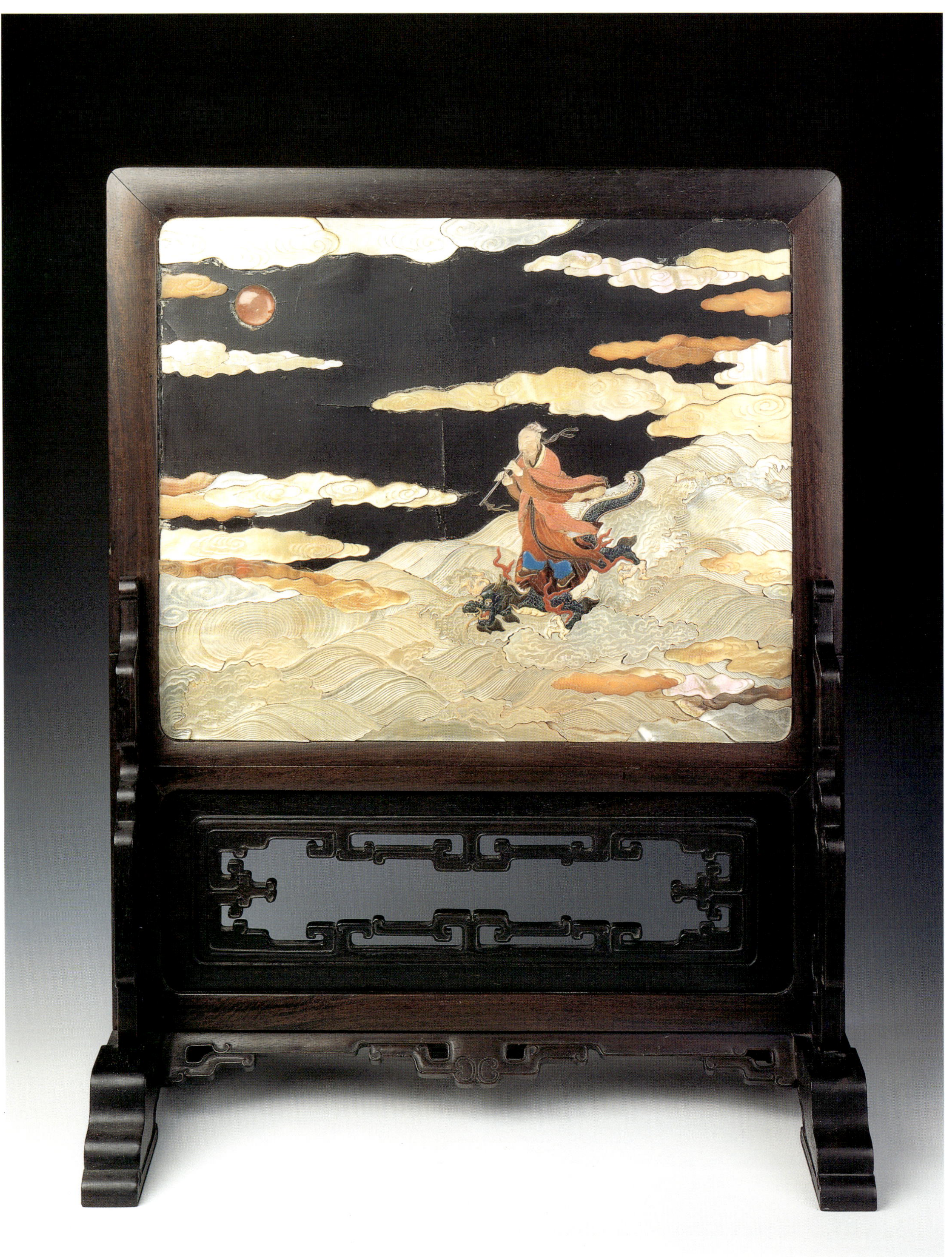

324

A BLACK LACQUER PLAQUE MOUNTED AS A SCREEN WITH MOTHER-OF-PEARL AND VARIOUS COLOURED STONE INLAYS DEPICTING AN IMMORTAL ON THE BACK OF A DRAGON CROSSING A SWIRLING OCEAN

QING
(FIRST HALF OF THE 18TH CENTURY)
HEIGHT : 44.4 CM
WIDTH : 36 CM

A black lacquer inlaid plaque mounted as a screen, one side decorated with an immortal borne on the back of a dragon, holding a flute in his hands, crossing a swirling ocean in mother-of-pearl and various coloured stone inlays. The reverse is decorated with the three friends of winter, bamboo, pine and prunus in coloured stone inlays on a black lacquer ground, the whole supported on an elaborate wood stand pierced with fretwork.

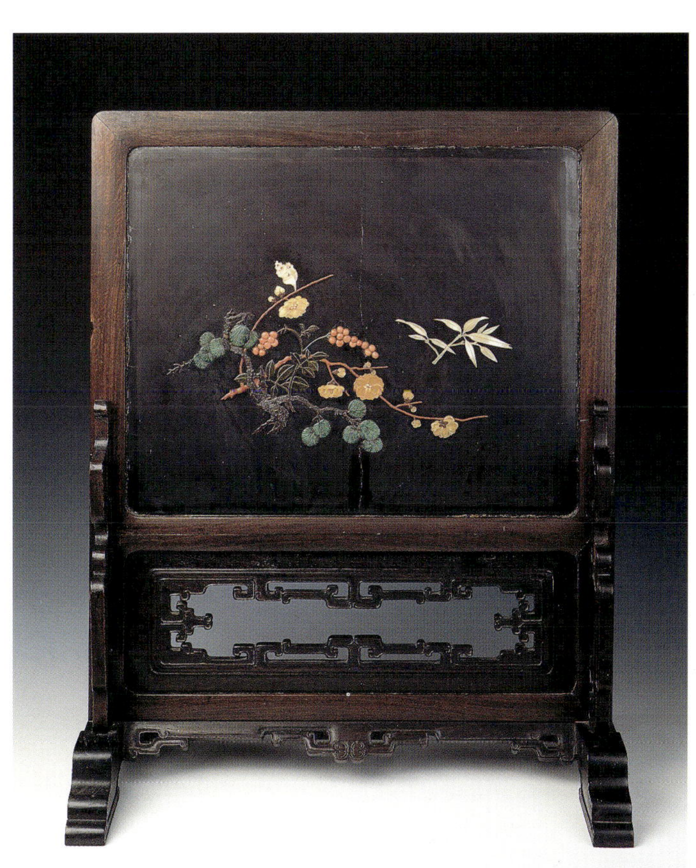

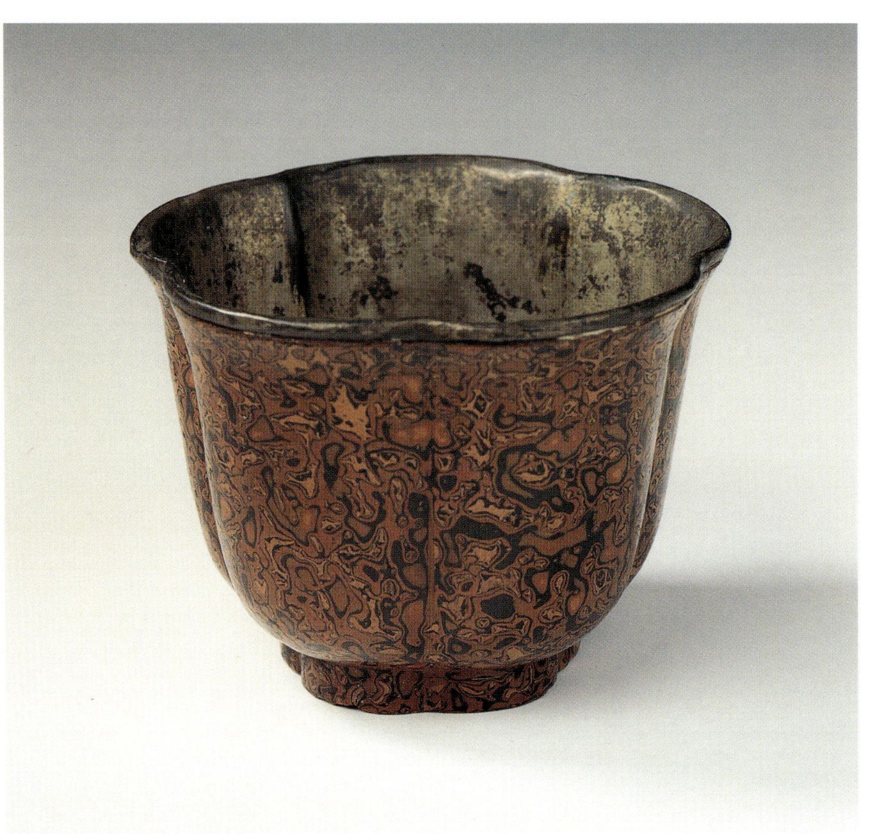

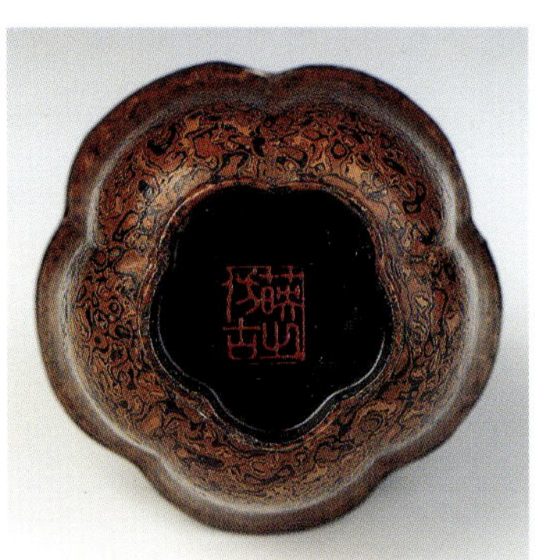

325

DEEP FIVE-LOBED MARBLED LACQUER METAL LINED CUP THE COLOURS OF THE MARBLED LACQUER BEING BLACK, YELLOW AND BRICK RED. MARK OF LU YINGZHI

QING (18TH CENTURY)
WIDTH : 8 CM
HEIGHT : 6.2 CM

Deep five-lobed cup, silvered bronze metal lined, the exterior covered with black, yellow and brick red marbled, relatively thin lacquer, the base black with a four character seal mark in red lacquer "Yingzhi fang gu" "Made by Yingzhi in imitation of the ancient" in archaic script. This mark is that normally used by the famous Yangzhou lacquerer, Lu Yingzhi.

326

Carved red lacquer box with design of horses amid waves

Qing, Qianlong mark and period (1736 - 95)
Length : 12.7 cm
Width : 12.7 cm
Height : 5.2 cm

A square red lacquer box carved all over with swirling waves and four prancing horses on the top with flames issuing from their front legs. A six character mark of Qianlong is incised and infilled with gold on the black lacquer interior. The four character mark "zema baohe" is similarly incised on the interior of the cover. This is one of a number of similarly incised lacquer objects produced to imperial order to which names were assigned by the Emperor Qianlong. He named about eighty different lacquer products.

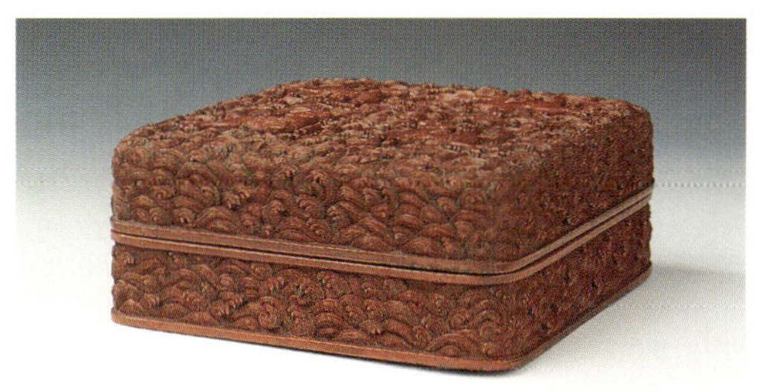

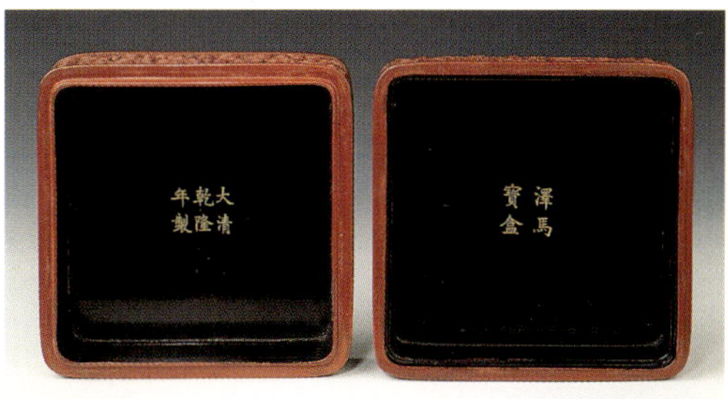

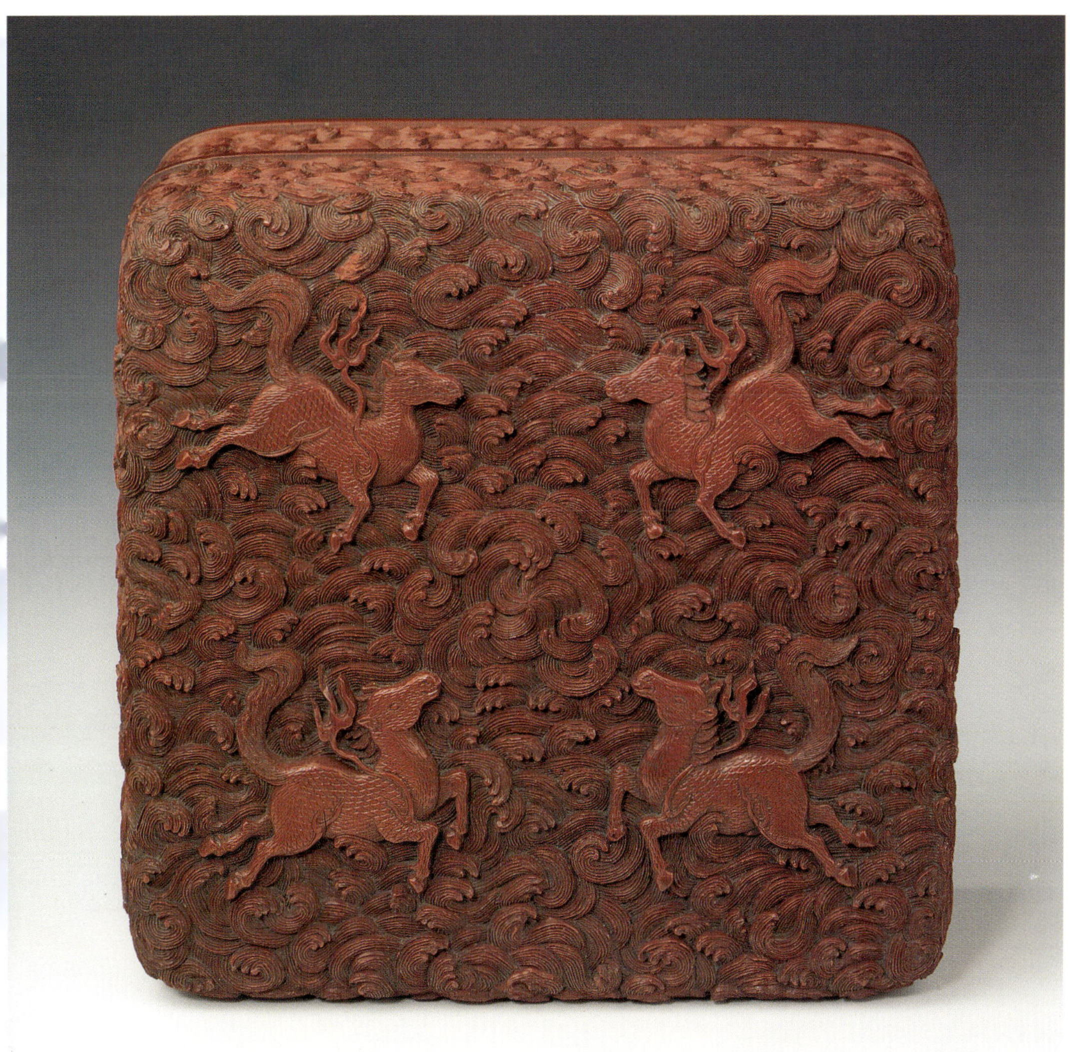

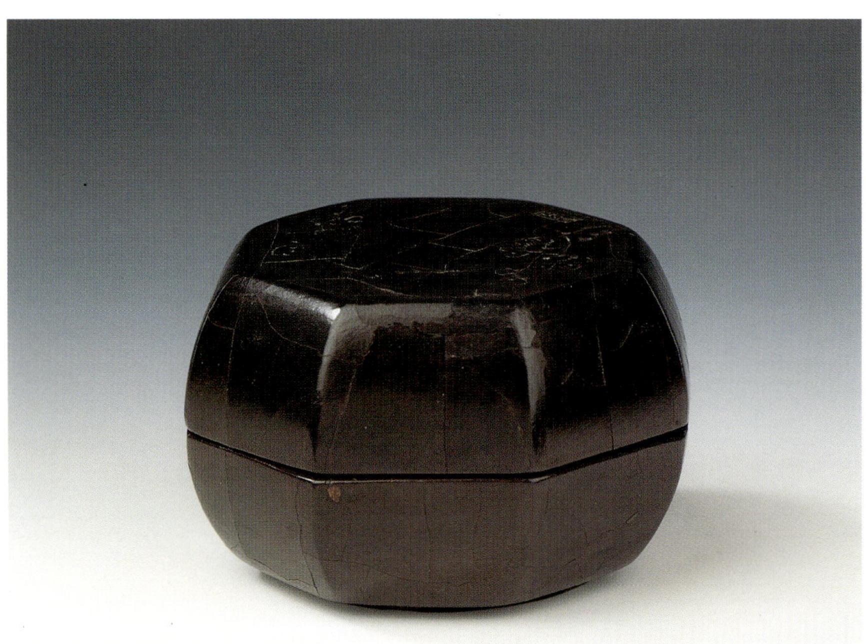

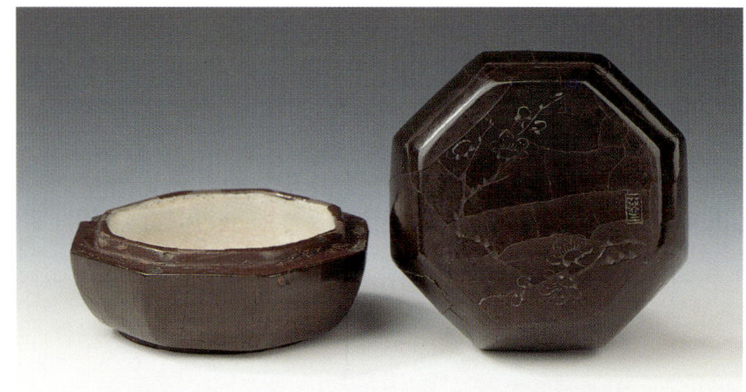

327

Yixing octagonal seal box covered with deep reddish-brown lacquer with incised prunus spray by Lu Dong (ante 1780 - *circa* 1850)

Qing dynasty
(early 19th century)
Diameter : 5 cm
Height : 3 cm

A small Yixing pottery octagonal seal box covered with deep reddish-brown lacquer. The top of the lid is incised with a prunus spray and the tiny seal mark of Lu Kuisheng (Lu Dong) (ante 1780 - *circa* 1850), the most celebrated Yangzhou lacquer artist of the early 19th century. Lu Dong was the grandson of Lu Yingzhi (see Exhibit 325). The interior and base of the Yixing pottery are covered with greyish-white enamel.

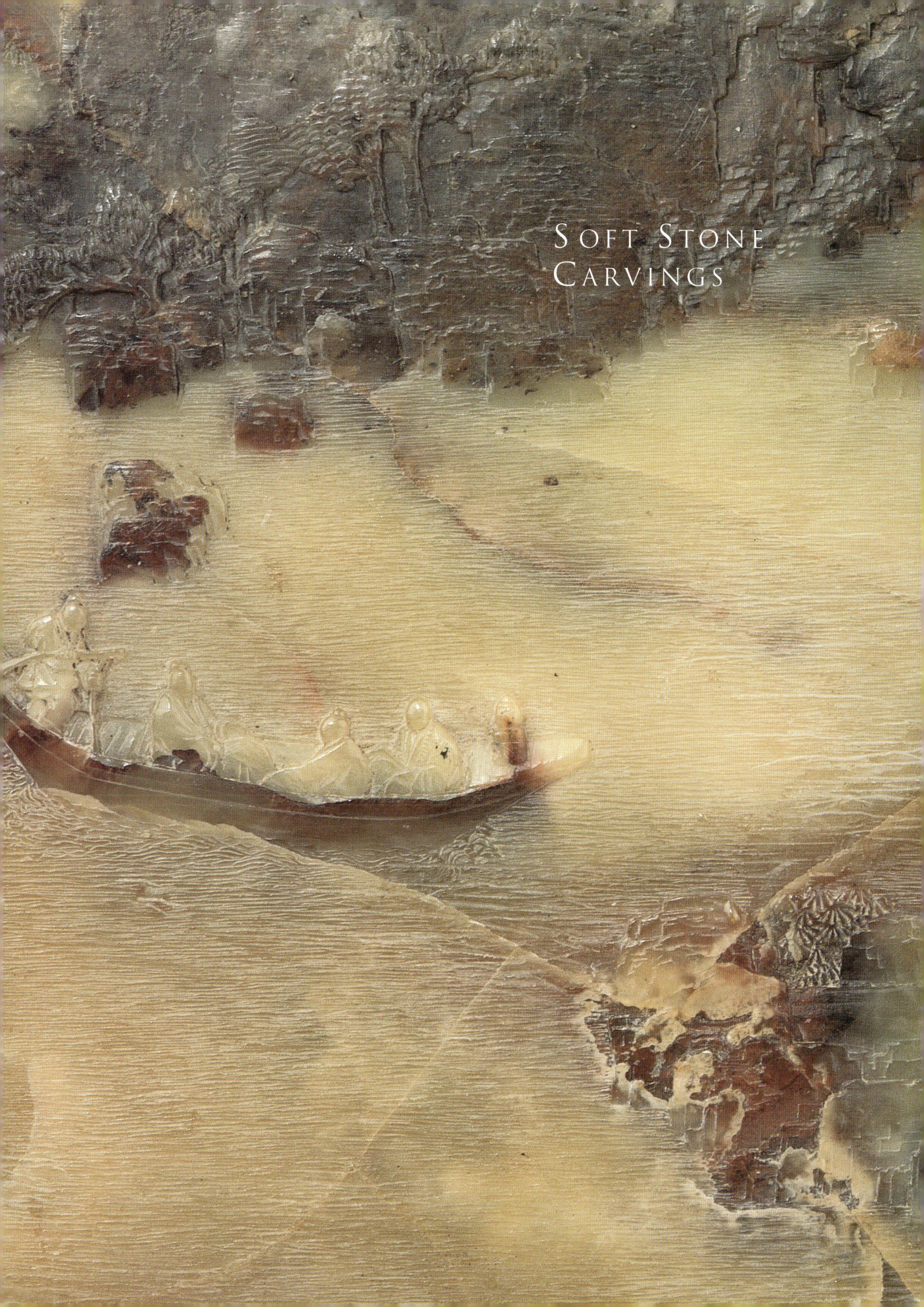

Soft Stone Carvings

Soft Stone Carving

Also included in this exhibition are a few soft stone carvings made from stones such as steatite, *tianhuang* and *Shoushan* stone ranging in date from the Six Dynasties period to the 18th century. Steatite pieces are of some rarity but the use of this stone from the Han dynasty on is well known. It was especially popular in the Tang dynasty. The three steatite pieces chosen demonstrate the wide variety of stone types involved in the steatite classification. The earliest piece (Exhibit 328) is a steatite scholar's palette in the shape of a tortoise with the carapace as the cover. Similar pieces to the present example but in pottery are known from the early Six Dynasties period. This piece with its long neck is difficult to date and I have dated it quite late in the Six Dynasties period but would not rule out an early Tang dynasty or an early Six Dynasties date. The other two examples (Exhibits 329 and 330) show two different types of steatite, which were used during the Tang period. The first is a pouring ladle with a long spout, probably derived from a metal prototype, with a dragon's head handle protrusion, which would originally have held a wooden handle. The type of steatite used here is a fine blue-grey slate-like material. Similar dragon's head handles on bronze or pottery ladles do occur from as early as the Han dynasty but the shape of the long spout and the use of steatite renders a late Six Dynasties or early Tang dating more likely. The other piece is a slightly greenish-grey circular covered ewer with hexagonal spout and circular vertical handle under a horizontal flower-shaped flange. This ewer and its cover are decorated with bunches of leaves with finely incised lines. Similar finely incised decoration has been found on parcel gilt silver of the late Tang dynasty. The hexagonal spout is also found on ceramic ewers (particularly those from the Changsha kilns) dating to the 8th and 9th centuries A.D.. The type of handle and flange found on this piece can also be paralleled in 9th century ceramics from southern kilns. A similar steatite ewer has recently been reported excavated from a late Tang site thus confirming the late Tang dating of this piece.

Tianhuang or heaven stone is a very fine soapstone of deep honey or amber colour, which in the best quality stone is quite translucent. Other commoner, similarly coloured soapstones are frequently confused with *tianhuang* but they are not translucent. *Tianhuang* has always been highly priced and I am told even before World War II used to fetch more than its weight in gold. It was particularly popular for carving into seals and other objects for the scholar's studio. The single example included in this exhibition (Exhibit 331) probably dates from the 17th century and is a typical *tianhuang* seal surmounted by a Buddhist lion and cub.

There are two *Shoushan* stone pieces, one of which is a marvellous figure in pale pink *Shoushan* stone of the finest quality, which bears the signature of Yang Yu Xuan (Exhibit 332). This famous artist, a native of Zhangpu in Fujian Province seems to have worked in the Transitional and early Kangxi periods in Fujian. Recent research dates his work to the period *circa* 1630 to *circa* 1670. The very high quality of the stone used here, the use of a cloth cap which is frequently depicted on

Chinese paintings from the mid Ming to the Transitional period, and the description of his works recorded in literary sources, with which this figure accords well, make it likely that this figure is by the master himself. The other *Shoushan* stone carving is a plaque showing an incident in the *Romance of the Three Kingdoms* which was an extremely popular subject in the late 17th and early 18th century (Exhibit 333). The piece is beautifully executed taking advantage of the colours in the stone even to the extent of the red crest on the stork in flight. This is a masterpiece by an unknown 18th century *Shoushan* stone carver.

滑石及壽山石刻等

展覽中有幾件滑石、壽山石及田黄雕刻，年代爲自六朝至十八世紀。

滑石雕刻頗爲罕有，遠在漢朝已有發現，至唐代尤爲流行。選展的三件製品顯示滑石有多種不同的種類。最早的一件（展品328）是一個硯台，形狀似龜，蓋刻成龜殼形。六朝早期的陶製龜硯便與這件相似。這件長頸龜硯的年份頗難決定，我認爲它是六朝末期的件品，但亦不排除它是早唐甚至是六朝早期所製的可能性。

其他兩件（展品329和330）滑石雕表現出不同的石質，兩者在唐代均有採用。一件是勺，有長流和突出的龍頭柄，原來可能插有木柄。形制可能是仿照金屬。這類滑石質細，呈灰藍色，看來與板石相似。類似這一帶龍頭柄的勺早在漢朝經已出現，但只有以銅或陶所製。根據長流的形狀和用滑石所製的事實，我們可以認定其年代大約是六朝晚期或唐朝早期；另一件滑石雕是圓形帶蓋壺，石色灰中泛緑，六角形流，圓垂直的柄，上覆以平放的花形唇。壺身及蓋皆飾以葉紋，上有陰刻細綫。類似的紋飾在晚唐鎏金器的局部上也可以見到，六角形的流也可以在八至九世紀的陶壺上見到（特別是長沙窑器），而花形唇和其下的柄也可以在九世紀南方窑器中找到類似的例子。據報導，類似的滑石壺最近在一個晚唐墓發現，因此，我們可以確定館藏的一件是晚唐這個時間的產品。

田黄是優質的粉石，色呈深栗黄或琥珀黄色。上等的田黄頗爲通透。其他較爲普遍而顏色相若的粉石往往與田黄相混，但主要區別是前者並不通透。收藏家對田黄珍同拱壁，據悉在第二次世界大戰以前田黄的價格比同等重量的黄金還要高。人們常以之刻成圖章及其他文房珍玩。展覽中惟一的一件田黄是一方圖章，上有佛教的子母獅紐，年代可能是十七世紀（展品331）。

展覽中有兩件壽山石刻。其一是一件鐫刻極精的人像，石質細滑，桃花紅色，上有楊玉璇款（展品332）。楊氏是活躍在明末清初至康熙間的名工，爲福建漳浦人。根據最近研究資料，他的作品年代約在自一六三〇年至一六七〇年間。觀乎石質的精美、人像的頭巾與中明至明末清初間畫作中所繪相同、文獻所載其作品風格與此件吻合，都表明此件極有可能是這位大師本人的作品無疑。另一件壽山石刻是一塊小屏，上刻三國時代的一段故事，是十七世紀末至十八世紀初流行的題材（展品333）。這一件鐫刻精美，巧妙地利用石本身的天然顏色構製圖案，甚至正在翱翔的鶴的丹頂，也是石的天然色澤，足見匠心獨運。這是一位不知其名的十八世紀壽山石工的一件傑作。

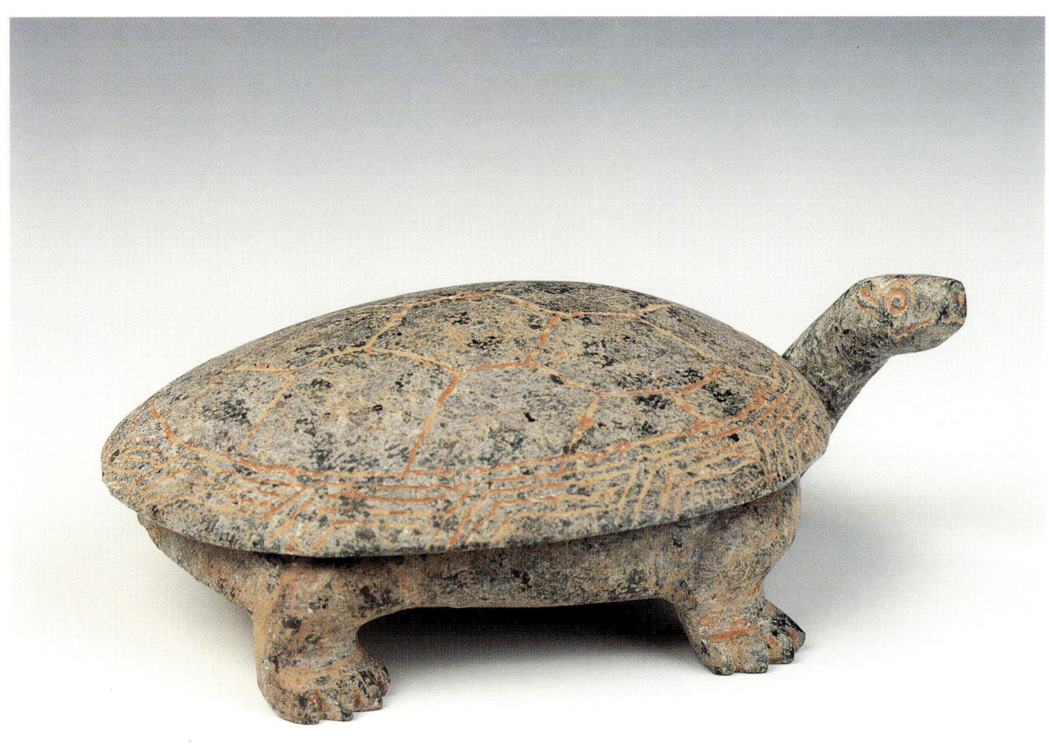

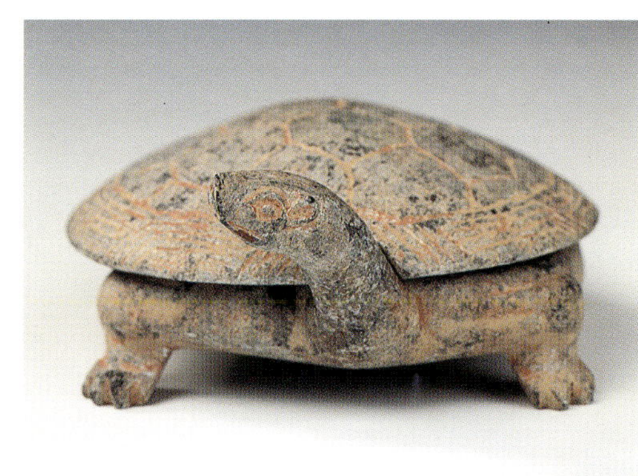

328

STEATITE COVERED INK PALETTE IN THE SHAPE OF A TORTOISE WITH CARAPACE

SIX DYNASTIES TO EARLY TANG
(7TH CENTURY OR EARLIER)
LENGTH : 13 CM
WIDTH : 10.1 CM
HEIGHT : 4.8 CM

Steatite covered ink palette in the shape of a tortoise, the carapace cover fitting neatly behind its long snake-like raised head and neck, incised to simulate the scales of the carapace, the base forming the palette shaped to hold fluid but not a separate ink stone. The tail, eyes and ears are all in relief. The whole is executed in greyish steatite with black flecks; traces of ink and cinnebar, the base with clawed feet.

329

Blue-grey steatite pouring bowl of plain circular shape with long spout of metal inspiration and dragon's head protrusion

Tang
(618 - 906) or earlier
Diameter : 11.6 cm
Length of spout : 6.5 cm
Height : 5.3 cm

Blue-grey slate-like steatite pouring bowl of plain circular shape with a long angular spout of typical metal shape. At right angles to the spout is a dragon's head extending 3.8 cm from the body, which probably originally held a wooden handle extension.

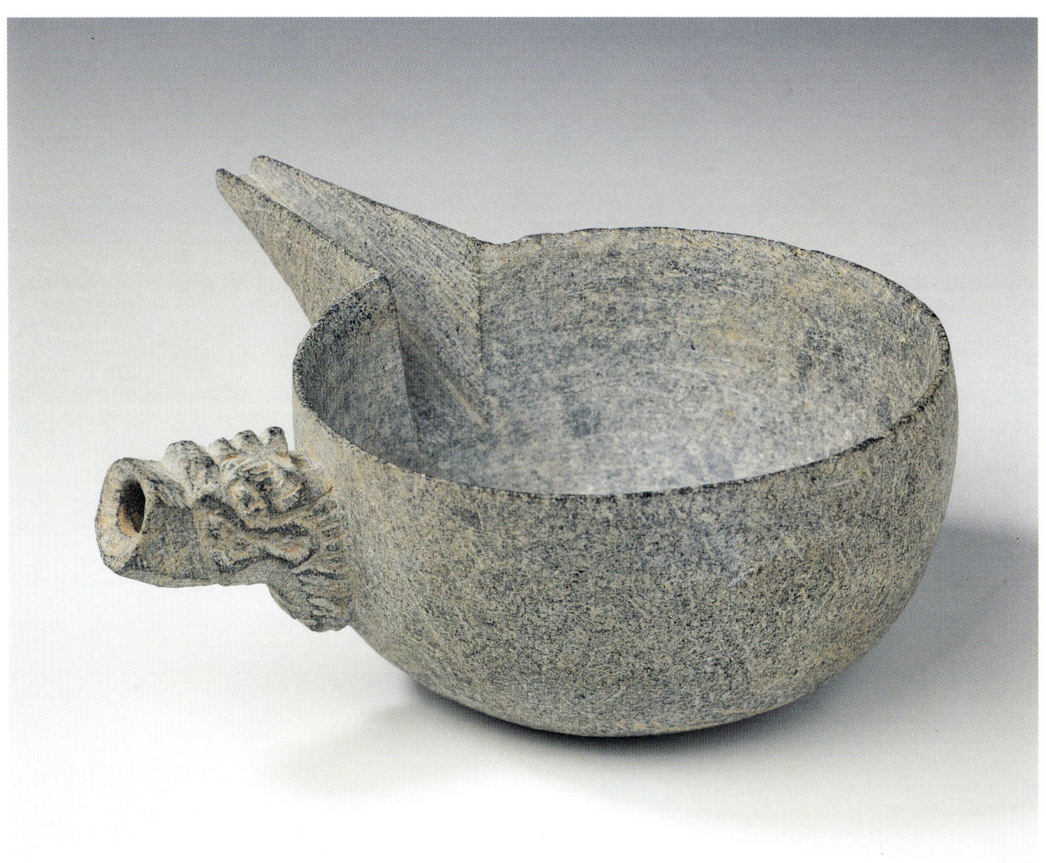

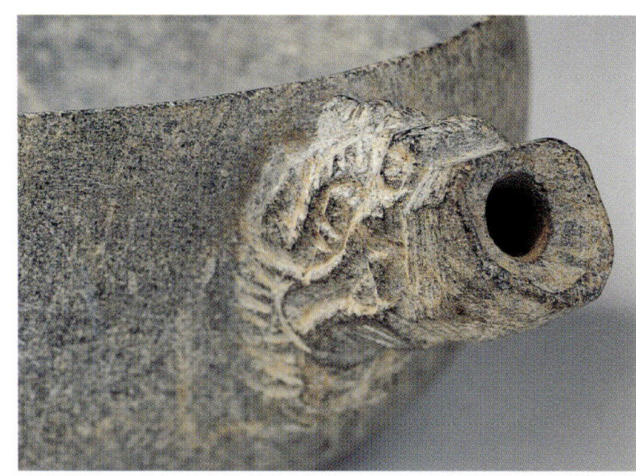

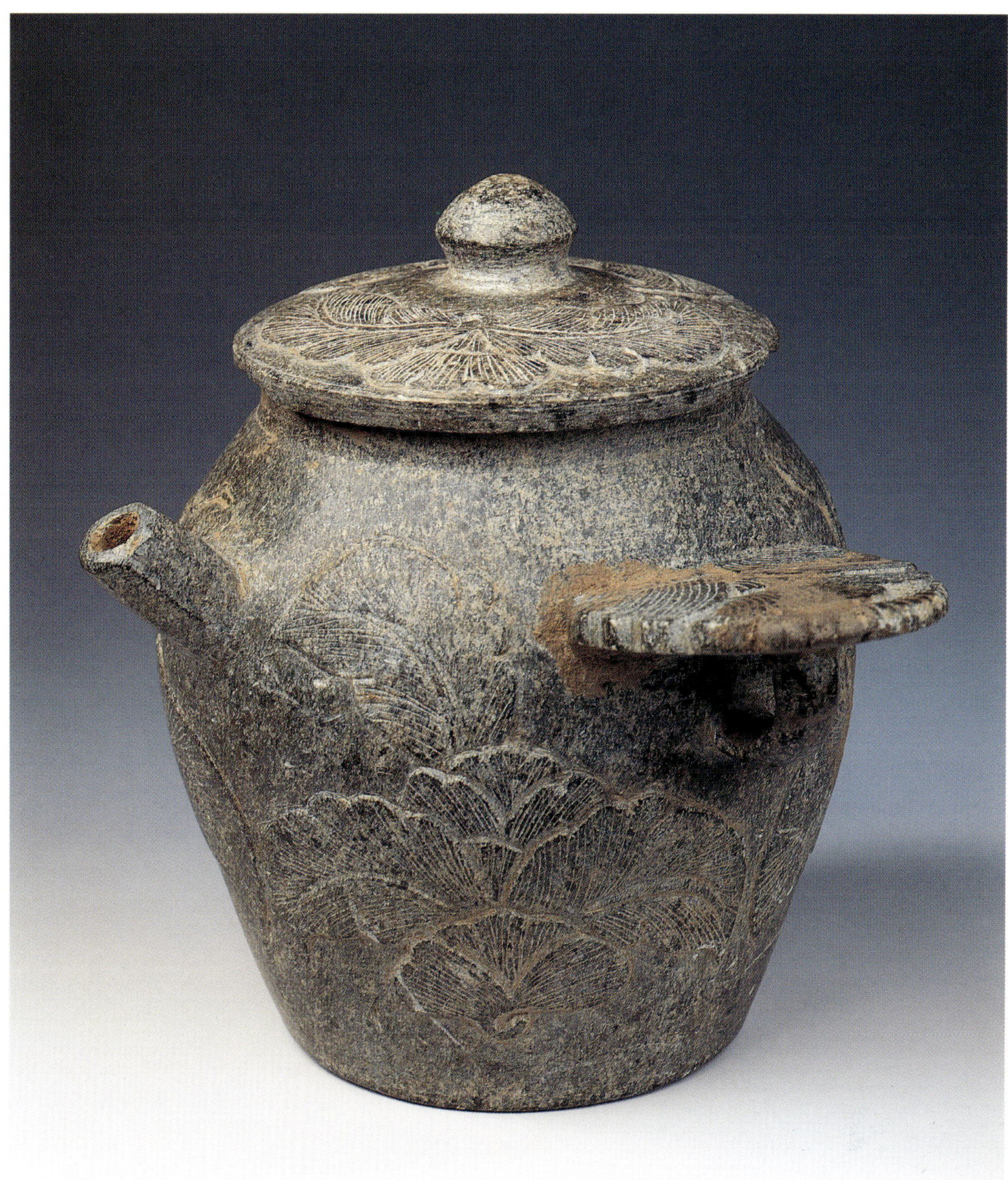

330

A STEATITE EWER AND COVER OF GREENISH-GREY COLOURED MICA-FLECKED STONE WITH SHORT HEXAGONAL SPOUT AND FLANGE COVERED HANDLE WITH INCISED CABBAGE-LIKE LEAVES IN RELIEF ON BOTH EWER AND COVER

LATE TANG
(9TH CENTURY)
HEIGHT : 18.5 CM
DIAMETER OF COVER : 10.6 CM

Steatite ewer and cover of greenish-grey coloured mica-flecked stone, the stubby 1.7 cm octagonal spout reminiscent of Changsha ewers, a flange 6.5 cm wide at 90° angle to the spout protrudes 5.8 cm from the body. The horizontal incised flange is decorated as a flower, with a vertical ring underneath. The wide mouth is 9.6 cm in diameter with an everted rim; the base solid without a footrim, the body decorated with three large and one small group of cabbage-like leaves in relief with many fine line incisions similar to the decorations found on late Tang to early Northern Song parcel-gilt silver; the cover with a circular somewhat pyramid-like knob also decorated in relief with two similar floral sprays with many fine lined incisions. A similar covered ewer has been excavated from a 9th century Tang tomb.

331

TIANHUANG SQUARE SEAL WITH BUDDHIST LION AND CUB FINIAL

PROBABLY FIRST HALF OF THE 17TH CENTURY
HEIGHT : 4.5 CM
WIDTH : 3.5 CM

Tianhuang square seal of pleasant honey-amber colour, the base carved with a four character seal, surmounted by a Buddhist lion with a cub on its back in Ming style.

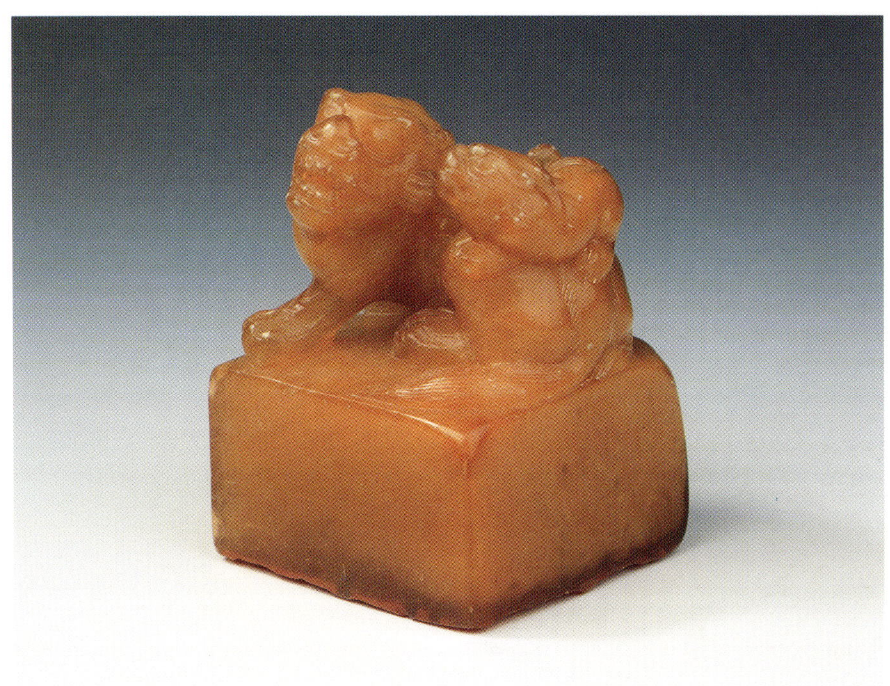

▶ ## 332

PINK SOAPSTONE FIGURE OF DONGFANG ZHUO BY YANG YUXUAN

LATE MING DYNASTY TO EARLY KANGXI PERIOD
(1630 - 1680)
HEIGHT : 11 CM
WIDTH : 7.5 CM

A pink soapstone seated smiling figure of Dongfang Zhuo with one hand holding a peach and wearing a cloth covering on his topknot. The face, beard and borders of the robes are intricately incised. The signature of Yang Yuxuan is subtly incised on the rock seat.

Yang was a native of Zhangpu in Fujian Province, but resided in the provincial capital, Fuzhou. The *District Gazetteer* of the Zhangpu area compiled in the Kangxi period described him as "a capable carver of Shoushan stone (soapstone), all his figures, birds and animals and his vessels are exquisite in the extreme". Recent research has discovered that Yang began work at some time in the late Ming dynasty and worked into the Kangxi period. The cloth covering on the topknot is a feature commonly found on figures of the late Ming period.

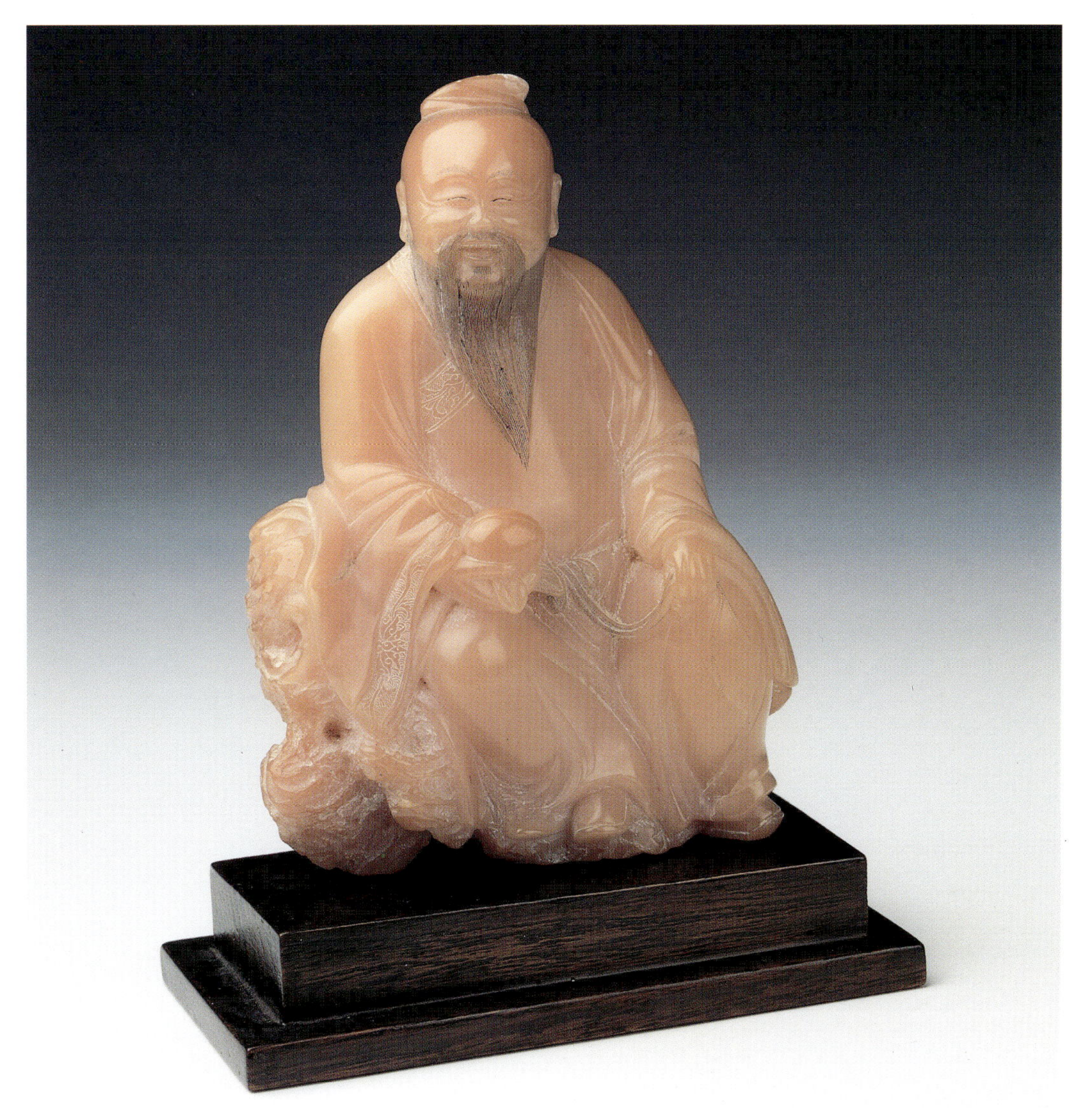

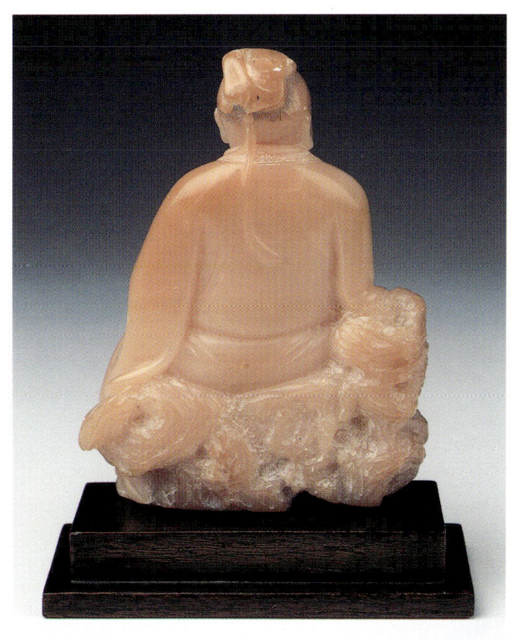

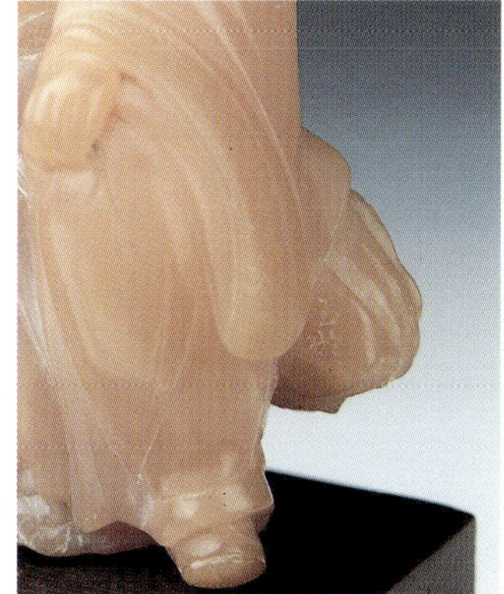

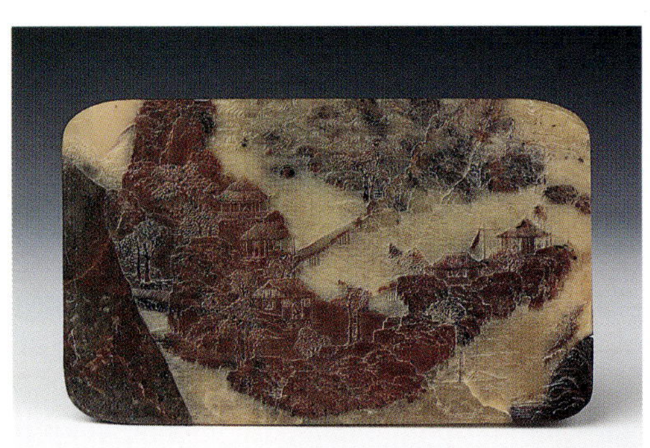

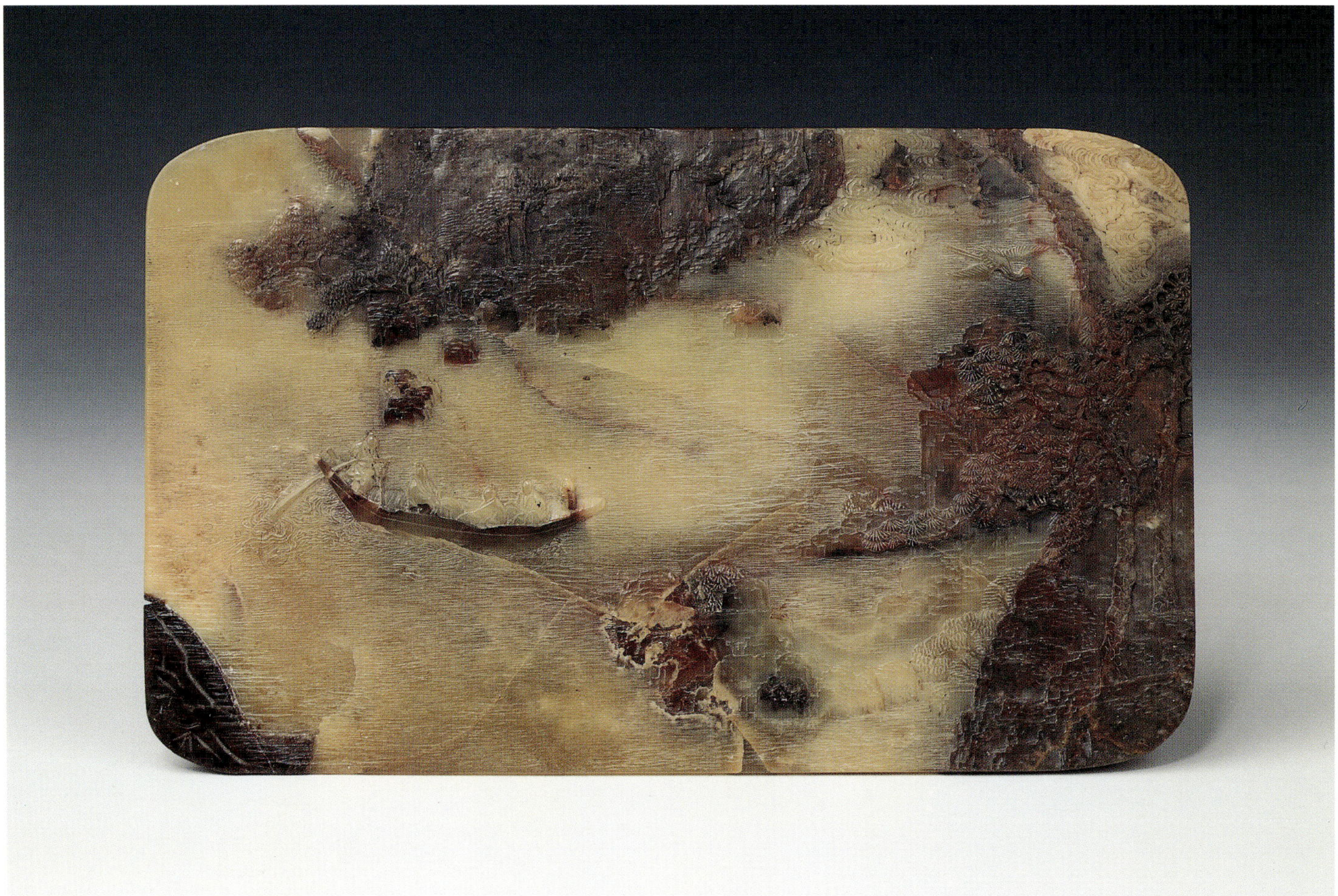

333

Soapstone plaque carved with historical and landscape scenes

Mid 18th century
Length : 14.2 cm
Width : 8.6 cm

A soapstone rectangular plaque of yellowish-green colour with extensive red and grey suffusions, carved on one side with a sampan with four occupants near pine clad cliffs with a crane and clouds above, depicting the well-known Song poet Su Shi boating under the Red Cliffs with his scholarly companions. The back is carved with a landscape scene of hills, trees, pavilions and a bridge.

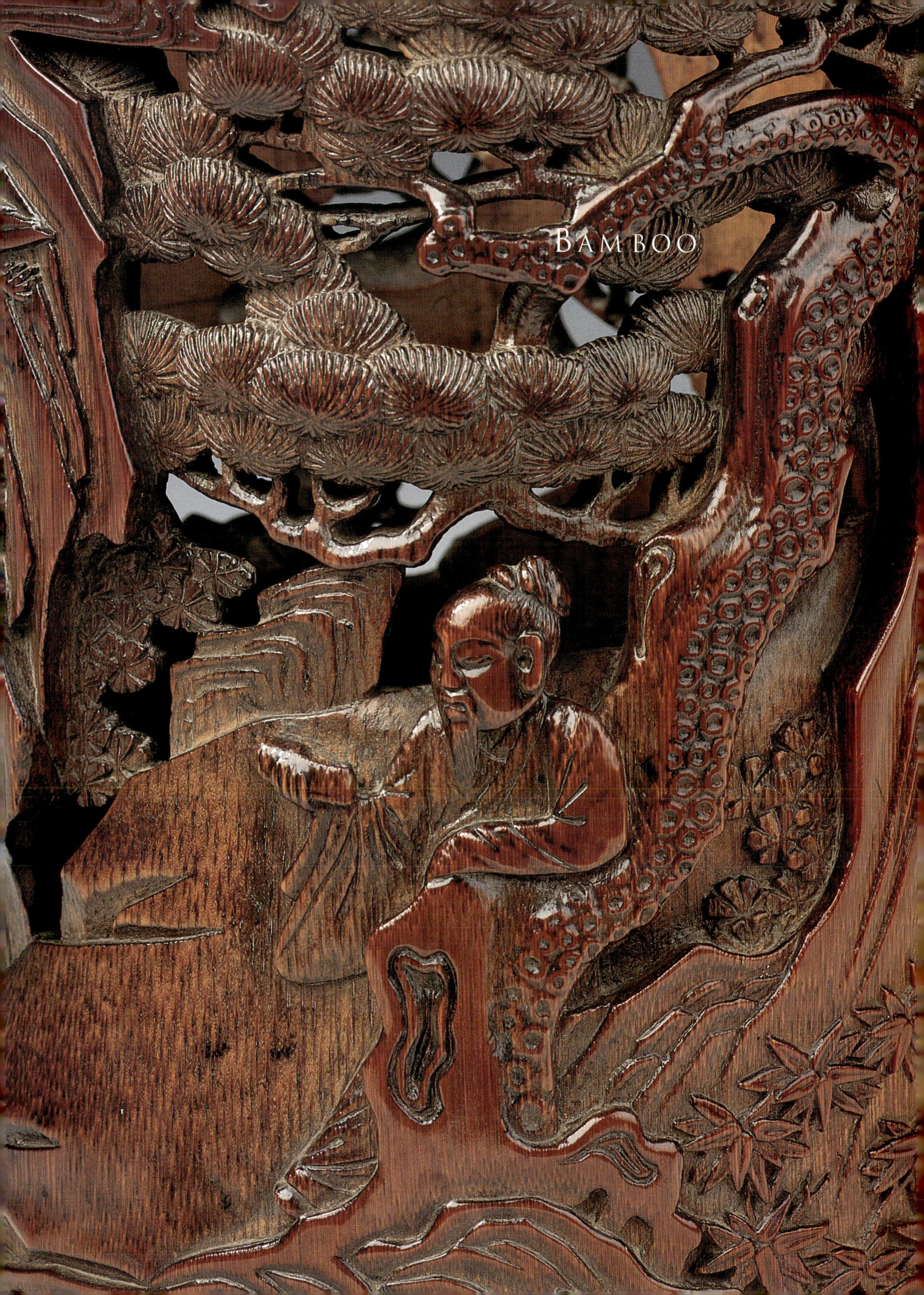

BAMBOO

Bamboo

Bamboo has been used extensively since the beginning of Chinese civilization and archaeological excavations of the past forty years have discovered that it was used in numerous interesting ways. Its use as a base material for lacquer vessels has also been known for many years. One of the more interesting archaeological discoveries of recent years, in so far as bamboo is concerned, is the discovery of bundles of bamboo strips with writing on them, in tombs dating from the Warring States period, which were the books of the time.

It was not, however, until scholars adopted this homely material sometime in the mid 16th century as suitable for use in their studios, that bamboo carving developed into a significant art form. Art historians and collectors outside China did not devote much attention to bamboo carving until about 1970 when it became the subject of serious study and collecting on a major scale, chiefly by Hong Kong collectors. The bamboo carvings in the collection of The Museum of East Asian Art, mainly collected in Hongkong in the early 1970s, despite being few in number, form a fine representative collection with excellent and important examples of most of the main categories.

Bamboo belongs to a group of perennial grasses, most of which have tall jointed stems or culms. The joints are marked internally by strong diaphrams and the internodes between the diaphrams are hollow. When it emerges from the ground, the bamboo is almost solid and the nature of bamboo, with its solid buds and hollow stems, dictates very largely the basic types of bamboo carving. Bamboo has to be stored in a fairly humid atmosphere since if conditions are too dry, the bamboo, other than the root section, has a tendency to crack.

The root, which consists of a solid section, often with gnarled or tendril-like protrusions such as on Exhibit 338, is used for making figurines, animals and landscapes, brush rests, seals and other solid objects, but the hollow stems are normally used for cylindrical forms such as brush pots, perfume holders and the like, with wrist or arm rests being made from vertical segments taken from the internodal sections.

Almost the entire output of the artist carvers and the commercial workshops that followed them, was confined to items suitable for the scholar and his pursuits and for the furnishing of scholars' studios – brush pots of various sizes, perfume and incense stick holders and other cylindrical containers, wrist and arm rests, brush rests, paper weights, boxes, sculptures of figures and animals, botanical subjects, miniature landscapes and mountains and objects such as *ruyi* sceptres, seals, drinking cups and fan frames. Fan frames made of bamboo became common in the late 19th and early 20th centuries.

Bamboo carvings are in many cases signed by the carver of the piece, and on some pieces, particularly in the 20th century, the designer's name is also mentioned. It is only rarely that pieces of Chinese decorative art are signed by the artist concerned and bamboo carvings are unusual in this respect. Four of the bamboo carvings included in this exhibition are signed examples by Shen Dasheng, Zhu Zhizheng, Pu Cheng and Wu Zhifan, some of the greatest Chinese bamboo carvers of all time

(Exhibits 334, 336, 337 and 339). The problem with signed pieces is deciding whether the signature is contemporary or a later addition. However, all these examples are of excellent quality and in the known styles of the artists concerned and are almost certainly true works of these masters. Exhibit 346, which is a fine representative example of its type, is also signed, but the signature is probably a later addition.

By far the most common use of carved bamboo before the mid 19th century was for carved brush pots of various sizes, perfume and incense stick holders and other cylindrical containers. These are found in all the various carving techniques that were employed from the mid 16th century on.

Before actually carving the bamboo, a considerable period is spent in preparation; it has to be boiled for half an hour and then left to dry for at least two years. The thin outer layer of soft material is generally scraped off with a knife or a piece of glass, save in the case of the *liuqing* technique of carving where the skin itself, which dries to a much lighter colour, is left in relief and carved to provide the decoration.Where the *liuqing* technique is not used after scraping, the inner bamboo is carved to create the desired pattern, such as on Exhibit 336.

The *liuqing* technique does not seem to have been employed until the late 17th century, and until the 20th century does not seem to have been common. In the 20th century, however, most of the finest pieces produced used this technique. Indeed I think it would be true to say that the finest work ever in the *liuqing* technique dates from the 20th century when such artists as Sheng Bingyun and Xu Subai produced outstanding works frequently done using designs by well known 20th century painters such as Tang Yun and Wu Hufan. Excellent work continues in this technique by such carvers as Xu Bingfang and Fan Yaoquig even to this day. Exhibit 346 is a box in *liuqing* technique from the early 18th century.

Another technique used is called *zhuhuang* where thin layers of bamboo skin are cut to form the design, and the designs so cut are then stuck onto a wooden (usually box wood) base as a veneer. Because of the delicacy of the veneer, few pieces in this technique have survived in reasonable condition. I am told that this technique was very much a palace product and was never the subject of commercial production. This technique was popular for only a limited time span from the late Qianlong period to about the end of Daoguang's region, in other words from about 1780 to 1850. A good example of this technqiue in the museum's collection is the *ruyi* sceptre Exhibit 347.

The earliest technique employed in the carving of bamboo by 16th and 17th century carvers, however, involved high relief work using the natural cylindrical shape of the bamboo. By far the most popular design was of a pine tree or section thereof, such as Exhibit 335, sometimes with figures or animals such as a scholar or deer in a landscape setting. Many of the designs used seem to have been inspired by the woodblock illustrations in printed books of the late Ming dynasty, and it is interesting to note that the designs chosen follow quite closely those found on rhinoceros horn cups of the same period which no doubt drew their inspiration from the same source (e.g. Exhibit 342). Indeed the close similarity in the designs on bamboo and rhinoceros horn cups extends throughout the 17th century.

The containers of the first half of the 17th century seem to have the flakes of the pine bark individually carved . By the second half of the 17th century, these seem to have been substituted by punched circles on the tree trunk of the pine (see Exhibit 344). The earlier brush pots generally follow the naturalistic and somewhat irregular form of the pine tree rather than the artificial and regular circle of the bamboo (Exhibit 335). This early group also has a rather greyish-brown colour.

In the second half of the 17th century, the cylindrical shape was maintained, but the greyish-brown colour of the early pieces ceased and a beautiful dark honey-coloured patina became the most common colour for bamboo carvings. Exhibit 336 which is signed by Zhu Zhizheng alias Zhu Sansong, and cyclically dated 1662, is an excellent example of such patina. Even the best of modern copies never seem to have the same lovely patina. Whilst late Ming pieces do exist with reticulated decoration (i.e. carved-through decoration), particularly in the case of perfume holders (Exhibit 336), it was not until the second half of the 17th century that reticulated brush pots became common (Exhibit 344). The carving of these was normally in high relief with excellent modelling.

In the second half of the 17th century, several new techniques seem to have become popular. The first was low relief carving. In some cases, the artist artifically made the bamboo swell into the pattern desired by the application of water. The inventor of this technique was the famous carver Pu Yang alias Pu Cheng born in 1582. A brush pot by this carver is included in the exhibition (Exhibit 337). He is regarded as the founder of the Jinling school and was still alive in the early Qing. Sometimes the low relief technique was enhanced by the carving away of the background, which was left plain, so that the low relief almost appears to be high relief. One of the masters of this technique was Wu Zhifan, a nativeof Jiading, Jiangsu, who was active in the Kangxi period (1662 - 1722). Exhibit 339 cyclically dated 1672 is an excellent example of his work.

Many of the early brush pots have three small legs as integral parts of the bamboo (Exhibit 337). Perfume holders were almost always bound top and bottom with fittings of ivory, horn or wood (Exhibit 336). This fashion was extended to brush pots towards the end of the 17th century. Many of the brush holders have over the years lost their diaphram bases and new bases have frequently been added later. However, some pieces, from the early 18th century on have always had different bases from the original diaphram which was discarded right from day one.

In the late 17th century, carving of figures and animals, water containers, cups, seals etc. became common. These all involved the use of the root section. The items in question were all for furnishing of scholars' studios. The cups frequently follow the shape and, in some cases, even the designs found on contemporary rhinoceros horn cups (see Exhibit 342). The nodules from which the roots grow are frequently left as a decorative feature as they provide an attractive colour contrast when polished (Exhibit 338). Several excellent examples of animals and figural root carvings in the museum's collection are included in this exhibition (Exhibits 334, 338, 340, 341 and 343). In the early 18th century, bamboo carvings of fruit and vegetables became popular and continued to be fashionable throughout the century.

All the techniques introduced in the 17th century continued into the 18th and early 19th centuries. However, there was a preference after the 17th century for carving in low relief and most of the high relief carvings from this time proclaim their relatively late date by the bindings in ivory, horn or wood.

There was also a tendency in the late 18th and increasingly in the 19th and 20th centuries to include long inscriptions on the pieces and indeed in the 19th and early 20th centuries, the sole form of decoration was quite often calligraphy and ancient scripts such as those found on oracle bones and bronze vessels. Many of the brush pots in the 19th century were also moulded into exotic shapes and rare types of bamboo such as squared bamboo or spotted bamboo were sometimes used. Fine work, however, was done in the early 19th century in this field.

For a short time in the period of Qianlong, some vessels were carved in the shape of archaic bronze vessels. Few examples of this group exist and none in the museum's collection.

The most famous bamboo carving in the collection is the brush rest formed by a group of frogs, one with a movable tongue, dated 1623, by Shen Dasheng, a famous late Ming carver. It has been included in several exhibitions and publications of bamboo carvings in the past (Exhibit 334). The perfume holder by Zhu Zhizheng (Exhibit 336) and the brush pots by Wu Zhifan and Pu Cheng (Exhibits 339 and 337) have also been previously published and are important examples included in the exhibition.

竹刻

中國有史以來便已普遍使用竹。根據過去四十年的考古成果我們發現竹有很多有趣的用途。用竹作爲漆器的胎身早已爲人所知。近年考古工作其中一個有趣的發現便是在戰國墓中出土了一束束寫上文字的竹條，這些竹簡相當於當時的書籍。

竹藝發展成爲一種重要的藝術形式是十六世紀中期的事。當時的仕人採用這種質樸的材料，放置在書齋之內。約在一九七〇年以前，中國以外的藝術史家和收藏家們對竹刻不大注意。自從香港收藏家大力搜羅之後，人們始對竹刻進行認真的研究。東亞藝術博物館的竹刻大部份是一九七〇年代早期在香港收集的，數量雖然不多，但主要類型已然齊備，而且精良重要，可說頗具代表性。

竹屬於多年生草本植物，中空有節，節間有韌膜，其間空洞。近地處實心。竹的空心節和實心芽決定了竹刻的基本類型。竹須存放在濕度稍高的環境中，這是因爲乾燥的環境會令中空的竹節部份裂開。實心的竹根部份則較少有裂開的情況。

竹根的實心的部份，往往帶瘿瘤或卷鬚狀的枝根，如展品338，可雕作人像、動物、山水擺設、筆架、印章及其他實心物件。空心節部則一般做成筒狀物如筆筒、香薰之類，而節與節之間的垂直部份可剖作臂擱之用。

竹雕藝術家和對其起推動作用的商業作坊所生產的竹刻製品絕大部份是適應仕人和他們的學業，裝飾他們的書房，如大大小小的筆筒、香薰和其他圓筒狀的盛器、臂擱、筆架、紙鎮、盒、人像和動物、植物形器物、小型山水擺設、如意、印章、杯和扇骨。扇骨在十九世紀末和二十世紀初頗爲流行。

長時間以來，雕竹的人會在作品上刻上自己的名字。在二十世紀，有些作品甚至會刻上設計人的名字。在中國裝飾藝術品上署款的例子不多，所以在這方面來說，竹刻上加款是頗爲不尋常的事。在這次展覽中的竹刻，其中有四件具款，它們是沈大生、朱稚征、濮澄和吳之璠，這幾位全是竹刻史上出類拔萃的人物（展品334、336、337、339）。具款竹雕的最大問題是如何分辨簽款是與竹雕本身同時抑或爲後來所加。然而，這幾件都是精品，具有該等竹刻家的典型風格，可以肯定是原作無疑。展品346具有該類的典型風格，具款，但款字可能是後人所加。

在十九世紀中葉以前最流行的竹刻可算是大大小小的筆筒、香薰和其他的直筒形盛器。在其之上可見各種不同的技法，而這些技法是自十六世紀中期開始採用。

在雕竹之前需一段頗長的日子進行準備：先是把竹泡煮半小時，待乾，這個程序至少要兩年時間。竹的薄薄表層通常用刀或玻璃片刮去，以便雕鏤。運用「留青」技法的竹刻則保留竹的表層，待乾至頗淡的色澤，匠人把擬刻的花紋刻上，去地使花紋呈淺浮雕狀。如果不採用留青法，那麼匠人則在刮去表層後在竹上進行雕鏤所擬刻的紋飾，就像展品336一樣。

留青法在十七世紀末才開始採用，但一直不大流行，直至二十世紀方始普遍，這時期有不少佳作都是採用這種技法。我認爲最好的留青作品都產於二十世紀，殆非虛語。當時竹藝家如盛丙云和徐素白，配上二十世紀名畫家唐雲和吳湖帆的畫作，創製出極爲上乘的作品。繼承這種風格的匠人有徐秉方和范遥青，時至今日仍在生產優秀的作品。展品346是用留青技法刻成的一個十八世紀早期的竹盒。

另一種技法叫做竹篁。其法是把竹的薄片切成圖案，之後把該圖案黏貼在木胎上，（木胎通常用黃楊木造成）。由於這些竹篁非常纖細，所以存世作品多剥落不全，因而極爲難得。據說用這技法製作的作品多屬宮廷所造，而非商業製製品。流行時期極短，僅自乾隆晚期至道光末，即公元一七八〇年至一八五〇年一段時間。館藏展品347的如意便是一精美之作。

十六和十七世紀竹刻家所運用最早的技法是高浮雕，利用竹本身自然的圓筒形。最常見的紋飾是松樹或是其中一段，如展品335，或刻上人物如名人高士或動物，如鹿，而背景則爲山水。大多數紋飾的靈感似乎都來自晚明時木板書籍插圖。值得一提的是這一類圖案與同時代的犀角杯上所刻的圖案非常接近。毫無疑問，後者的靈感也是來自同一出處，參見展品342。竹刻與犀角雕的風格酷似，這現象在十七世紀一直存在。

十七世紀前半葉的盛器上的松樹鱗片是一片一片地刻成。到了十七世紀下半葉，這些片狀鱗紋已爲圓圈所取代（參看展品344）。早期的筆筒通常仿效天然略不規則的松樹造型，而非造作和規整的圓筒狀，一如展品335。這一組早期竹刻都呈灰暗的棕褐色。

在十七世紀下半葉，直筒形繼續流行，而早期灰暗的棕褐色則不復見，當時最常見的竹色是一種美麗的深栗黃色。展品336的簽款是朱稚征。朱稚征又名朱三松。這件帶干支紀年款，相當於公元一六六二年，是這種栗黃色皮殼的最佳樣本。甚至當今最好的仿品也難以造出同樣可愛的皮殼。鏤空的技法在晚明已經出現，特別是應用在香薰之上（展品336）。直至十七世紀下半葉，鏤空筆筒方始流行（展品344）。這些竹刻一般都是高浮雕，刻工精細。

在十七世紀下半葉，似乎有幾種新技巧開始流行。最初流行的是淺浮雕。這類雕刻中有部份是用水使竹膨脹，並使之在模中形成紋飾。發明這技法的竹藝家是有名的濮陽，又叫濮澄。濮氏生於公元一五八二年，在這次展覽中有他的一件作品（展品337）。人們尊他爲金陵派的創始者，清初時尚在。製作淺浮雕作品的另一種方法是去地，竹地不加雕飾，所以淺浮雕看來便像高浮雕一樣。擅長這種技法的竹刻家有吴之璠，江蘇嘉定人，活躍於康熙時期（公元一六六二至一七二二年）。展品339是吴氏的一件佳作，上有紀年款，相當於公元一六七二年。

大部份的竹刻筆筒都帶有三個小足，與筆筒本身一併刻成（展品337）。香薰的頂部和底部則往往配上用其他質料如象牙、牛角或木製成的蓋和座（展品336）。十七世紀末期的竹刻筆筒亦趨於流行這種工藝。有很多竹筆筒因年代久遠而致使底部的隔膜殘缺，所以往往會加上其他質料的底以取代原來的底部。有些十八世紀早期的筆筒常常配有不同的底，因爲自製作之初，竹節間的隔膜已經棄去不用。

十七世紀末，竹刻人像、動物、水丞、杯、印，開始流行。這些器物都是用竹根部份製成，藉供書齋所用。杯的造型甚至圖案都仿效同時期的犀角杯（展品342）。竹根伸出部份的結節經打磨後所呈現的顏色，與原來的竹色形成美麗的對比，所以竹刻家往往利用這些結節作爲裝飾（展品338）。館藏之中有好幾件精美的竹根動物和人像在這次展覽中展出（參見展品334、338、340、341和343）。自十八世紀初開始，竹刻蔬果流行，持續整個世紀而不衰。

自十七世紀肇始的所有技法經十八世紀至十九世紀早期還一直沿用。但十九世紀初趨於流行淺浮雕。即使是高浮雕的作品也可以根據其上所鑲的象牙、牛角或其他木料看出它們是較晚時期的作品。

自十八世紀末以來，特別是十九世紀和二十世紀盛行在器物上刻上較長的題識，整個紋飾部份常常僅以書法和古代文字，如甲骨文和鐘鼎文構成。很多十九世紀的竹刻筆筒都是用模子制成奇形怪狀。罕有的品種如方竹和斑竹也屢見不鮮。但這方面的產品以十九世紀初的作品較爲精美。

乾隆年間中的短時期製作了一些仿古銅器的竹刻，存世不多，館藏也付闕如。

這裡最有名的一件竹刻是沈大生所刻的蛙形筆筒。此物是由一組青蛙構成，其中一隻有活動的舌頭，上有紀年款相當於公元一六二三年。沈大生是江蘇嘉定人，晚明名匠之一。這筆筒曾經展出過多次並見於幾個著録之中（展品334）。這次展出的朱稚征（又名朱三松）香薰上有紀年款，相當於公元一六六二年（展品334），吴之璠筆筒，上有紀年款，相當於公元一六七二年、濮澄（展品339和337）等都曾經著録，是難得的精品。

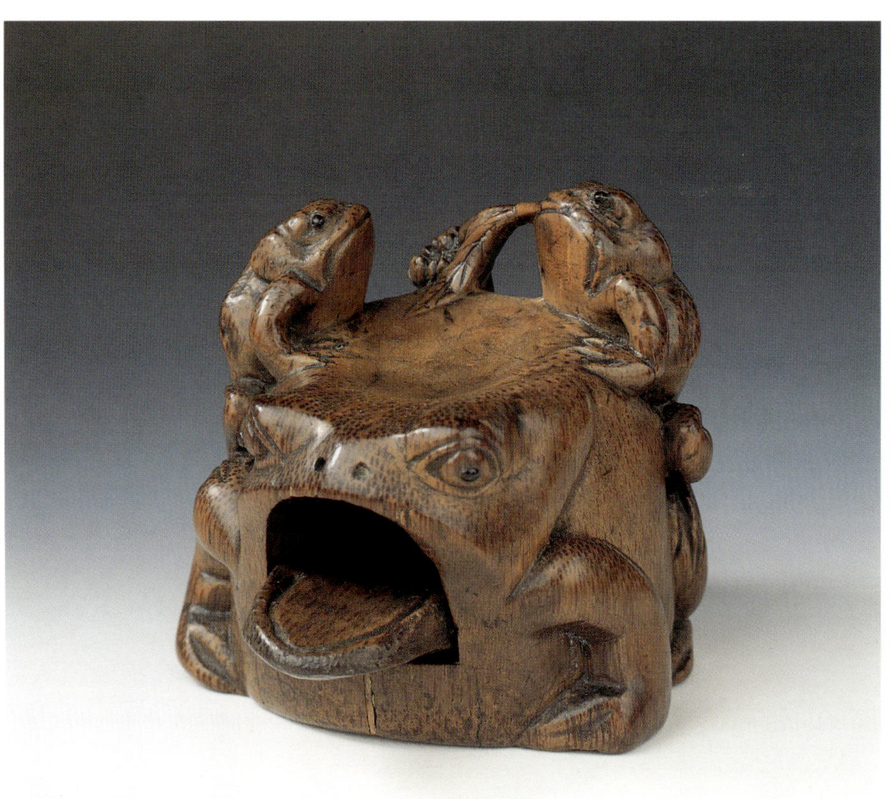

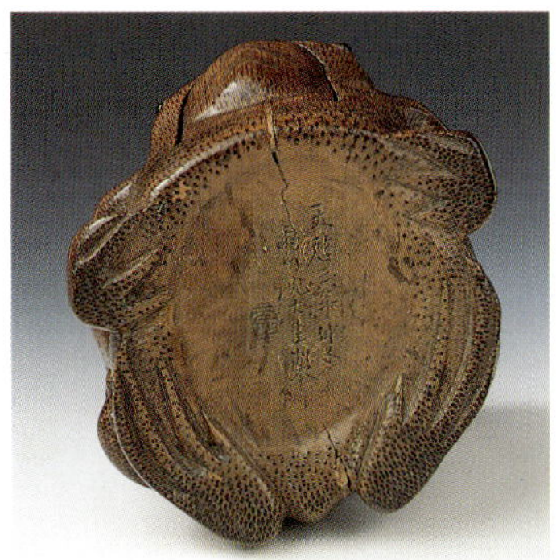

334

Dated bamboo toads carved in the round by Shen Dasheng

Ming dynasty, Tianqi period (1623)
Length : 7.6 cm
Height : 6.7 cm

Three bamboo toads carved in the round. The tongue of the big toad is fitted at the base to slots and can be moved up and down. The two smaller toads, one with a rice spray, are clambering onto the flat back of the big one. Inscribed by Shen Dasheng with his studio seal on the bottom of the piece. It is dated to the third year of Tianqi (1623). The carver Shen Dasheng was a leading bamboo carver of the late Ming period. Probably intended as a brush rest for the scholar's studio.

335

Small bamboo brush pot carved as the section of a pine tree with two pendant branches

First half of the 17th century
Height : 9.5 cm
Width : 5.5 cm
Depth : 3.6 cm

A small bamboo brush pot carved as the section of a pine tree with smooth but knobbled trunk, two knarled pine branches, one small, one long and forked with individually done scales, both branches free standing desending from the rim, the longer almost extending as far as the base.

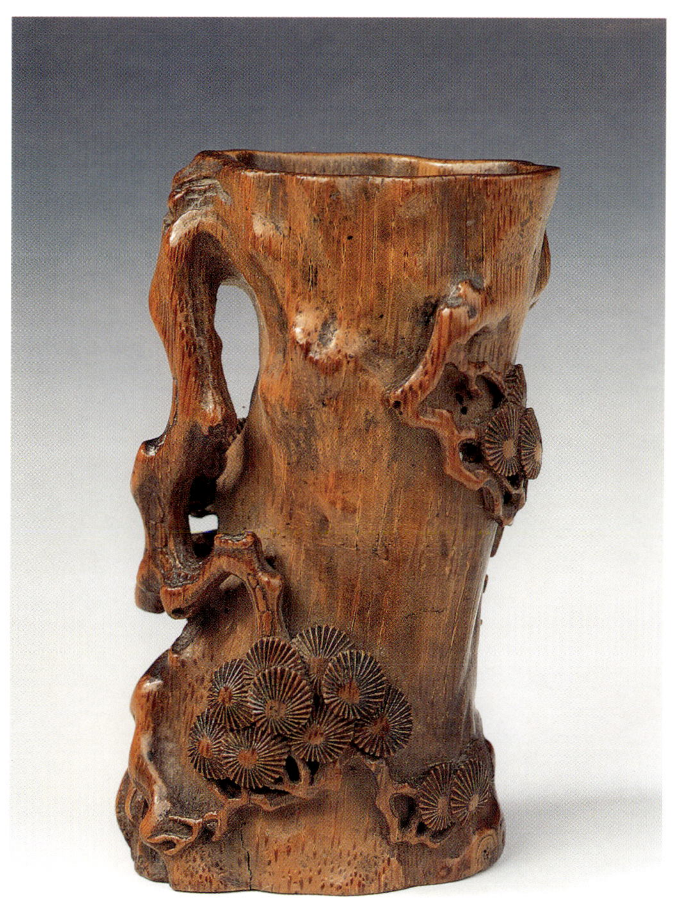

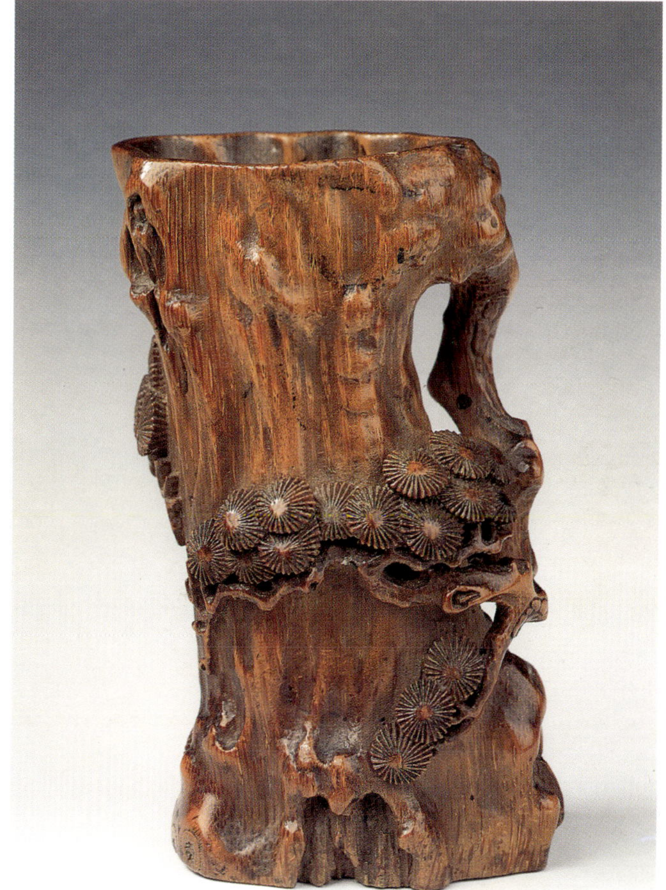

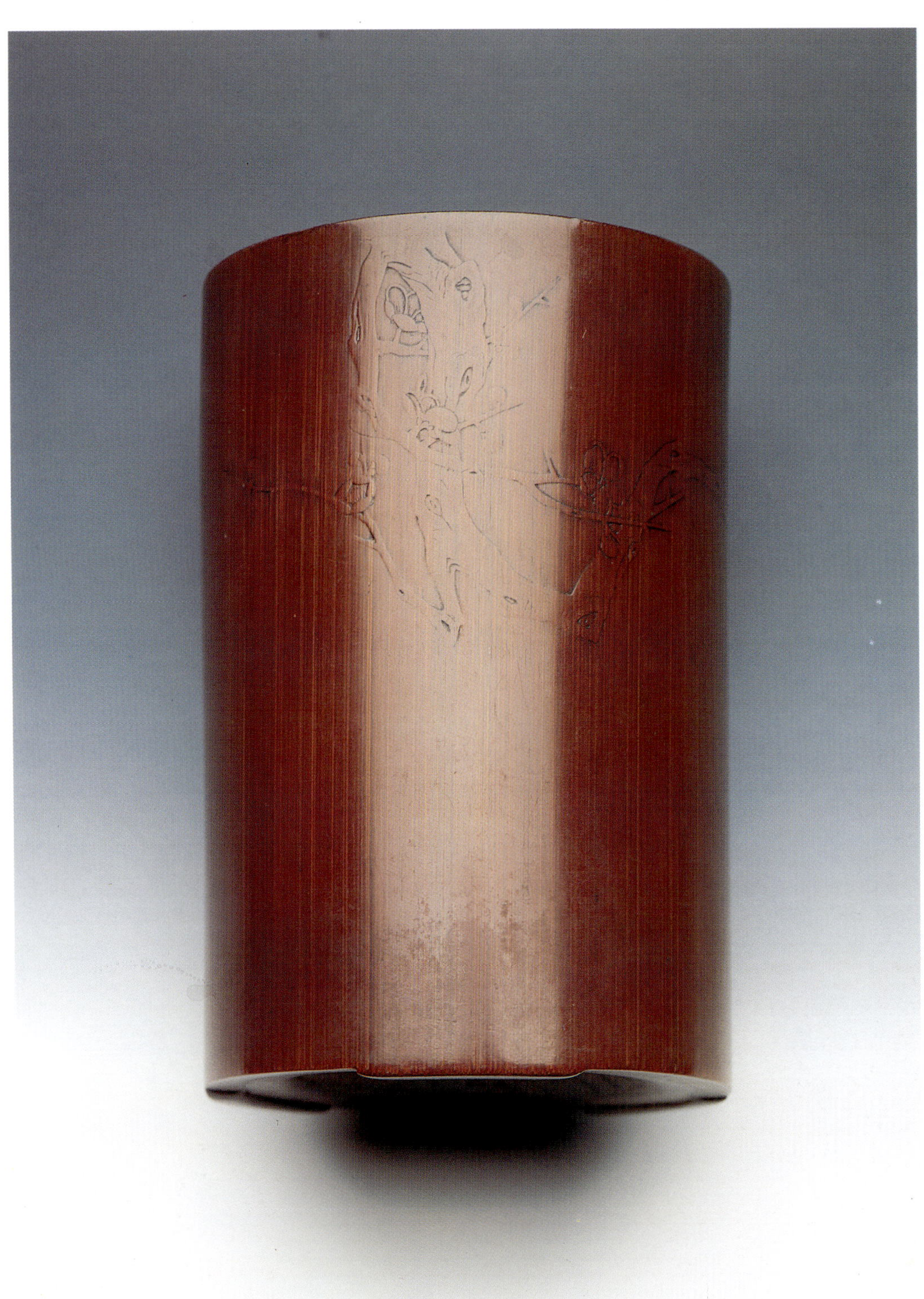

336

Bamboo brush pot decorated in low relief with prunus and incised poem by Pu Cheng

Early Qing
(mid 17th century)
Height : 14 cm
Diameter : 7 cm

A bamboo brush pot, the body of oval section resting on three low feet, delicately carved in very low relief with a pendant branch of flowering prunus, beside an incised poem and incised signature Zhong Qian, the pen name of the famous carver Pu Cheng (b. 1582) regarded as founder of the Jinling school who survived into the early Qing dynasty. The bamboo is well patinated.

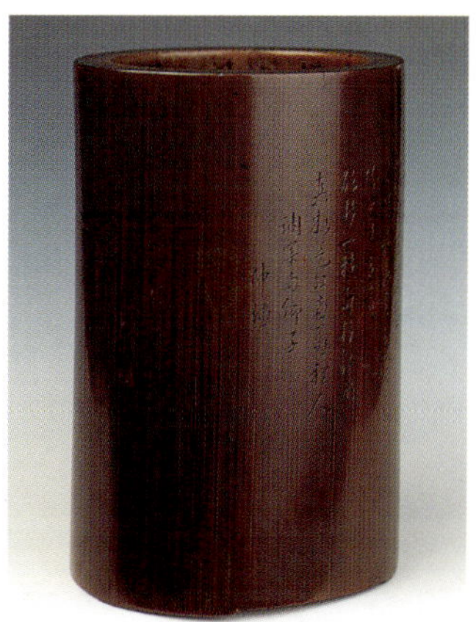

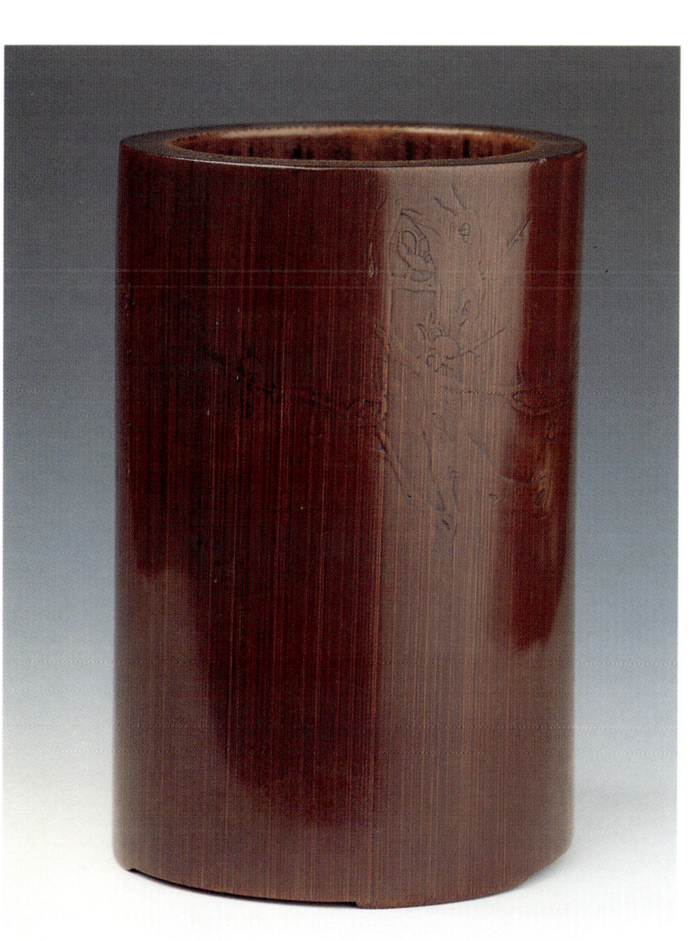

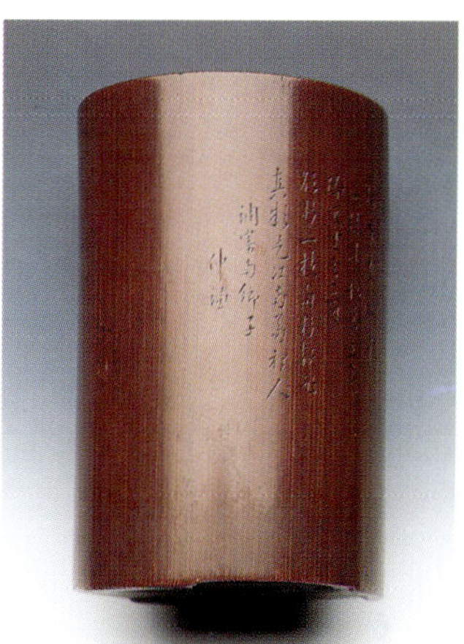

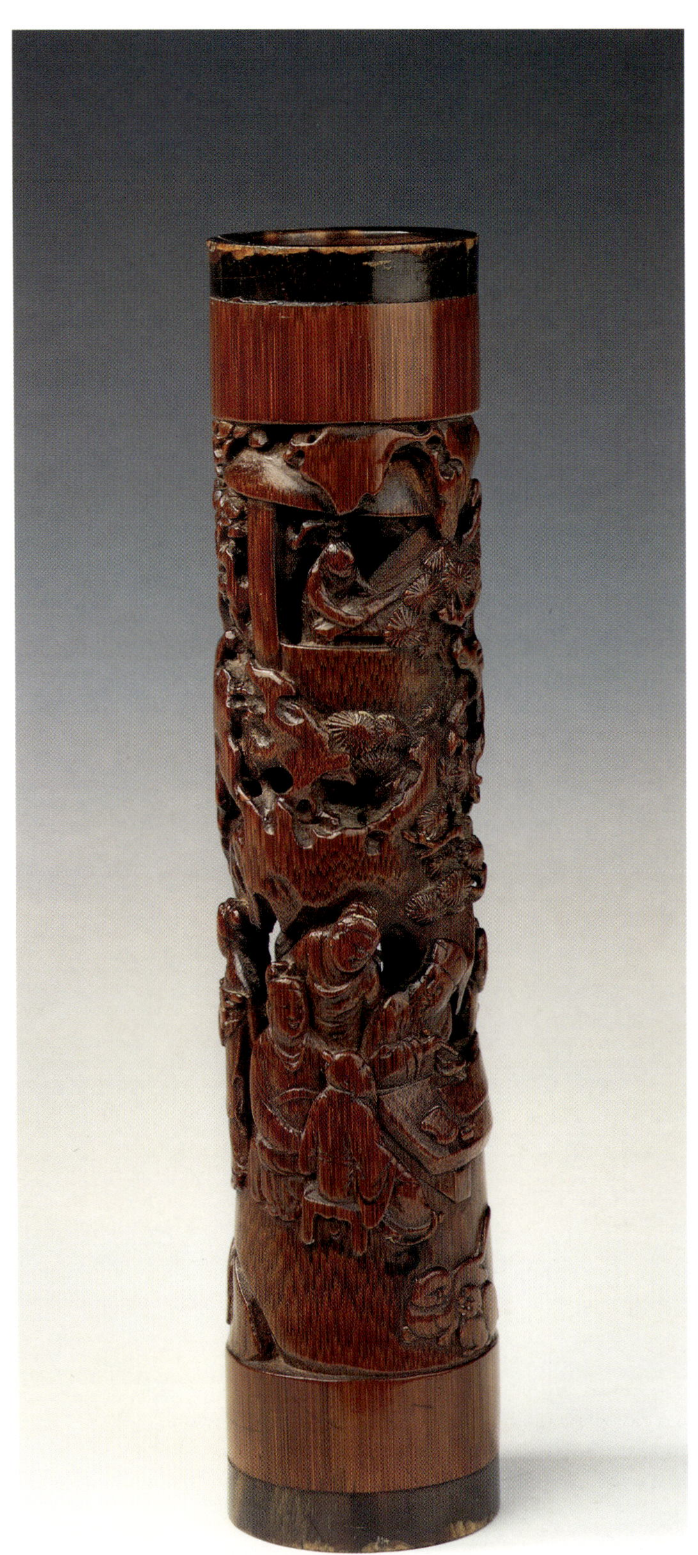

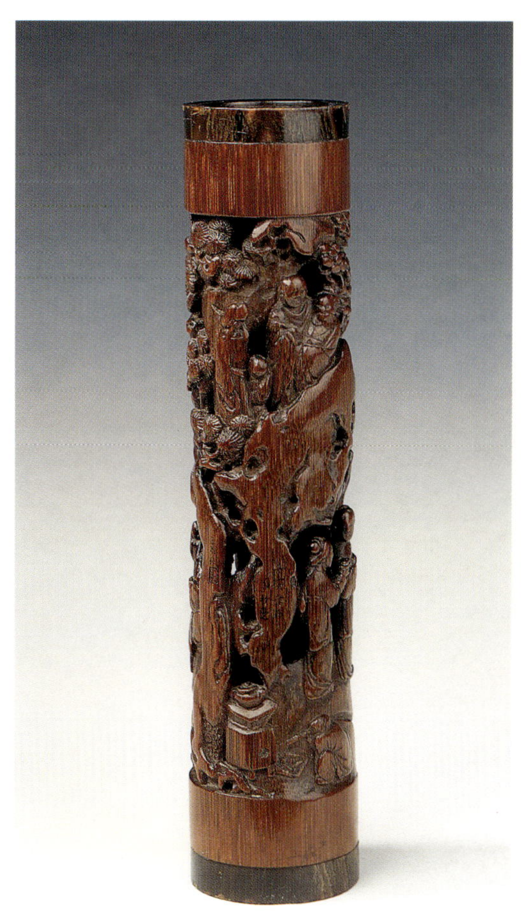

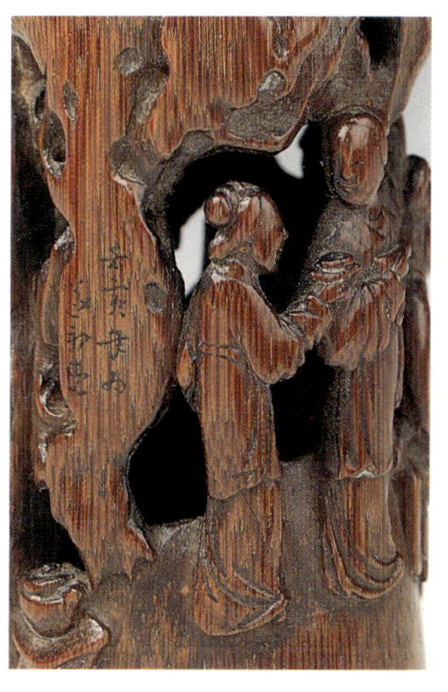

337

RETICULATED BAMBOO PERFUME HOLDER SIGNED BY ZHU ZHIZHENG AND CYCLICALLY DATED, PROBABLY 1662

17TH CENTURY, 1662
HEIGHT : 17.1 CM
DIAMETER : 3.5 CM

Reticulated bamboo perfume holder with five scholars under a single knarled pine crowding round a table on which are writing materials. To one side is a servant cooking tea. Two female servants and two cats playing above three scholars, one writing on rock with a servant, another servant in a pavilion; inscribed signature of Zhu Zhizheng alias Zhu Sansang and date probably 1662. Zhu Zhizheng is the third generation of a very famous family of Ming bamboo carvers and is believed to have still been alive in the early Qing.

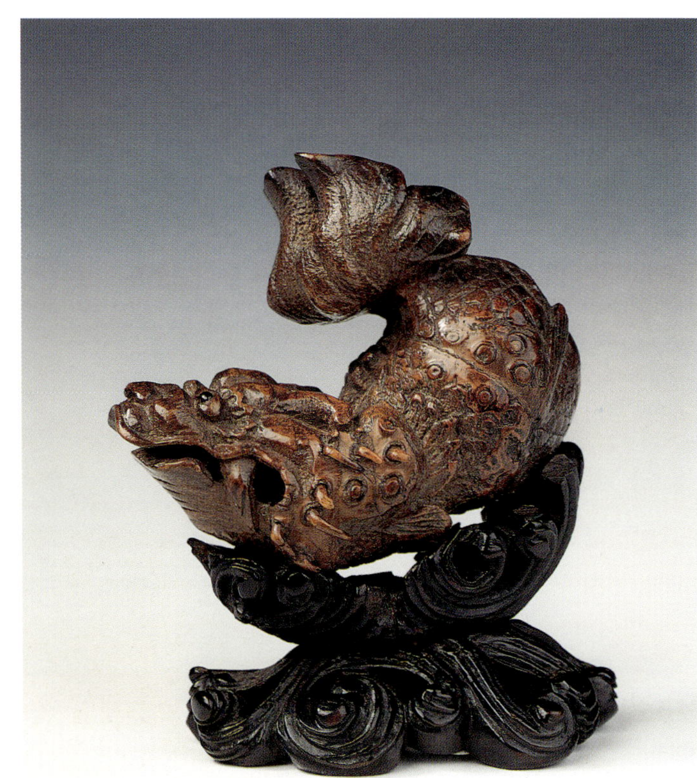

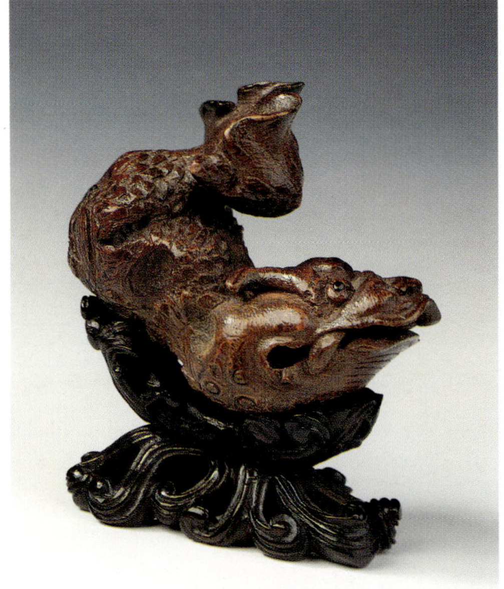

338

Root bamboo carving of a twin-horned dragon-headed carp

Second half of the 17th century
Length : 7.5 cm
Height : 6.5 cm

Root bamboo carving of a twin-horned dragon-headed carp with tail up over the head, some roots retained as prickly spines and fins. This carving depicts the moment when the carp going up the waterfall changes into a dragon, a subject popular in the 17th century.

339

Bamboo brush pot decorated in low relief against a plain ground with the figure of Laozi on a buffalo with inscription, signature of Wu Zhifan and cyclical date, probably 1672

Second half of the 17th century
Height : 16 cm
Diameter : 10.8 cm

Nicely patinated bamboo brush pot decorated in low relief with figure of Laozi on a buffalo with inscription, signature of Wu Zhifan, a native of Jiading, Jiangsu Province and a noted carver active in the Kangxi period. He is generally regarded as the first to carve figures in low relief on an almost plain carved-away background making the design appear almost as high relief.

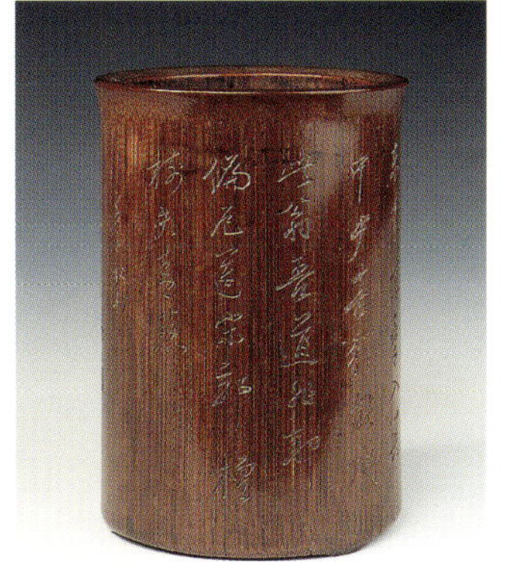

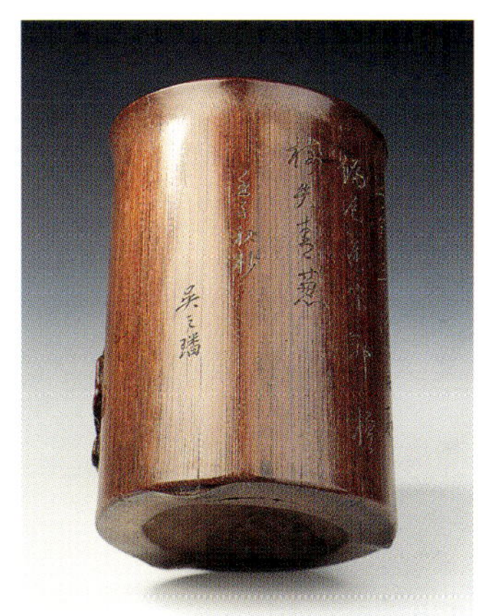

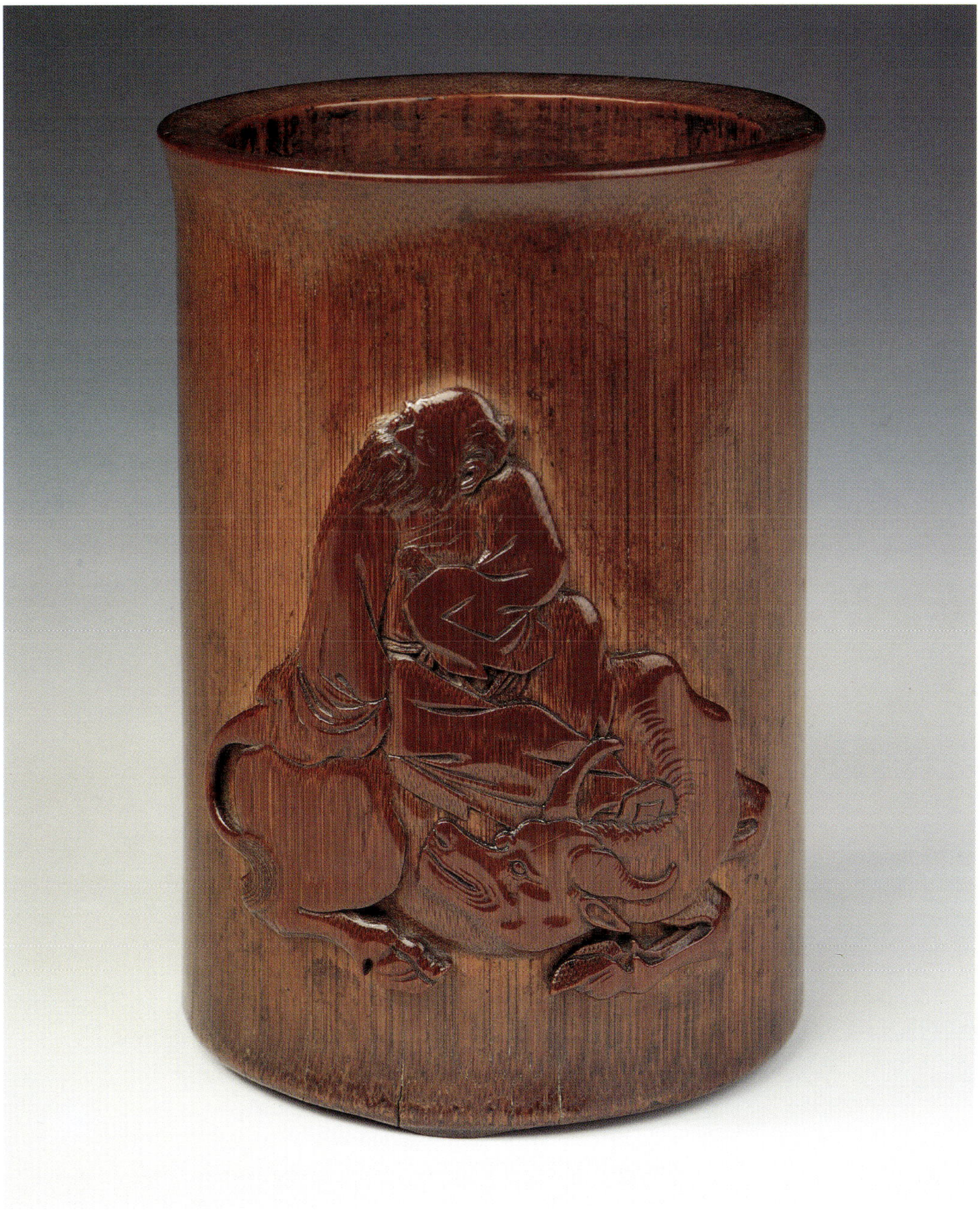

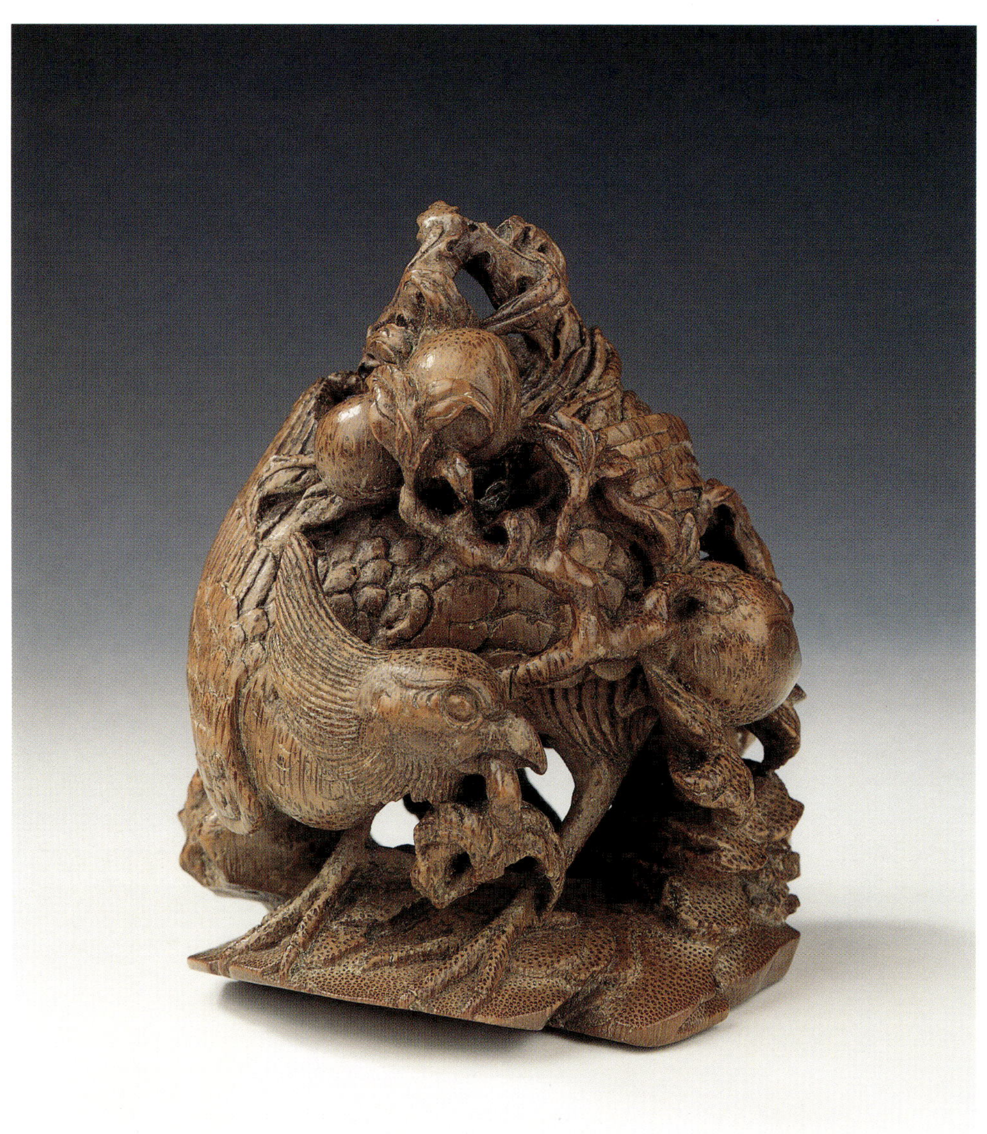

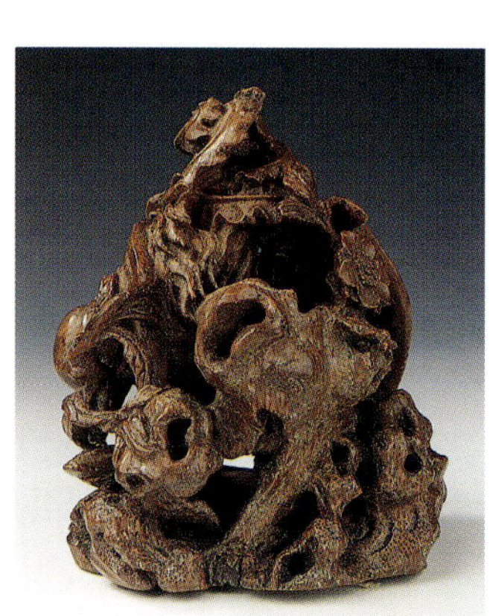

340

Bamboo phoenix with peach spray by perforated rock

Second half of the 17th century
Height : 10.7 cm
Width : 7 cm

A bamboo root carving of a phoenix with a long tail standing beside a perforated rock, holding in its mouth a peach spray.

341

Root bamboo Box carved in the form of a female crab

Kangxi
(1662 - 1722) (late 17th century)
Length : 12.3 cm
Depth : 7.5 cm
Height : 4.3 cm

Bamboo carving of a female crab, its claws and legs held close to the body, the eyes protruding and lacquered black, the carapace removable to form a shallow box.

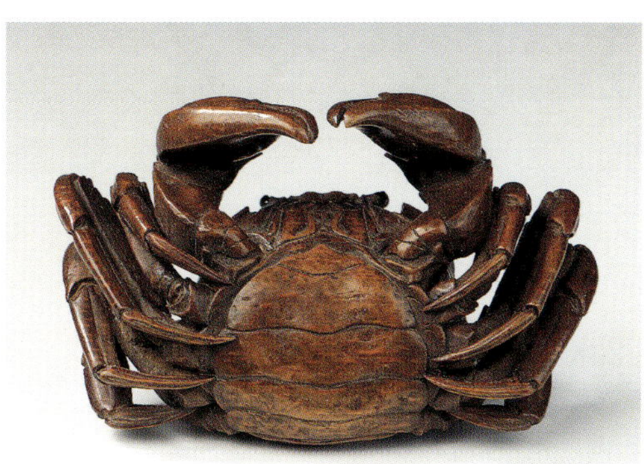

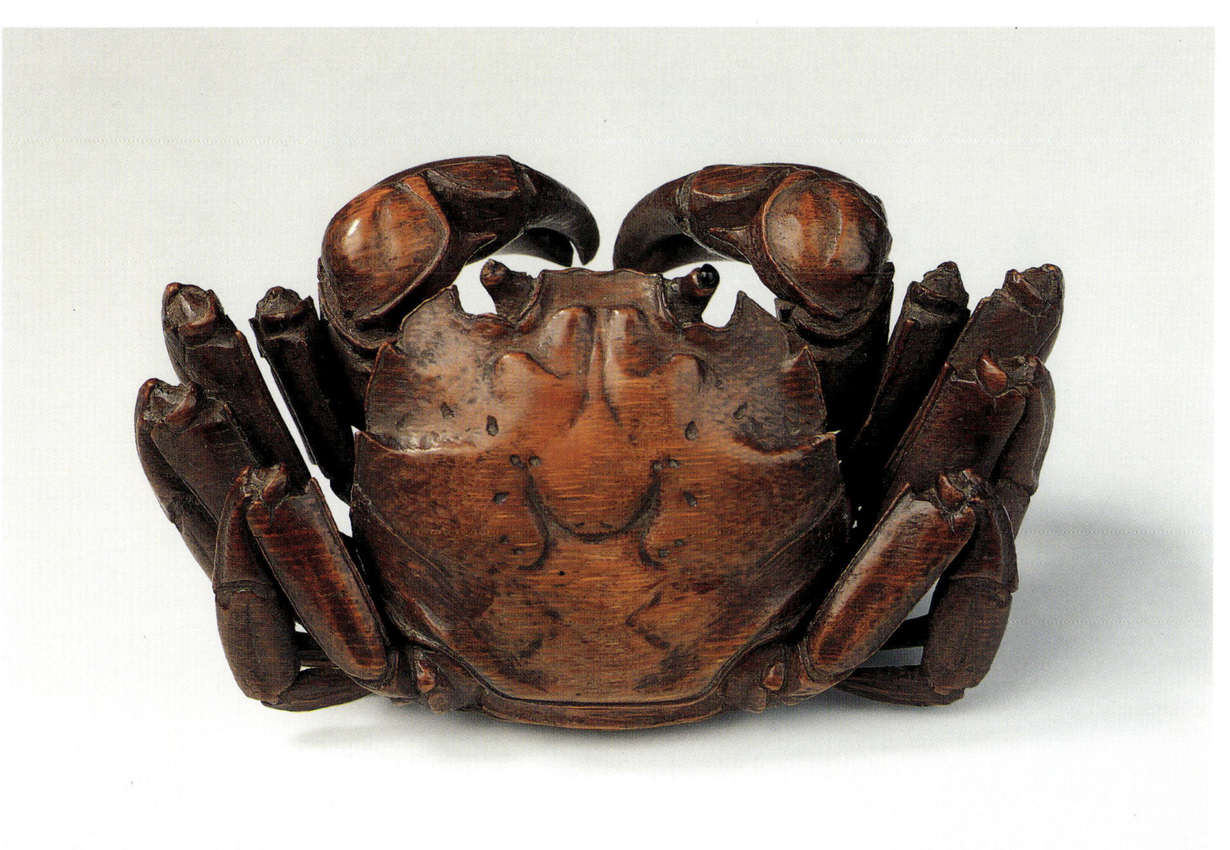

342

BAMBOO CUP
CARVED AS A SECTION
OF A MAGNOLIA TREE

KANGXI
(1662 - 1722)
LENGHT : 10.3 CM
HEIGHT : 8.9 CM

Bamboo cup carved as a section of a magnolia tree with branches of magnolia flowers in bloom and bud. Comparable with rhino-horn carvings of the same subject.

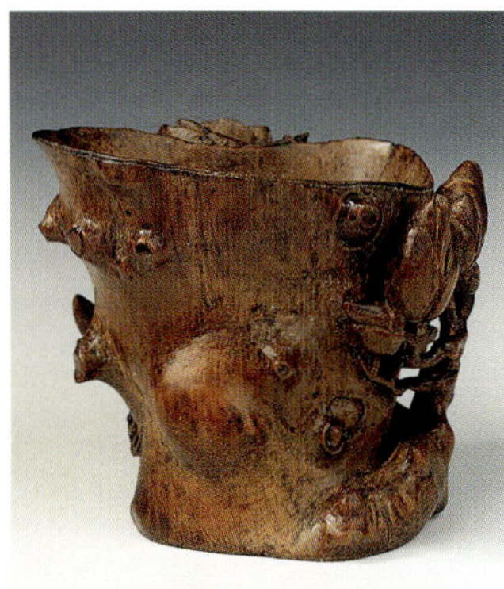

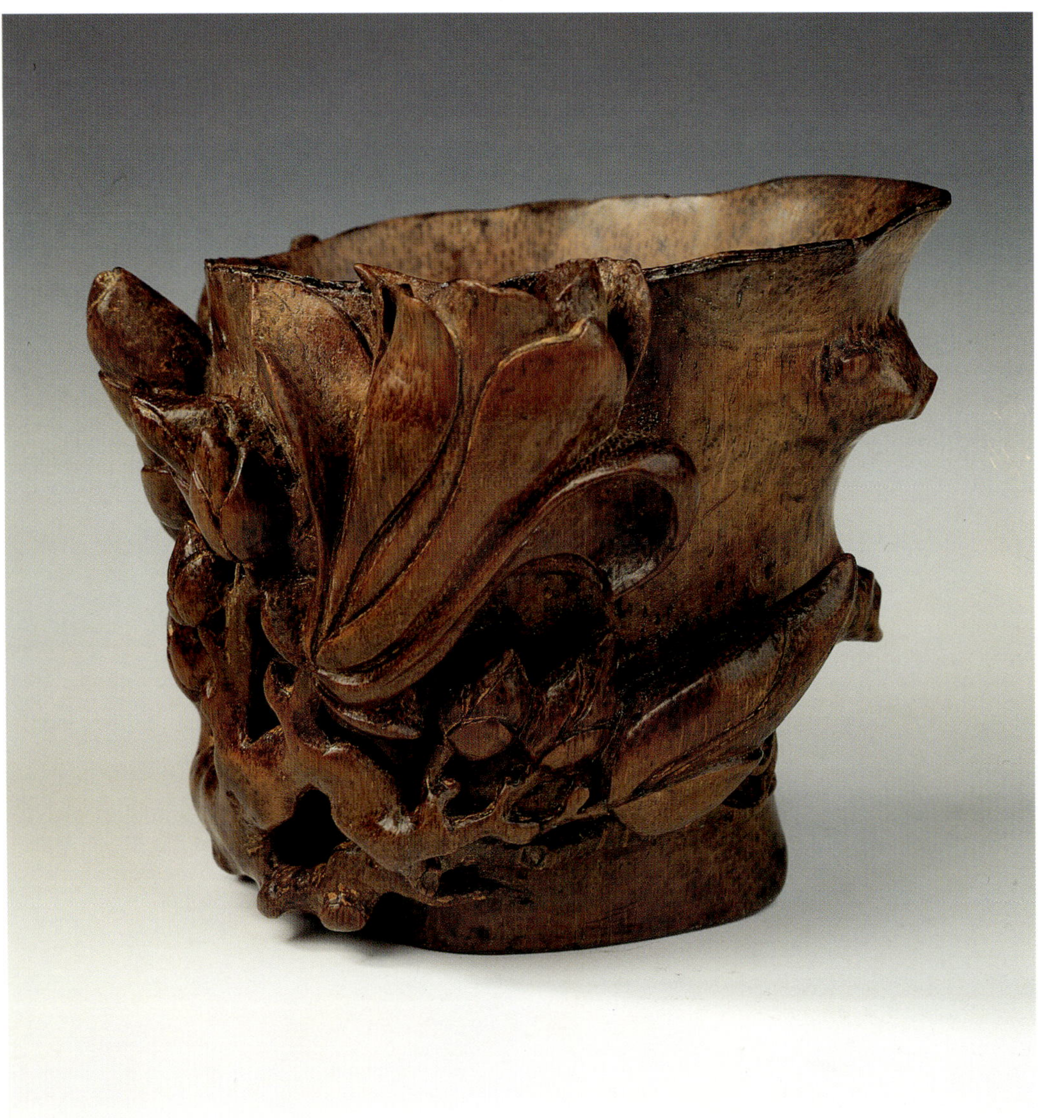

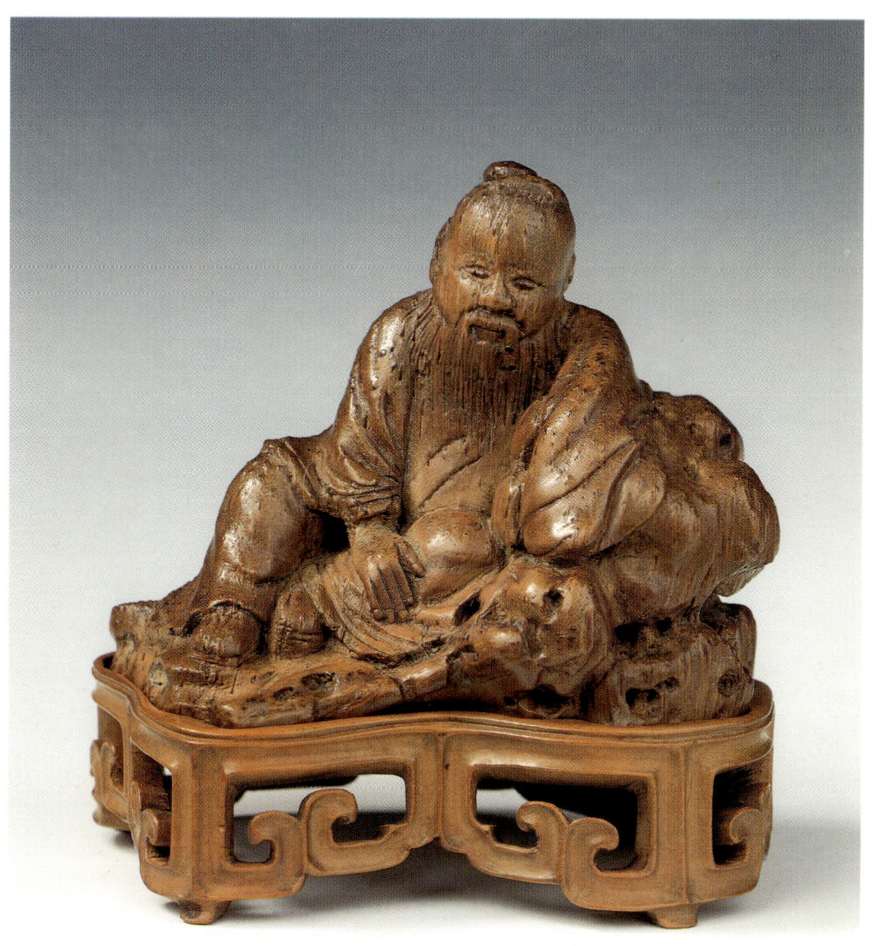

343

BAMBOO ROOT CARVING OF A SCHOLAR LEANING AGAINST A ROCK

KANGXI PERIOD
(1662 - 1722)
WIDTH : 7 CM
HEIGHT : 5.6 CM

Bamboo root carving of bearded scholar leaning against a rock, one leg over the other.

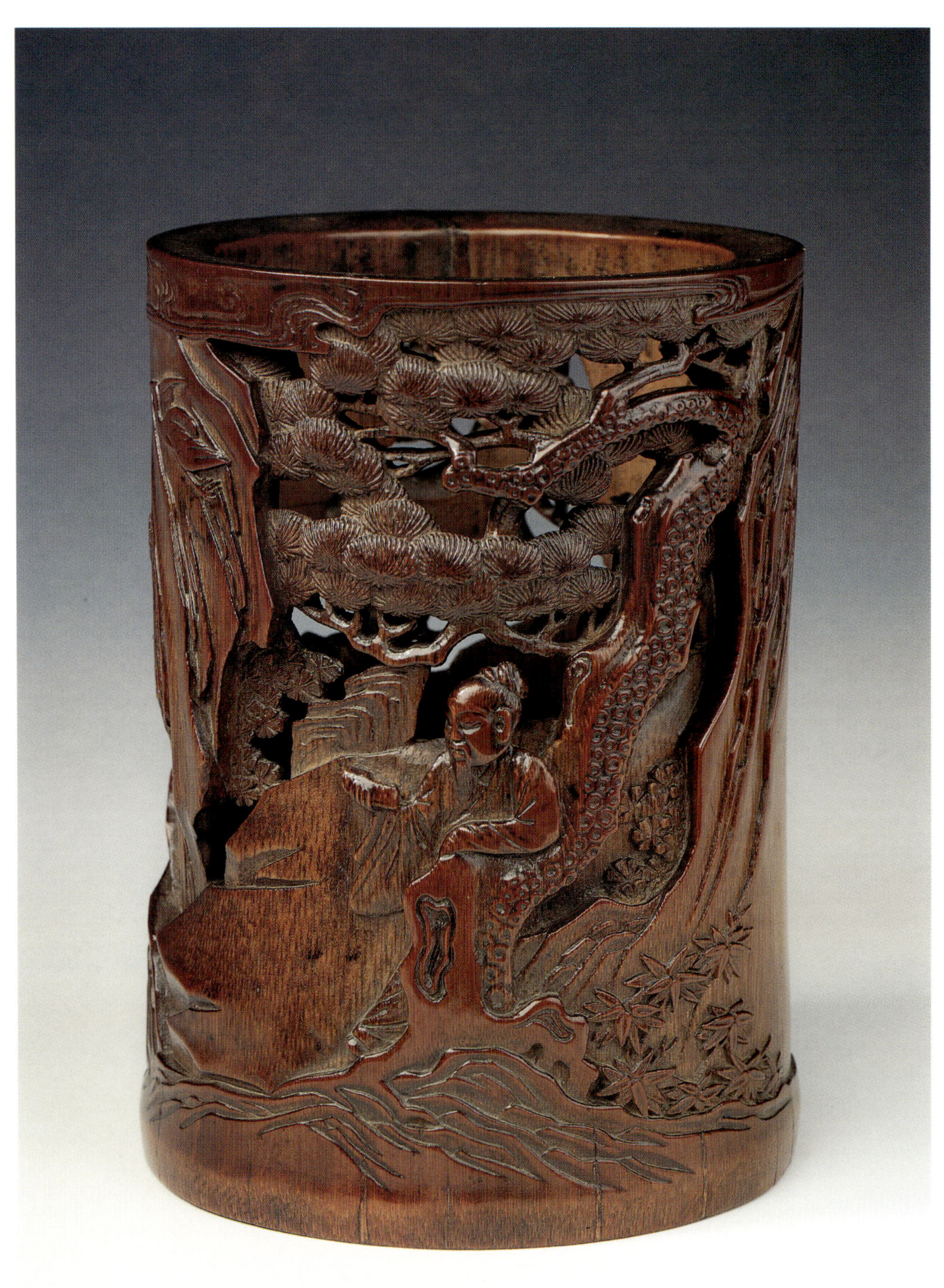

344

RETICULATED BAMBOO BRUSH POT DECORATED WITH A SCHOLAR LEANING AGAINST A PINE IN LANDSCAPE

FIRST HALF OF THE 18TH CENTURY
HEIGHT : 14 CM
DIAMETER : 9.6 CM

Bamboo brush pot of pierced work with a scholar leaning against a knarled pine tree, his left arm bent at the elbow holding in his other hand a shoe, the reverse with tree issuing from rocks amid swirling clouds, tiered rocks with vegetation and a flying stork.

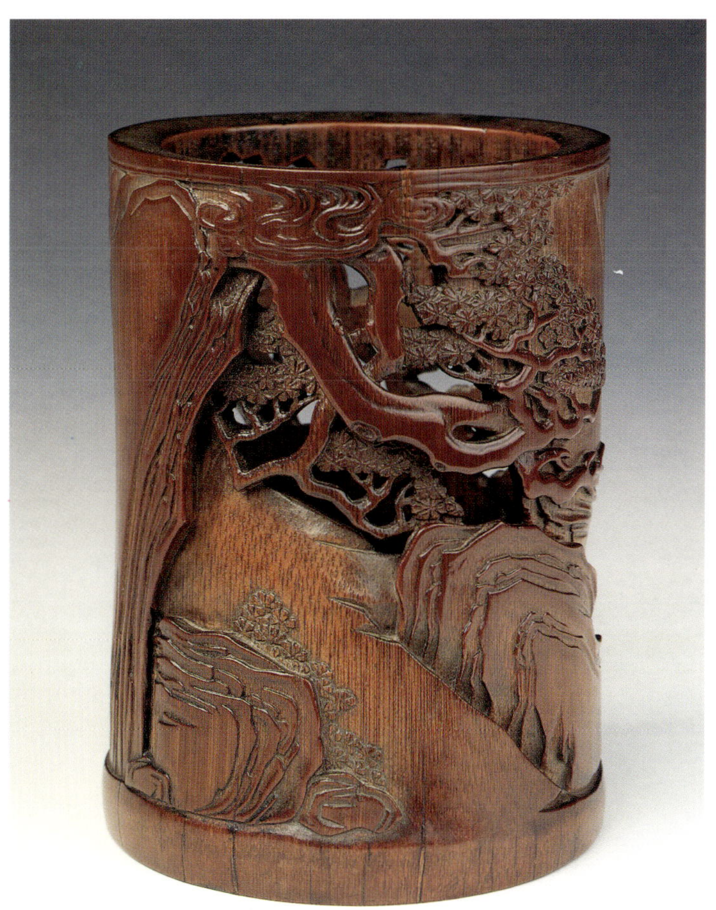

345

BAMBOO ROOT CARVING OF SINGLE-HORNED FABULOUS ANIMAL WITH YOUNG ANIMAL

LATE KANGXI/YONGZHENG PERIOD
(1710 - 1735)
HEIGHT : 11 CM
WIDTH : 9.5 CM

A bamboo root carving of a standing adult single-horned fabulous animal with long fluffy tail and wide open mouth. A young animal by its side looks up at the adult.

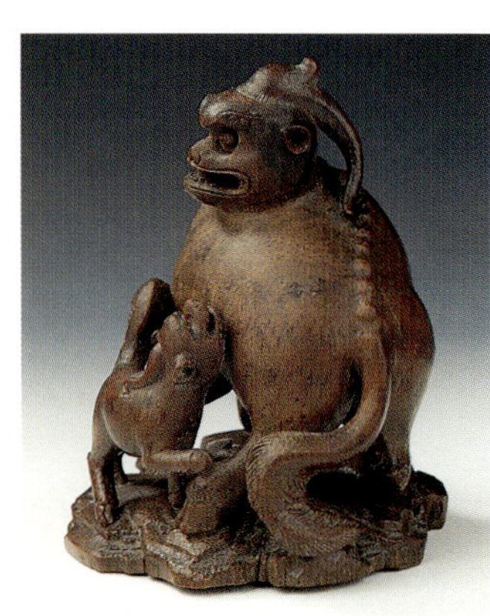

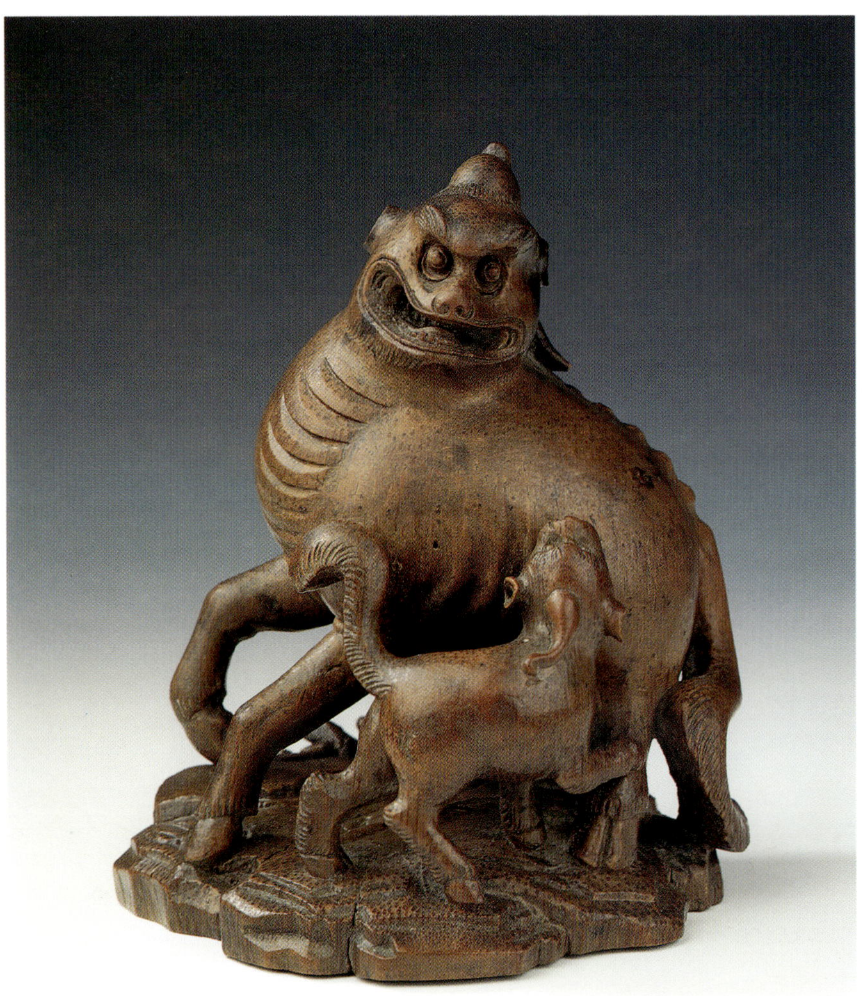

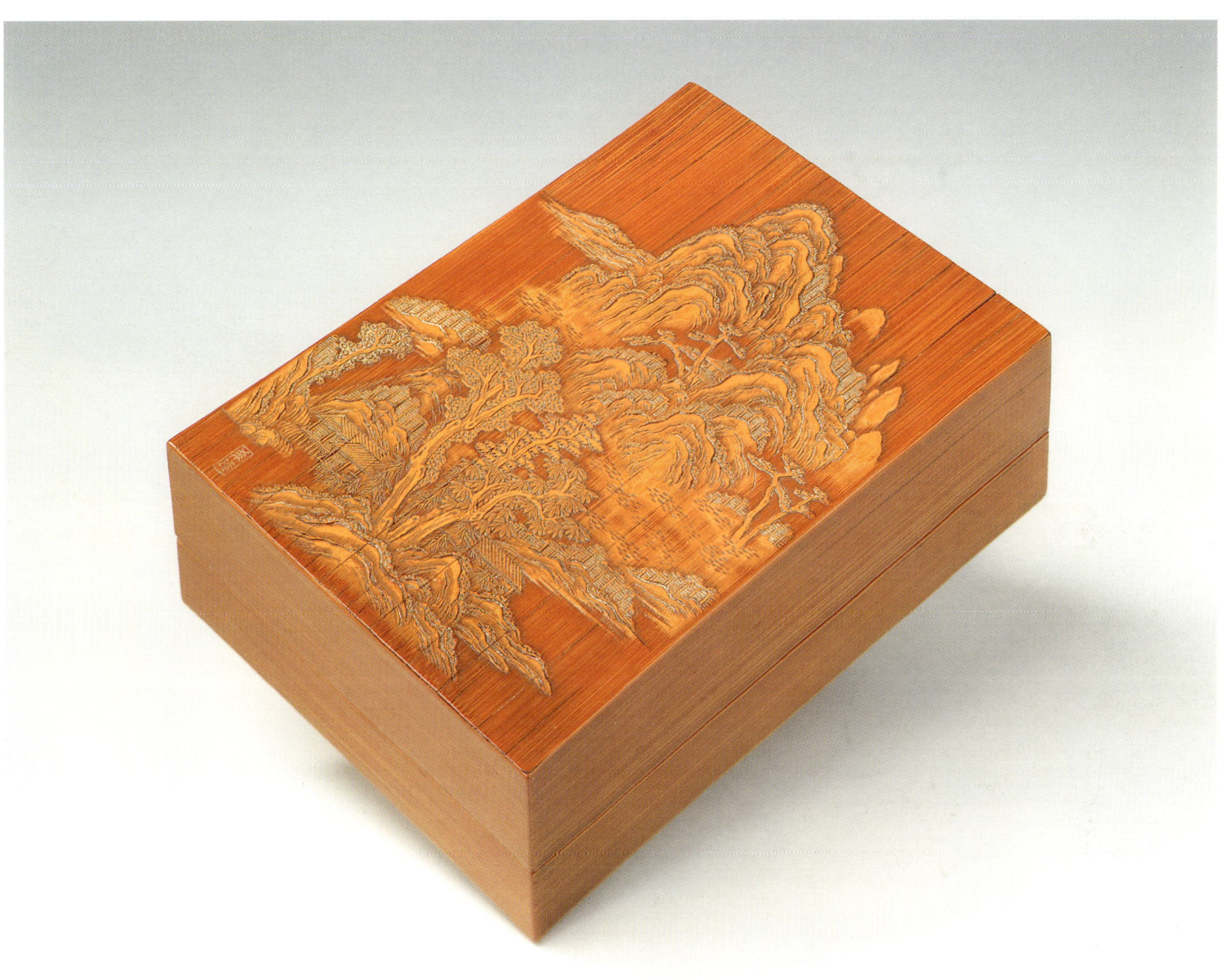

346

RECTANGULAR BAMBOO BOX DECORATED WITH LANDSCAPE SCENE IN *LIUQING* TECHNIQUE

18TH CENTURY
LENGTH : 10.4 CM
WIDTH : 8 CM

A rectangular bamboo box, the skin of the bamboo carved with a landscape of pavilions near a stream with trees and soaring mountains, the background plain, the skin having been removed from the background portion.

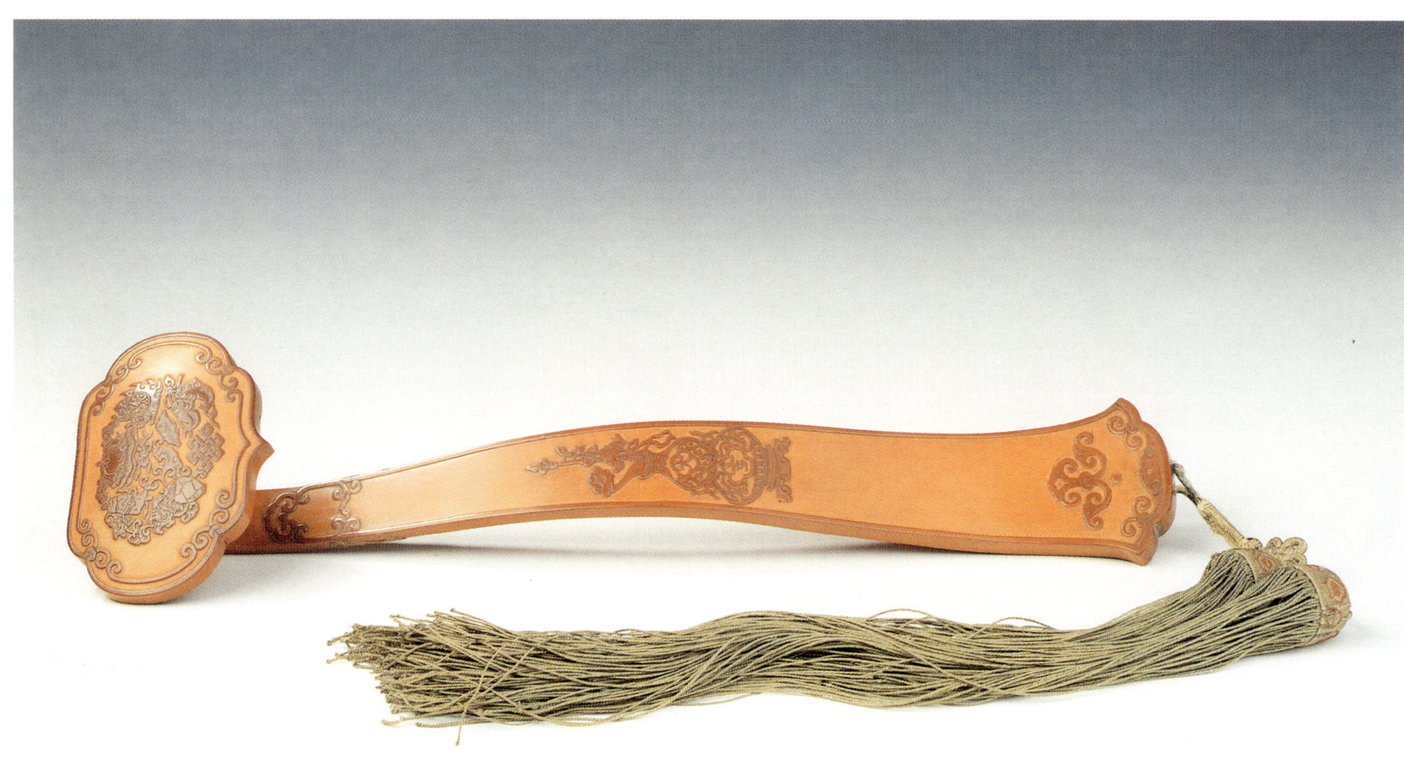

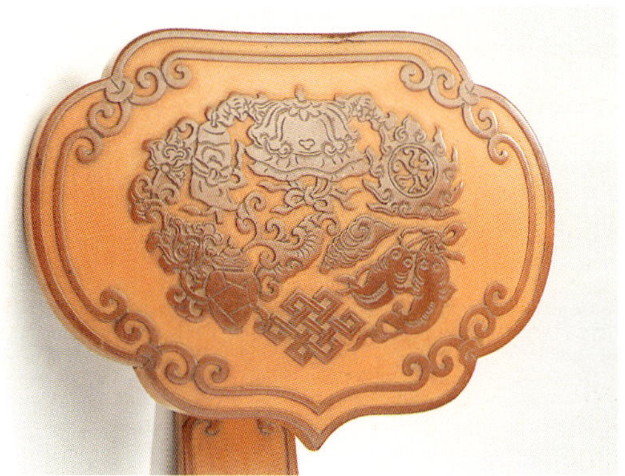

347

Bamboo veneered boxwood based ruyi sceptre of straight form with decoration of Buddhist emblems

Late 18th to early 19th century
Length : 33.6 cm

Bamboo veneered boxwood base *ruyi* of straight form, the tail slightly splayed, the boxwood of nice honey colour, the head and tail with cut out bamboo skin veneer depicting on the head some of the eight precious Buddhist emblems, the tail has formal veneer and in the middle is bamboo veneer of a double gourd vase holding a *ruyi* and other items with bamboo veneer skin borders.

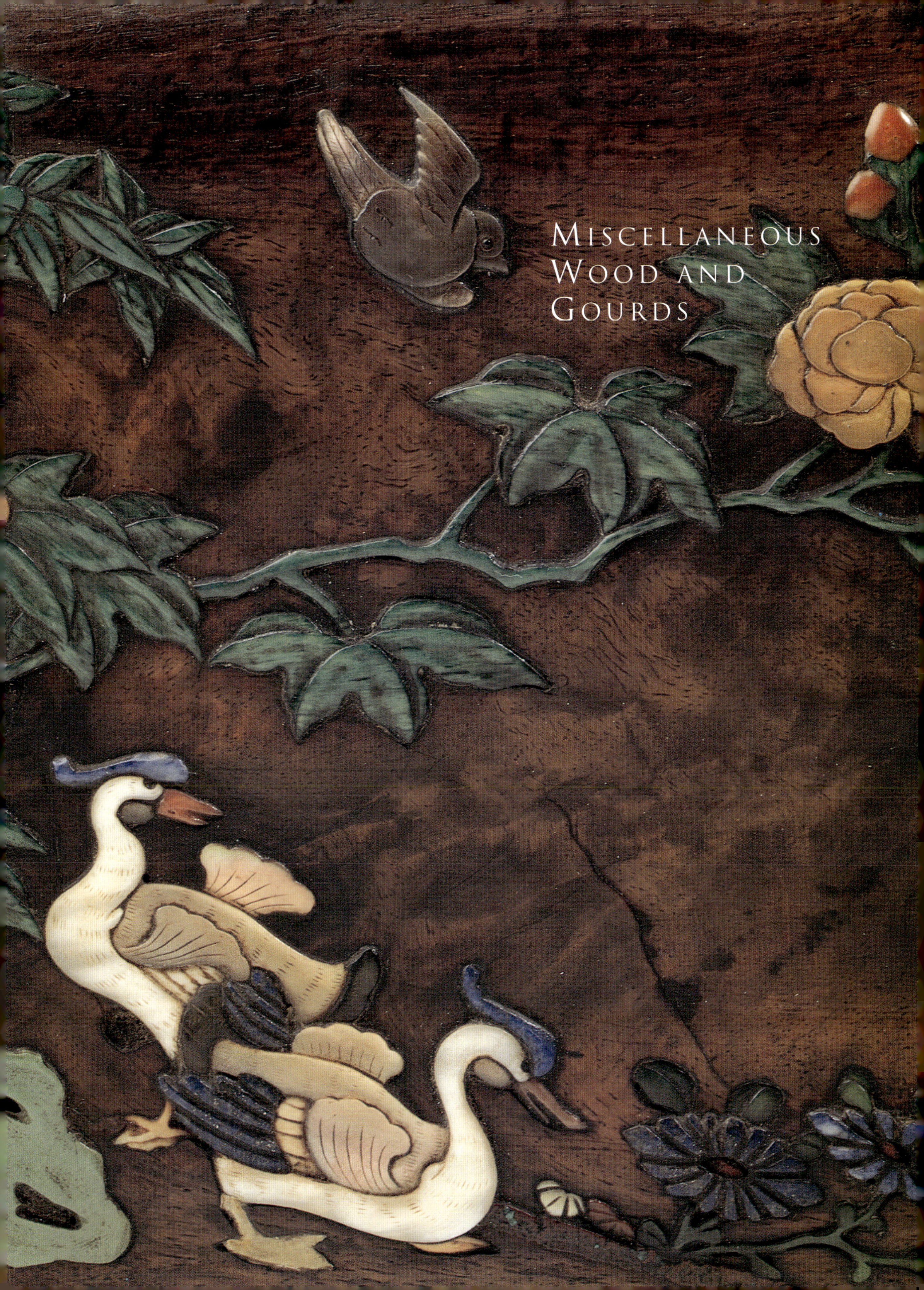

Miscellaneous Wood and Gourds

Miscellaneous Wood and Gourds

One of the interesting decorative art forms developed in China in the Qing period, involved the moulding of gourds into scholars' objects or vessels of various kinds. It was an art form apparently particularly linked with Daoism. This art form is rare, and as far as is known, there are no Ming examples. It also seems initially to have been a palace product and all the marked pieces I have seen have had a four character imperial mark in Chinese characters, "shang wan" meaning "made as a plaything for the Emperor [named]". Two of the four gourds in the exhibition (Exhibits 348 and 350) bear imperial marks in this form, one of the Emperor Kangxi and the other of the Emperor Qianlong.

In the making of such gourds the fertilized flower is first clamped into a mould (probably of clay) which is in the form, size and decoration of the object desired. The gourd then grows into the mould. When the mould is completely filled, it is cut off the vine and the mould removed. In the Kangxi period the mould generally appears to have been used only once and was broken to remove the object, but by the mid 18th century, the moulds were invariably made in sections so that they could be used over and over again. The use of reusable moulds is evidenced by traces of the joins in the mould appearing on the gourd. This is particularly evident on the Qianlong marked piece (Exhibit 350). However, I have recently seen a believably genuine, marked Kangxi shang wan, bowl with moulded decoration similar to (Exhibit 350). It also showed traces of a reusable mould. The use of reusable moulds would seem from such evidence to have started in the late Kangxi period *circa* 1720.

The other two pieces in the exhibition are a square moulded piece dated to the mid 18th century, which also shows traces of the mould joins and a plain eccentrically shaped water container from the 19th century (Exhibits 349 and 351).

By the 19th century gourds had ceased to be palace products and apart from such eccentric pieces as Exhibit 351, they were being commercially produced almost entirely for use as cricket cages, and were frequently mounted with ivory, tortoise-shell, coconut shell, or, in rare cases, rhino horn additions. Many of these mountings were beautifully carved. Some of these gourd cricket cages bear the signature of Chen Jintang. He seems to have worked over a relatively short period and unfortunately his dated pieces are only cyclically dated and the exact cycle is presently uncertain. The dates are probably 1862 to 1868. One of the dated pieces mentions Chen as being 75 years of age.

It should be noted that besides moulding, the Kangxi piece (Exhibit 348) also has some carved details. Carving remained popular throughout but always played a secondary role to moulding until the second half of the 19th century. At that time gourd cricket cages were frequently decorated solely with etched landscapes done with the aid of a heated instrument. Ji Banlu from Shanxi is most commonly associated with such work.

匏器

清代在中國興起的有趣的造型藝術形式之中，匏器是其中之一。其法是把葫蘆瓜放在范裏制造成各種文房用品。這種形式明顯地與道教有關係密切。所產數量不多，似乎最早出現在清代，因爲存世未見明代樣本。原先可能是宮中產物，個人見到的所有帶款匏器均有不同的皇家款記如「××賞玩」，意即給皇帝所制造的玩品。展出的四件匏器中有兩件帶有類似以上的款記（展品350及353），一件是「康熙賞玩」，另一件是「乾隆賞玩」。

製作這些匏器的方法是先將受精的花放入范中（范可能是陶土造成），范的形狀、尺寸和裝飾與所製的器物相同，葫蘆瓜在范中生長直至完全填滿整個范時，割斷瓜藤並把范除去。在康熙時代，這種匏范似乎只能使用一次，在取出成品時便須把范打破。至十八世紀中葉，匏范均是分段制成，所以可以重複使用多次。這種情況可從成品上面的范痕顯示出來，在帶乾隆款記的器物上愈益明顯（展品353）。可是，最近我見到一件帶「康熙賞玩」款的葫蘆碗，其模印紋飾與展品353帶「乾隆賞玩」款的一件相似，年代相信是康熙時期無疑。其上亦見可重複使用的范的痕跡。基於以上的發現，我認爲重複使用瓜范的技法是自康熙晚期、即約一七二〇年時開始。

展覽中還有兩件匏器。其一呈四方形，模製，年代是十八世紀中葉，此物之上亦見分范痕跡；另一件是造型奇特的素身水丞，年代是十九世紀（展品352和354）。時至十九世紀，匏器已再不是宮廷產品，同時趨於商業化，而大量製造，所產幾乎全是蟈蟈罐。這些罐的口部往往加上用象牙鑲飾的玳瑁或椰殼的蓋。犀角製造的蓋也有，但爲數極少。這些蓋大多鐫刻精美。有些蟈蟈罐帶陳錦堂的款記。陳氏活躍時間似乎很短，同時所見紀年器物僅具干支款，沒法決定屬那一個干支，因此只能推斷其年代是公元一八六二年至一八六八年。有一件帶干支款的器物提及陳氏其時是七十五歲。

必須一提的是「康熙賞玩」的這一件匏器（展品350）。雖是模製，但上面也有細緻的雕刻。雕刻技法其後一直流行，但總是作爲模製的輔助，而非主要。直至十九世紀下半葉，雕刻這種技法始成爲主流，其時的蟈蟈罐往往飾有山水紋飾，其法是用炙熱的金屬器具烙在匏器表面而成。山西的籍班録便精於此技。

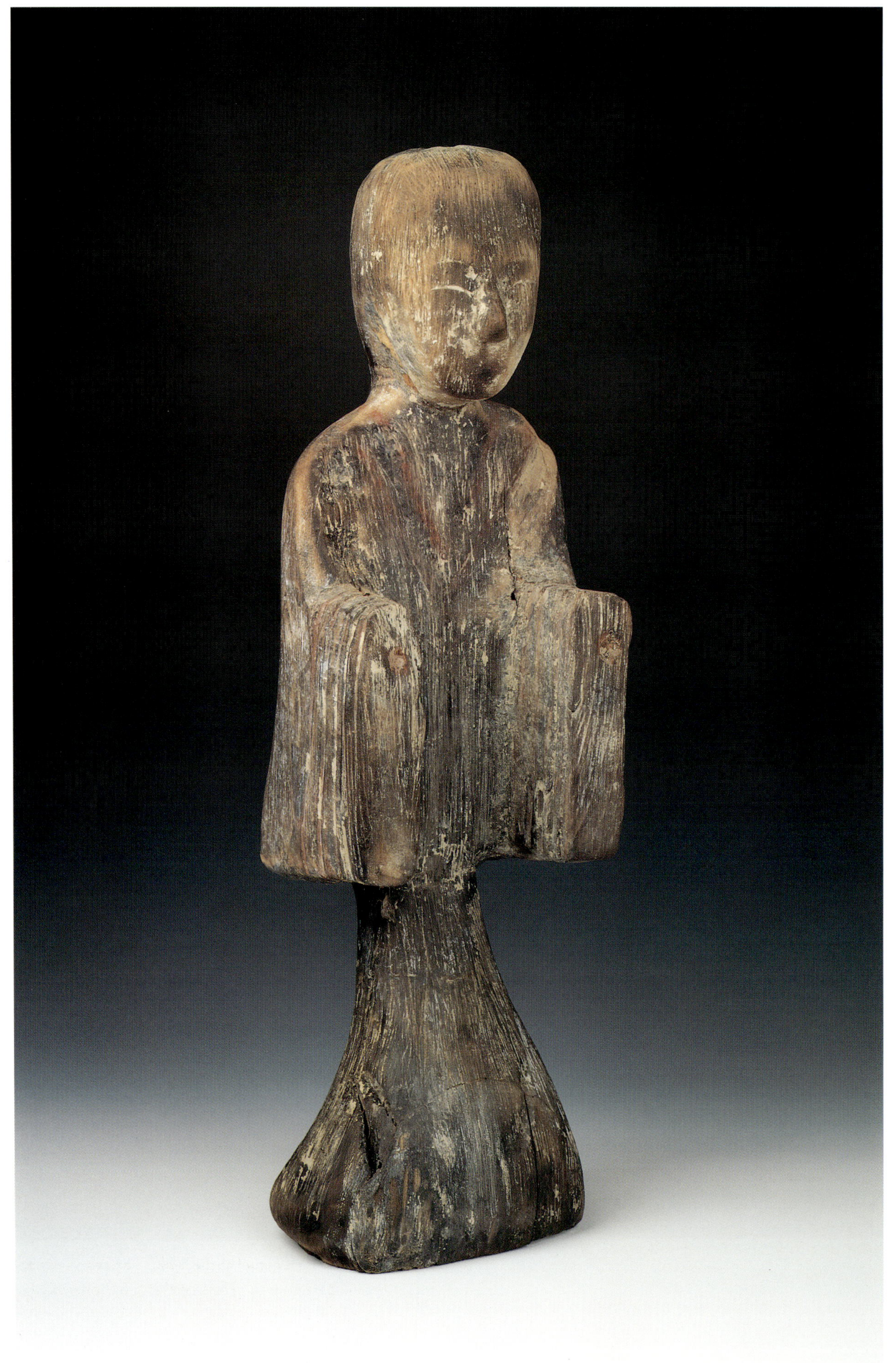

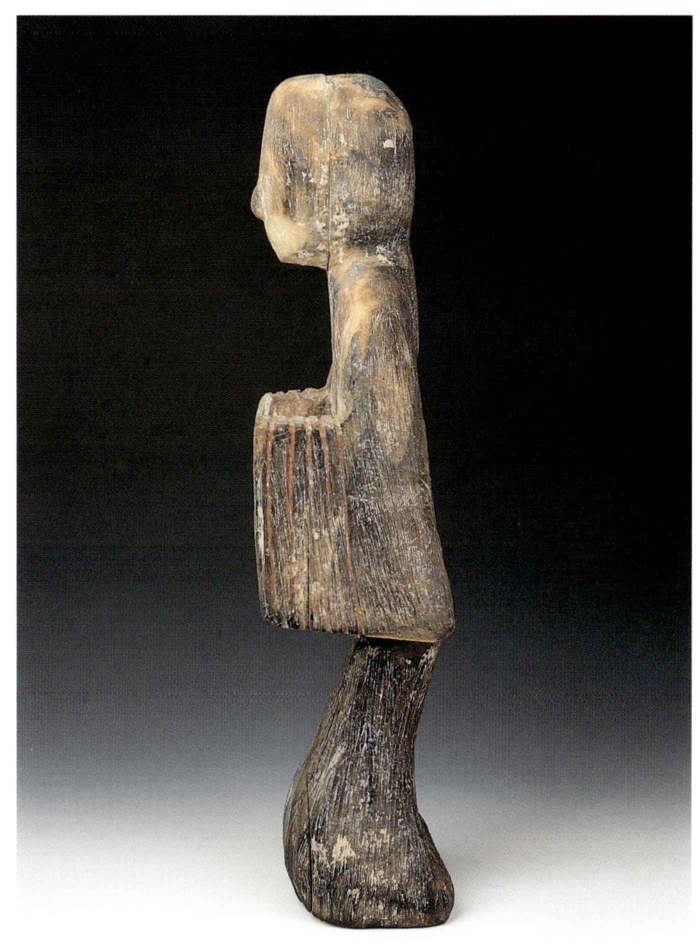

348

A wooden standing female figure

Eastern Han (25 - 220 A.D.)
first century A.D.
Height : 55 cm

A large camphor wood standing figure of a lady in Eastern Han style with a close fitting dress covering the legs and a rather flat face with a pigtail at the back. The arms bent at the elbow, with hanging sleeves. The lower part is represented in a pyramid-like form with knees slightly bent. The figure is painted extensively on the body with red and white pigments. The face, arms and protrusions of this figure are built up of wood blocks fused to the basic flat central wood plane.

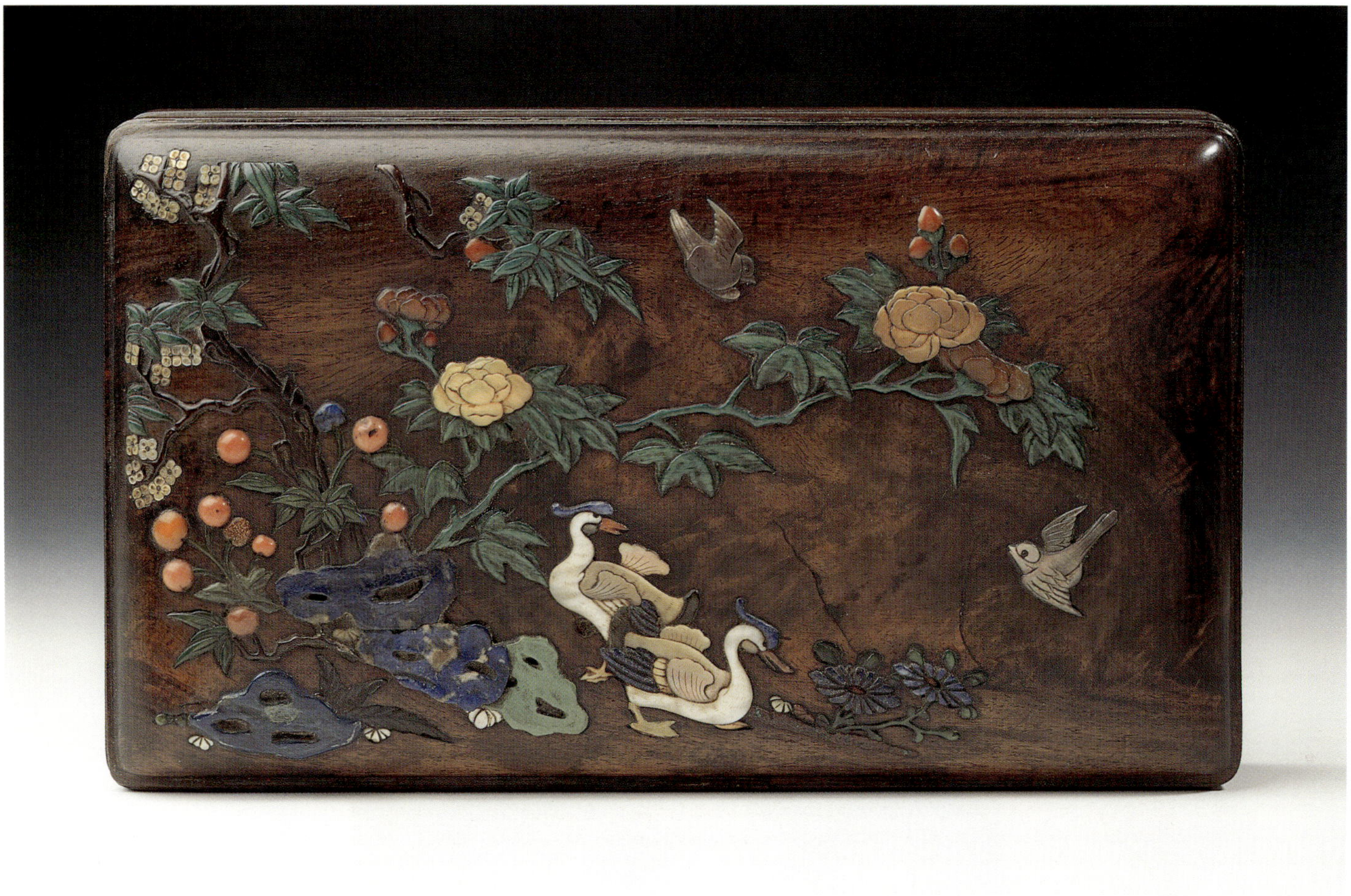

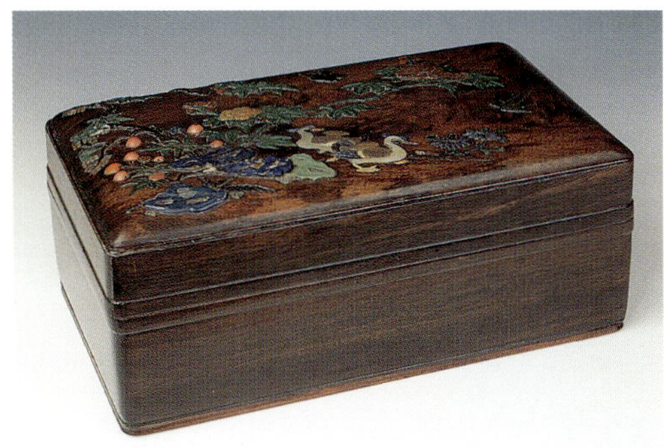

349

ZITAN WOODEN BOX WITH INLAYS OF MOTHER-OF-PEARL, COLOURED STONES AND GREEN-STAINED IVORY IN A DESIGN OF MANDARIN DUCKS AMONG ROCKS AND FLOWERING TREES

QING, KANGXI PERIOD
(1662 - 1722)
LENGTH : 24.5 CM
WIDTH : 14 CM
HEIGHT : 9 CM

Rectangular *zitan* covered box, the cover of which is decorated on the top with pieces of inlaid green stained ivory, coral, lapis, soapstone and mother-of-pearl depicting a pair of mandarin ducks beside rocks framed by overhanging sprays of flowering tree, chrysanthemums, peonies, berries, a prunus tree and two birds. The interior of the box is fitted with a plain detachable tray.

350

Gourd moulded with gourd and vine pattern with carved details

Qing, "Kangxi shang wan" mark
(1662 -1722)
Length : 14.5 cm

A gourd with reddish-brown patina moulded in low relief over the whole body with double gourd vine pattern with carved details. Four character mark "Kangxi shang wan" i.e. "made as a plaything for Emperor Kangxi" in square double-bordered cartouche on the base. The mould of non-reusable type typical of the period.

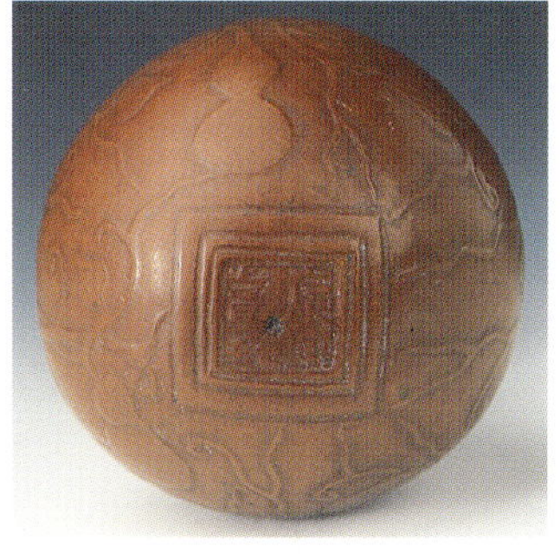

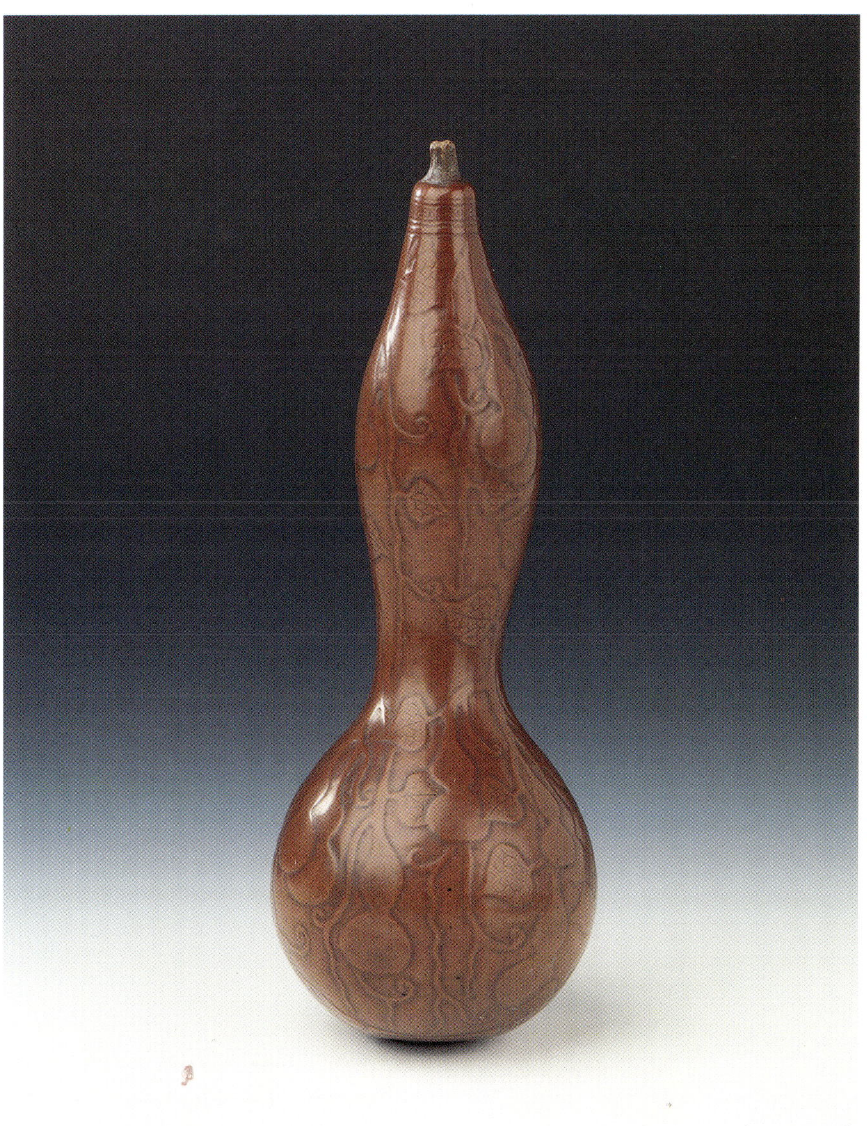

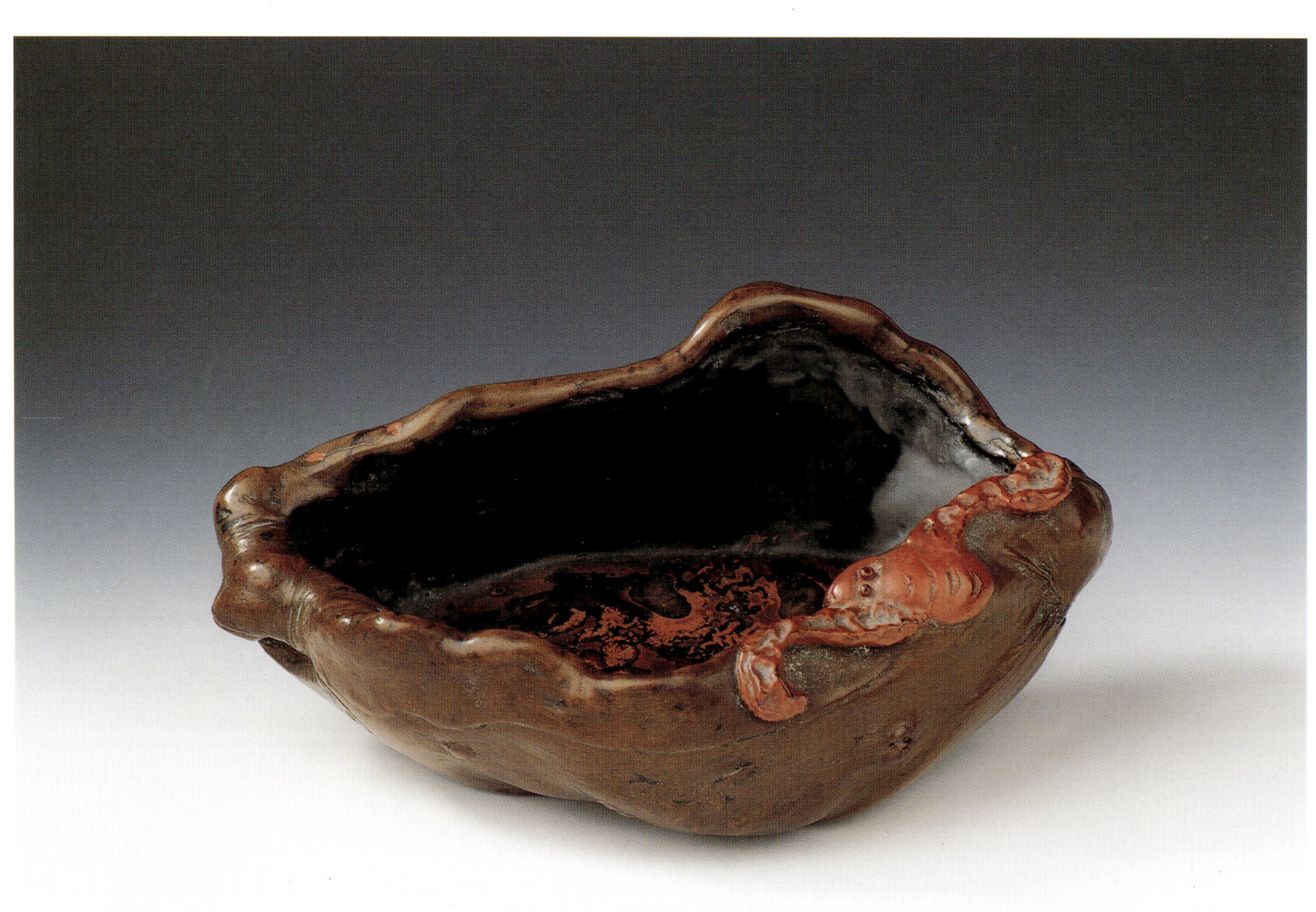

351

Red and black lacquered wood rustic drinking vessel

Qing, Kangxi/Qianlong period
(18th century)
Length : 10.5 cm
Width : 6 cm
Height : 3 cm

A natural wood root waterpot lacquered in the interior with black, orange and red lacquer. A bat in red lacquer decorates the rim. The base is inscribed in lacquer "For the elegant appreciation of Huantianyi" in black lacquer within a large rectangular red bordered cartouche. It is not known who Huantianyi was.

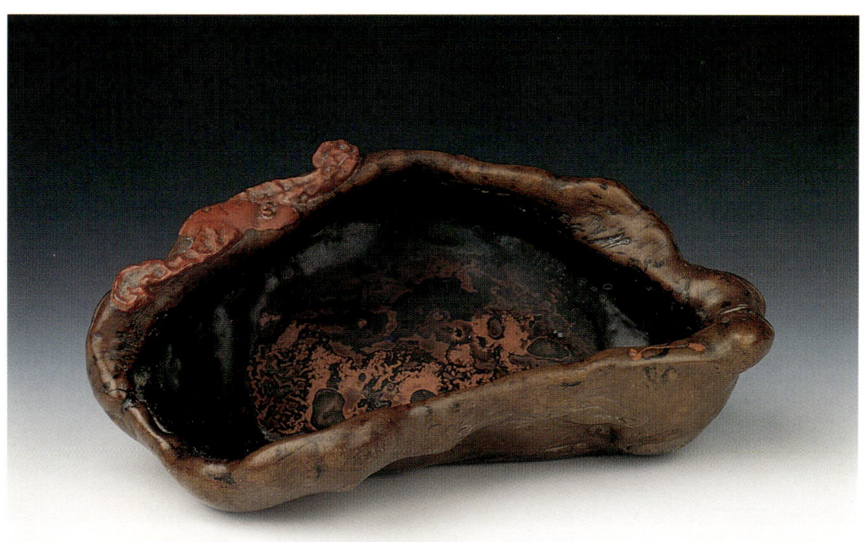

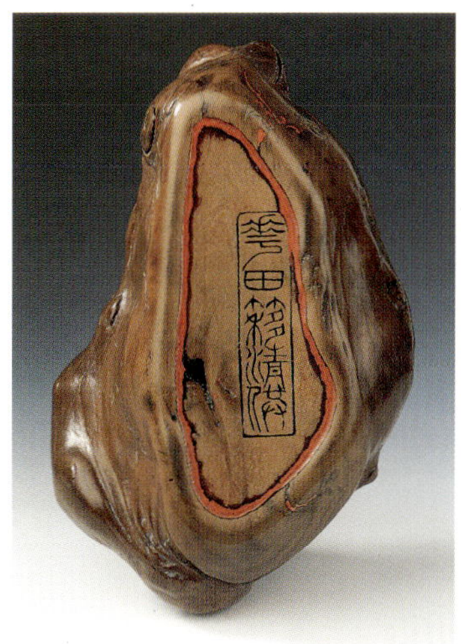

352

Gourd plaything moulded with scenes from the story of the cowherd and the fairy

Qing dynasty
Yongzheng/Qianlong period
(mid eighteenth century)
Length : 5.6 cm
Width : 5.6 cm
Height : 3.5 cm

A small square gourd box of yellowish colour moulded in low relief with a cow and a cowherd in a landscape on one side, with a fairy and a pagoda on the opposite side separated by a cricket on bamboo and a cricket on a vine on the remaining sides. The mould is of a reusable type typical of the period as evidenced by traces of mould joins on the piece.

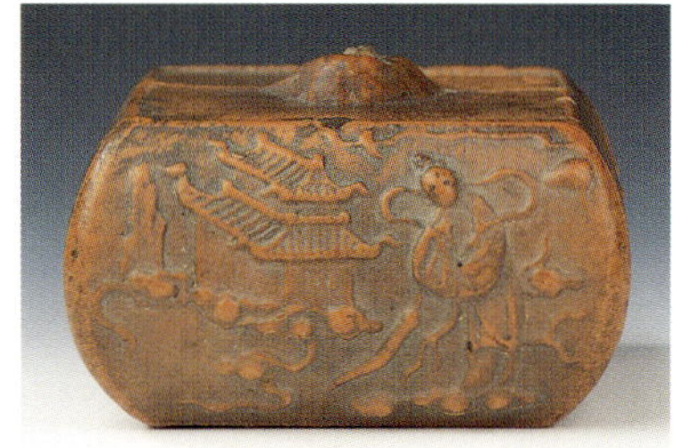

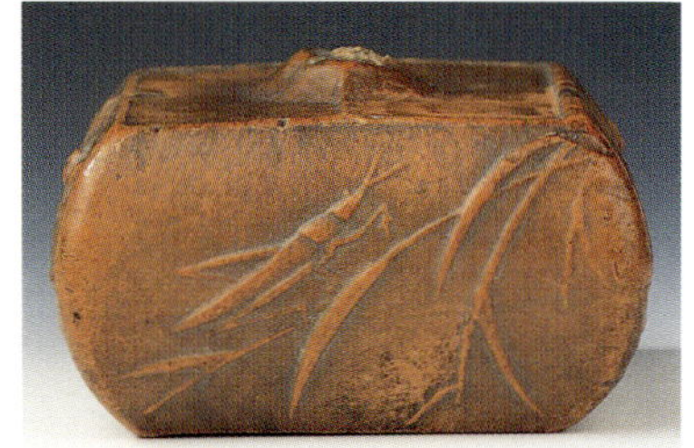

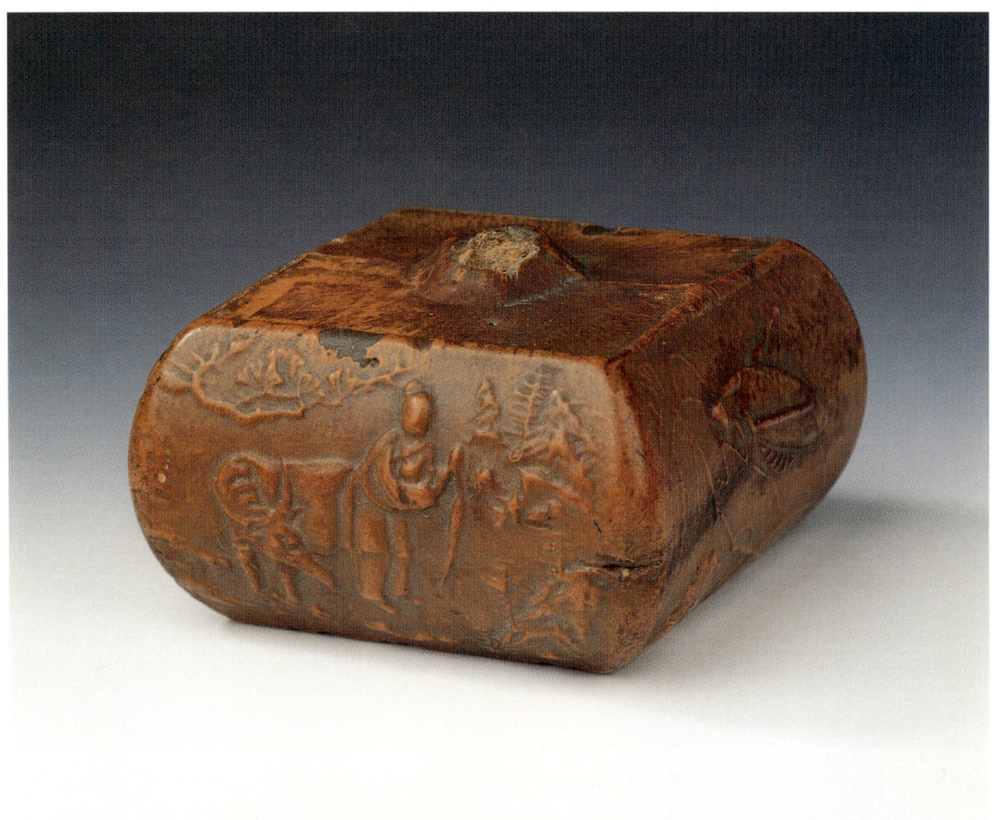

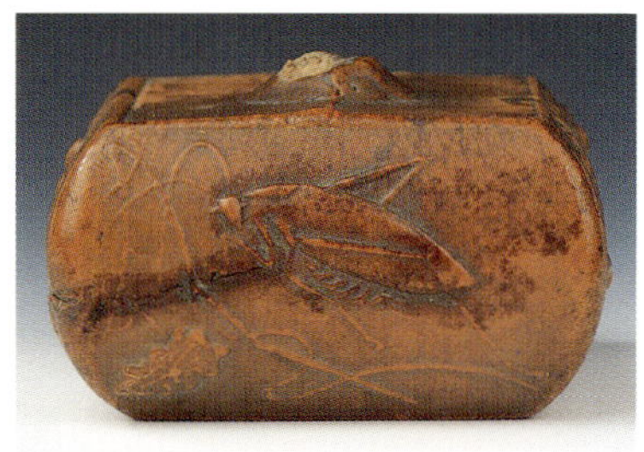

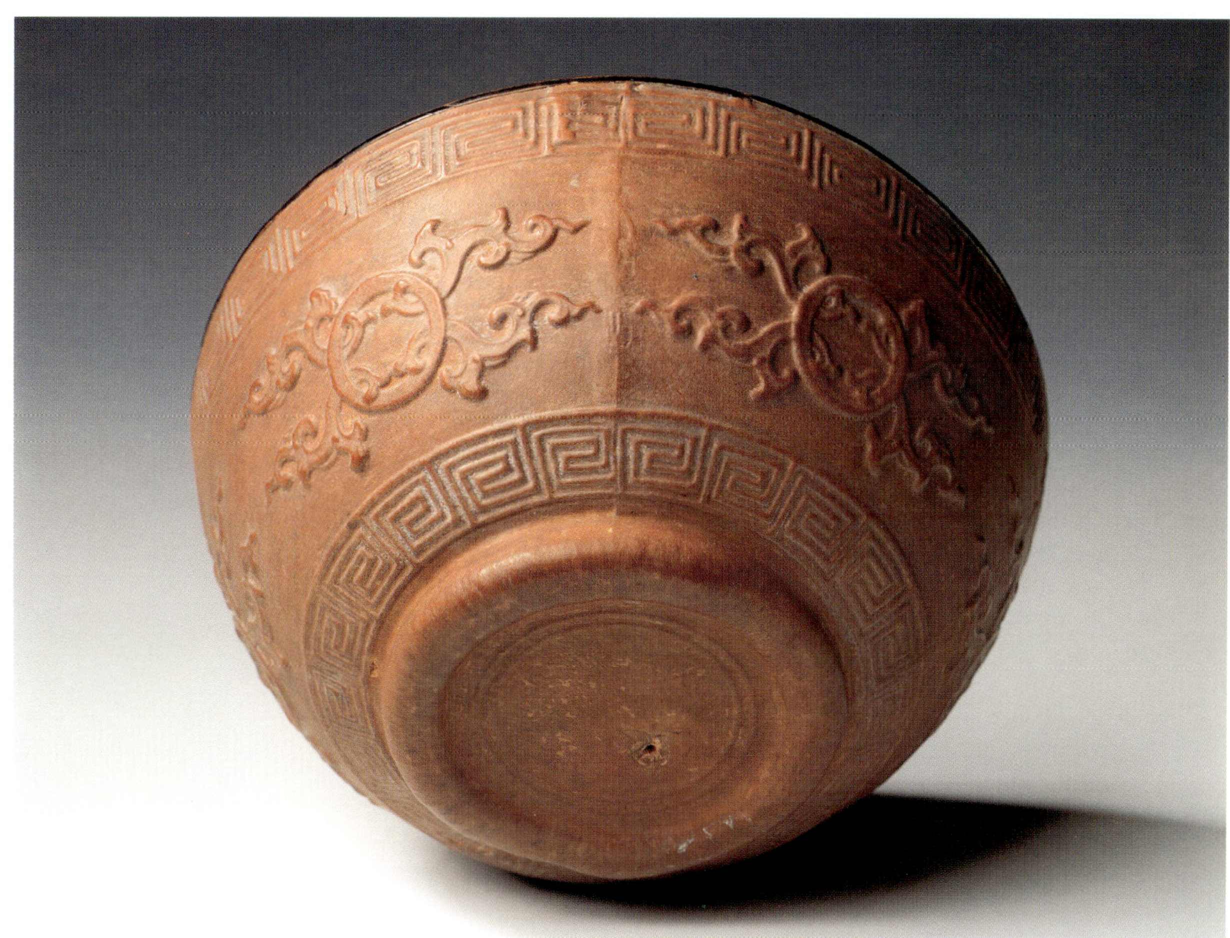

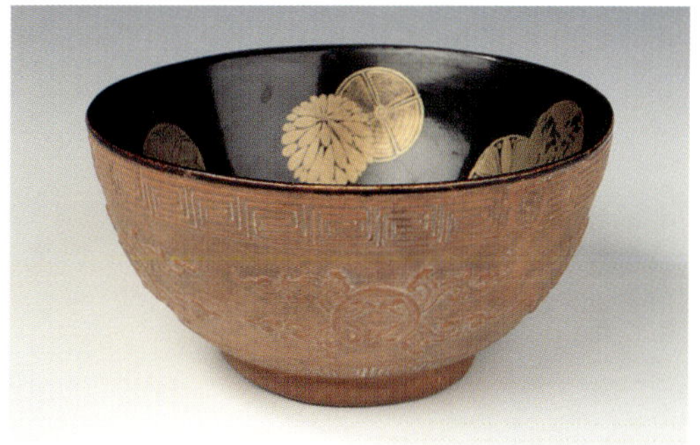

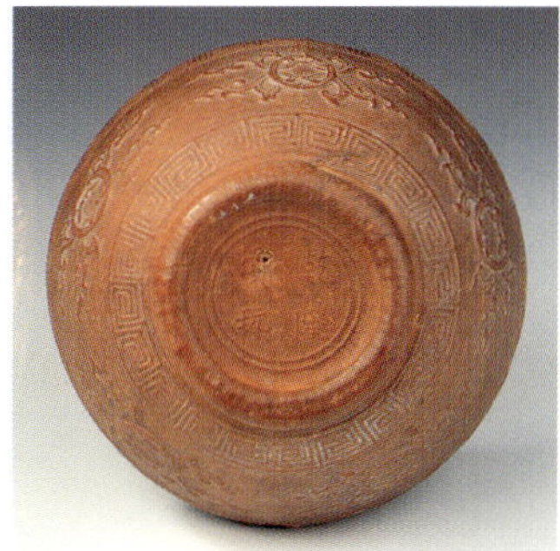

353

Gourd-moulded circular bowl decorated with stylised ribbon-threaded circles, the interior with black lacquer and gold lacquer roundels

Qianlong (1736-1745) "shang wan" four character mark and of the period
Diameter : 11 cm
Height : 5.3 cm

Gourd-moulded circular bowl, the exterior moulded with design of stylised ribbon-threaded circles and a Buddhist emblem between key fret borders, the base with "Qianlong shang wan" mark in a double line bordered square, the interior with black lacquer and circular gold lacquer roundels. The piece clearly shows that it was made using a reusable mould.

354

Gourd medicine bottle in goose-like eccentric shape

Qing dynasty Jiaqing period (1795 - 1820)
Height : 17 cm

A moulded plain gourd medicine bottle in goose-like eccentric shape with a carved coral stopper.

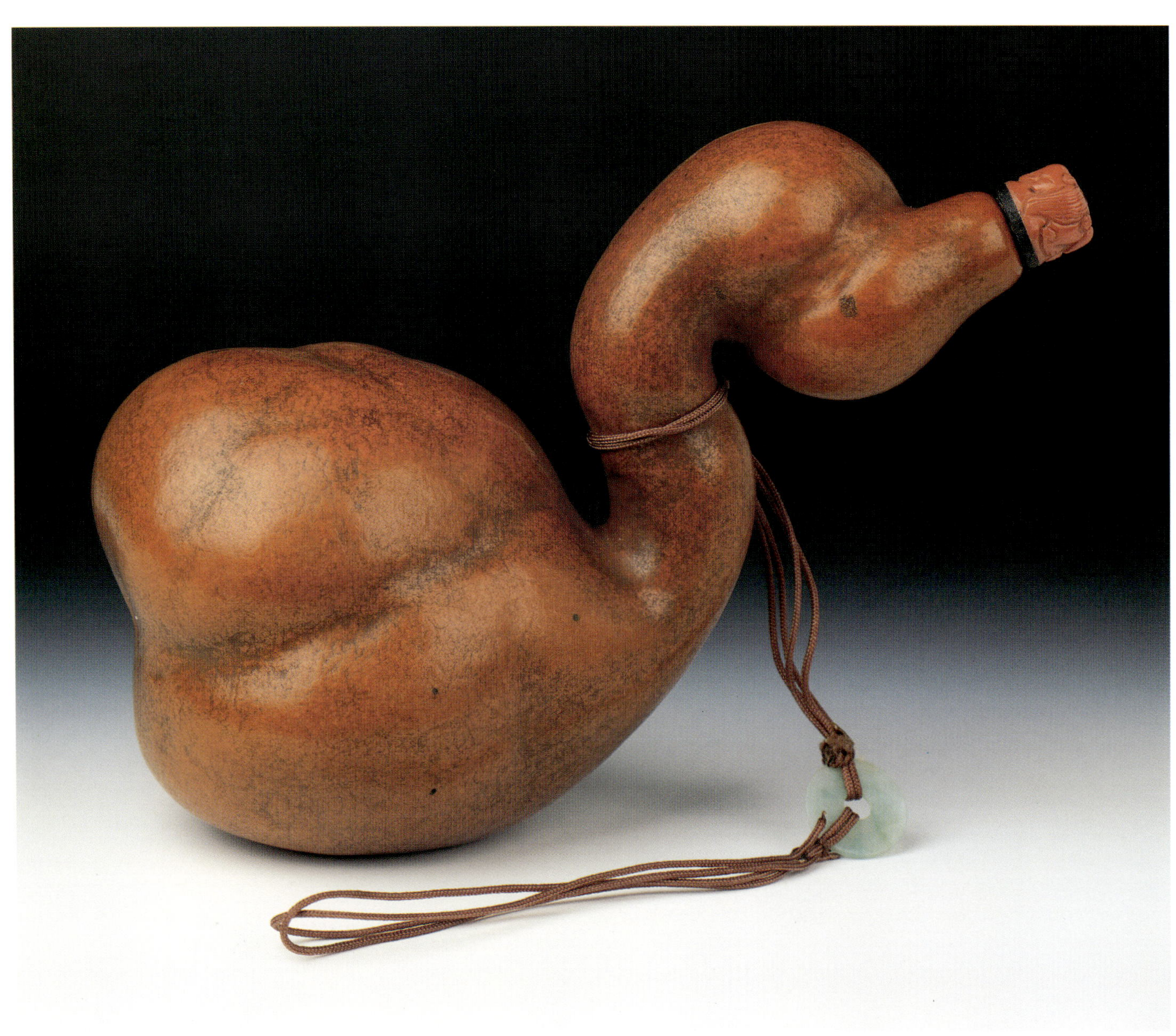